Ponyvill

DEC   2017

Ponyville Confidential

*The History and Culture
of* My Little Pony, *1981–2016*

SHERILYN CONNELLY

McFarland & Company, Inc., Publishers
Jefferson, North Carolina

LIBRARY OF CONGRESS CATALOGUING-IN-PUBLICATION DATA

Names: Connelly, Sherilyn, 1973– author.
Title: Ponyville confidential : the history and culture of My little pony, 1981–2016 / Sherilyn Connelly.
Description: Jefferson, North Carolina : McFarland & Company, Inc., Publishers | Includes bibliographical references and index.
Identifiers: LCCN 2016044897 | ISBN 9781476662091 (softcover : acid free paper) ∞
Subjects: LCSH: My little pony 'n friends (Television program : 1986–1987) | My little pony : friendship is magic (Television program : 2010–) | Popular culture—United States.
Classification: LCC PN1992.77.M875 C66 2016 | DDC 791.45/75—dc23
LC record available at https://lccn.loc.gov/2016044897

BRITISH LIBRARY CATALOGUING DATA ARE AVAILABLE

ISBN (print) 978-1-4766-6209-1
ISBN (ebook) 978-1-4766-2686-4

Front cover image © 2017 InhaSemiankova/iStock

Printed in the United States of America

McFarland & Company, Inc., Publishers
  Box 611, Jefferson, North Carolina 28640
    www.mcfarlandpub.com

For Daria,
because the things she enjoys have value.

Acknowledgments

My deepest gratitude goes out to the strangers and friends alike who helped make *Ponyville Confidential* happen: Bonnie Zacherle and Lauren Faust, whose work has made this world a slightly less horrible place. Ellen Seiter, for writing *Sold Separately*. Ryan Borromeo, for his stealth research assistance. Sister Edith, for being able to recognize russet and ochre. Summer Hayes, for her reference works on *My Little Pony* Generations 2 and 3. David Gerrold for writing the nonfiction books *The Trouble with Tribbles* and *The World of Star Trek*, which I read countless times growing up and which taught me how to think critically about the pop culture I love. Doris Kearns Goodwin, whose *Team of Rivals: The Political Genius of Abraham Lincoln* was an inspiration on a structural level. The staff of the South San Francisco Public Library (Juv Team Represent!). Amid Amidi, Jerry Beck, Maria Bustillos, Hal Erickson, David Perlmutter, Kathleen Richter, and Sethisto and all of Equestria Daily's contributors and commenters for speaking their truth. Debra Hansen, my History of Books and Libraries instructor at San Jose State University, who called me "an excellent historian!" (I hope she knows how much both the sentiment and the punctuation meant to me.) And perhaps most importantly, those who represent the magic of friendship in my life: Clare Marie Myers, for being there when it all began. Helena Lukas, for being there before the beginning and after the end. Pete and Sarah Goldie, for making me feel like I'm part of their herd. KrOB, for his trust and for listening to me talk at length about this book. And my mother, for her unwavering support of her daughter's dreams. I love you all, even the haters.

Table of Contents

Introduction

This is a history and scholarly study of My Little Pony, with an emphasis on the television series *My Little Pony: Friendship Is Magic* and the *My Little Pony: Equestria Girls* movies.

Ponyville Confidential will examine how My Little Pony has been the recipient of a pervasive cultural sexism in the United States regarding children's entertainment: that shows created for boys are considered universal, but those for girls are considered to be for girls only, and are expected to be kept segregated from more respectable—i.e., masculine—toys and cartoons, and outgrown in a way that boys' entertainment is not. It will also demonstrate how My Little Pony has also long been a scapegoat for a wide variety of societal ills, with cultural critics projecting their own fears and anxieties onto the franchise.

This is not a book about the organized fandom known as the Bronies, and though I am a fan of *My Little Pony: Friendship Is Magic* and the *My Little Pony: Equestria Girls* movies, I do not identify as a Brony. They will be discussed in terms of the media coverage and how their existence sometimes overshadows the series and movies, as well as the part they've played in some of the specific controversies, but they are not the focus. When I would humblebrag to a friend that I was writing a critical study of My Little Pony, after they were done laughing they would usually start going on about something they'd read or seen about the Bronies, as though the subjects were interchangeable. The hope is that this book will reframe the discussion about My Little Pony by putting the franchise in its historical and social context, and allow *Friendship Is Magic* and *Equestria Girls* to be considered for what they are beyond the knee-jerk reaction of "Ha ha Bronies!" It should also be noted that the words "Brony" and "fan" are *not* used as synonyms.

* * *

As a child, I was in a big hurry to grow up. When I was treated like the five- or six-year-old that I was—say, when I was handed a children's menu at a restaurant—I felt like I was being stripped of what little dignity I had. (And if the waiter tried to give me crayons, I wanted to curl up in a ball under the table.) Even worse were the things that kids were expected to watch. The 1970s and 1980s were not a golden age of children's fare, and I was offended to my core by being expected to watch most of the cartoons being produced, or inexplicably popular Sid & Marty Krofft shows like *The Bugaloos*. Seriously, did they think we were stupid, or what?

It helped that I grew up in a permissive family, and I wasn't forbidden from watching things meant for grown-ups. Admittedly, most everything made for broadcast television up to that point was designed to be non-offensive, but *M*A*S*H* and *Star Trek* were my favorite shows because they were what my siblings and parents enjoyed. (Both the live-action and animated versions of *Trek* were in regular rotation for a while, and they were equally valid to me.) My parents were early adopters of home video, and one day when I was seven, my mother directed me over to the children's section of our neighborhood's video store. It was mostly Disney movies for and about children, and being limited to that section felt like a punishment. I chose a now-forgotten live-action Disney movie called *The North Avenue Irregulars*, because the cover picture showed two suburban women (of the sort that many would later describe as "soccer moms") tying up some criminal-looking men in an auto junkyard. It looked like it might not actively insult my intelligence, unlike more traditional Disney fare such as *Pete's Dragon* or *The Apple Dumpling Gang,* both movies that I refused to watch because they just looked so ... childish. (In the case of the latter, I wasn't about to watch a movie named after a kind of food that I found disgusting.)

The only new cartoon I watched with any kind of regularity in the 1980s was *Inspector Gadget*, because it was the voice of the guy from *Get Smart* (another favorite of my family), it had interesting stories that were set in something resembling the real world, and most importantly, the real hero of the show was Gadget's young niece, who inevitably saved the day using her intelligence and her confidence. That, I could appreciate.

I started watching *My Little Pony: Friendship Is Magic* in mid–2011, shortly after the end of Season 1. I'd been vaguely aware the show existed and that it had a rabid fanbase in corners of the Internet that I generally ignored, but the tipping point was an article by Todd VanDerWerff on the A.V. Club, my favorite pop culture website. He compared it to the recently concluded *Battlestar Galactica* series in that they were both remakes and far superior to their source material, yet with legacies and titles that made it difficult to recommend without adding an "I know how it sounds, but trust me" disclaimer.[1] (Plenty of people in the months to follow laughed in my face when

I told them that *My Little Pony: Friendship Is Magic* was actually really good, and also more recently when I told them I was writing *Ponyville Confidential*.)

Though VanDerWerff ultimately praised the show, the tone of the article was hesitant at best; in addition to describing it as "a show built to advertise a toy line" and "a way to create new toy ponies to sell to little girls," and that "in some respects, it may be a toy commercial, sure," he cited *Friendship Is Magic*'s greatest obstacle as being the fact that it's about "fucking cartoon ponies."[2] He was distrustful of what he described as the show's "sheer and utter joyfulness," but that his inclination to watch it with an "ironic sneer of detachment" was worn down by the time he was "giggling maniacally at a tiny cartoon pony being dragged against her will toward a giant rock, adorable frown affixed firmly to her face. She was such a cute little pony! Yes she was!"[3] The scene was a flashback of the character Rarity (who is the best) from the one of the best episodes of Season 1, and it is indeed funny, but the infantilization of the character makes no sense. Further A.V. Club coverage of the show would similarly indulge, such as a January 2012 article about an online character generator in which Genevieve Koski wrote that "regardless of what you think of the series and its attendant web-phenomenon status, it's hard to deny that those ponies are da kewtest widdle ponies eva yes dey are!"[4] Though she clarified that she was not a fan of the show, I still found myself wondering, was she even referring to the same *My Little Pony: Friendship Is Magic* that I watched? And if so, where did the baby talk come from?

What I had discovered when I started watching is a show that featured well-developed characters, strong writing—even if I could tell where an episode was going, I could never tell *how* it was going to get there, or what might happen next—and a deeply humanistic, occasionally morally ambiguous worldview which eschewed the "magic" of the title. It was beautifully animated and nice to look at, with a purple-heavy palette which appealed to my own aesthetics, but prettiness without substance gets pretty boring pretty fast.

What's more, *My Little Pony: Friendship Is Magic* has a strong feminist bent, showing its cast of female ponies as fully rounded individuals with their own strengths and weaknesses. They gain much of that strength from their friends, but are also able to work out problems on their own, often under extreme duress. They can do anything a boy can do, and never need one to save or complement them.

There were some strong indicators of children's television, of course, such as an often ham-handed attempt to shoehorn in a moral at the end of each episode during Season 1, often followed by the deeply hacky Everybody

Laughs Ending—you know, the kind where someone makes a weak joke, everybody laughs, and the credits roll. But I never felt condescended to while watching *My Little Pony: Friendship Is Magic*, or like I was watching something which presumed the viewer was unintelligent or immature, regardless of their age. Nor, even, that I was watching something inappropriate for a taxpaying grown-up in her late 30s. This wasn't the *Bugaloos*, nor did it resemble the bits and pieces I'd seen of the 1980s series *My Little Pony 'n' Friends*. This was something new, different, and a notable alternative to what was still a largely male-oriented animation world.

I also found a show which rewarded close attention, with a season-long arc in the first season that ended with "The Best Night Ever" (S01E26), one of the best-written, most emotionally-satisfying half-hours of *Friendship Is Magic*. Or any other show.

Sure, *My Little Pony: Friendship Is Magic* is about fucking cartoon ponies, and the *Equestria Girls* movies are just about teenage girls, but by that same logic, all that needed to be said about the critically acclaimed *Battlestar Galactica* reboot—which *Time* had frequently listed as one of the best shows of the given year—was that it was about sexy killer robots in space. See? Being reductive is never wrong.

*   *   *

This book is divided into five parts. Part 1, "Family Appreciation Day," looks at the history of the franchise from the release of Generation 1 in the early 1980s through the late 1990s, showing how long after both the toys and cartoons had ceased production, My Little Pony continued to be criticized in the media as the worst of children's entertainment in a way that similar brands marketed toward boys were not.

Part 2, "The Lost Generations," details the first attempts at reviving the brand, including the failed Generation 2 and the far more successful Generation 3, and how they set the stage for Generation 4 and the game changing *My Little Pony: Friendship Is Magic* series. (This is not a detailed production history of *Friendship Is Magic* or the *Equestria Girls* films, though that is a book which I hope to write.)

Part 3, "Twilight's Kingdom," is a reference guide to Seasons 1–5 of *Friendship Is Magic*, as well as the feature films *My Little Pony: Equestria Girls*, *My Little Pony: Equestria Girls—Rainbow Rocks*, and *My Little Pony: Equestria Girls—Friendship Games*.

Part 4, "The Foal Free Press," examines the reaction in the media first to the mere existence of *Friendship Is Magic*, the head-scratching over how a show intended for young girls can possibly appeal to anypony else, and how the show has helped to break down rigid cultural notions about gendered entertainment.

Part 5, "Battles of the Brand," studies in detail two of the biggest Brony dramas surrounding *Friendship Is Magic*: the saga of a background pony with misaligned eyes, and the introduction of a spinoff set in a world populated by humans, not ponies. (Note to parents: there is a fair amount of profanity in this section.)

The scope of this book is up through Season 5 of *My Little Pony: Friendship Is Magic*, and *My Little Pony: Equestria Girls—Friendship Games*; please keep that in mind before writing to say I "forgot" to mention revelations that occurred in later seasons or movies. Other contemporary television shows I consumed while writing this book included *BoJack Horseman, Mr. Robot, Steven Universe, Veep, Rick and Morty, Fargo, Wander Over Yonder, Better Call Saul, Unbreakable Kimmy Schmidt, Gravity Falls*, and the final seasons of *Parks and Recreation, Mad Men, Cougar Town, Justified*, and *Hannibal*.

Indefinite personal pronouns on *Friendship Is Magic* take the form of "anypony," "somepony," and so forth, and they also will in this book.

Much of the research was done via scholarly and news databases available via the San Francisco and San Mateo County Public Library systems. I also made use of the bibliographies of existing works, what historians call "source mining," to find as many primary and secondary sources as possible. I hope other researchers of the history of My Little Pony find this book's bibliography useful for their own mining.

And, in the interest of full disclosure: (1) Rarity. (2) Twilight Sparkle. (3) Sunset Shimmer. (4) Fluttershy. (5) Applejack. (6) Pinkie Pie. (7) Rainbow Dash.

Welcome to Ponyville. Don't be afraid.

March 2017

PART 1

Family Appreciation Day
(1981–1998)

Ponies: Grosser by the Gross

Hal Erickson's reference book *Television Cartoon Shows: An Illustrated Encyclopedia, 1949–1993* was published in 1995 by McFarland, the same publisher as the work of scholarly sparkliness you are now reading. It's an astonishing tome (*Television Cartoon Shows*, not *Ponyville Confidential*), containing approximately 600 entries over the course of 659 pages.

Multiple shows from the same franchise are grouped together, and this is how the joint entry for the 1986 series *My Little Pony 'n' Friends* and the 1992 *My Little Pony Tales* begins:

> Together with *G.I. Joe* (q.v.) and *He-Man* (q.v.), *My Little Pony* was Hasbro Toys' principal source of income in the mid–1980s. The *Pony* marketing strategy was founded on gender-role notions that purportedly were outdated by 1984: If boys would respond to a line of action-figure soldiers, girls would enthuse over an equally overpopulated line of toy horses. Perhaps it wasn't in the best interest of sexual equality to assume that girls would bypass warrior dolls to purchase toys that looked like pretty ponies, but that assumption proved accurate. This writer knows of several otherwise rational high school and college-age young ladies of 1994 (some within the family) who have My Little Ponies by the gross tucked away in their attics.
>
> The characters weren't simply horses, of course, but humanized representations of various traits like vanity, pride, courage, and so forth (see *Care Bears*). All were gifted with magic powers, all were bedecked with flowing hair styles of various pastel colors, and all were evidently regular customers of Ponyland's Institute of Eyelash Elongation. Ponyland was of course the idyllic mythical land (with background art apparently based on the Beethoven Pastorale sequence in Disney's *Fantasia*) whence the tiny pony dolls owned by a human girl named Megan would retreat and come to life.[1]

There are nits to be picked, if one were inclined to pick nits, and this book (*Ponyville Confidential,* not *Television Cartoon Shows*) will indeed engage in a great deal of nitpicking. Details matter in criticism, and conclusions drawn from faulty assumptions and inaccurate readings of the text being criticized—

as is the case with a vast amount of criticism of My Little Pony—must be called into question.

Not mentioned by Erickson in this entry, the Transformers range outsold My Little Pony by a wide margin in 1984,[2] 1985,[3] and 1987,[4] thus making it a far more principal source of income for Hasbro at the time. He-Man was a Mattel property, not Hasbro, though Erickson's entry on the *He-Man* cartoon doesn't make that mistake, referring to He-Man action figures as "rolling off the production lines of Mattel Toys."[5] Also, though there was a biped girl named Megan in the 1986 *My Little Pony: The Movie* and subsequent *My Little Pony 'n' Friends* series, the ponies were not her own dolls come to life *à la Toy Story*, nor were they tiny. This misrepresentation reinforces the narrative of all My Little Pony animation being a commercial for the toys which preceded it, a concept which we'll call My Little Pony's Original Sin.

Those are all minor details, the sort of thing which can be corrected in later editions. (These errors were *not* corrected in the updated and expanded edition of *Television Cartoon Shows* in 2005, but they *can* be.) His snark about the feminine characteristics of the ponies *vis-à-vis* their eyelash length is not paralleled in his *He-Man* or *G.I. Joe* entries, neither of which contain similar comments about the exaggerated masculine characteristics of their biped heroes. Prince Adam in *He-Man* is already pure beefcake before he transforms into the even more beefcakey title character, but Erickson refers to He-Man as "superpowered" and leaves it at that, without suggesting Prince Adam is a charter member of Eternia's 24-Hour Fitness or anything of the sort.[6] And considering that the landscapes in *Fantasia* were inspired by the work of Grant Wood, painter of *American Gothic*, an animated series could do worse for inspiration.[7]

Most troubling is the hostility in *Television Cartoon Shows* toward both the My Little Pony toys and their young female owners, a hostility that had already been going strong elsewhere by the time of that book's publication in 1995, and would continue for the next two decades.

To say the female-oriented marketing of My Little Pony perhaps "wasn't in the best interest of sexual equality"[8] is a terrible burden to put on a toy that became available around the time the Equal Rights Amendment officially failed to be ratified.[9] Erickson's statement that the marketing strategy was "founded on gender-role notions that purportedly were outdated by 1984" raises the question of *who* was purporting such a thing.[10] The Supreme Court's first female justice in its 200-year history had only been serving for three years,[11] and a woman was nominated for Vice President for the first of only two times as of 2016—and, as nominee Geraldine Ferraro pointed out in her acceptance speech to the Democratic National Convention on July 19, 1984, women were still getting paid 59 cents on the dollar compared to men for the same work at the time.[12]

While a great deal of progress had been made thanks to the rise of feminism in the 1960s and 1970s, there's no evidence that gender role notions were anywhere close to being considered outdated in the early-to-mid 1980s, or that My Little Pony was counterrevolutionary to the cause. Furthermore, this book will demonstrate that both the content and popularity of *My Little Pony: Friendship Is Magic* is contributing to the necessary job of dismantling rigid gender roles in the United States.

Erickson's "best interest of sexual equality" statement also presumed that masculinity is the universal norm, and equality among the genders equates to girls liking boy-oriented things, but not the other way around.[13] There's no similar statement about gender equality in his entries on *He-Man* or *G.I. Joe*, nothing to the effect of "Perhaps it wasn't in the best interest of sexual equality to assume that *boys* would bypass *toys that looked like pretty ponies* to purchase *warrior dolls*, but that assumption proved accurate." This double-standard is at the heart of the disconnect surrounding *My Little Pony: Friendship Is Magic*: that something intended to appeal to young girls cannot be enjoyed by people of all ages and genders, and if somepony outside the prescribed demographic does enjoy it, that means there's something wrong with the consumer, and not something right with the product.

In her 1993 book *Sold Separately: Children and Parents in Consumer Culture*, Ellen Seiter devoted a chapter to My Little Pony, observing that while *My Little Pony 'n' Friends* and other girl-oriented cartoons such as *Rainbow Brite*, *Strawberry Shortcake*, and *The Care Bears* were not only "denigrated as the trashiest, most saccharine, most despicable products of the children's television industry"—a wave of denigration which only got stronger after 1993, by which time those shows had long since left the airwaves—but they were also the first cartoons "that did not require girls to cross over and identify with males."[14] Seiter argued that "some of the most virulent attacks on the licensed character shows were in fact diatribes against their 'feminine' appeal" (e.g. Erickson's snark two years later about the ponies' hair and eyelashes), and that these shows were about the emotional lives of the characters, much like soap operas, family melodramas, and other disreputable female-oriented genres.[15] She quoted Tom Engelhardt's essay "The Shortcake Strategy" in the 1987 collection *Watching Television: A Pantheon Guide to Popular Culture*, in which Engelhardt bemoaned the "endless stream of these happy little beings with their magical unicorns in their syrupy cloud-cuckoo lands" which "have paraded across the screen demanding that they be snuggled, cuddled, nuzzled, loved, and adored," as though that was the worst of all possible worlds.[16]

A previous borrower of the San Francisco State University library's copy of *Sold Separately* underlined the following quoted text regarding the importance of *My Little Pony 'n' Friends*, then drew an arrow pointing at it:

> Little girls found themselves in a ghettoized culture that no self-respecting boy would take an interest in; but for once girls were not required to cross over, to take on an ambiguous identification with a group of male characters.[17]

While McFarland does not encourage the defacement of library books, the passage was indeed worthy of highlighting. (If this is your personal copy of *Ponyville Confidential*, however, deface it to your heart's content! May we suggest a sketch of Rarity pointing at the above paragraph?)

Consider also Erickson's reference in *Television Cartoon Shows* to the many "otherwise rational" young women of his acquaintance, some of whom he's related to, "who have My Little Ponies by the gross tucked away in their attics."[18] While the suggestion that those young women have them by the gross (a square dozen, 144) may be exaggeration for effect, something *this* writer would never do in a million billion *kazillion* years, let's take the economics of that statement at face value. My Little Pony dolls had a suggested retail price of $4 in 1984, and Hasbro sold an estimated $70M worth of them that year alone[19] and another $95M in 1985.[20] This means there were at least 40 million of the 4-inch dolls out in the world by 1986—though as we'll see later, Congressional testimony quotes a much higher number—making it more feasible for them to be collected by the gross by 1994.

Most troubling is the implication that women having collected My Little Pony dolls without discarding them at whatever age Erickson deems appropriate constitutes a sign of irrationality. Of the other television shows from that era known to be based on toy ranges—the aforementioned *He-Man* and *G.I. Joe*, as well as *Transformers*—he makes no such judgments about the collectors of those products. Indeed, though he uses the *He-Man* and *Transformers* write-ups to discuss the "program-length commercial" phenomenon which we will discuss at greater length below, he praises those boy-oriented shows, suggesting that without *He-Man* "to show the way," there'd be no *DuckTales*, *Tiny Toon Adventures*, or *Batman: The Animated Series*.[21]

The second edition of *Television Cartoon Shows* was published in 2005, and covered an additional 450 shows spread out over two volumes totaling more than 1,000 pages. As mentioned, it did not fix the factual errors in the first two paragraphs of the My Little Pony entry, though Erickson did update "several otherwise rational high school and college-age young ladies of 1994" from the 1995 edition to "several otherwise rational young adult women" for the 2005 edition, suggesting that retaining one's Pony collection will never *not* be irrational.[22]

It's also worth noting that one such grown and "otherwise rational" woman (though probably not of Clan Erickson) who held on to her far-less-than-a-gross of childhood My Little Pony dolls well into adulthood was Lauren Faust, the creator of *My Little Pony: Friendship Is Magic*.[23] And considering that she's been a creative force on no fewer than four successful television cartoons (*The Powerpuff Girls*, *Foster's Home for Imaginary Friends*, *Friendship Is Magic*, and *Wander Over Yonder*), she's done quite well for herself in spite of her apparent irrationality.[24]

A Foal Is Born

Controversies regarding commercialism in children's television go back as far as there's been children's television to be commercialized. In November 1952, an educational show called *Ding Dong School* premiered on NBC.[25] The televised preschool session was well-received for its educational value, but by the following April the *New York Times* criticized how host Dr. Frances Horwich pitched her sponsors' products on the air, encouraging her young viewers to persuade their mothers to buy the items, which *Times* columnist Jack Gould described as "hucksterism at its most callous level."[26] Similar charges would be leveled against the various My Little Pony cartoons in the decades to come, even though they lacked that direct approach, and Gould's "please think of the children" plea in his April 1953 *Times* column would also be echoed, though seldom with such an Eisenhower-era pro-capitalism bent:

> Free enterprise can flourish magnificently without abusing the innocent faith of children. Even in this age of television with all its materialistic outlook, little boys and girls between the ages of 2 and 5 are still something special—and precious.[27]

The phrase "program-length commercial" dates back to the 1969 cartoon series *Hot Wheels* based on the Mattel toys; it was yanked off the air for violating an agreement with ABC and the National Association of Broadcasters forbidding cross-referencing between program content and commercials.[28] (It was a replaced on the schedule in September 1970 with the animated *Will the Real Jerry Lewis Please Sit Down*, which was product placement of a different sort.[29]) Following a 13-year study of children's television, the Federal Communications Commission issued a policy document in 1984 which concluded that television stations already provided sufficient children's programming, and there was no need to mandate how much such programming a given station should broadcast—or for limitations on how much advertising could be bundled with it.[30]

This ruling was under the watch of Chairman of the Federal Communications Commission Mark Fowler.[31] Appointed in 1981 by Ronald Reagan and as big a fan of deregulation as his president, Fowler was quoted in *The Nation* as referring to television as "just another appliance," little more than "a toaster with pictures."[32] The 1984 ruling under his watch would be overturned by 1991, but the wheels were in motion.

* * *

Like everything else about My Little Pony, the exact origin of the brand is a matter of some debate. According to Sydney Stern and Ted Schoenhaus's *Toyland: The High-stakes Game of the Toy Industry*, the genesis was Hasbro conducting "blue-sky research" (i.e., research which is exploratory and without any particular outcome in mind): they asked little girls what they see when they go to bed and close their eyes, and a common answer was "horses."[33] While the authors don't cite a source for this story, it does reflect many anecdotal origin stories before and since, that My Little Pony was purely the cold, calculated fruit of marketing meetings and focus groups. More likely, however, is that a woman named Bonnie Zacherle created My Little Pony, since Hasbro has referred to her as the creator[34] (even if they misspelled her name in the process), and it's Zacherle's (properly spelled) name on U.S. Patent D269,986 for a Toy Animal, published on August 2, 1983[35]:

[57] CLAIM: The ornamental design for a toy animal, substantially as shown.
[75] Inventors: Bonnie D. Zacherle, Norwood, Mass; Charles Muenchinger, Providence; Steven D. D'Aguanno, Greenville, both of R.I.
[73] Assignee: Hasbro Industries, Inc. (Pawtucket, RI)
[**] Term: 14 Years
[21] Appl. No.: 298,018
[22] Filed: Aug., 31, 1981

The patent was filed under Class D21/620, defined by the U.S. Patent Office as "Design for toy representation of four-legged animal with flowing main and tail."[36] It's a prescient typo, considering how much mileage the franchise would get out of mane/main homophones over the years.

According to an August 2006 interview with the *Faquier Times* which was later reprinted on the collector site My Little Pony Trading Post, Zacherle was the Director of Studio Cards at a Massachusetts greeting card company in the late 1970s while also doing freelance work for Hasbro.[37] She went on to work full-time in Hasbro's Research and Development department, a job which allowed her to create the toys she would have enjoyed as a child, and she later reflected, "a pony or horse was the only thing I ever wanted."[38]

In spite of opposition from her department's male Vice President of Research & Development, who informed her that little girls were more interested in domestic work than they were in horses, Ms. Zacherle worked with sculptor Charles Muenchinger to design what would be known as My Pretty Pony.[39] Whatever the name, there was further pushback, as she later explained: "My Little Pony was on the verge of not making it to market. It didn't do anything. That's the beauty of My Little Pony. You put yourself in it. You comb it. You dress it."[40]

Released through Hasbro's Romper Room subsidiary in 1981, My Pretty Pony was much larger and harder than the eventual My Little Pony dolls, approximately 10 inches tall and presented in realistic colors.[41] The suggested retail price was $17.99, which is approximately $47 in 2015 dollars.[42]

Though millions of My Pretty Ponies were sold, the wife of the aforementioned vice president suggested it should be smaller, softer, and with a combable mane.[43] Zacherle designed miniaturized versions, and though she was a self-described "purist" regarding verisimilitude—her original designs were based on palominos and pintos, one of which was black—Hasbro's marketing director, Marlene Souza, suggested making the ponies pink and purple, colors which tested much better.[44] After this, Zacherle moved on to Parker Brothers, and was no longer involved with her equestrian creation.[45] (But not forever; she would go on to be a guest at My Little Pony collector conventions in the 2000s, as well as doing an autograph and sketching session at the Hasbro booth at the 2009 San Diego Comic-Con,[46] and met the only person as important as herself in the history of the franchise when she spoke on a panel with *Friendship Is Magic* creator Lauren Faust at the Equestria LA Convention in September 2015.[47])

The now-rebranded My Little Pony dolls are referred to by modern collectors as Year One of Generation 1, more commonly written as G1 / Year One (1982–1983).[48] (*Friendship Is Magic* is Generation 4, and its products and characters will frequently be referred to as G4 in this book.) Individually named Cotton Candy, Blue Belle, Butterscotch, Minty, Snuzzle, and Blossom, My Little Pony sold well enough that the My Pretty Pony range was discontinued, though there's some uncertainty over the official first year of My Little Pony.[49] Collectors cite them as having been introduced in 1982,[50] as did Hasbro's 2006 *Annual Report*,[51] but in January 2012 Hasbro's official timeline listed the range as having originally been released in 1983, while confusingly citing 1992 as the 10th anniversary.[52] My Pretty Pony was still appearing in newspaper advertisements as late as December 1982,[53] and My Little Pony was being advertised the following October,[54] so 1983 seems most likely. My Little Pony collector and historian Kimberly Shriner has written that she remembers "purchasing my first pony Cotton Candy in early spring of 1983, when they first appeared in stores."[55]

For certain, in November 1983 Hasbro brought in advertising firm BBDO Direct to devise a plan to use direct marketing techniques to sell their toy ranges, including but not limited to My Little Pony.[56] (When asked about his inspirations, *Mad Men* creator Matthew Weiner has said that his show's ad agency Sterling Cooper is "most like BBDO," bringing to mind the wonderful image of a Don Draper–type developing a My Little Pony pitch.[57] Come to think of it, he'd probably hand the client off to his Peggy Olson equivalent.) Not that sales were sluggish; in the December 11, 1983, issue of the *Evening News* in Newburgh-Beacon, New York, the now-defunct Zayre department store ran an ad during the Christmas rush apologizing that toy ranges including My Little Pony, G.I. Joe, and Masters of the Universe "may not be available in sufficient quantities due to greater than anticipated demand."[58] According to the journal *Playthings*, this scarcity continued into the New Year, except for one West Side discounter who stocked up early in 1983 and was having a good January 1984, citing "My Little Pony at $4.96" ($11.31 in 2015 dollars) as being his best item.[59] Meanwhile, My Little Pony was not a big seller at the Midwestern department store chain Pamida, though GoBots and Cabbage Patch Kids were.[60]

The dolls themselves were not the only manifestation of the brand even at this early stage, as licensed products were coming into their own in the early 1980s. Property owners and licensors formed an industry association called the Licensing Industry Association, while the manufacturers created the Licensing Merchandiser's Association, and according to industry lore, both held events called "Licensing Shows" at the same time in 1984 in two different Sheraton Hotels in New York.[61] However, according to the June 1984 *Playthings*, at least one of those Licensing Shows was held in Atlantic City, New Jersey, where Hasbro's Jon Gildea defined the four corners of the licensing market as "toys, apparel, publishing, and domestics."[62] He also cited overexposure as a concern, and said Hasbro had already stopped granting My Little Pony licenses for that very reason.[63] One licensor who made it in under the wire was the footwear company PONY (no relation), who announced at the National Shoe Fair Volume Exposition that they were launching a line of My Little Pony shoes for infants through youth sizes in color combinations that matched the toys, and with the specific intention of "[competing] directly with Strawberry Shortcake and Cabbage Patch."[64] As it happened, one of the main concerns at the event was how "the glut of branded merchandise being dumped into the market and discounted by retailers had cut into volume sales," according to the June 1984 *Footwear News*.[65] Another article in that same issue also described the movie *Gremlins* as well as Hasbro's My Little Pony, G.I. Joe, and Transformers ranges as examples of the "latest phase of a recent marketing revolution" in which an imaginary character "invades the media and children's product market at the same time for maximum profit"—an unsubtle choice of verb on *Footwear News*' part, "invade"—and that in some cases "the character is born not in an animator's imagination but in product form, around which a suitable entertainment vehicle is devised."[66]

As for the dolls themselves, the G1 / Year Two (1983–1984) range had been introduced by this point. Winged Pegasus and horned Unicorn ponies were established along with Rainbow ponies and Sea ponies, retroactively classifying the original unadorned six as Earth ponies. Among the new Earth ponies was Applejack, whose orange hide, yellow hair, and five red apples on her flank presaged her G4 incarnation, and a Unicorn named Twilight featured a stripe in her mane and stars on her flank, but otherwise bore no resemblance to G4's Twilight Sparkle. (Her design was the basis for Twilight Sparkle's mother in "The Cutie Mark Chronicles" (S01E23), however.[67]) Along with the rest of the G1 / Year Two ponies, Applejack and Twilight were also given backstories—literally, stories printed on the back of the packaging which deigned to give some depth to their characters. It was not always successful, as Applejack's story told of her getting stuck in a tree ("like a monkey," which must be offensive in their universe) due to her gluttony for apples and needing to be rescued by a passerby,[68] while Twilight's involved her making a deal with the moon to make "every single star that existed" shine brightly on a given night every year, presumably a night in which nopony else gets any sleep.[69]

Friendship Is Magic creator Lauren Faust has indicated that the personality of this Unicorn was indeed the template for Twilight Sparkle (who would become quite the stargazer herself, with a fondness for the constellation Orion), but they're far from the sharply defined characters of G4.[70] Other G1 / Year Two ponies that Faust has cited as inspirations for her G4 designs include Glory for Rarity,[71] Firefly for Rainbow Dash,[72] Ember for Apple Bloom,[73] and Majesty for Princess Celestia.[74]

It may not be fair to hold G1 to G4 standards in terms of the characters and the storytelling considering that they were made with different goals, political and otherwise, but it's necessary since much of the bias against *Friendship Is Magic* is based on lingering and often unreliable memories of the original toys and series. In both cases they're written with a young audience in mind, but there's a far more juvenile bent to the G1 work.

This deepening of their characters via backstories—and, indeed, the toys being given characters at all—resulted in one of the first moral panics involving My Little Pony. It was one of many toy ranges mentioned in a December

1984 *New York Times* article titled "Toy Makers Frolic **in Fantasy Land**" (the last three words in bold type to convey the weight of the threat), which referenced unnamed sources who worried that "this new marketing concept could rob children of their imagination," as well as unspecified parents and children's advocacy groups who worried that "background stories may stop children from developing their own fantasies."[75] (At best, this is a misunderstanding of how imagination works.) The *Times* article also described toys with backstories as irresistible to collectors, with anonymous "analysts and toy manufacturers" agreeing that the 1977 *Star Wars*, with its toy range "at one point numbering nearly 50" (which seems low), "gave new life" to the concept of toys as collectibles.[76] There's no question that *Star Wars* caused as much of a seismic shift in licensed merchandise as it did in the rest of pop culture—the August 1978 issue of *Starlog* listed leather and suede Star Wars shoes and R2-D2 cookie jars as well as "posters, buttons, patches, souvenir programs, 8mm home movies, and bubblegum cards" among the officially licensed products available—but the argument disregarded the existence of other 1970s toy ranges based on sci-fi properties such as Star Trek or Planet of the Apes.[77] It also ignored the history of Disney, as many do when criticizing the commercialism of My Little Pony; the merchandise associated with Disney's Davy Crockett franchise in the 1950s, aimed at the Star Wars–aged audience and younger, is estimated to number in the hundreds,[78] including realistic-looking guns and knives.[79] Other violent and/or adult-oriented shows from the mid–20th century which had licensing agreements with toymakers included *Dragnet* and *The Life and Legend of Wyatt Earp*.[80]

There were some who appreciated the non-violent aspect of My Little Pony, such as family psychologist John Rosemond. In his syndicated column from November 29, 1984, he compared the creative value, flexibility, and durability of ten of the most popular toys that Christmas season; My Little Pony was one of the only two which he gave a durability rating of "Excellent" (hence all those dolls taking up space in attics by the gross), describing them as "great, soothing, quiet-time toys" which "will stimulate neither violent nor sexual fantasies."[81] As we'll see, those who defend the various aspects of the My Little Pony franchise tend to be people like Rosemond, who work with children on a professional level. A *San Diego Union-Tribune* article the following week about a daycare center's panel of seven children from ages 5 to 11 "scrutinizing" that year's hottest toys offered the parenthetical note that while My Little Pony and Cabbage Patch Kids were the favorites of the two girls on the panel, "Some of the boys confessed they would have been keen to see a Cabbage Patch boy."[82] "Confessed" is an apt verb; I recall there was no small amount of controversy that same Christmas season when the 10-

year-old son of a family friend expressed interest in owning a Cabbage Patch Kid. A young boy in the 2010s asking for a Rainbow Dash doll would perhaps not cause quite as much consternation among the grown-ups, though as we'll see in "Are You Now or Have You Ever Been a Brony?," peer bullying is still a concern.

And speaking of the sexual fantasies which Rosemond said that My Little Pony would not stimulate, the dolls were described in a United Press International article on Christmas Day as "the sellout hit" in England.[83] In the years to follow, the press in the United Kingdom would sexualize the franchise on a regular basis.

From Dream Valley to the Devil's Backyard

G1's Applejack and Twilight figure prominently in the first My Little Pony cartoon, a 22-minute special broadcast in the spring of 1984. As was the custom with cartoon specials, it tended to be shown in the afternoon and evenings. WCBS in New York broadcast it at 7:30 p.m. on Monday, March 31[84] and again on Saturday, April 7 at 7:30 p.m.[85]; the self-described Super-Station WTBS presented it to basic-cable subscribers throughout the nation on Monday, April 9 at 2:35 p.m. in the Mountain Time Zone[86] and 4:35 p.m. in the Eastern Time Zone[87]; the independent station WTTG in the Washington, D.C., area put it on at 4:30 p.m. on Friday, April 13[88]; and NBC affiliate KING in Washington State showed it at 4 p.m. on Saturday, April 14.[89] This is by no means a comprehensive list of all the stations which carried the special, but it does establish that it was not a Saturday morning cartoon, which will become an important detail in the years to come.

Set in Dream Valley and titled simply "My Little Pony," Spike the Dragon also makes his first appearance in the special, though like Applejack and Twilight, he doesn't resemble his G4 incarnation, and is not indentured to his generation's Twilight. (Hasbro lost the copyrights and trademark rights for all the character names from G1 except for Applejack and Spike by 2010, hence theirs being the only names to be revived for *Friendship Is Magic*.[90]) Even more jarring by modern standards is the presence of the young biped Megan. She acts as a surrogate for the audience, unlike in *Friendship Is Magic*, whose characters can't even conceive of *homo sapiens* until the first *Equestria Girls* movie.

Retitled "Rescue at Midnight Castle" when re-edited for the 1986 television series, this initial one-off retained the unadorned name "My Little Pony" for its original 1984 VHS release, which made no attempt hide its provenance: the front cover proudly declared "Everyone's Favorite Toy!" and the first line of the back-cover text described My Little Pony as "the wonderful series of toys that children love."[91] The special is also aggressively mediocre as most animated children's television was at the time, and while that was the extent of the brand's animated presence, the *Philadelphia Daily News* referred to the My Little Pony VHS release that December as "newly coined cartoon legends."[92]

Other, soon-to-be-coined cartoon legends such as *Transformers* and *G.I. Joe* were being sold to television stations by John Claster, president of the modestly-named Hasbro subsidiary Claster Television, Inc., at the National Association of Television Program Executives (NATPE) convention held in San Francisco in January 1985.[93] He also spoke at a seminar called "The Future of Children's Programming," moderated by *Good Morning America*'s Joan Lunden and including FCC Commissioner Henry Rivera.[94] Most significantly, *Broadcasting* reported that Claster's booth was "generating attention" for the second special based on those wonderful toys that children love, "Escape from Catrina," which Claster predicted would clear 115 markets.[95] Among those markets were KBSI in Cape Girardeau, Missouri, that March[96] and WPIX in New York in April,[97] both of which broadcast it on a weekday evening as a double feature with "Rescue at Midnight Castle."

A few months prior, a series that would be a lightning rod for controversy had just exhausted its run of original episodes, though they'd continue to be re-run for years: *He-Man and the Masters of the Universe*.[98] While there's no evidence that animation had ever been part Hasbro's original My Little Pony strategy, Mattel did ask the studio Filmation to create a television series based on their He-Man toys *before* they hit the market.[99]

When ABC passed on *He-Man*, it was sold directly to television stations via syndication and debuted in September 1983 on weekdays, becoming the first program-length commercial series since 1969's *Hot Wheels*.[100] Mattel is reported to have raked in $500M from the sales of 35 million He-Man toys in 1984[101] and over $1B in 1985 from the sale of not just toys but all manner of licensed products, such as toothbrushes, belts, and wallpaper.[102] The show was distributed via the controversial barter system, in which the producers offered the more-expensive-than-it-looked program to stations for free (along with lunch, one imagines), and of the four minutes of commercial time, two minutes were already allocated for the show's producer.[103] In this case, all of the bartered commercial time would be for Mattel products—with the exception of He-Man itself, since "host-selling," i.e., commercials featuring the same characters and products as seen on the show itself, was still illegal.[104] Also in effect through the premiere of *My Little Pony 'n' Friends* in 1987 and still present in *My Little Pony Tales* in 1992 was the "clear separation" principle, established by a 1974 Federal Communications Commission Report and Policy Statement and requiring broadcasters to clearly delineate where the program ended and the commercials began, as in "*My Little Pony 'n' Friends* will return after these messages."[105]

An estimated 70% of children's programs were distributed via the barter system in 1983.[106] Speaking before Congress on March 17, 1988, at the second of the two hearings regarding three bills which would require the FCC to reinstate restrictions on advertising during children's television programs, John Claster cited *My Little Pony 'n' Friends* as proof that program-length commercials didn't work nearly as well as commercial-length commercials:

> My Little Pony, the product, was introduced into the market in 1983. It was a successful product for Hasbro. In fact, since its introduction almost 100 million My Little Ponies have been sold worldwide. In 1986, we were able to clear a My Little Pony animated series in first run syndication. During the first four months that the series aired, sales of My Little Pony products declined significantly, while the show was popular from its inception. In response to sagging sales, Hasbro adopted a new advertising campaign which was effective in restoring product sales. The programming was not changed and had no impact on sales.[107]

Claster went on to suggest that *My Little Pony 'n' Friends* and other Hasbro series not having new episodes produced for the 1988–1989 television season was due to "increasing production costs and decreasing audience," and that this was further evidence that their programming decisions were not influenced by product sales.[108] In spite of that declining audience, Claster had placed a full-page ad in the previous month's *Broadcasting* to promote the series at the NATPE convention, declaring that "THESE STEEDS ARE GATHERING SPEED! Pulling Away from the Field with Bigger Numbers than Ever!" with no exact numbers given but citing "NSI Overnights, November '86 and '87."[109]

Indeed, elsewhere in the 1988 hearing he made the dubious claim that his was the only company he knew of in the broadcasting industry which contractually forbade host-selling commercials from being shown during the series proper—and if it *did* happen, it was a mistake made by computers.[110] In 1988, "computer error" was still a valid excuse, even when testifying in front of Congress.

In addition to the fears that computers would take over, the 1980s were also the years of the Satanic Panic, the belief that devilish forces were on the prowl in the entertainment industry and beyond. In his 1986 book *Turmoil in the Toy Box*, evangelist Phil Phillips asserted that "My Little Pony toys may be cute, but they definitely are based on occult symbolism."[111] (Other titles by the same publisher listed on *Turmoil*'s copyright page include *The Great Pre-*

tender and the delightful-sounding *To My Jewish Friends with Love.*[112]) In bold text, Phillips insisted that unicorns are a symbol of the Antichrist, citing the reference to a small horn rising among a group of larger horns in Daniel 7:8.[113] However, when deconstructing "Rescue at Midnight Castle" to demonstrate that it was "also laden with the occult," he referred to the rainbow in bold text as **"a symbol representing the 'New Age Movement,'"**—and, surprisingly for an Evangelical Christian, he made no reference to Genesis 9:13, in which the rainbow represents the covenant between God and humanity after the flood.[114] It was not the last time that the usage of rainbows in My Little Pony was gleaned to have negative connotations, and not simply because rainbows are a beautiful natural phenomenon that children are naturally drawn toward; critics looking for surface elements of *Friendship Is Magic* representing sinister themes would latch onto the rainbow not as a sign of the "New Age Movement," but as sign of homophobia, while the unicorn's horn would not represent the Antichrist but instead be referred to simply as a phallic symbol. By some standards the definition of wholesomeness, even rainbows and unicorns become dangerous when they're associated with My Little Pony.

I Don't Know Your Name, But the Mane Is Familiar

Of the more than 3 dozen ponies released in G1 / Year Four (1985–1986), none had names similar to anypony on *Friendship Is Magic*. The names included Lickety-Split, Truly, North Star, Skippity Doo, Hippity Hop, and Whizzer, and while the previous two years had been subdivided among breeds—Earth, Pegasus, Unicorn, Sea, and Rainbow, as well as a few Baby variations of specific characters—Year Four expanded it further with ranges that were less about identifiable breeds and more about the physical attributes of the dolls themselves, such as the extra-fuzzy So Soft Ponies, or the gem-eyed Twinkle Eyed Ponies. Many of the dozens of G1 ponies only appeared once as one of these forms, such as the aforementioned Whizzer (Twinkle Eyed) and Skippity Doo (So Soft).

Launched in 2010, Generation 4 would also have many such variations. In addition to So Soft, there's also Fashion Style, Shine Bright, Playful, Glimmer Wing, Traveling, Royal Wedding, and far more than can be discussed here. While there are plenty of Whizzer-esque one-off characters in G4 (even dedicated viewers of *Friendship Is Magic* such as myself who don't immerse themselves in the merchandise or Brony fan fiction may not have the foggiest idea who Sunny Rays or Dewdrop Dazzle are), the strong emphasis on the characters in *Friendship Is Magic* results in the primary characters—Twilight Sparkle, Rarity, Fluttershy, Applejack, Pinkie Pie, and Rainbow Dash, hereafter referred to collectively as the Mane Six—being represented more frequently in the varying ranges than were any given characters in G1. *Who* the pony is that's being represented is no less important, and possibly even more important, than it being a toy pony at all. (Your humble author has several different Rarity dolls from the biped *Equestria Girls* range in her office, because whether genus *equus* or *homo*, Rarity is the best.) It also speaks to a change in the concept of casual collectability over the decades; it's possible to purchase several iterations of the same character without it being redundant. (Depending on one's level of commitment or what particular political point that they're attempting to make at the time, as we'll see later in "No (Equestria) Girls Allowed, Part III: Daily v. Girls, Round 2.")

While the *Friendship Is Magic* series was a huge leap forward from the original series and movie in terms of character development, and its characters are more mature than their G1 forebears, this was seldom reflected in the G4 merchandise introduced in 2010. As such, the backstories and accessories for the G4 toys do not line up with the characters as they appear on the show. For example, Applejack's hat on *Friendship Is Magic* is missing from her official merchandise, and of the few dolls which do include a hat as an accessory, none look like the natty brown hat she habitually wears. (Applejack's hat's only appearance by mid–2015 had been in a licensed vinyl doll from Funko, and indeed, the Funko range made an effort to closely replicate the appearance of the characters in a way the official products did not.[115]) Meanwhile, the Fashion Style Applejack released as part of the G4 / Year One (2010) range came with a number of frou-frou accouterments that the Applejack of the show would find distasteful; the back of the package stated that "Applejack has found the perfect outfit to wear while apple picking."[116] It suggested that the customer could style Applejack's hair with "with pretty barrettes and her favorite cowgirl hat"—a pink number which bore no resemblance to *Friendship Is Magic*'s Applejack's brown hat, the one she's so dedicated to she even makes a point of sneaking it on while a bridesmaid for Princess Cadance in "A Canterlot Wedding, Part 2" (S02E26).[117] In its exhortation to style the pony's hair, the G4 merchandise maintained the "My" aspect of "My Little Pony," emphasizing the play of the child with the pony, while the possessive "My" in the *My Little Pony: Friendship Is Magic* series refers to the relationship between the characters, in particular Twilight Sparkle; as expressed in that show's theme song, her friends are the "my little ponies" of the title.

My Little Pony, Destroyer of Cinema

Though there wouldn't be another show of any kind until the debut of the series in September 1986, 18 months post–"Catrina," My Little Pony was still listed in a December 1985 *Seattle Times* article about television influencing what kids want for Christmas.[118] It was the last in a nine-item list—after, among others, Transformers, Voltron, He-Man, and the all-but-forgotten M.A.S.K.—and while there was no regular television presence other than commercials, My Little Pony was still considered to have a pernicious influence on youngsters. The article also reprinted a contemporaneous *Toy & Hobby World* list of 1985's best-selling toys: Cabbage Patch Kids and Transformers were tied for the first, while My Little Pony came in number 8, after M.A.S.K.[119] Not a bad showing for a toy range without a regular series to back it up, but then again, Cabbage Patch Kids had no television presence beyond commercials and a holiday special. By July 1987, My Little Pony would drop to number 10 on the *Toy & Hobby World* list.[120]

With the debut of the television series a few months off, *My Little Pony: The Movie* was released to theaters in June 1986. In a *San Jose Mercury News* summer movie preview, film critic Glenn Lovell called it "another animated feature whipped up by merchandisers to cash in on a popular toy," and after quoting the logline's promise to "transport children to a magical dimension of loveable ponies and fantasy creatures," he added a personal aside: "Yeee-uk!"[121] Whether or not Lovell reviewed *My Little Pony: The Movie* is unclear, but in his review of *The Care Bears Adventure in Wonderland* the following year, he proudly described himself as "one who can barely tell a Care Bear from a My Little Pony."[122] (Helpful hint from three decades into the future to Mr. Lovell: a Care Bear is the one that looks like a cartoon bear, and a My Little Pony is the one that looks like a cartoon pony.)

The *New York Times* addressed the *Pony* movie's origins in the first line of its review, referring to the movie as "probably the longest self-advertisement since [1985's] *The Care Bears*," and that these "sticky-sweet creations typify a new idea in marketing"[123]:

> Invent the toy, blitz the children with television commercials for it, maybe throw in a television special that shows the toy in action, and finally top it all off with a full-length cartoon movie that will sell the toy and the movie tickets all in one gooey package.[124]

That's a passable description of the process up to that point, even if it incorrectly suggested that a toy was included with the price of the ticket like a latter-day Prince album.[125] In a degree of over-intellectualization that would not be out of place in this book, the *Times'* critic does refer to the film's villain—a witch who intends to obliterate the ponies—as "a basic nihilist."[126] Charles Solomon's *Los Angeles Times* review described the movie as "like being immersed in cotton candy for an hour and a half," and while he praised the songs contributed by composer Tommy Goodman and lyricist Barry Harman, that wasn't the music that leapt out at him[127]:

> …the real theme song is the ring of the cash register, as Hasbro attempts to turn unwitting young viewers into customers. The sugary cuteness of the Little Ponies masks a corporate greed as cold and sharp as a razor blade.[128]

Elanor Ringel's *Atlanta Journal-Constitution* review was no less angry, describing the film as an "unabashed 90-minute plug" for the recently introduced Flutter Ponies range (in spite of the fact that they don't appear until the end), and took an apocalyptic view of the impact on the young viewers while making a broad assumption about their parents[129]:

> But something has to be done about this toy-into-TV-series-into-tot-movie syndrome. It's an ugly '80s phenomenon and I'll bet years from now, those same kiddies who begged to see "My Little Pony" are going to be teenagers trading parental resentments like, "When I was little, my mom never bothered to take me to the good stuff like the Disney classics. She just dumped me at whatever was easy—crud like 'My Little Pony'—and that's why I'm so messed up now."[130]

There weren't any Disney classics in wide re-release at the time, a detail a professional film critic like Ringel had to have been aware of, but that still didn't excuse parents for taking their future teenage malcontents to *My Little Pony: The Movie*. Meanwhile, in his *Philadelphia Inquirer* review, Desmond Ryan warned that the film entering the Top 10 in its first weekend "ought to give us all pause for thought"; he also referred to the film as "pap that scrupulously avoids any real attempt to engage children," because that might "distract from the main order of business, which is to put their money on more horses."[131] In his effusive review of Disney's new *The Great Mouse Detective* a few days later, Ryan took time out to call *My Little Pony: The Movie* and other similar films "inanimation," and "shoddily made and cynically motivated feature length commercials for toy lines."[132] He does not mention that the non-classic *Great Mouse Detective*, like all Disney films before and after, had plenty of ancillary merchandise.[133] And, clever though Ryan's wordplay may be, "inanimation" is not a fair description of *My Little Pony: The Movie*'s style. Rather than using the limited-animation process common to television cartoons in which the characters remain static except for their limbs or mouths (Hanna-Barbera's *The Flintstones* being the classic example), the traditionally-animated yet under-budgeted *My Little Pony: The Movie* suffers the opposite problem, in which all the characters move and gesture more than is motivated by the action, and often have a persistent wobble. On the plus side, almost every shot has motion on the screen; the camera frequently pans and zooms, and there's even some clever direction, such as the otherwise unremarkable song "Go It Alone" in which the dueting Baby Lickety-Split and Spike the Dragon gradually approach the camera, eventually sharing an extreme close-up. It's not up to the standards of Disney or Don Bluth, or even all that good, but whatever else one can say about the picture—and for the most part, all anypony wanted to say about the picture was to shame it for its Original Sin—*My Little Pony: The Movie*'s animation is always animated. Indeed, for a rush job in which the 300,000 cels were created in 10 weeks as the first job of the newly formed AKOM Studio in Seoul, South Korea, which a few years later would go on to produce the animation for *The Simpsons,* it could look much worse than it does.[134] (Another *Simpsons* connection: Nancy Cartwright provided the voice of Gusty in both *My Little Pony: The Movie* and *My Little Pony 'n' Friends*, and would go on to use that same voice for Bart Simpson.[135])

The *Ottawa Citizen*'s Richard Martin did acknowledge the merchandising aspect of the Disney empire in his *My Little Pony: The Movie* review, which he wrote as a history of licensed products in a faux-Biblical style, though it was given the prosaic headline of "Movie Sure to Give Toy Sales a Boost."[136] (Editors!)

> Soon, the image and likeness of The Mouse was seen throughout the land on lunch pails and watches, and his face sprang up in Mousketeer clubs everywhere as the dandelion in early summer.
> And people marvelled at the marketing genius of Uncle Walt, saying, we need a product like that, one to make us all rich beyond our wildest expectations.
> And so there came to pass Smurfs and Care Bears, Strawberry Shortcake and Dolls of the Cabbage Patch, Go-Bots and Transformers.[137]

While he acknowledged that there had only been two My Little Pony half-hour specials thus far, he still referred to the great cultural evil known as "Saturday morning cartoons" three times in a 441-word review:

> These creatures inhabited a magical world called the Saturday morning cartoon where their adventures caused squeals of delight from innocent children who had never seen a real cartoon in their life and were defenceless.[138]

Though he did not directly compare it to Disney, that chauvinism still slipped into the reference to "defenceless" children who squeal in delight because they don't know what a "real cartoon" is. This suggests that a child who has seen whatever Martin would deem to be "real" would thus not *also* be capable of enjoying the far less accomplished animation of *My Little Pony: The Movie* just because Martin himself cannot. Indeed, the fact that children are capable of enjoying the good and the not-so-good equally, to still squeal in delight at a cartoon that isn't up to the standards of a big-budget Disney feature, is not a sign of defenselessness, but the opposite—it's a strength, and one which many film critics lack.

> …and the marketing men at Hasbro Toys saw that it was good. So they dreamed up a product called My Little Pony and advertised it in the magical world of the Saturday morning cartoon until all the children wanted one…[139]

Again, the narrative is reinforced that My Little Pony was conceived and developed by not just men but *marketing* men, and that children were drawn to it because it had been advertised to them—during Saturday morning cartoons, no less, though the majority of the commercials were likely run during the bartered children's programming on weekdays—and not because it was a cute, attractive product that struck a nerve.

> …and the drawing and animation were as crude and simple as they are in the magical world of the Saturday morning cartoon and the songs were completely forgettable and the happy ending was utterly sweet and sticky.[140]

To an adult, sure. But it wasn't for adults, let alone those with such a strong beef against Saturday morning cartoons.

A few critics grudgingly enjoyed *My Little Pony: The Movie*, or at least admitted that its target audience might enjoy it more than themselves, though seldom without mentioning the merchandising aspect. The *Seattle Times* allowed that "as kiddie-matinee marketing ploys go these days, *My Little Pony* isn't that bad."[141] The *Providence Journal-Bulletin*'s critic said that as much as they hated "the idea of a movie based on a line of toys, this movie makes the most of its limited premises," while also referencing John Milton's *Paradise Lost* Satan *vis-à-vis* the movie's villains (which is nearly as pretentious as referencing Eugene O'Neill when discussing an episode of *Friendship Is Magic*, or using the phrase *vis-à-vis*).[142] And not only did the *San Diego Union Tribune*'s critic bring along a seven-year-old girl and four-year-old boy to gauge *their* reactions (the girl enjoyed it more than the boy), at no point in the 736-word review did he mention the merchandise.[143]

Identifying herself as the mother of a three-year-old girl, Baton Rouge *Advocate* critic Norma Dyess described the film as "so adorable and so well-done, I didn't even mind being set up by the toy's manufacturers as a captive test market for a whole new crop of Ponies."[144] Recapping the summer's films that September, Dyess wrote of both the My Little Pony and Care Bears movies, "Sure they're commercial as all get-out, but they're well-done, beautiful to look at and a sure winner for preschoolers. And they're cute."[145] In a January 1987 *New York Times* piece with the no-bones-about-it title "In Animation for Children, the Old Days Were Best," Janet Maslin made a prediction: "It seems highly unlikely that today's children will be looking back as fondly three decades hence on Fievel, let alone He-Man, the Care Bears, My Little Pony or Rainbow Brite."[146] She was speaking more of the potential nostalgia value rather than longevity of the brand, but four out of five ain't bad, and He-Man, the Care Bears, and Rainbow Brite would all experience a rebirth of sorts in the 1980s nostalgia boom of the 2000s. An October 1987 *People* piece about the 50th anniversary of *Snow White and the Seven Dwarfs* also predicted that My Little Pony would be forgotten by its golden anniversary, calling it and one of its contemporaries to the floor: "And what will you be doing in 2037, Strawberry Shortcake and My Little Pony?"[147] It is impossible to predict its status 20 years from the time of this writing, but not only did My Little Pony manage to hang in there for the previous 30, it seems likely that the kids growing up on *Friendship Is Magic* will have fond memories of it as they approach middle age.

As had been the case with the toys, those who worked professionally with children were often less hostile to the franchise than those who did not. Reviewing the video release of *My Little Pony: The Movie* for the April 1987 *School Library Journal*, librarian Constance Dyckman wrote that while the "substance and charm of a good story is lacking," the story is "limitless in imaginative words, particularly names," and she didn't mention the toys or the marketing angle that so angered most film critics.[148] This was not the case across the board; a review in the March 1986 *School Library Journal* of the picture book *My Little Pony Under the Big Top!* began by calling it "yet another blatant cash-in on a popular toy," and concluded that "there is no reason for this book to be on any shelf, except perhaps in the supermarket."[149]

Five months after his colleague Elanor Ringel predicted that future teenagers would specify *My Little Pony: The Movie* as the reason they're so messed-up, the *Atlanta Journal-Constitution*'s critic Scott Cain's November 1986 review of the video release (which listed the retail price as $79.95 on Beta and VHS) adopted a tone of weary resignation[150]:

> Pre-school girls don't know and don't care that this cartoon feature is a 90-minute toy commercial. Complaining about blatant commercialism is a waste of time. If we must have these toy promotions, "My Little Pony" is one of the more palatable.[151]

He probably considered *Transformers: The Movie* to be one of the less palatable. Released in August 1986, three months after the *Pony* movie, Cain hated the *Transformers* picture; his review focused on the incomprehensibility of the movie's plot (the opposite of the problem many critics had with *My Little Pony: The Movie*, when they deigned to discuss the text at all), and while he acknowledged the commercial tie-in, that was not his main issue with the film:

The fact that children appreciate "The Transformers" proves only that non-stop action is sufficient for kiddie audiences, but I am irate anyway. I am offended that "The Transformers" is a 90-minute toy commercial. Even worse, it paints a future in which war is incessant. The only human child among the characters is in tears almost constantly. Whenever he enjoys a laugh, it is only during a momentary lull in the battle.[152]

In the *Philadelphia Inquirer*, film critic Carrie Rickey objected to the film's male-centrism:

On purely sex-specific grounds, Transformers is masculinism on the rampage. All the characters but one have male traits and voices—most notably those of the mellifluous Robert Stack and the sonorous Orson Welles. Does Transformers really believe that outer space (and the future) is a man's world?[153]

In spite of *My Little Pony: The Movie* having spent a few weeks in the Top 10—according to the *San Francisco Chronicle*, by its third and final week on the chart, it had grossed $2.9M[154]—both it and *Transformers: The Movie* were financial failures, losing Hasbro about $10M in an otherwise profitable year.[155] An August 1987 *Los Angeles Times* article on the decline and fall of the DeLaurentiis Entertainment Group listed *My Little Pony: The Movie* as having grossed $2.8M on a $5M budget, while *Transformers: The Movie* only grossed $2.6M on a $5M budget, so My Little Pony won that race by a photo finish.[156] Three decades later, a live-action *Jem and the Holograms* film produced by Hasbro's Allspark Pictures division would continue the not-so-proud tradition by grossing $2.25M on a $5M budget.[157] It would also be savaged by not only critics, but the general public long before it was released.[158]

Looking back on the poor performance of G-rated films in 1986, the *Atlanta Journal-Constitution*'s Cain described these Hasbro properties and others as "crass attempts to cash in on a TV show or a line of toys" which "richly deserved to fail,"[159] though it should be noted that *Transformers* was rated PG due to its violence and use of the word "shit."[160]

In *Television Cartoon Shows: An Illustrated Encyclopedia*, Hal Erickson wrote of *Transformers: The Movie* that "the animation style that passed muster on TV seemed inadequate when blown up to the 35-foot dimensions of a movie screen" and that "the film's ear-shattering rock music score was also a drawback."[161] He did take mild issue with the film receiving a "BOMB" rating in *Leonard Maltin's TV Movies and Video Guide,* saying that "he wouldn't go that far," while also acknowledging that he wouldn't have paid five 1986 dollars to see the movie in the theater.[162]

Here's the entry for *Transformers: The Movie* in the 1990 edition of the Maltin book:

Obnoxious animated feature about the title good guys, who defend the universe against an evil planet (which has a voice of its own ... provided by Orson Welles). That deafening rock score certainly doesn't help. Little more than a feature-length toy commercial.[163]

Erickson did not mention Leonard Maltin's review of *My Little Pony: The Movie*, perhaps because Maltin gave it two stars out of four, and skipped the *de rigueur* gripe about the commercialism:

> Animated fantasy pits the good Little Ponies against an evil witch. Highlight is an encounter with the Smooze, and evergrowing mass of living lava—a good idea hampered by bad animation. Too "cute" for anyone over the age of 7. Followed by a TV series.[164]

Nostalgia for *Transformers: The Movie* is much stronger. This is partly because entertainment geared toward male children tends to have a more positive presence in the public consciousness, though it also helped that Stan Bush's song "The Touch" was later repurposed in Paul Thomas Anderson's 1997 *Boogie Nights*.[165] This was not because it was a good song—quite the opposite—but it still had the effect of lionizing the *Transformers* movie.

My Little Pony, Destroyer of Television

In November 1985, *Broadcasting* reported that Claster Television had cleared 65 episodes of *My Little Pony 'n' Friends* in the fall of 1986 in "61 markets covering 56% of the country," including KCOP in Los Angeles, WLVI in Boston, and WTTG in Washington.[166] Eight runs of those 65 episodes were scheduled, and they were sold on a barter basis, with four minutes of the commercial time going to the station and another two to Claster.[167] *Broadcasting* reported that by January the number of markets had increased to 87, though it still trailed behind Claster's just-renewed shows *G.I. Joe* (126 markets) and *Transformers* (142 stations).[168]

My Little Pony 'n' Friends premiered in September 1986. The friends in question were other characters based on Hasbro toys who appeared in their own unrelated segments, such as Potato Head Kids,[169] Moondreamers,[170] and Glo Friends.[171] Subsequent reruns and video releases would only feature the *Pony* segments, and the name of the series was shortened to *My Little Pony*. However, it will continue to be referred to in this book as *My Little Pony 'n' Friends* to differentiate it from *My Little Pony Tales* and *My Little Pony: Friendship Is Magic*.

Spike and the human Megan appear in both the movie and the *My Little Pony 'n' Friends* series, now set in Ponyland rather than Dream Valley, while Applejack and the Unicorn Twilight only appear in "Rescue at Midnight Castle," the re-edited version of the original My Little Pony animated special. Elsewhere in the series there's a different Twilight, a Pegasus rather than a Unicorn. This winged Twilight is part of the Year Five (1986–1987) range of toys, but of the approximately 40 different ponies that have speaking parts throughout the two seasons of *My Little Pony 'n' Friends*, the majority stem from Year Four (1985–1986) and prior, probably due to the long production time for animation. Beyond that, no further ponies with names similar to major *Friendship Is Magic* characters would be released throughout the rest of G1, which ended in 1992.[172]

My Little Pony 'n' Friends is cloying and treacly on the surface, written to be unchallenging to young children at a time when the boundaries of what was considered "appropriate" were much narrower than they are now, and perhaps worse, all the characters are voiced not so much as young children as what adults think young children sound like. (By contrast, the school-age Cutie Mark Crusaders on *Friendship Is Magic*, though not the Mane Six, are voiced by teenagers, doing characters but non-exaggerated voices.) But the series also needs to be considered in the context of its original run. Whatever one's feelings about its status as a program-length commercial, those who owned the toys had a different relationship with the show, a connection that's not shared by those not emotionally invested in their own toy horses. In that respect, *My Little Pony 'n' Friends* can be viewed now as a part of a multimedia presentation which only made sense in its original context, like a film loop that loses its meaning outside of an art installation. *Friendship Is Magic*, on the other hand, can be appreciated by viewers who have no familiarity with the tie-in merchandising—and, as previously discussed, the merchandising's connection to that show is tenuous.

This is not to say that *My Little Pony 'n' Friends* was all that good, but it did have its moments, mostly by outside writers who brought a little individuality to their scripts. The most notable was Linda Woolverton, who wrote "Crunch the Rockdog (Parts 1–2)," and went on to write the screenplays for the blockbuster Disney films *Beauty and the Beast* (for which she was the first woman to have sole screenwriting credit on a Disney film), *Maleficent*, and *Alice in Wonderland* (for which she is thus far the only woman to have sole screenwriting credit on a film, Disney or otherwise, to gross a billion dollars worldwide).[173]

Established science fiction and fantasy novelist Diane Duane wrote two of the series' better episodes, "The Great Rainbow Caper" and "The Masterpiece." She also co-wrote what's considered to be one of the first good episodes of *Star Trek: The Next Generation*'s dismal first season, "Where No One Has Gone Before," which aired a month after *My Little Pony 'n' Friends* exhausted its run of original episodes in September 1987. And as further evidence that the *Pony* producers were not without taste, they fired future *Big Bang Theory* and *Two and a Half Men* creator Chuck Lorre before he was able to complete a filmable script.[174]

In *Sold Separately*, Ellen Seiter analyzed three episodes of *My Little Pony 'n' Friends*: "Mish Mash Melee," "Baby, It's Cold Outside," and "The Glass Princess," examining the actual content of the show in a way that's almost never done elsewhere. She noted in her analysis of "The Glass Princess," for example, that the character of Shady—whose "high-pitched, sing-song" voice, she acknowledged, is "especially grating to adults," a formalistic element of the show which has been a barrier to serious study—expresses feelings of insecurity and inadequacy, which are not to be found in cartoons intended for boys.[175] Seiter pointed out that if Shady's character "represents a masochistic response to the problem of being a little girl, she at least represents an acknowledgment of that identity as problematic."[176]

In the book's first chapter, Seiter discussed how because "very young children are now sufficiently immersed in a consumer culture," they're likely to strike up a conversation with another child in public based purely on them holding a favored toy or wearing branded t-shirt.[177] In this, she described what is now commonly known as a *fandom*, a term which wasn't in broad use at the time. Perhaps most controversially, she wrote that it's a mistake "to see marketers as evil brainwashers and children as naïve innocents, as they are so often depicted in journalists' accounts of the toy industry," and argued that "children's desire for toys and media is more than the direct fulfillment of the designs of manufacturers and marketers, however attractive this notion may be in its simplicity."[178] That simple notion would indeed continue to be irresistible, up through and including *Friendship Is Magic* and *Equestria Girls*.

A March 1994 *Women's Review of Books* review of *Sold Separately* took Seiter to task for not acknowledging My Little Pony's Original Sin. The critic wrote that Seiter didn't go far enough in her analysis of the damage caused by toys marketed to children, and of consumer culture "becoming the currency or language of a peer culture" (again, what we now call a fandom).[179] They were also troubled that Seiter herself wasn't troubled enough by the inevitable future of My Little Pony fans:

> If little girls are using My Little Ponies to identify with each other and to declare their membership in a group, it seems reasonable to assume that they can be seen as "in training" for using other, more expensive products to establish group identities in the future. The 3-year-old whose heart is set on a lavender pony can easily grow into the 13-year-old who must have a $50 pair of Guess jeans, the 23-year-old who can only find clothes she really likes at The Gap and the 33-year-old for whom only a BMW will do.[180]

In addition to stretching the definition of "reasonable" to the breaking point, this scenario raises the question of whether those hypothetical girls whose desire to bond with other girls with like interests lead to them becoming Gap-wearing, BMW-driving 33-year-olds were the same ones who were messed-up teenagers because of their parents dumping them at *My Little Pony: The Movie*. It may be decades before we can fully determine the damage caused to the first generation of women who grew up with My Little Pony, even if they appear to have done just fine for themselves.

My Little Pony, Destroyer of Everything

Another way My Little Pony wrought havoc in 1987 was demonstrated by a September 21 *Orange County Register* article about the local chapter of the Cartoon Fantasy Organization (CFO), a club that held marathon screenings of series like *Dirty Pair* that are now called anime, but were still called Japanese animation in the United States press.[181] In spite of the word "cartoon" being right there in the name of their organization, a spokesperson explained that they shunned the C-word: "We don't call the programs 'cartoons' because that implies a low level of intelligence, like 'My Little Pony' or 'Rainbow Brite.' In Japan, animation isn't just for children; consequently, their stories have more depth and the characters are more realistic than ours. The CFO provides an alternative to most of the animation people see on their TV sets."[182] In fact, there was animation being produced in Japan for children, just as there was animation for adults being made in the United States (though it wouldn't be on television until the end of the decade).

Things that people were seeing on their TV sets in those days included the still-relevant MTV, and music videos were always a reliable scapegoat. Speaking to Association of Independent Television Stations President Preston R. Padden during the second of two hearings on the commercialization of children's television on September 15, Illinois Representative Terry L. Bruce referred to the Bruce household as being "blessed by cable," since it meant that his 15-year-old and 11-year-old children had never seen "one of those programs you ran through," i.e. program-length commercials on broadcast television.[183]

No video of the hearing is readily available to the public, but one can imagine a flop-sweating Padden's eyes lighting up at the mention of cable as "blessing" for children, since that gave him a greater cultural evil to point at, one which would be politically dangerous for anypony to defend.

> I've got to jump in on your comment about being blessed with cable. Because whatever arguments we may have about the social utility of children's programs like "My Little Pony" or "Charmkins," I think everyone would agree that they are a lot less harmful to children than are the music videos that are available 24 hours on demand for children on cable. And I have been in cable homes when there were quality programs available for children on independent stations, and you walk in, and the kids are sitting there watching some depraved music video with violence and sex, and bizarre behavior.[184]

Instead of taking the moral-outrage bait and agreeing that yes, of course, music videos are far more dangerous to children than My Little Pony, Representative Bruce slapped Padden down, albeit in a somewhat muddled way: "Well, obviously you'd be upset because if they're not watching independent stations, none of your independent stations are selling commercials to whoever watches the independent network."[185]

Also speaking at the hearing was Action for Children's Television (ACT) President Peggy Charren, who went on to describe My Little Pony in an October 1987 *USA Today* article as a "half-hour commercial" that should be banned, ending a list including *GoBots, Transformers,* and *G.I. Joe.*[186] Charren, who did good work and was quite noble in her desire to create more diverse and less commercially-driven television for kids, disbanded ACT in 1992 after the passage of the Children's Television Act of 1990.[187] (When she passed away in January 2015, a *Variety* article about her life's work titled "How Peggy Charren Overpowered the Children's TV Establishment" referenced 1980s children as being bombarded with "ads aimed at getting them to run in and demand their parents buy them He-Man action figures or My Little Pony," yet the picture at the top of the article was from *My Little Pony: Friendship Is Magic* in 2010.[188])

Sales of Generation 1 were declining by 1987, likely due to the overexposure and rampant licensing which Hasbro had sworn to avoid in 1984 when product scarcity was also an issue. Things were different now: the December 1987 *Playthings* quoted an Illinois toy store owner as saying that My Little Pony in particular had "an overabundance of product," while a store owner in New Jersey said that G.I. Joe, My Little Pony, and Rainbow Brite had all been disappointments that year, citing "the 10 or 20 point difference in price" as a probable cause.[189]

G1 / Year Seven (1988–1989) did show signs of creative fatigue, with new categories including the Windy Wing Ponies and Perfume Puff Ponies, and the Poof 'n' Puff Perfume Palace, which the February 1988 *Playthings* (probably quoting verbatim from a Hasbro press release) described as a "playset shaped like a perfume bottle with a real atomizer that sprays a fragrant scent."[190] The article also referred to the range as "about to gallop into their sixth season," implying that My Little Pony was introduced in 1983 rather than 1982.[191] And while the Pony range was in decline, 1989 would go on to be a record year for Hasbro, with sales growth in games and puzzles resulting in a net revenue of $1.410B and a net income of $92M.[192]

In a January 1989 *Providence Journal* article titled "Holiday Gifts Rated: Love It or Loathe It," a 5-year-old girl is described as giving the cold shoulder to My Little Pony "in favor of the Little Miss Makeup and Sun Island Barbie

Dolls she got for Christmas," and her mother points out that "'she had really outgrown My Little Pony anyway, and she couldn't wait to get the Barbie.'"[193] (Left unexamined was a 3-year-old boy's mother's description of how her son was enthralled with a *Ghostbusters*-branded toy gun, marveling that "the gun replaced all his stuffed animals. He sleeps with it!"[194] It was a toy gun based on a make-believe weapon that shoots proton beams to capture ghosts, but the boy was sleeping with a representation of a firearm nonetheless.) A December 1989 *New York Times* article about children who collected all manner of objects (not just toys) described a pair of 10- and 8-year-old sisters in Jersey City who had 104 My Little Ponies between them, while an 8-year-old Bakersfield girl won Hasbro's official "My Little Pony Mommy of the Year" contest with her collection of 364 dolls.[195] (For the record, that's 2.5 gross.) A brief *USA Today* piece in 1988 about the Bakersfield girl was headlined "My Little Obsession," marking one of the first times that a fan and/or collector would be referred to as obsessed,[196] while the 1989 *New York Times* article referred to Hasbro as My Little Pony's "perpetrators," a word popularized on *Hill Street Blues* and other police shows of the era as a synonym for criminals.[197]

When those perps became the first Western business to mass-market toys in the Soviet Union, the *Providence Journal*'s December 1989 headline on the front page was "Guess Who? My Little Pony to Trot into Soviet Toy Market," even though the focus of the article was the now-forgotten Sindy doll.[198] It came as a surprise to many in the industry that My Little Pony was not already forgotten by the end of the 1980s; ruminating in *Marketing* that June on how long the new-to-them Teenage Mutant Ninja Turtles would remain viable, the toys and games buyer for Harrod's in the UK pointed out that "no-one thought My Little Pony would last as long as it has."[199] That September, *New England Business* referred to My Little Pony as a "modern classic" along with Transformers and Cabbage Patch Kids, and at least two of those have proven worthy of the description.[200] The following September, *Adweek* called My Little Pony a "perennial," evidently unaware that the perennial in question was on the verge of going to seed for a decade.[201]

A March 1990 *Toronto Star* column by Nancy White described the difficulty of finding things to rent at the local video store that would appeal to her 1- and 4-year-old daughters—the latter of whom she referred to as "the dominatrix of the VCR," an unfortunate choice of words—and which White could listen to in the background while retaining her sanity.[202] She cited John Huston's critically-reviled 1982 musical adaptation of *Annie* as "one of the best" for those purposes, and went on to list many of the film's positive and negative qualities, such as the villains trying to kill Annie, the fact that "politically, it is not my glass of tea," and concluded with this[203]:

Annie is not really a children's movie. Miss Hannigan is played as a mean lush who comes on to every man she meets in a way that can only be described as overt. And the dance she does with her brother (Tim Curry) and his tarty girlfriend (Bernadette Peters) is pretty raunchy. It's a nice antidote to My Little Pony. Our 4-year-old loved My Little Pony, but [my husband] and I found it a stomach turner.[204]

In short: with its violence, children in peril, and overt sexuality, the PG-rated *Annie* is not appropriate for a toddler and a 4-year-old ... but at least it ain't *My Little Pony*! A profile of White in the *Globe and Mail* the following year described her kitchen as "tastefully decorated with My Little Ponies, colorful fridge magnets and tiny underpants," though she assured the reader that while she'd hoped that motherhood would make her a nicer person, "My writing hasn't changed at all. I'm as mean-spirited as ever."[205] Hooray?

*   *   *

As the debate raged on in Congress and elsewhere about acceptable percentages of advertising in children's television, Hasbro was getting into trouble in other ways. According to the July 17, 1989, edition of *Adweek's Marketing Week*, they had recently violated Better Business Bureau guidelines "when it offered a movie based on its My Little Pony Toy for 'only' a dollar," and that Hasbro agreed to follow the guidelines in future ads.[206] Unfortunately, there are no further details available as to exactly what the ad offered, or what the movie in question was; it may have been the 1986 *My Little Pony: The Movie*, which was slated to drop in price from $79.95 to $19.95 that September,[207] though it was more likely to be the 1985 special "Escape from Catrina," which was also $19.95 but might have been considered more disposable and thus more appropriate as a loss leader for the promotion.[208]

Thanks in no small part to the efforts of Peggy Charren and ACT, the Children's Television Act of 1990 (H.R.1677) was passed by the 101st Congress in September 1990, and by October it had become Public Law No. 101–437.[209] (President George Herbert Walker Bush did not approve of the bill and refused to sign it, but he also chose not to veto it.[210]) Rules were adopted by the FCC on April 9, 1991, to carry out the law, rules which wouldn't take effect until that October and limited the number of commercials during children's shows to 12 minutes per hour on weekdays, and 10.5 per hour on weekends.[211] Broadcasters would also be required to provide summaries of their educational programs, without specifying a required minimum amount of educational broadcasts, while the definition of a "program-length commercial" was now limited to any toy-based show featuring paid advertising for the toy in question—i.e. host-selling, which had been prohibited all along.[212] As Assistant Professor of Radio-TV Pamela Colby at George Washington

University later pointed out, at most the Act served as a reminder that host-selling was (still) illegal.[213]

The new television series *My Little Pony Tales* was probably not impacted. Its single 26-episode season originally ran from August through December 1992 on the Disney Channel while it was transitioning from a premium service to a basic cable channel, thus marking the first *Pony* series to debut on a network, though a network with far fewer viewers on average than any given independent station.[214] It was not much of an improvement over *My Little Pony 'n' Friends* in terms of production quality, but it did try some new things: Ponyland now resembled suburban America—if anything, it foreshadowed the biped world of the *Equestria Girls* movies—and the characters' lives more resembled that of their young viewers, with no human interlopers like Megan. *My Little Pony Tales* also tried to approach real-world problems in a way that the previous incarnations had not, if nowhere near as successfully as *Friendship Is Magic* would; in *Tales'* "The Great Lemonade Stand Wars," when the local mean boy ponies (also, there are mean boy ponies in *Tales*) decide to compete against the girls' lemonade business, one of them shrugs off any namby-pamby ethical concerns by quoting their teacher: "Free enterprise and competition make the economy stronger."[215] It's a far less nuanced take on economics than, say, *Friendship Is Magic*'s "The Super Speedy Cider Squeezy 6000" (S02E15). The 1992 *My Little Pony Tales* does have a direct behind-the-scenes connection with the 2010 *Friendship Is Magic*: the credited director of singers on *Tales*, Cathy Weseluck, provides the voice for Spike and others on *Magic*.[216]

The Long Dark Saturday Morning of the Soul

Hasbro stopped producing both *My Little Pony Tales* and the toys in English-speaking countries in 1992, though the 26 episodes of *Tales* remained in circulation on the Disney Channel in weekday afternoon slots through at least 1995.[217] The series was also offered to broadcast stations as a weekly show at the January 1993 NATPE Convention, but it's unclear whether it was ever shown outside of Disney.[218] But much like after the end of *My Little Pony 'n' Friends*, the brand never disappeared from the public consciousness, and North American newspapers often treated it like a collective trauma.

The *Ontario Star*'s April 1992 review of *FernGully: The Last Rainforest* referred to the film as "good, but not goody goody," and that "as adult survivors of Care Bears and My Little Pony know all too well, that makes it a small miracle."[219] In May, *Ren & Stimpy* creator John Kricfalusi told the *Austin*

American Statesman that part of his inspiration to start his own production company was that he figured "there had to be millions of kids out there as sick of Ducktales and The Flintstones and My Little Pony as we were."[220] Most oddly, that same paper later bemoaned the current lack of real-life horny toads, which in the 1950s and 1960s were "everywhere, spitting blood from their eyes" and "lurking implacably under porches," concluding that "as childhood pals went, they beat My Little Pony hands down."[221]

Stretching even further, the *Ottawa Citizen's* August 1993 review of John Woo's *Hard Target* began with, "Right from the start, you can tell this ain't going to be My Little Pony."[222] Left unexplained is why a viewer sitting down to watch a film called *Hard Target* starring Jean-Claude Van Damme might possibly expect that it would be My Little Pony; the joke would have made the same amount of sense had it referenced *Children of Paradise, Gone with the Wind,* or *Citizen Kane.* Or perhaps the critic was just being prescient: in 2015, Jean-Claude Van Damme released green-screen footage of himself doing action-hero-esque things, and YouTube user TechPony inserted Van Damme into the most violent *Friendship Is Magic* episode, "A Canterlot Wedding, Part 2" (S02E26).[223]

Throughout the 1990s, *My Little Pony 'n' Friends* was frequently held up as an exemplar of the worst of 1980s Saturday morning cartoons, in spite of it having been independently sold to television stations as a weekday show, and Saturday morning cartoons being a network phenomenon. Writing about the Children's Television Act for *Adweek's Marketing Week* in September 1991, David Kiley described Saturday mornings as having been "loaded with cartoons, many of which center around toys such as GI Joe and My Little Pony, or carry heavy merchandising tie-ins such as Teenage Mutant Ninja Turtles."[224] A January 1992 *San Francisco Chronicle* article about screenwriter Linda Woolverton referred to her as having been successful at "freelancing Saturday morning cartoons show scripts ("The Berenstain Bears," "My Little Pony"),"[225] while a March *Los Angeles Times* article about former Marvel Productions CEO Margaret Loesch described her as having "brought My Little Pony, Jem, G. I. Joe, Spiderman and Transformers to Saturday morning cartoons."[226] A review of *Tom and Jerry: The Movie* in the *Grand Rapids Press* the next year referred to the producers as trying to make the film "look like a Saturday morning television cartoon a la 'Care Bears' or 'My Little Pony.'"[227]

My Little Pony continued to be associated with not only the Saturday morning slot it never occupied but also the Care Bears by people looking to make a point about what they represented. In 1998, the president of the "adult-oriented" animation studio International Rocketship in Vancouver declared that "people are tired of Care Bears and My Little Pony," several years after those brands had ceased to have a broadcast television presence.[228]

In January 1999, *Los Angeles Times* writer Booth Moore's review of Timothy and Kevin Burke's *Saturday Morning Fever: Growing Up with Cartoon Culture* claimed that "the book also acknowledges that much of Saturday morning programming was weak and taught consumerism. Remember 'My Little Pony' and 'Care Bears?'"[229] *Saturday Morning Fever* itself only made one reference to any *My Little Pony* series, in the context of gendered entertainment rather than weakness and/or consumerism:

> …in some households, low-level war raged constantly on Saturdays. Fragile truces were made and broken with the space of an hour. Boys and girls in these homes struggled mightily with each other to get the television turned to "their" programs, a dilemma which became more acute in the 1980s with the rise of highly gendered programs like *My Little Pony and Friends* or *The Real Ghostbusters*. Veterans whose memories include struggles of this sort tell us that each week, a different range of programs might be seen, depending on which sibling was more wily or feral.[230]

Along with being one of the few instances beyond the era of the original broadcasts that the show is referred to by its full title, this anecdotal account only implied that *My Little Pony 'n' Friends* was a Saturday morning show ("each week") without stating it outright. The book's discussion of "furry, fuzzy, cute, or otherwise unpleasantly wholesome" Saturday morning shows focused on *The Smurfs* (NBC) and *The Care Bears Family* (ABC, for its first two seasons), both of which were categorically Saturday morning network shows.[231] And in spite of Moore citing *My Little Pony* and *Care Bears* as examples of "Saturday morning programming" that "taught consumerism" in their review of *Saturday Morning Fever*, the closest that *Fever*'s authors came to such a thing was a passing reference to how from 1983 to 1990, "kidvid schedules were choked with programming whose primary purpose was to flog lines of toys like the Transformers or the Care Bears."[232] It was one of the rare occasions that My Little Pony *wasn't* included in such a list.

Balancing that out was a March 1999 *Billboard* article about the 96th annual American International Toy Fair, which began with a history of licensed products that was almost as inaccurate as it was brief:

> In the early 1980s, when Hasbro's My Little Pony made the leap from retail to Saturday-morning cartoons and then video, the small plastic horse with its bushy, colorful mane was seen as trotting in the wrong direction.
>
> Until then, licensed toys had generally been born of TV and video programming, not the other way around. But at the 96th annual American International Toy Fair, held Feb. 8–15 in New York, it was apparent that My Little Pony's journey had paved the way for numerous others.[233]

They weren't wrong about the implied controversy, but otherwise, almost every detail is incorrect. To fact-check: there were television specials broadcast on weekday afternoons or evenings that were subsequently released on VHS prior to the debut of the series in 1986; 1986 is not the early 1980s; *My Little Pony 'n' Friends* was not a Saturday morning cartoon; and it was preceded by the *Transformers* and *He-Man* television series, so it by no means "paved the way" for other such shows, instead coming at the tail end of that particular cycle.

These frequent references to *My Little Pony 'n' Friends* as a Saturday morning network show when it was a syndicated weekday show demonstrate how the franchise in all its forms became the default when discussing the worst of animation and children's toys, such as the reviewer of *Saturday Morning Fever* making a point with it which the book they're reviewing does not. Ellen Seiter's *Sold Separately*, it should be noted, is one of the few texts to establish that the various *My Little Pony* cartoons were only broadcast in syndication, and were never on the networks on Saturday morning.[234] However, that *My Little Pony 'n' Friends* was not a Saturday morning show does not mean it was never on before noon; it was a fixture on weekday mornings (but not on weekends) in many markets from September 1987 to September 1989, including WNYW in New York,[235] KUSI in San Diego (and again in the afternoon),[236] WFTS in Sarasota, Florida,[237] and WCGV in Milwaukee, Wisconsin.[238] But those were the exceptions, and for cartoons, weekday mornings were a different market than the network-dominated Saturdays. The first *My Little Pony* television series to be a Saturday morning network show was *Friendship Is Magic* on the Hub, and not until Season 2 in 2011; Season 1 was broadcast on Friday afternoons at 1:30 p.m.[239] (In a March 2012 *Christian Science Monitor* article about the dangers of creators paying too much attention to fans, James Turner referred to a particular scene in *Friendship Is Magic*'s "The Last Roundup" [S02E14] as "typical Saturday morning nonsense." Judginess aside, at least the episode really was broadcast on a Saturday morning.[240])

Though International Rocketship had name-dropped both the Care Bears and My Little Pony in 1998, the latter was the only reference most animation producers needed. Speaking to the *Chicago Tribune* about his new Cartoon Network series *The Powerpuff Girls* that fall, Craig McCracken confirmed that it's no "girlie" show, specifying that it is not "My Little Pony."[241] He also suspected that girls would take to show more readily than boys, offering as it does "girls being heroes, and they're not being too girlie," thus reinforcing the false dichotomy between heroism and femininity.[242] In a November 2000 interview on NPR's *Morning Edition* after *Powerpuff* had become Cartoon Network's most popular show, host Madeleine Brand observed that "now 11 year-old boys, six year-old girls and an untold number of adults are hooked."[243] That such a wide-ranging audience was possible for a girl-centric show would be all but forgotten a decade later, and McCracken's response, while again fashionably slamming My Little Pony, would prove to be applicable to *Friendship Is Magic*:

> What a lot of people have found out about "Powerpuff Girls" is initially they just think it's this little girl thing that's lame like My Little Pony or whatever. Then they watch it and they're like "Wait a minute, this is really funny, and this is really good, and it's actually, you know, entertaining."[244]

The specter of the long-moribund My Little Pony cartoons continued to loom over Cartoon Network, in one case literally; a 2001 *Atlanta Journal-Constitution* profile of Cartoon Network head of programming and development Mike Lazzo described his office like so:

> Painted on two walls is a herd of toy ponies, from the "My Little Pony" cartoon series. Each pony wears a frown.
> "They're there to remind me how to screw it up," Lazzo says. "They're a perfect example of, 'Hey, let's make a cartoon for girls and let's make 'em little ponies and we'll give 'em combable hair.' That's not a great cartoon. That's a great toy."[245]

Sadly, no pictures of his office wall seem to exist on the Internet, though in the plus column, he called the G1 My Little Pony toys "great." That's a first!

The following year, in a *Chicago Tribune* article about a new *He-Man* series intended to tie into Mattel's revival of the toy range—a cartoon which Mattel's vice president of entertainment-marketing explicitly called "an education tool to reach kids who don't know about He-Man"—Cartoon Network senior vice president of development Sam Register said that while they were also developing new shows based on other masculine 1980s toy ranges such as the Transformers and Thundercats, there were limits: "I personally don't want to see 'My Little Pony' if I don't have to."[246] (A decade later, *My Little Pony: Friendship Is Magic* would indeed be seen on Cartoon Network's UK Boomerang channel, though not on their American flagship channel.[247])

That boys didn't want anything to do with My Little Pony was accepted as a given, but North American newspapers also used it throughout the 1990s as a litmus test for femininity in girls, and/or the extent to which they had grown to an acceptable level of maturity. One of the more promising such examples was an October 1991 *New York Times* article about the gender-defying appeal of the Teenage Mutant Ninja Turtles, as a mother described her 8-year-old daughter as a "very girly girl" who always wore dresses and liked Barbie and My Little Pony, and yet one day apropos of nothing shouted "Cowabunga!"[248] The article also quoted an Associate Professor of Clinical

Psychology who said that a little girl in 1991 may play with both boy-oriented toys as well as those intended for girls, "because she doesn't see it as an either/or situation."[249] (Which is the ideal, to be sure.)

My Little Pony was often the deciding factor of whether a girl was a tomboy, and 1996 was a big year for that sort of analysis. In a rather heart-breaking *Providence Journal-Bulletin* article that January, the mother of an 8-year-old described her recently murdered daughter as "part tomboy and part little girl," in that "she could play with dolls but also play football," and the ponies were among her preferred dolls.[250] An *Orange County Register* profile that March of a 9-year-old horseback-riding expert called her "an admitted cowgirl and tomboy," and that she played with "fanciful My Little Pony toys" from the age of 3 until her parents bought her the real thing.[251] That same month in the *New York Amsterdam News*, an 11-year-old girl described her older brother as having always directed her "toward sports and other 'tomboy' things," and that while she hated Barbie and My Little Pony, she hated G.I. Joe as well.[252]

In an August 1997 *Santa Fe New Mexican* article about the University of New Mexico Football Clinic (described as a "night of slight instruction on America's favorite sport"), the reporter prided herself "in never having owned a My Little Pony as a girl," and that she was "destined to be a tomboy the moment my father realized none of his children would ever write their name in the snow."[253] The head of a "clique of *Star Wars*-lovin' gals at San Clemente High School" told the *Orange County Register* in January 1999 that she "never considered herself a tomboy," since "she collects My Little Pony figures, too."[254]

How much has what it means to be a tomboy changed, and to what extent can *Friendship Is Magic* be seen as an example of a culture whose attitude about such things is changing for the better? An October 2013 *San Mateo County Times* article about a young girl who had been battling a rare pediatric cancer since she was 18 months old described her as "a 4 year-old tomboy who loves the color blue, Rainbow Dash from 'My Little Pony,' and singing along to 'The Lion King.'"[255] A tomboy, *and* she likes My Little Pony! Wonders, they never cease.

Ponies What Are British

Meanwhile, the UK press never failed to find a reason to reference My Little Pony. Perhaps because *My Little Pony 'n' Friends* hadn't been the presence on British television that it was in the United States, it was seldom referenced as a cartoon, but instead largely as a toy and an aesthetic, and often in a prurient manner. For example, the July 1992 "Advice to the Lovelorn" column in the *Times* offered as advice to teenagers that "sex is absolutely the most wonderful thing in the whole world, more wonderful even than My Little Pony, but that perhaps you ought to wait a year or six before you find out just how wonderful it is for yourself."[256]

In that same paper, an April 1993 review by Suzanne Moore of the pop-culture reference book *Fads, Fashions & Cults* fretted that the book would result in people 20 years down the line thinking that "the citizens of the 1990s were so brainless that they gave equal value to My Little Pony and post-structuralism, rave grannies and the Gaia hypothesis."[257] (If all goes well, taking My Little Pony as seriously as post-structuralism and the Gaia hypothesis will be considered a folly of the 2010s rather than the 1990s thanks to *this* book.) The *Fads, Fashions & Cults* entry is brainy enough, considering the physical properties of the dolls in a thoughtful way, though no source is given for the statement about the selection process of the skin:

> A craze among pre-teen girls in 1983, My Little Pony was a toy designed especially to feature tactile attractions. The Pony's plastic skin texture was chosen to provide maximum pleasure to the touch, while the long silken mane and tail were for caressing and combing. The miniature Pony was un-lifelike (some had detachable hooves), but served as an idealized object of affection. As a "promotional toy" or manufactured and merchandised fad, the Ponies were a milestone in 1980s mass marketing.[258]

As is so often the case with anything My Little Pony-related, the entry seems to have given offense to Moore less for its content than for its existence. As for "rave grannies," they were not grandmothers who still shook their groove thangs like Studio 54's famous septuagenarian Disco Sally,[259] but rather young British women who wore "a loose black dress over heavy boots—hence the comparison with an archaic peasant/grannie."[260] Speaking as somepony reading the book two decades after Moore's review, not only do I *not* consider the inclusion of such things a sign of Thatcher-era brainlessness, I'm happy to realize that I've done the rave grannie look a number of times over the years without knowing it.

The UK press also associated My Little Pony with androgyny, as in a November 1993 *Guardian* Terence Trent D'Arby concert review titled "This Little Pony" in which the writer was preoccupied with the way D'Arby blurred boundaries, "be they of race, gender, or musical genre."[261] The writer concluded that D'Arby was "wayward, nervy, and most of all, strangely equine," finally asking, "Could it be that he has come out as the My Little Pony of rock?"[262] A *Guardian* review of a performance by aging female impersonator Danny La Rue the following month bafflingly called it "a perfect candyfloss Christmas treat for the My Little Pony generation."[263]

At least one member of said generation rejected the designation, as an August 1994 article in the *Independent* quoted a 9-year-old North London girl who "did not admire her peers' reading tastes. 'My Little Pony! Yeuch! Too girly.'"[264] That it's their *reading* tastes further suggests that neither the *My Little Pony 'n' Friends* nor *My Little Pony Tales* series made it to Britain, though the books did.

The *Guardian* enjoyed comparing UK-famous political mistress Bienvenida Buck to that icon of girliness, such as Catherine Bennett describing her in June 1995 as "[standing] out like a life-size My Little Pony: all long legs, baby-blue, and a whouffed-up swirl of impossibly blonde hair."[265] Hair continued to be a trend; in November 1995 the *Independent* wrote that British Comedy Awards host Jonathan Ross "[guaranteed] a few extra laughs, if only for his My Little Pony hairstyle,"[266] while in January 1996, *Good Housekeeping* editor Pat Roberts Cairns described herself in an interview with the *Times* as having "ghastly My Little Pony hair, like spun nylon."[267] In an interview with Demi Moore in the *Observer*, the writer observed that Moore, "or someone, had curled her shiny hair into ringlets secured with clips, which reinforced the impression of a pre-teen or, perhaps, My Little Pony."[268]

In February 1997, the *Guardian* referenced a *Zest* magazine article about a study purporting to show that "tomboys grow up to be more assertive and self-reliant than girlie-girls," which the *Guardian* concluded was "yet another reason to buy your daughter or niece a footie kit instead of a My Little Pony."[269] A "footie kit" is a British soccer uniform, so it's not quite as adorable as it sounds, and while the study in question did say that "tomboyism was positively related to some instrumental qualities assertiveness and self-reliance," it neither made any purchasing suggestions nor said that girliness was an empirically bad thing.[270]

The ascendancy of the Spice Girls gave the UK media many more opportunities, such as Simon Hoggart writing in the *Guardian* in October 1996 that "their stage names, such as Ginger Spice, remind you of My Little Pony."[271] That November, Bernice Harrison wrote in the *Irish Times* that the Spice Girls "are simply huge with the My Little Pony set."[272] (Whether the "My Little Pony set" is the same as the "My Little Pony generation" for whom the 66-year-old Danny La Rue's drag performance was "a perfect candyfloss Christmas treat" is uncertain.) As late as 2006, when Posh Spice—by then best known by her married name, Victoria Beckham—cut her long hair, Susannah Frankel was relieved, writing in the *Independent* that there had "always been rather too much of the My Little Pony" about Beckham's tresses.[273]

The United States press didn't pick up on the Spice Girls / My Little Pony connection until the release of the feature film *Spice World* in January 1998.

Los Angeles Daily News film critic Glenn Whipp, who called it "the worst movie I have seen in a very long time," wrote that the movie's "prime audience of 8- to 16-year-old girls would be better off watching their old 'My Little Pony' videos."[274] Jay Boyar of the *Orlando Sentinel*, meanwhile, grasped for various metaphors to best "describe the transcendently puerile cinematic experience known as *Spice World*," such as "getting mauled by the Care Bears" and "drowning in a sea of My Little Pony sweat."[275] Press on both sides of the Atlantic who referenced My Little Pony in regards to the Spice Girls also made a point of what they perceived as the group's unsexiness; in the article in which Simon Hoggart compared stage names such as Ginger Spice to My Little Pony, he also observes that "the cunning trick is that they are not particularly gorgeous; any teenage girl with a nice hairdo and make-up could look like one."[276] And in his *Spice World* review, Glenn Whipp observed that "despite the tight, short dresses, the Spice Girls are pretty much asexual—probably a marketing decision so they won't frighten or offend their prime audience of 8- to 16-year-old girls," the same ones he recommended should watch their My Little Pony videos instead.[277]

But the history of My Little Pony is nothing if not a study of cycles: in a 2013 *New York Daily News* article about a backlash among New York mothers regarding the Mane Six "losing their manes and tails for mini-skirts and hooker boots" in the first *Equestria Girls* film, a disapproving 40-year-old Upper West side mother is quoted as saying "they're a little too sexy," and that "they look like the Spice Girls."[278] For as much as My Little Pony was used as a negative cultural touchstone during its own fallow period in the 1990s, it's appropriate that now-moribund icons of that decade would be trotted out to criticize the revitalized brand in the 2010s.

PART 2

The Lost Generations
(1998–2010)

Rebuilding the Stable

It is a law of pop-culture thermodynamics that My Little Pony cannot exist, or be announced to soon exist, without somepony being angry about the fact of its existence. On January 18, 1998, around the time that *Spice World* was being flagellated for crimes including but not limited to making critics think of My Little Pony, Teena Lyons's column for the *Sunday Mirror* in the UK featured a list called "7 Deadly Whims," a Seven Deadly Sins spoof.[1] The entry under "Wrath" should come as no surprise at this point:

> HOW can they do it? Prepare to froth at the mouth as you learn that My Little Pony, the tackiest toy of the decade, is back. They were last on sale in 1993 but makers Hambro UK have decided that we're ready for them to return. Cupcake, Flutterbye, Sundance and Tulip are on their way. You have been warned.[2]

A January 30 *Daily Mail* article credited the return to "an Internet petition by British and American fans" which "attracted hundreds of names," though Hasbro spokeswoman Alison Berry said the petition was merely one of many factors in the decision to revive the range.[3] She also explained that G1 sales had declined for multiple reasons, "one of which in particular was that the girl's toy market wanted smaller things like Polly Pocket. We simply did not match up to the pace of change."[4] The petition's British coordinator also spoke of how she came to be a fan of the franchise, noting that while she'd been a collector for a while, she hadn't realized that there was a massive fanbase until she got involved with the petition.[5]

Hasbro made it official with a February 6, 1998, press release titled "Hasbro Unveils a World of Fun at American International Toy Fair," which announced what would come to be known as Generation 2 as "an all-new collection of My Little Pony(R) ponies and playsets reminiscent of the 1980s favorite that won millions of girls' hearts worldwide."[6]

There are four new My Little Pony assortments. Secret Surprise Friends(TM) features ponies with special accessories highlighting each pony's individual personality. Magic Motion Friends(TM) are ponies that appear to come to life, swishing their tails and moving their legs with a turn of their heads. And for portable pony fun, Pony Magic Playsets(TM) and the Pony Garden Play Case(TM) fold and go wherever girls go with their collection of My Little Pony ponies.[7]

In spite of mentioning the accessories which would highlight a given pony's personality and the names of the two different lines, they did not mention the names of the ponies that would constitute G2 / Year One (1997): Berry Bright, Clever Clover, Morning Glory, Petal Blossom, Sky Skimmer (the Secret Surprise Friends), and Ivy and Sundance (the Magic Motion friends). Much like G1, the exact year that G2 began depends on where you look; though Hasbro didn't announce it until 1998, collector Summer Hayes's book *The My Little Pony G2 Collector's Inventory* cites G2 / Year One as beginning in 1997.[8]

The official setting was now Friendship Gardens, reflected in the October 1998 release of the first Pony-related video game and only G2 animation of any kind, the Windows-only *My Little Pony: Friendship Gardens*.[9] The game is perhaps the most overt example of the "My" aspect of the brand, as the game requires the player to feed, brush, and otherwise take care of a pony which they also design and name. Though other ponies are encountered who have voices and personal lives, the player's pony never speaks or displays any personality other than that which the player projects onto their equine avatar.

The April 1999 edition of *FamilyPC* gave the game a "Recommended" rating, saying that "the younger set will relish this opportunity to feed, play with, and tend to their own pony."[10] And while there was no mention of the toys, there was another, more important point made:

Some parents may find the pastel graphics and squeaky-voiced enthusiasm of My Little Pony a serious deterrent. But once you get beyond these elements—elements that younger girls, incidentally, had no problem with—you'll discover that there's a lot of fun to be had in Ponyland.[11]

The "incidentally" aside is an important one, because so few reviews or references to My Little Pony at all in the media had acknowledged the fact that it was intended for young girls, and that it's okay for things intended for young girls to appeal *only* to them. Along with the petition and the CD-ROM game, the technological connection that would come to define Generation 4 in 2010 had its dial-up equivalent in the form of still-futuristic-seeming websites such as Kimberly Shriner's collector site Dream Valley—which, at the time of this writing, continues to be updated while remaining charmingly Web 1.0.[12]

Brandweek reported in February 1999 that the G2 relaunch cost $1.5M, and that while "awareness of the property is widespread," Hasbro made a deal that would put "25 million Little Pony and [Transformers] Beast Wars premiums" in McDonald's Happy Meals, while a separate "collectible program" would be "driven by bursts on 4 million packages."[13] A Hasbro executive was quoted saying that "not many classic brands for girls can come back," and that they had "analyzed the marketplace and realized there has been a huge gap, and there's potential for huge global growth."[14]

Sometimes potential goes unfulfilled, and Generation 2 did not last in the United States or the UK beyond 1999. Covering the launch of Generation 3 in 2003, the UK edition of *PR Week* would write that it was "understood" that G2 relied too much on nostalgia, and that the toy itself wasn't sufficiently updated to appeal to modern children.[15] The most overt sign of Hasbro's lack of faith in G2 and/or their willingness to pretend that it never happened is the fact that My Little Pony is not mentioned in any of Hasbro's *Annual Reports* from 1997 through 2001. The 2000 *Annual Report*'s letter to the shareholders began, "We all know that 2000 was a very disappointing year for Hasbro," without singling out any specific brand that failed to deliver.[16] It was also missing from the September 1999 press release announcing the formation of the Hasbro Properties Group, which was created "to maximize the Company's vast intellectual properties in a wide-range of entertainment-based categories."[17] Hasbro brands and products listed throughout the release are Furby, Action Man, Monopoly, Tonka, Centipede, Playskool, Kenner, Oddz-On, Super Soaker, Milton Bradley, Parker Brothers, Tiger, Hasbro Interactive and Galoob—but not My Little Pony, which less than two years after its failure to relaunch, may have been considered too toxic to mention.[18] The first post-millennial reference to the brand came in the 2002 *Annual Report*, which announced that they would continue to "expand our core brands beyond our toy and game segments through our Hasbro Properties Group," and to "look for a big push with MY LITTLE PONY in 2003."[19]

G2 may have promptly disappeared down the memory hole, but the brand continued to be a handy symbol for consumerism, girlishness, and other such evils (which shows no sign of letting up well in to G4). In the January 2001 *Columbia Law Review,* Katherine M. Franke described the expenses mothers face when raising a child to include "Pokémon accessories, My Little Pony dolls, Barbies, fancy sneakers, and other expensive articles of consumption that are aggressively marketed to children these days."[20] While it was indeed the height of the first Pokémon wave, and Barbie had never gone out of production, My Little Pony was off the market in the United States. The *Columbia Law Review* is a peer-reviewed journal, but nopony is ever going to suggest that My Little Pony *isn't* an example of aggressive marketing to children at any given moment.

The same thing had occurred after the end of Generation 1; speaking to *Marketing* in March 1994, the media director of the marketing firm Oglivy & Mather said that the recent research had shown that kids were growing increasingly savvy about advertising, so it's necessary to "create a whole world of interest for them—that is why My Little Pony works so well."[21] Which is reasonable enough, except the line wasn't working at all by then, though it does foreshadow the later retroactive application of the word "lifestyle." The article's author did express the common fear of how the Kids Those Days would turn out: "If today's children are marketing sophisticates, we may wonder what sort of adult consumers they will make. Finding out will not be child's play."[22]

In 2001, Hasbro decided to give My Little Pony another shot.[23] According to the exuberantly-titled journal *License!*, Hasbro held a pitch meeting for "potential and existing licensees" in November 2002 to lay out their vision for the brand, which they described as having been launched in 1983 and "generated worldwide retail sales in excess of $1 billion" over the course of a 10-year run.[24] *License!* also related that Hasbro said that "a large licensing initiative is already underway with a global toy launch, a publishing program, and a series of films. Yes, My Little Pony in theaters."[25] *My Little Pony: The Movie* had of course already been in theaters to the chagrin of many in 1986, and *License!*'s "Yes, My Little Pony in theaters" aside was the first of many such faux-unbelieving comments going forward. They would pick up steam in *Friendship Is Magic* era.

Cheryl McCarthy of Hasbro's "Fantasy Factory" division announced that their plan for the revived My Little Pony was for it to be no less than "a positive influence for little girls all over the world for the rest of time."[26] She acknowledged the ambition of such a statement, adding that it was "a property that can have an impact on little girls," 3- to 7-year-olds in particular. It would require "little girls to be little girls," and that the marketing campaign would reflect a "magical and innocent world for young girls, with no makeup, no belly buttons, just My Little Pony."[27] Hasbro's Senior Brand Manager Alpana Virani told *Marketing Week* in July 2003 that "the young girls market is becoming more focused on fashion, glamour and glitz but we are looking for a return to innocence for young girls with this new look range."[28] These were most likely references to the introduction of sexualized bipedal dolls such as the bare-naveled, pouty-lipped and makeup-heavy Bratz line, as well as the new My Scene Barbie, which was similarly bare-naveled, pouty-lipped and makeup-heavy.[29] (When the *Equestria Girls* line of bipedal dolls would be released a decade later, they were inevitably compared to Bratz as well as the Monster High range, and unfairly so in both cases.) Hasbro's vice president of North American Consumer Products suggested that the goal of the relaunch was to "create the world of My Little Pony and make it a lifestyle brand," the first time the word "lifestyle" would be associated with the brand.[30] The first time it was *positively* associated as a marketing tool, to be precise; in a June 2000 *Publishers Weekly* article in which the publisher Scholastic defined "lifestyle brands" as "properties with which the company's target audience identifies and that are part of readers' lives," *The Powerpuff Girls* was described as "focusing on girls' individuality," unlike My Little Pony, which was just "a horse with colored hair."[31]

The first Generation 3 / Year One (2003) ponies announced at the November 2002 pitch meeting were Sparkleworks, Minty, Sweetberry, Wysteria, Kimono, Sunny Daze—and most importantly—Rainbow Dash and Pinkie Pie, names that would be used in Generation 4, though the characters would be different.[32] (The first Fluttershy would also be part of G3 / Year One.) HarperCollins was announced as Hasbro's global publishing partner, with "storybooks, coloring books, and board books" being rolled out at the same time as the toys, and with "mass market, book clubs, and specialty" among the slated channels of distribution.[33]

As for the films—My Little Pony in theaters, a thing like that!—a planned series of CGI-animated movies was described as a component of the relaunch, "though not a driving force."[34] The stated ambition was to release four to six films per year to play in national theater chains, "1,000 to 1,500 screens, preferably near or around retail locations," as weekend matinees for eight to twelve weeks per film.[35] In spite of the success of other aspects of the G3 launch, this ambitious plan of thousands of screens every weekend for two to three months at time never came to pass, and no G3 My Little Pony films were released to theaters until 2005 after the Hasbro Properties Group inked an arrangement with family-film distributor Kidtoons Films and onscreen advertising company Screenvision.[36] On the subject of unrealized plans, a few weeks after the November 2002 pitch meeting, *Variety* reported that film distributor Fat Rock Entertainment was partnering with SD Entertainment to "create several G-rated digital animation/live action pics based on Hasbro properties, including 'My Little Pony' and 'Super Soakers.'"[37] No Super Soaker films were made, perhaps because developing stories around souped-up water pistols proved too difficult a narrative nut to crack, in addition to just being a bad idea.

The first G3 My Little Pony theatrical release to open to the public, *A Very Minty Christmas,* played matinees from October 2–23, 2005, as a promotion for its October 25 release on VHS and DVD.[38] (Though it can be called a movie with little fear of contradiction, at 44 minutes long, it can't quite be called a feature film; while the exact definition of "feature-length" is a matter of debate, it's generally agreed that at least 60 minutes is required.) There was no mention of home video in *License!*'s coverage of the November 2002 pitch meeting, and it would appear that in the ensuing years, the profitability of the burgeoning DVD market rendered Hasbro's already-unlikely theatrical plans moot. Indeed, according to *Entertainment Marketing Letter* in July 2005, "coupons toward the purchase of the DVD" were to be handed out at the *Very Minty Christmas* screenings later that fall.[39] (If that did happen, then it's as close as the 1980s critics' criticism of *My Little Pony: The Movie* as nothing but a toy commercial came to being true, though in the case of the screenings of *A Very Minty Christmas*, it was a commercial for the product itself.) *License!*'s article did report that "a co-op marketing campaign, coupons, goody packs, premiums, samples, and video on packs will be part of the theater experience," but it was also in the context of Hasbro's unrealized four-to-six-theatrical-films-per-year ambition.[40]

Hasbro's initial press release about the theatrical screenings in September 2005 promised that "children will receive a MY LITTLE PONY party hat and favor for a before-the-show Pony Party,"[41] while in a 2007 interview with ANIMATIONWorld not long after the release of a DVD gift set containing *A Very Minty Christmas* as well as the subsequent movies *The Princess Promenade* and *The Runaway Rainbow*, Cheryl McCarthy said that "every child attending a My Little Pony movie receives a fun gift, such as a sheet of My Little Pony cutie mark temporary tattoos."[42]

Though the toys, books, and films were the talking points of the November 2002 pitch meeting, they were not the whole of the planned marketing juggernaut. A February 10, 2003, press release stated that Hasbro had "agreements in principle" (i.e., precursors to actual contracts) with Springs Industries to produce My Little Pony–themed bedding, while Franco Manufacturing was slated to make blankets, bath, and beach towels, Accessory Network to make backpacks, headwear, and cold weather accessories, and ES Originals would make athletic shoes, slippers, and sandals, all of which would allow the brand "to be a part of nearly every aspect of a little girl's life—from home to school, and everywhere in between."[43] The release also announced that Fat Rock had signed Loews Cineplex, Cinemark and Carmike Cinemas to a "unique broadcast schedule" of early mornings and midday matinees for a new *My Little Pony: The Movie*, promised to debut that October.[44] Yes, My Little Pony in theaters! October 2003 came and went without it happening, though the 20-minute *A Charming Birthday*—the first new Pony cartoon since *My Little Pony Tales* a decade prior—was available by then, either by mail order or packaged with certain dolls.[45] Indeed, by June 2003 Hasbro was no longer promising a theatrical release that would "give fans an entertaining glimpse into the world of MY LITTLE PONY"[46] as they had been in February, but instead that select toys "will include a special video that will really bring the world of MY LITTLE PONY to life for girls."[47]

In the United Kingdom, the public relations firm Mason Williams won a head-to-head pitch against Brazen PR in January 2003 to oversee the My Little Pony relaunch.[48] According to the UK edition of *PR Week* that June, Mason Williams was briefed to not only make the "cuter and funkier" new ponies "relevant to today's little girls," but also to promote it as "'bringing back innocence' and being 'really girlie' with pony names such as Pinkie Pie and Tink-a-Tink-a-Too," and "to exploit the huge gay following enjoyed by the My Little Pony brand."[49] This last detail does not figure in to Mason Williams' official case study of the relaunch, which cited Hasbro's objectives as to "Raise awareness and position MLP as the best toy—the latest craze," "Communicate the new range and the additional features," and the *rasion d'etre* of the whole rodeo, "Drive Sales."[50] They were not fools about their own country's media; Mason Williams knew they had to tread lightly:

> To get the ball rolling we arranged an deal with The Independent on Sunday Magazine for a guaranteed amount of coverage in return for an exclusive visit to Boston, home to "Pony-town." We had to be careful in our choice of journalist—and had to brief the client very carefully. There is a cultural difference between USA and UK and their enthusiasm for the project could easily have resulted in a mickey-take from a cynical hack.[51]

A "mickey-take" is British slang for talking trash, and as we've seen, in spite of those cultural differences, there had been plenty in both the UK and North American press. The resulting *Independent on Sunday* piece in July 2003 was quite positive compared to most British (or American) press coverage on the subject up to this point. (And it did its job, though Eugen Beer of the PR agency Kazio would later criticize that aspect of the Mason Williams campaign: "It was disappointing to see that there had been no attempt to reach little girls directly. The Independent on Sunday is a fine newspaper, but how many little girls read it?"[52])

Writer Jonathan Thompson visited Hasbro's headquarters in Providence, Rhode Island (not Boston), where he described the mood as "buoyant, if slightly surreal," particularly the boardroom, "what appears to be the real-life incarnation of Ponyville"—marking the official introduction of Ponyville as the new setting—"bedecked in pink, lilac and green My Little Pony banners, with Pony-themed cakes, accessories, play sets, and of course dolls, littering the tables and alcoves."[53] Vice President of Marketing Valerie Jurries filled in one of the gaps as to why G1 ended when it did: not just because of the aforementioned

Polly Pocket, but also the Troll doll making the mini-doll market that much more competitive. No mention was made in the article of the failed 1998 relaunch, just that "the time is right for a renaissance, thinks Hasbro."[54]

Though sales in both the UK and the U.S. weren't shabby the first time around, specified as 8 million units in Britain and upwards of 100 million in the United States, Hasbro tailored the G3 strategies for each market differently[55]:

> In Britain, where collectability is thought to be a higher priority, 14 of the new characters will be introduced this year, whereas American audiences will only see eight. In September, London will play host to a Pony Parade, where 20 Pony effigies, each 4ft high, will be decorated by a selection of celebrities, fashion designers and artists and placed at strategic locations in the city.[56]

That little girls were meant to identify with the ponies was emphasized.

> My Little Pony is not designed to be a pet, I am told when I ask. She is designed to be a little girl's best friend. Ponies aren't horses, says Jodie Neville, brand manager for girls toys, indignantly. We don't ride ponies, they don't work they just play. They're just like little girls.[57]

This was a distinct change from the G1 cartoons in which the audience surrogate was the biped Megan (and to a lesser extent her brother and sister), and arguably the Generation 2 game *Friendship Gardens*, in which the player adopted a caretaker role with their pony. In both cases the "My" had signaled the relationship between the consumer and the product, but now the girls were intended to identify with the ponies. And *today's* little girls, at that; G3 designer Jen Long is quoted as saying that her charge was to "contain the essence of the Ponies, but update them, making their faces and poses more engaging," to preserve the flavor while serving it up to a new audience.[58] But why now, and why this new approach? Beyond the simple nostalgia or appealing-to-parents angle, John Radcliffe Hospital's clinical child psychologist Dr. John Richer is quoted as suggesting the "escalator model"[59]:

> Die-cast toy cars, for example, were all the rage in the 1950s for boys of nine or 10, but now babies are given them. Older children don't want to be seen playing with the same toys as younger kids, and the toys move down the age range, year on year, until they fall off the bottom. Then, the manufacturers have to wait for that generation to pass before they can reintroduce the toy to the older children again.[60]

Dr. Richer is also quoted as saying that My Little Pony had the best chance to succeed out of all the revived toy ranges because it "puts together in one package a number of different elements which girls like," combining "pastel colours, grooming and a girl's natural liking for ponies with an innate desire to nurture."[61] The largely mickey-free article ended with a line reminiscent of many past articles about the fear of a return of My Little Pony: "Let's hope, for [parents'] sake, that the decision is not taken to relaunch the Troll."[62]

Somepony always has to be at the bottom of the ladder, and for once, it *wasn't* a pony.

The return of My Little Pony as a force to be reckoned with caused some consternation within the trade magazines regarding its new audience. On June 9, 2003, *DSN Retailing Today* observed, "That properties like My Little Pony and Superman are checking well simultaneously with different audiences—juniors customers, children and moms—is highly unusual."[63] That same day, T.L. Stanley in *Brandweek* painted a more vivid picture in an article titled "Irony Giants," after observing goth kids wearing *Saved by the Bell* t-shirts and "post-post-modern punks" with Care Bears backpacks[64]:

> The same teenagers who have grown up seeing violent acts on television (and now emulate them in Grand Theft Auto: Vice City) are embracing a gaggle of warm and fuzzy, geeky and cutesy characters. They are making room in their otherwise dank wardrobes for the sunny likes of Strawberry Shortcake, My Little Pony, Snuggle bear, Curious George, Rainbow Brite, Sesame Street, Dr. Seuss and Tinkerbell, bought at their favorite trendy retailers.

"Trendy" is an apt word for the retailers, as Stanley makes use of the trendy fear that kids who've grown up watching violence on television and/or have played violent video games are somehow damaged, certainly too damaged to want anything to do with "warm, fuzzy, geeky, and cutesy characters," as if the children themselves are one-dimensional creatures who are not capable of appreciating more than one kind of tone in entertainment.[65] (He was not the first to evoke My Little Pony when discussing violent video games, or even *Grand Theft Auto* in particular. Reviewing *Mortal Kombat: Deadly Alliance* that January for the *San Francisco Chronicle*, Peter Hartlaub wrote that just because the Mortal Kombat series had been rebooted, that didn't mean it was "suddenly appropriate for the My Little Pony crowd," and that "even the Grand Theft Auto: Vice City champion of the world might feel a little dirty after watching all the blood and bone chips flying."[66]) Stanley in *Brandweek* went on to ponder whether it's just a fashion statement, or if the kids are "honestly touched by the cloying kiddie characters and looking for comfort in the (vaguely) familiar." His main theory was that there was a "'wink' factor driving the trend," which he called "the ironic license."[67] Whether or not the consumers are simply being "ironic" would be a recurring theme in the press coverage of *Friendship Is Magic*'s diverse viewership.

Generation the Third

After a soft launch of some toys and books over the summer, Generation 3 was officially launched on September 19, 2003, with an appropriately jovial

Hasbro press release titled "It's Time to Celebrate! Hasbro's MY LITTLE PONY Brand Makes Its Long Anticipated Return."[68] Along with Sparkleworks, Minty, Sweetberry, Wysteria, Kimono, Sunny Daze, Rainbow Dash, and Pinkie Pie as originally mentioned in the November 2002 pitch meeting, all available individually for $4.99 each, four new ponies were also announced: Razzaroo, Moondancer, Cotton Candy, and Pink Sunsparkle, each as part of larger assortments or playsets.[69] Many things will necessarily change through the course of any product launch, particularly when a slew of products are launched at once, so it's no surprise that the *Independent on Sunday*'s tidbit that American audiences would only see eight ponies did not pan out.[70] Similarly, there was no longer any hint of theatrical releases, instead using the same language as the June press release, that select toys would "include a special video that will really bring the world of MY LITTLE PONY to life for girls."[71]

"Life," and the styles thereof of little girls, was a recurring theme of the announcement: "Little girls around the world have reason to celebrate as Hasbro, Inc. (NYSE:HAS) brings the MY LITTLE PONY brand to life for a new generation"; how both the new website mylittlepony.com and the "extensive line" of products would allow little girls "to live the MY LITTLE PONY life" (to the extent that "girls can always feel a part of the magical world" even when away from their ponies); and how after the launch in 1983, the range "blossomed into a true lifestyle brand," thus allowing little girls to experience My Little Pony "in everything from apparel and bedding to a feature film and cartoon series."[72] It wasn't referred to as a "lifestyle" in the 1980s, though the introduction of the word at this point was a clever marketing ploy: don't buy all the things just because you like them, buy them because it's a *lifestyle*.

The smaller core cast of G3 allowed for a stronger emphasis on character and backstories than in G1, hence books being far more important than in the past, and they began arriving in stores that August.[73] In addition to the HarperCollins storybooks, coloring books, and board books, there were novelty books by Running Press Kids, boxed activity books from Bendon Press, sound books from Publishers International, and how-to-draw books from Walter Foster.[74] Hasbro's Vice President of Global Publishing and New Business Development Tom Klusaritz told *Publishers Weekly* in August that Hasbro pitched to publishers before any of the other licensed categories: "We had decided that story and character would become a very strong component of the relaunch strategy of My Little Pony. The content, with the video and with the publishing, was really one of the central focal points."[75] This book-first approach tended to be the case with the girl-oriented properties; HarperCollins had already successfully relaunched the

Care Bears and Strawberry Shortcake before taking on My Little Pony, whereas publishers would usually come on later in the reintroduction of boys' properties, and then they would focus on comic books rather than the more interactive nature of the girls' books.[76] By the end of 2003, Bendon was expected to have more than a million activity books in print each of My Little Pony and Transformers, though it's notable that Transformers had been relaunched the year before.[77] In November 2004, HarperCollins Children's Books announced that since the 2003 relaunch they had sold more than 3.5 million units of the 17 titles in the My Little Pony book line, describing them as "colorful and fun books that boast an eye-popping palette of girl-friendly pinks and purples."[78]

Not everypony was on the nostalgia kick; though Random House had published My Little Pony books in the 1980s (including the maligned *My Little Pony Under the Big Top!*), they chose not to pick up any retro properties in the early 2000s, also passing on Cabbage Patch Kids, Muppet Babies, and Transformers, all licenses they'd once carried.[79] Random House/Golden Books for Young Readers vice president and publishing director Kate Klimo told *Publishers Weekly* that while she could understand the appeal, she questioned their longevity and creativity: "These burned hot, but can you reheat them? I think this retro redux is more to do with poverty of imagination than anything else."[80]

Though the official demographic of G3 was three-to-six-year-old girls rather than G1's intended range of up to nine years old, it was also the first time that My Little Pony was associated with grown-ups, particularly mothers who'd had the dolls as children.[81] London Fashion Week 2003 designers Tracey Boyd and Michiko Koshino created outfits for My Little Pony dolls which were later auctioned off for the children's charity Barnardo's, and a 1985 picture of four-year-old Beyoncé Knowles in a masked My Little Pony costume printed in *People* the previous November proved timely.[82]

The G3 launch was a success by any standard. During Hasbro's Q3 2003 Earnings Conference Call in October, president and CEO Alfred Verrecchia reported that U.S. toy sales were up 23% from the year before, and My Little Pony was among the reasons why[83]:

> It is fair to say that My Little Pony is exceeding our expectations, we launched this brand globally in the third quarter, with an aggressive media program, complimented by an extensive merchandising program from our Hasbro Properties Group. HPG has signed up 30 licenses, you can expect to see My Little Pony in apparel, home goods, publishing, and visual entertainment in addition to the strong portfolio of games, toys and puzzles.[84]

That the hard launch occurred in the lead-up to the Christmas season was not a coincidence; according to the December 1 *Advertising Age*, a

National Retail Federation survey found that both My Little Pony and Care Bears were expected to be among the top toys given to girls for the holidays, and both brands were also on the trade publication *Toy Wishes*'s "All Star" list, along with Strawberry Shortcake and Teenage Mutant Ninja Turtles.[85] But you can't have My Little Pony without incredulity, hence an eBay spokesperson being quoted in that day's *Hollywood Reporter* that along with other big sellers such as G.I. Joe, Legos, remote-control cars, and Lord of the Rings action figures, "My Little Pony is making quite a comeback, if you can believe it."[86] Legos date back to the late 1940s, and G.I. Joe, remote-control cars, and Lord of the Rings were all introduced in the 1960s, but it was the property from the early 1980s whose comeback beggared belief.

According to the UK edition of *PR Week* in September 2004, more than a million My Little Ponies had been sold in Britain since the previous year's relaunch, which was covered by all the national newspapers, as well as "nine TV news shows, 46 national magazines, 90 regional newspapers, and 39 radio programmes."[87] In October, Hasbro said that after My Little Pony's return "as a highly popular lifestyle brand for little girls ages three and up" the previous fall, more than eight million ponies had "reached the U.S. marketplace," and three million books had been sold. The second G3 cartoon, the 20-minute *Dancing in the Clouds*, became the first to fulfill the dream of My Little Pony returning to theaters, though to a very specific audience: in a partnership with the Starlight Starbright Children's Foundation, the video was shown to hundreds of seriously ill children on November 13, 2004, in "special MY LITTLE PONY movie celebrations hosted exclusively for them at Loews Cineplex Theatres in Los Angeles, New York City and Chicago."[88] (Quite coincidentally to their successors' prominence in G4, Rainbow Dash and Pinkie Pie are name-checked in the first line of dialog.) *Dancing in the Clouds* was also distributed to hospitals nationwide (hospitals serviced by the Foundation, that is) to reside in their video libraries, and to be shown at viewing parties called "Hospital Happenings" before being released to the general public.[89]

Released with far less fanfare that fall (and long out of print at the time of this writing) were four My Little Pony music CDs by Genius Products, made in association with Minnesota Public Radio: *Friendship Songs*,[90] *Pony Party Favorites*,[91] *Musical Treasures*[92] (itself a double-disc set of the first two), and the classical *Sweet Classics in Ponyland*.[93] These were licensed by the Hasbro Properties Group, and were in essence standard children's music with a coat of My Little Pony shellac; unlike the G4 soundtrack albums of music from *Friendship Is Magic* and *Equestria Girls*, there were no new shows or movies to draw from, though *Friendship Songs* did pad out its running time by including the entire audio of *A Charming Birthday*. *Pony Party Favorites* was a mix of traditional children's songs such as "I'm a Little Teapot" and originals, though a spoken intro to "The Birthday Song"—for which acquiring the rights to "Happy Birthday," still a decade away from entering the public domain,[94] must have eaten up much of the album's budget—does reference Fluttershy having received a camera for her last birthday.[95] G3 / Year One Fluttershy's backcard story established that she was an avid photographer, perhaps because "Fluttershy" is an anagram of "Shutterfly."[96] (Fluttershy's G4 namesake would be horrified by the thought of invading other ponies' privacy with a camera.) *Friendship Songs* was a more mature collection of songs, thanks to the four contributions of Annette Summersett. Her "Pony Palace Ball" is a bouncy children's ditty which is overtly My Little Pony–themed, but "Riding Rainbows" and "Hot Air Balloon" are both very well-produced pop songs. The standout is the Beatles-esque "You Are a Rainbow," which could well have made a mark on the Adult Contemporary charts had it not been buried on a children's record from a disreputable franchise, and it's by far the best song to be released on a My Little Pony album until "The Art of the Dress" on Daniel Ingram's *Songs of Friendship and Magic* in 2013. Genius's *Sweet Classics in Ponyland,* beyond having an erroneous title (Ponyland not having been the setting since G1), was a collection of chamber music "perfect for little ballerinas and their favorite ponies," and performed on the piano, flute, and violin.[97]

In a comparatively rare instance of mainstream critics being kind to My Little Pony products, Johnny Loftus of Allmusic gave *Friendship Songs* a positive review, praising the accordion-led version of "You Are My Sunshine" and describing the original instrumental "Dreams of Cotton Candy" as being "as misty and atmospheric as you'd expect from a song with such a great name,"[98] while Mackenzie Wilson wrote in her review of the *Musical Treasures* compilation that the songs overall "nicely highlight a merry playtime atmosphere."[99]

The first My Little Pony computer game since 1998, the *My Little Pony PC Play Pack*, was released that October by Atari (a perfect convergence of 1980s iconography, by some standards.[100]) Unlike *Friendship Gardens*, in which the player created their pony more or less from scratch, the *PC Play Pack* allowed—or restricted—the character to play as either Sunny Daze, Sky Wishes, Pinkie Pie, or Sparkleworks, which kept with the stated goal of allowing girls to identify with the ponies.[101] As had often been the case, those who worked with children were kindest; that month's issue of *Scholastic Parent & Child* listed it among their Teacher's Picks for Best New Tech, saying it "encourages care, compassion and creativity."[102] The *PC Play Pack* would later be repackaged as *My Little Pony: Best Friends Ball*; reviewing it for the UK magazine *Computer Act!ve* in 2006, Scott Colvey wrote that while it was "very twee, and suffocatingly sweet to boot," it would no doubt "seem utterly magical" to the target market, and perhaps have appeal beyond them: "In fact, even though we're quite removed from the target market, we really enjoyed it. It's a bit like taking the director's chair to create a My Little Pony cartoon."[103]

Perhaps inspired by the success of the London Fashion Week 2003 experiment, in October 2005 Hasbro collaborated with the Brooklyn-based creative agency Thunderdog Studios to create the Pony Project, in which a few dozen female artists such as Junko Mizuno and Betsey Johnson customized 18-inch ponies; the final products were then displayed for five days at the Milk Gallery in New York, and half of the proceeds from the art sales were donated to the Paul Newman–founded children's charity Hole in the Wall Camps.[104] Hasbro's press release referred to My Little Pony as "a favorite among girls and young adults," and quoted Thunderdog's media director as describing the Pony Project as a great way to introduce the brand "into the world of art and pop culture," though Hasbro left out the detail that all the artists were female, referring to them simply "nearly 50 of today's leading and up-and-coming artists."[105] Which was accurate, but also rather vague; the official Pony Project website launched earlier that year, as well as much of the promo material, described it as "an exhibition inspired by every girl's favorite toy, featuring some of today's leading female artists."[106]

As with everything having to do with My Little Pony, the Pony Project was viewed with skepticism; the business magazine *Fast Company* later described it as similar to the outsourcing of jobs, but "more sinister"[107]:

> Companies are outsourcing cool. They're paying other companies—smaller, more-limber, closer-to-the-ground outsiders—to help them keep up with customers' rapidly changing tastes and demands. Talk about a core competency! It's like farming out your soul—or at least, asking someone what you should wear in the morning.[108]

Before the art show, a more traditionally-sized Pony Project pony was sold in a limited run of 2,000 at the 2005 San Diego Comic-Con.[109] It was successful enough that Hasbro would continue to sell exclusive "Special Edition" ponies at Comic-Con from 2007 onward, though for as large as that convention already loomed in United States pop culture in those days, it was not the only destination for My Little Pony fans.[110]

Pony Conventions Lead to Press Confusion

The first International My Little Pony Collectors' Convention was held on November 27, 2004, in Morecambe, Lancashire, England.[111] It was the sub-

ject of a cover story in the *Sunday Telegraph Magazine* in December, and the
dek below the headline set a tone that, give or take the specified gender, would
be revisited in countless articles, essays, and rageful rants over the next
decade: "What compels grown women to collect toy horses obsessively, travel
thousands of miles to show them off, even write plays for them?"[112] Though
Mason Williams listed the article among the successes of their relaunch campaign,[113] it existed squarely on the mickey-take end of the spectrum, as writer
Rebecca Tyrell remained incredulous about the age of the attendees:

> Grown women are here today at this convention to trade ponies, compare ponies and covet
> ponies they can't have but, apart from saying how much they love their ponies, they won't
> give a satisfactory explanation for their obsession.[114]

Why they should *have* to "give a satisfactory explanation for their obsession"
was not satisfactorily explained, instead taking as given that there was something unbecoming of these grown women devoting time to childish things.
To Tyrell, that level of inexplicability qualified as an obsession, and the issue's
cover referred to the attendees as "The Cult of My Little Pony."[115] "Obsession"
was a recurring word in the British press; in her coverage of the Birmingham
2006 PonyCon for the *Sunday Mercury*, Claire Morrall asked a young Norfolk
woman what "her friends think of her obsession,"[116] while Cole Moreton in
the *Independent on Sunday* asked a 2008 PonyCon attendee if her boyfriend
had any obsessions of his own.[117] The attendee replied, "No. He's doing a PhD
in plant metabolism," which ignored that her boyfriend was obsessed with
the metabolism of plants—it was just a more socially acceptable obsession.[118]

  In her 2004 *Sunday Telegraph Magazine* article about the My Little Pony
Collectors' Convention, Tyrell found it peculiar that "many of these adult My
Little Pony enthusiasts, oddly, are goths or at least sub-goths."[119] (Not to speak
for the entire subculture, but all I can say is, it makes perfect sense to us.)
She also maintained a tone of aggressive literalism, refusing to meet the attendees halfway or even acknowledge any degree of play or imagination, no
doubt because she was a grown-up who had expectations of how grown-ups
should be:

> Most people would think it weird that grown women are playing with plastic ponies, espe-
> cially the kind of plastic pony Lorna Dounaeva from London shows me. "It is a Surprise
> Twins pony," she explains.
>   "If you push this button, it releases a catch and she simulates giving birth to twins." Actu-
> ally, she doesn't because in real life ponies don't give birth by opening a hatch in their tum-
> mies.
>   Surprise Twins pony is not surprisingly not programmed to writhe in agony. Lorna likes
> to take the romantic view, though. She used to work at the Home Office but is currently
> taking time out to write a book. "It's a novel," she says. "A romance thriller."[120]

(Dounaeva did indeed become a published novelist, so good on her for that.[121]) Speaking of things that are actually surprising, Tyrell was blasé about the only man that she reported as attending, who was there with his wife and daughter, and offered a "humanoid" pony for the customized pony competition.[122] Similarly, Morrall in the *Sunday Mercury* failed to make hay of the fact that the 2006 PonyCon chairman (whom she asked "to make some sense of it all," because it is an inherently nonsensical thing) was male, only noting that he was a "married 22-year old," thus implying that he was at least heterosexual.[123] The sexual orientation of male viewers would go on to be a major press obsession in G4.

Though it may well have been the first event to call itself the International My Little Pony Collectors' Convention, the Morecambe gathering was not the only My Little Pony convention in 2004: the first My Little Pony Fair was held that July at the Imperial Palace in Las Vegas,[174] a two-day event with more of a community angle, but without the direct involvement by Hasbro which the English event enjoyed.[125] Also, both events were focused on the toys, with little if any attention paid to the past cartoons. This can be contrasted with later *Friendship Is Magic* fan conventions which were centered on that series—or, more accurately, on the segment of the fans who called themselves Bronies, hence such solipsistic convention titles such as the Eastcoast BronyCon, or the Brony Fan Fair in Texas. The underlying theme changes from "Let's celebrate this show we like!" to "Let's celebrate that *we* like this show!," which can be alienating to fans who do not identify as Bronies and/or are disinterested in that aspect of the organized fandom. Not all *Friendship Is Magic*–era convention titles are like that, and some are more directly related to elements of the show—such as Everfree Northwest in Seattle, Nightmare Nights in Texas, or Czequestria in the Czech Republic—but all still assume a degree of inside-baseball knowledge, while BABSCon, which at first glance seems to be a reference to Apple Bloom's troubled cousin from Manehattan first introduced in "One Bad Apple" (S03E04), is reverse-engineered to stand for "Bay Area Brony Spectacular."

In addition to having less of a mickey-taking tone about the age of the attendees than the *Sunday Telegraph*, an August 2005 *Minneapolis Star Tribune* article about the second annual My Little Pony Fair treated the cartoons as almost an afterthought, and acknowledged gender diversity without making a big deal about it (and voted for 1982 being the first year):

> First mass-produced by Hasbro in 1982, millions have now been sold, capturing the imagination of little girls (and some boys) for more than two decades. There was even a television show and movie based on the shy plastic equine with the silky hair.[126]

Parenthetical though it is, the notion that boys might have possibly also enjoyed My Little Pony on some level was unheard of, since as we've seen, it had previously been used as the dividing line between masculine (universal) and feminine (for girls only) entertainment.

Hasbro was nowhere close to acknowledging such a thing, probably because their research didn't dictate it. Their March 2005 press release about the "build-your-own MY LITTLE PONY" display at the Once Upon a Toy store at Walt Disney World referred to the "creativity and imagination that My Little Pony brings to little girls," described how "the experience begins as little girls are greeted by multiple interactive displays," and concluded that My Little Pony is "truly a lifestyle experience for little girls."[127] Contemporaneous press releases referring to male-oriented ranges such as Transformers and Duel Masters frequently used the generic "fan" when referring to their customer base, seldom associating it with gender.

As the media slowly began to reckon with the concept of boys liking My Little Pony long before the premiere of *Friendship Is Magic*, the knee-jerk tendency was to associate it with homosexuality. A June 2008 *Providence Journal* article about the fifth annual My Little Pony Fair adopted the "What's the deal with these adults interested in toys for little girls?" stance from similar past coverage—the opening paragraph was "There were thousands of toys. But where were the children?"—with an emphasis on how many of the adult female collectors kept their hobby a secret for fear of being laughed at, a fear which was exacerbated by the tone of this kind of article.[128] He also quoted original My Little Pony designer Bonnie Zacherle, who described her creation as having taken on a life of its own: "What you see here are girls who grew up with My Little Pony and taken it beyond the initial play."[129] But the writer seemed most intrigued by a 25-year-old Singapore man named Juecong Chai with a collection of 1,300 ponies; Chai acknowledged that "in Western countries, they think I'm gay," though the article stated that, "for the record, Chai is not gay."[130] Whew!

The following month, proudly gay *Doctor Who* and *Torchwood* actor John Barrowman hosted a BBC documentary called *John Barrowman: The Making of Me*, in which he explored the question of whether his homosexuality was a product of genetics or environment.[131] He met 12-year-old twins Adam and Jared, the former of whom preferred traditionally feminine toys and pursuits such as Barbie and the Care Bears, while the latter collected war toys and the like. According to their mother (who described herself as "not feminine," disdaining dresses and makeup), the gender-nonconforming Adam had said she was a girl since the age of two, which strongly suggests that she is transgender, or at least genderqueer, rather than simply homosexual.[132] Though there's a not a My Little Pony in sight among her collection, Barrowman later muses that homosexuality is clearly a matter of genetics, since it was Adam "who chose to have the My Little Pony and the Bratz."[133] The deeply-rooted problem of homosexual men reducing gender identity to just another aspect of sexual orientation (which it is not) and/or disregarding the existence of transgender women altogether is beyond the scope of this book, but it is unsurprising that Barrowman would go out of his way to mention My Little Pony in this context.

In November 2006, the *Mail on Sunday*'s Suzanne Moore—who, 13 years previous in her review of *Fads, Fashions & Cults,* had worried that future generations might think people in the 1990s took My Little Pony as seriously as they did post-structuralism—wrote this in a piece criticizing what she considered to be the UK media's overly sentimental reaction to the death of the racehorse Desert Orchid: "Clearly, I am not a horsey type. I even find My Little Pony a bit weird. A pink plastic horse you can put make up on? What psychosexual fantasies are we playing with here?"[134] Only the ones Moore brought with her, considering that makeup was never an integral part of the My Little Pony range. A (literal) handful of the several hundred G1 ponies did come with lipstick, but they were by no means representative, any more than they were all pink. There's nothing actively *preventing* somepony from putting makeup on a doll if they were so inclined, though the small size of the features would make it difficult, and it was never the point. It's akin to reducing Barbie to "a doll whose nose you can wipe" just because three particular Barbie ensembles in the early 1960s included a white handkerchief.[135]

Picking up the psychosexual fantasy thread was the Spring 2007 issue of the United States magazine *Bitch*, in which Jesse Rutherford argued that the G3 ponies "look more like sexually available human children than anything remotely equine," and that the message Hasbro was sending to young girls is that they too can be a "hot sex pony," and the toys are "training them in sexual display before they are capable of understanding the meaning of the signals they send."[136] Lest somepony think that Rutherford might be reading too much into it (or to perhaps suggest that young biped girls are not inclined to replicate the poses of their toy animals), she offered this thought experiment, all in bold text: "**Just take off the pony's tail and add hands to the front legs, and what you have is a human doll that could be used in a stop-animation pedophilic porn flick.**" Which is also true for many dolls that represent mammals, but few toys are known to be as dangerous as My Little Pony. Presented at the Thinking Gender conference in February 2008, Natalie Corinne Hansen's paper "Queering the Horse-Crazy Girl: Part II" picked up from where the *Bitch* article left off.[137] Hansen described both the

Breyer line of model horses as well My Little Pony as objectifying horses for human consumption, with My Little Pony conflating "girl bodies and horse bodies, reducing difference by, again, employing a standardized body type (all MLPs have the same basic shape) and by fetishizing hair as a fashion accessory."[138] After quoting from the *Bitch* article's litany of the sexualized aspects of the G3 ponies ("Today's My Little Pony displays upturned, accentuated buttocks; smooth, glittery skin; a tilted head; an exposed neck; long eyelashes; lowered eyelids; dilated pupils; long, slim legs; shifted weight; accentuated hair—even, in some cases, parted lips"), she put it in her own words[139]:

> Today's My Little Pony is actively seductive, selling a certain version of pre-adolescent female sexuality. The images these toys offer girls, along with the scripts that accompany each toy, are fantasies of female sexual availability, very much reflecting heteropatriarchal consumer culture, quaintly packaged in the "innocent" body of a little pony-girl.[140]

No points for a lack of tattoos or makeup, it seems.

The Promenade to Equestria

The second G3 My Little Pony movie, *The Princess Promenade*, played weekend matinees in January 2006 along with the 20-minute *Friends Are Never Far Away*.[141] *Promenade* was released on VHS in February, and while at 50 minutes it still didn't qualify as feature-length, it proved quite durable: not only was it still on the *Billboard* charts in June,[142] it was on the media research company Rentrak's list of the Top 10 VHS sellers for the week ending November 6, 2006.[143] *A Very Minty Christmas* had reached No. 1 on the *Billboard* VHS Sales and Top Kid Video charts the previous November,[144] and while both found success during a time in which the format's death rattle grew deafening—David Cronenberg's *A History of Violence*, also released on video in 2006, was the final major studio film to be released on VHS—it was still a sign that the new wave of My Little Pony animation had staying power, and was finding its audience.[145]

As had been the case with their appearances in *Dancing in the Clouds*, the characters in *The Princess Promenade* with G4 names were different from how they would be portrayed in *Friendship Is Magic*, Rainbow Dash in particular. Instead of the roughhousing tomboy she's best known as, G3 Rainbow is a Rarity-style high femme with a tendency to say "Darling" at a rate that not only surpasses G4 Rarity's use of the word, but which even Edina and Patsy on *Absolutely Fabulous* would find excessive. Spike the Dragon also makes his first appearance since *My Little Pony 'n' Friends*, though like the ponies, he bears no resemblance other than his name to G4 counterpart, reintroduced here as a British-inflected dandy with a deep knowledge of the arcane ways royalty is conferred.

The Princess Promenade is also significant for being the DVD which Hasbro gave to Lauren Faust when she pitched a project called Milky Way and the Galaxy Girls in 2008.[146] They declined her Galaxy Girls pitch, asking instead if she might have any ideas for a My Little Pony reboot series.[147] But *Friendship Is Magic* was still a half-decade away when *The Princess Promenade*'s follow-up *The Runaway Rainbow* played weekend matinees in August 2006 prior to its DVD release that September, becoming the first My Little Pony cartoon to be released only on DVD, not VHS.[148] It also marked the G3 introduction of Rarity, who would of course go on to be the best *Friendship Is Magic* character, and as with Pinkie Pie and Rainbow Dash, this Rarity shares a name with her superior G4 incarnation and little else. The video coincided with the release of the *Runaway Rainbow* game on the Game Boy Advance platform, the first of the video games to be directly related to the G3 animations, in this case allowing the player to "take on the role of Princess Rarity as she tries to return to Unicornia in time to create the season's first rainbow."[149] The system having proven successful thus far, a fourth movie—the 45-minute *A Very Pony Place*, consisting of three short episodes rather than a single narrative—played weekend matinees in January 2007[150] before debuting on DVD that March.[151] It would be the last My Little Pony movie to receive a theatrical release until the lone G3.5 cartoon *Twinkle Wish Adventure* in 2009.[152]

In addition to the movies and video games, the publication angle was still going strong in 2006, with a magazine launching in the UK that July with the aim of "[making] learning fun through a range of educational activities," such as "a pull-out workbook with rewards stickers to help the reader work through it," as well as "loads of stories, activities, and codes to crack."[153] There were 100 My Little Pony titles in print by that September, and according to *Publishers Weekly*, Hasbro had "repositioned some of its brands as content-driven intellectual properties, instead of simply toys" through the use of characters, artwork, and backstories.[154] According to Tom Klusaritz, then Hasbro's Vice President of Licensing and Retail Development, publishing was vital to the successful revival of the line: "We made My Little Pony into more than just a toy, and we couldn't have done that without our publishing partners, especially HarperCollins."[155] This concept of My Little Pony being more than just a toy would prove to be elusive in the years to follow.

45 books were slated for release worldwide that year, and a buzzword-heavy press release in June announced the latest incursion of My Little Pony into the real world[156]:

Fall 2006 will be an exciting time for little girls who are devoted MY LITTLE PONY fans with the debut of MY LITTLE PONY: THE WORLD'S BIGGEST TEA PARTY live stage show. Under license with VEE Corporation, the highly interactive 90-minute musical production will feature singing, dancing and playing along with all the ponies. The fun-filled experience will immerse young girls into PONYVILLE as they are surrounded by PINKIE PIE and friends, as well as teapots, rainbows, castles, balloons, fancy dresses and unicorns. The tour is set to kick off this fall at theaters and arenas nationwide.[157]

"Branded merchandise" was also sold at the venues, at long last materializing the decades-old fear of My Little Pony entertainments encouraging the audience to go right out and buy the products.[158] The occasional references to boys also being interested in My Little Pony up to this point were always regarding the toys, not the cartoons or this live show, and *My Little Pony Live!: The World's Biggest Tea Party* was explicitly intended for three-to-six-year-old girls. Unlike *Friendship Is Magic*, it had a limited perspective on that age range, hence the promise to surround young girls with "teapots, rainbows, castles, balloons, fancy dresses, and unicorns," which sounds less like a description of a show and more like a whiteboard list generated during a "Things We're Pretty Sure Little American Girls Like" brainstorming session.[159]

A November 2007 *Baltimore Sun* editorial reflecting on the 25th anniversary of My Little Pony referred to it as having "spawned an entire ancillary culture, with twinkly cartoons and Halloween costumes and a traveling show called the World's Biggest Tea Party (yeccch!)."[160] The writer, who was anonymous but gave all indications of being a childless male, also mused, "Some might argue that My Little Pony is the first real wedge driven between a girl and her parents," and that the parent may choke on the toy's "terminal cuteness" and "gender imprinting."[161] One man's "gender imprinting" is another corporate spokesperson's celebration of girlhood, as Hasbro Properties Group President Jane Ritson-Parsons described *The World's Biggest Tea Party* as "a rock concert for little people," with Pinkie Pie as the biggest star.[162] She echoed the earlier sentiment from the initial G3 launch about maintaining innocence in the age of Bratz: "We're not supporting belly-button rings or makeup. This is about being a little girl, which is fabulous."[163]

This also makes it all the more of a shame that at the time of this writing, the only full-length versions of the out-of-print DVD of the live show available on YouTube include default commentaries by largely teenage-to-adult male Bronies (and the occasional girlfriend thereof) amusing themselves by saying horrible, expletive-filled things about the show.[164] As an interactive entertainment designed to be enjoyed by three-to-six-year-old girls accompanied by their mothers, *My Little Pony Live!: The World's Biggest Tea Party* is fine for what it is, and the audience seems to be having a good time. While it's never fair to compare a video recording of a live show to something which was meant to be watched on a screen, it's a distinct improvement over *My Little Pony 'n' Friends* and *My Little Pony Tales*. And most importantly, *The World's Biggest Tea Party* is not *for* snarky teenagers and/or adults—but sadly, there is no shortage of videos on YouTube of Bronies harshly criticizing the G1 and G3 material.

My Little Pony Live!: The World's Biggest Tea Party ran through February 2009.[165] It's arguably one of the last times that the phrase "tea party" had a wholesome connotation in United States vernacular, considering that the modern Tea Party political movement was birthed that very same month, but that's not My Little Pony's fault.[166]

*   *   *

The signs that Generation 3 would be a sprint rather than a marathon came early; the Littlest Pet Shop range, reintroduced in 2005, was outselling My Little Pony by 2006.[167] In June 2007, Hasbro announced that as part of the 25th anniversary celebration of the brand in 2008, a "fresh new cast of MY LITTLE PONY characters will come skipping into little girls' lives, including PINKIE PIE, RAINBOW DASH, TOOLA-ROOLA, STARSONG, SWEETIE-BELLE, CHEERILEE and SCOOTALOO."[168] At the Licensing Show that month, Hasbro rep Shelly Eckenroth told *Playthings* that the roughly 300 G3 characters would be whittled down in 2008 to "a core seven ponies"[169]:

> "It's really about the characters and the depth of those characters," she said, noting that the strategy for the brand will see it move into products that are designed to develop the core characters in more detail.[170]

(Though released during G3 / Year Six (2008), we'll refer to this set of ponies as Generation 3.1 for sake of clarity.) Pinkie Pie and Rainbow Dash were arguably not "fresh," in that the character names had been in use since G3 / Year One, and the name Cheerilee had been introduced in Year Four. But those seven names would be retained for G3.5, and except for Toola-Roola and Starsong, were used for significant characters on *Friendship Is Magic*.

It was also not the first time that story and character were posited as the linchpin of a new generation; in 2003, Tom Klusaritz had told *Publishers Weekly* that those elements would be "a very strong component of the relaunch strategy of My Little Pony."[171] One of the promo books available at the Licensing Show featured pictures of the G3.1 cast with a headline reading, "Hasbro Spotlights Seven Distinctive Ponies That Will Set the Stage for Your Business!"[172]

As would happen so many times in G4, the response from the fans to the announcement of the change was not positive, and viewed by many as a sign of the end times. On the My Little Pony Arena forum in 2007, user RobynGraves opined that focusing on only seven ponies "sounds like MLP going down the toilet,"[173] while on the My Little Pony Trading Post, Firebyrd predicted that G3.1 would "destroy the line."[174] In 2008, user Archer06 on the Trading Post eulogized My Little Pony, albeit prematurely: "To put it simply, Core 7 is the death of MLP's."[175] (According to Summer Hayes's *The My Little Pony 2007–2008 Collector's Inventory*, a panel of Hasbro employees at the 2008 My Little Pony Fair assured the assembled collectors that while the main focus of the range would always be young girls and "that the Core Seven focus was here to stay," there would still be special edition sets intended for adult collectors.[176])

In any event, the franchise-killing G3.1 ponies were overshadowed in 2008 by Hasbro's focus on the "year-long global celebration" of the 25th anniversary of the brand: The My Little Pony Project: 25 Ponies for 25 Years, not to be confused with the Pony Project from 2005.[177] For the *My Little* Pony Project, "international pop culture influentials such as celebrities, fashion designers, brands, artists, collectors, and kids"—a peculiar list which feels like as much of an unpolished whiteboard brainstorm as "teapots, rainbows, castles, balloons, fancy dresses, and unicorns" had for the *World's Biggest Tea Party* announcement—would design one of 25 custom dolls to be displayed in a gallery show that September.[178] Special new ponies were announced, such as the limited-edition and very-purple Twinkle Hope designed by the non-profit Give Kids the World Village, as well as Hasbro's own Silver Pony made of (wait for it) silver, while the commercially-available G3.1 ponies Pinkie Pie, Rainbow Dash, Toola-Roola, Starsong, Sweetie Belle, Cheerilee, and Scootaloo were kept out of the spotlight.[179] This 25th anniversary was intended to celebrate the franchise, not individual ponies, particularly individual ponies who were already on the chopping block, as Lauren Faust had already been approached to reboot the brand. (It seems likely that the 35th or 40th anniversaries will focus on G4 characters as much as the 25th anniversary ignored G3.1 characters.)

Though the June 2007 announcement suggested that the G3.1 ponies wouldn't appear until 2008, they were featured in the video game *Pinkie Pie's Party Parade* released for the PC in October 2007,[180] and for the Nintendo DS as simply *Pinkie Pie's Party* in September 2008 during the height of the 25th anniversary festivities. Parties also factored into the lone G3.1 animation, a series of 4-minute webisodes focusing on each of the characters planning a themed party. First made available for streaming on Hasbro's website in July 2008,[181] they were later collected in a DVD titled *Meet the Ponies* which was packaged with certain dolls.[182]

Generation 3.5 was first referenced a month after the announcement of the network that was not yet known as the Hub:

> Not only is MY LITTLE PONY earmarked to be one of the many Hasbro brands to arrive on U.S. television as a result of the Hasbro and Discovery Communications joint venture, almost 150 licensees are on board to bring new products to market in 2009 focusing on the core cast of seven pony friends—SWEETIE BELLE, CHEERILEE, PINKIE PIE, RAINBOW DASH, SCOOTALOO, STARSONG, and TOOLA-ROOLA—and their new look.[183]

The names were the same as G3.1, and it's uncertain whether Lauren Faust's concurrent design work for *Friendship Is Magic* had any direct influence on the G3.5 ponies, but there are some strong similarities; most noticeably, the ponies now had somewhat smaller bodies, and larger heads with larger eyes.[184] In terms of the illustrations of the ponies rather than the dolls themselves, the further enlargement of the ponies' eyes to *anime*-like proportions in *Friendship Is Magic* was a vast improvement. The smaller eyes of previous Generations may get points for the verisimilitude Bonnie Zacherle originally strived for, but they've always looked unsettling to this writer's own myopic eyes, and the short-lived G3.5 is my favorite pre–G4 design animation-wise. (Also, G3.5 Cheerilee has the best hair of anypony this side of G4 Rarity.)

Animated shorts continued to be produced; a DVD with the unwieldy title *Once Upon a My Little Pony Time* was packaged with the My Little Pony Newborn Cuties Family Convertible in the UK in January 2010,[185] and by March, the G3.5 webisodes "Sweetie Belle's Gumball House Surprise" and "Pinkie Pie's Ferris Wheel" shared real estate on Hasbro's My Little Pony Videos page with the G3.1 webisodes.[186] The 44-minute *Twinkle Wish Adventure* received limited matinee showings in November 2009, and would be the last My Little Pony theatrical release until *My Little Pony: Equestria Girls* in 2013.[187]

G4 was creeping up on this brief generation: not only was Lauren Faust announced as the new "creative steward" two days before the *Twinkle Wish Adventure* premiere, the back cover of Hasbro's 2010 G3.5 catalog featured an ad for *Friendship Is Magic* which referenced neither the name of the show nor the network, simply to "Watch for My Little Pony on TV later this fall! (U.S. Only)."[188]

The Worst News Ever

On April 30, 2009, a joint television venture between Hasbro and Discovery Communications was announced in which the former would invest $300M for a 50% stake in the latter's existing Discovery Kids channel.[189] During a Q&A session, Hasbro's president and CEO Brian Goldner said they were going to "look at programming that's for kids and tweens," but also pointed out that many of their brands "are enjoyed by so many multi-generations and it's really that process of the sharing of those brands," specifying "the passing of the My Little Pony experience from moms to kids" providing "great opportunities for co-viewership."[190] It was just one of the many Hasbro properties that were mentioned, and the Transformers brand was discussed at greater length in terms of the recently-launched film franchise, as well as the "9 plus TV series we've created over the history of the brand since the '80s," including the series that was already running on Cartoon Network.[191]

In spite of the emphasis in the Q&A session on the Transformers range and the many program- and feature-length commercials for it which already existed, My Little Pony was the first against the wall when the backlash began. An article by Sam Schechner and Joseph Pereira in the next day's *Wall Street Journal* began, "The 1980s toy My Little Pony and others in Hasbro's stable may end up on their own cable network, and some consumer-advocacy groups aren't happy about it."[192] The only Transformers reference in the article was to the upcoming *Transformers: Revenge of the Fallen*, itself the second in a line of violent, mega-budgeted, feature-length toy commercials which horribly objectified women. (That is a criticism lodged by your humble and young-looking-for-her-age author, not by Messrs. Schechner and Pereira.) The only Hasbro property the *Journal* article specified as having been a television show previously was My Little Pony, even though there had only been two series since the 1980s (*My Little Pony 'n' Friends* and *My Little Pony Tales*) and no television presence at all for the past 15 years, while by Hasbro's own math in the Q&A, there had been more than nine Transformers shows.[193] Titles of Transformers series listed in the 2005 edition of *Television Cartoon Shows* are the original 1984 *Transformers*, followed by *Transformers: Generation II* in 1993, *Beast Wars: Transformers* in 1996, *Beast Machines: Transformers* in 1999, *Transformers: Robots in Disguise* in 2001, and *Transformers: Armada* in 2002[194]—and even without including the Transformers series which premiered *after* 2005, that's three times as many program-length Transformers commercials than the My Little Pony franchise had managed to produce. But Original Sin has always been the burden of My Little Pony, not the Transformers; after all, it's Eve who gets the flak for the Fall of Man, not Adam.

Lauren Faust was announced as the new creative steward of My Little Pony during Hasbro's Investor Day webcast on November 5, 2009.[195] Margaret Loesch, who had been the CEO of Marvel Productions during the *My Little*

Pony 'n' Friends era and had recently been brought on as the president and CEO of the still-unnamed network, was open about the new series being tied into a new line of merchandising, but also said part of that process involved "creating a compelling story that would introduce young girls to our core cast of ponies."[196] This was the third time that a new generation was promised to have a strong focus on story and character, and the first time it would prove successful.

The name of the new network was announced as the Hub in a January 14, 2010, press release by Discovery Communications.[197] For better or worse, this also is where the animation news blog Cartoon Brew enters our story.

Cartoon Brew was co-founded by animation historians Jerry Beck and Amid Amidi in 2004, a year before the publication of Beck's *Animated Movie Guide*. A February 2005 *Booklist* review of the *Guide* said it "describes films from all of the major and relatively unknown studios, running the gamut from the most vapid of children's fare (*My Little Pony*) to the adult features of the swinging 1970s, such as Ralph Bakshi's X-rated *Fritz the Cat*."[198] Unlike the *Saturday Morning Fever* review, this was not the critic projecting their own feelings about My Little Pony, as Beck used it as the bottom rung for his ratings system:

> 0 stars: **Pure Torture**. Kiddie-show hell. (Example: *My Little Pony*.)[199]

For a film which was so significant as to be the epitome of hellish torture, Beck's attention to detail in his synopsis was roughly on par accuracy-wise with Hal Erickson's in *Television Cartoon Shows*:

> A trio of wicked witches hatches a plot to turn peaceful Ponyland into a dark and dreary wasteland. Ponies Lickety Split, Wind Whistler, and North Star team up with the furry Grundles and children Megan, Molly, and Danny to take on the witches and a purple goose named Snooze.[200]

The monster in *My Little Pony: The Movie* is in fact a sentient purple goo called the Smooze, not a purple goose named Snooze, though he does spell "the Smooze" correctly in the film's cast list, and the accompanying picture is of the definitely-not-a-goose Smooze.[201] (A far more genial version of the character would appear in the *Friendship Is Magic* episode "Make New Friends but Keep Discord" [S05E07].) Again, a single-author reference book covering such a broad spectrum cannot be reasonably expected to get every single detail right, but it does suggest that the decision to rank *My Little Pony: The Movie* as the worst of the worst was done without re-watching the movie during the research and writing of the book, and fact-checking has never been a concern with journalists or critics where My Little Pony is concerned. (Beck did not care for *Transformers: The Movie,* either; he described it as "a feature-length high-tech toy commercial," "not 'user-friendly,'" and "for fans only," and then spent the remainder of the entry describing the history of the franchise, and the backlash against the film killing off the show's hero, but he nonetheless gave it a one and a half stars, without hinting at *why* it received one and a half stars more stars than *My Little Pony: The Movie*.[202])

The first mention of Lauren Faust on Cartoon Brew was a picture of her and her husband Craig McCracken in Beck's coverage of the CTN Animation Expo in November 2009, three weeks after she was announced as the creative steward of the new My Little Pony series.[203] Faust is on the left side of the picture, closer to the foreground, and is wearing a green t-shirt which draws the eye, while McCracken is in a black shirt on the right side of the picture toward the background, with his face mostly obscured by his hair. In an article intended for a Western audience which instinctively looks from the left to the right, the caption read: "Craig McCracken (right) and his wife Lauren Faust (left) look over some of their notes."[204] It bears repeating that they had also been creative partners for several years by that point, having collaborated on *The Powerpuff Girls* and *Foster's Home for Imaginary Friends*.

Beck followed this up in January with a post in which he apologized for being "overdue in reporting on the current activities of cartoon creator Craig McCracken (*Powerpuff Girls, Foster's Home*) and his wife, animator Lauren Faust (*Iron Giant, Cats Don't Dance*)," referring to having chatted with them at the CTN-Expo back in November, citing their current projects as Wander Over Yonder and Milky Way and the Galaxy Girls, respectively.[205] A debate then raged in the comments about the ethics of them selling merchandise from Wander (t-shirts) and Galaxy Girls (limited edition dolls at FAO Schwartz) before either property had become a television series, with one commenter griping: "Has making money from Fosters and the Girls worn off?! Are they really that strapped for cash?"[206] As if it weren't bad enough that these two artists were selling their new, original work, he was also disdainful of those who might be inclined to purchase such merchandise based on a fondness for the creator's past work: "Move ON! And create you're on thing."[207] Original Sin is not limited to My Little Pony, though that's where it's strongest.

The third reference was by Amid Amidi on April 13, eight months before the premiere of *Friendship Is Magic*, in the opening lines of an article titled "Ruby-Spears and Sid and Marty Krofft Team Up":

> Pray for animation, these are scary times. The animation industry has been experiencing a nasty relapse into the crumminess of decades past. First, there was the news that Hasbro is launching its own toy-driven animation network and recruiting talented artists like Lauren Faust to shill My Little Ponies.[208]

The rest of the article had nothing to do with Hasbro or My Little Pony, but it was addressed in the comments by animation character design artist Chris Battle, who'd previously worked on *Samurai Jack*, *The Powerpuff Girls* and others.[209] He objected to referring to Faust as "shilling," asking if by that same logic the producers of *G.I. Joe: Resolute* and *Clone Wars* were also shilling, before getting to the issue at the heart of it all: "Just 'cause it's a girl's toy doesn't mean it's any less valid a project than *Transformers* or whatever…"[210] Choosing to ignore Battle's references to the masculine G.I. Joe and Transformers franchises, both which started as toys before they were television shows yet lacked My Little Pony's Original Sin, Amidi took offense at the *Clone Wars* mention: "Are you suggesting that My Little Ponies is the equivalent of Star Wars?"[211] He went on to explain in no uncertain terms that while "Star Wars is rooted in the integrity and creative vision of an artist's work" and thus gets a lifetime pass, "MLP was designed be a faceless corporate entity for the sole purpose of emptying wallets," and since "the only goal of updating that piece of junk is to move more product," it's a "questionable role for any self-respecting artist to find themself in."[212]

It is no secret among fans that part of George Lucas's deal with Twentieth Century–Fox for the original *Star Wars* was that Lucas would have control of the merchandising. According to Dale Pollock's *Skywalking: The Life and Films of George Lucas*, moving product was already on the artist's mind even during the most integrity-filled period in which he was working to fulfill his creative vision:

> While writing *Star Wars*, Lucas fantasized about R2-D2 cookie jars, Wookiee mugs, and wind-up robots. "Gee, it would be nice if we could do it," he remembers thinking. "And if we do it, I want to make sure that it's done right."[213]

He was also angry about Twentieth Century–Fox's decision to sell the rights to all Star Wars toys in perpetuity to Kenner Toys, reportedly fuming, "We've lost tens of millions of dollars because of that stupid decision."[214] (Kenner was acquired by Tonka in 1987, Hasbro acquired Tonka in 1991, and Generation 2 was released under the Kenner label, creating yet another My Little Pony / Star Wars equivalency.[215]) Lucas was also quoted as saying that he took control of the merchandising "not because I thought it was going to make me rich, but because I wanted to control it."[216] That's as may be, but it does not change the fact that the toys were being planned before the script was finished, long before a single frame of film had been shot. An argument could be made that Amidi's slam that the only goal of updating a piece of junk like My Little Pony is to move more product could also be applied to the poorly-received Star Wars prequels, which were even more "rooted in the integrity and creative vision of an artist's work" than the original trilogy.

Lauren Faust herself stepped into the comments of the April 13 Cartoon Brew post, graciously thanking Amidi for calling her "talented" before proceeding to point out that the Hub "is the only place in town interested in making and airing cartoons for girls," and after correctly predicting that "most people will write off the MLP cartoon as dumb, girly crap whether they watch it or not," she explained that if the only shot she's given to create things for girls that they'll actually enjoy is through updating an existing property, then she was going to take it.[217] Faust's spouse Craig McCracken then ruminated on the time he spent as a kid "playing with the artistically rooted pieces of junk that George [Lucas] was selling me," pointing out that the only difference between that and the junk Faust was playing with at the time was that hers "was pink and had combable hair," and that on a personal level to each of them, the toys were far from junk: they stimulated their young imaginations, creating new characters and adventures, and that "Lauren's My Little Pony world was no less valid than My Little Star Wars world."[218] As if it weren't bad enough to keep putting My Little Pony on the same level as Star Wars, he further suggested that after the disappointment Faust felt at *My Little Pony 'n' Friends* as a child (which "was only bad because it was produced by a bunch of dudes who couldn't believe they were working on My Little Pony, uggggh"), it was a net positive that she now had the opportunity to "bring that world she's had in her head since she was a little kid to life," and "finally inject a little artistic integrity and creative vision into it and make a MLP that girls will actually really like"—adding, "Heck I even like it now and I hated that lame Pony junk, it wasn't cool like my Star Wars junk."[219]

Amidi was having none of this nonsense about the difficulty of women finding companies that will allow them to make quality cartoons for girls being a sufficient reason for Faust to work on a show based on an existing product, even one which had already been animated numerous times over the past three decades. He instead asked if their dream back at CalArts was "really to remake My Little Ponies," whether they used to "nerd out" at the prospect of someday being able to "take this toy designed in a corporate boardroom and make a prettier version of it."[220] He informed Faust and McCracken what *they* thought and felt, while taking continued offense at any conceivable equivalency between the two franchises—"My Little Ponies and Star Wars revivals (if you insist on lumping them together) wasn't [your] dream"—and scolded them that "it wasn't why any of you guys got into animation," concluding facetiously but no less tastelessly that "what I really need to do is come to LA and slap some sense into everybody!"[221]

In addition to the fact that it is *never* acceptable for a man to threaten to hit a woman, no matter how jokingly or how opposed he may be to her working on a series which had its origins as a toy, it's worth noting that Amidi always referred to the franchise in the plural as "My Little Ponies" even when it was grammatically incorrect. Intentionally misspelling the name of your philosophical adversary as a means of demeaning them is a cheap tactic, and unbecoming of an otherwise respectable site like Cartoon Bruise.

*   *   *

After the initial flurry surrounding the April 2009 announcement of the new network, another storm of controversy formed as the launch date approached eighteen months later. Peggy Charren and ACT were long out of the game, but on October 5, 2010, the director of the Campaign for a Commercial-Free Childhood was quoted in the *Los Angeles Times* as saying that "the notion of a toy company owning a television channel for the sole purpose of promoting their toys is egregious practice," though she acknowl edged that she had not yet seen any of the shows in question.[222] Her associate director told the *Wall Street Journal* that they were urging parents to not let children watch the Hub, describing it as "an escalation of the use of TV as nothing more than a way to promote products to kids."[223] Although the FCC rules from 1991 limiting the number of commercials during children's shows to 12 minutes per hour on weekdays and 10.5 per hour on weekends were still in effect by 2010, the Hub said that they would only carry six minutes of com- mercials per hour in shows aimed at preschoolers in order to "ease an outcry," while Margaret Loesch promised that the percentage of Hub programs based on Hasbro products would be less than 20%.[224] She also pointed out that lost in all the furor around the Hasbro connection to the Hub was the fact that it was a joint venture with Discovery Communications, "and we have pro- gramming from them and are using their DNA."[225]

While Hasbro wouldn't officially announce the show's title until June 7,[226] the first public appearance of the words *My Little Pony: Friendship Is Magic* and of the characters as they would appear on the show (Twilight Sparkle and Pinkie Pie in particular) was in the "Cable Guide 2010" supple- ment of the May 3 issue of *Advertising Age*. It was also the first of many times that a description of the show would fail to do it justice:

> Emmy-winner Lauren Faust ("The Powerpuff Girls," "Foster's Home for Imaginary Friends") presents a unique peek into the magical world of Equestria, where "Twilight Sparkle," a uni- corn pony with a talent for magic spells, co-exists with her pony friends. Each episode follows "Twilight Sparkle" and pals as they embark on wondrous adventures.[227]

"Co-exists" is an odd word choice by any standard, but whoever wrote the copy can't be blamed for not knowing that even in the augural season, Twi- light Sparkle (or "Twilight Sparkle," as they insisted on scare-quoting her) would sometimes be relegated to a cameo at the end, and that as early as the eighth episode, the "wondrous adventure" would take the form of holing up during a storm and watching two of her friends tear into each other emotionally. (It would be difficult to promote a show whose official target demographic is three-to-six-year-old girls and their mothers in those terms.)

That *Friendship Is Magic* was intended for girls and girls only was reinforced by Hasbro's September 28 press release which announced that "fans and kids can bring home the fantasy of IRON MAN 2" and "STAR WARS fans can celebrate the 30th anniversary of THE EMPIRE STRIKES BACK" with toys specifically geared to those properties, while "girls will have the opportunity to make some new friends with the introduction of new MY LITTLE PONY figures based on the original 'My Little Pony Friendship is Magic' animated series."[228]

Perhaps having a better idea of what they had on their hands, Hasbro's October 7 press release was dedicated to *Friendship Is Magic* and the accompanying "new product line, strong licensing program, and social media presence" which will "connect the brand with fans of all ages," describing the premise of the show as following "a core cast of six pony friends through funny, offbeat experiences, lessons in friendship and exciting, enchanted adventures."[229] Curiously, for as much attention as had been paid to pony names for the G3.1 and G3.5 launches in the previous few years, the names of the "core cast" were not mentioned: Twilight Sparkle, Rarity, Fluttershy, Applejack, Pinkie Pie, and Rainbow Dash. The September 28 press release did describe the "My Little Pony Friendship Is Magic Gift Set" as including "PINKIE PIE, TWILIGHT SPARKLE, PRINCESS CELESTIA, APPLE JACK and SPIKE THE DRAGON figures in addition to a storybook that reveals the fun-filled story behind these wonderful pony friendships," but only three of them were part of the new core cast, Applejack's name was misspelled, and not mentioning Rarity at all is burying the lede.[230]

It's all the more surprising considering that so much of the success of the relaunch would depend on the series in which they starred, but their names were evidently less important than the fact that their new look was promised to "win the hearts of 'Pony Girls' everywhere," while the press release also claimed that the new series "marks the first episodic MY LITTLE PONY animation since the original series in the 1980s."[231] Which was not true, but also an understandable oversight, since nopony wants to be reminded that 1992's *My Little Pony Tales* existed.

Co-produced by Hasbro Studios and DHX Media, *My Little Pony: Friendship Is Magic* debuted with "Friendship Is Magic, Part 1" (S01E01) at 2:30 p.m. EST on October 10, 2010, as part of the Hub's "Sneak Peek Sunday."[232]

Tara Strong provided the voice for Twilight Sparkle, Tabitha St. Germain for Rarity, Andrea Libman for Pinkie Pie and Fluttershy, and Ashleigh Ball for Rainbow Dash and Applejack. Though the threat of a new My Little Pony show had raised the most alarms in the press, it was by no means the Hub's premier series, nor even its premiere; the first program to be broadcast was *The Twisted Whiskers Show* at 10 a.m. EST, and *Friendship Is Magic* was sandwiched between *Pound Puppies* and *Strawberry Shortcake's Berry Bitty Adventures.*

Things had changed, but nopony knew it yet.

PART 3

Twilight's Kingdom (*Friendship Is Magic* and *Equestria Girls* Reference Guide)

Episode or movie titles are followed by the name of the credited writer, original broadcast/release date, a brief description of the episode or movie, and a letter grade based on a scale of *Friendship Is Magic* from its best ("Look Before You Sleep," "Twilight Time," *My Little Pony: Equestria Girls—Rainbow Rocks*) to its worst ("The Last Roundup," "Daring Don't," "Slice of Life"). That these are the subjective opinions of the author makes them no less definitive.

Season 1

S01E01: "Friendship Is Magic, Part 1." Lauren Faust. October 10, 2010. Princess Celestia sends Twilight Sparkle to Ponyville against her will to make friends. (B-)

S01E02: "Friendship Is Magic, Part 2." Lauren Faust. October 22, 2010. The Mane Six set out to defeat returned supervillain Nightmare Moon. (C)

S01E03: "The Ticket Master." Amy Keating Rogers and Lauren Faust. October 29, 2010. Twilight Sparkle must decide which of her five needy friends to take to the Grand Galloping Gala. (A)

S01E04: "Applebuck Season." Amy Keating Rogers. November 5, 2010. Applejack works herself to the point of delirium. (C)

S01E05: "Griffon the Brush Off." Cindy Morrow. November 12, 2010. Pinkie Pie confronts Rainbow Dash's childhood friend Gilda, a bullying griffon. (C+)

S01E06: "Boast Busters." Chris Savino. November 16, 2010. The showboating Great and Powerful Trixie wreaks havoc in Ponyville. (B-)

S01E07: "Dragonshy." Meghan McCarthy. November 26, 2010, Fluttershy's chronic phobias hinder a mission to confront a dragon. (B+)

S01E08: "Look Before You Sleep." Charlotte Fullerton. December 3, 2010. The animosity between Rarity and Applejack boils over during a dark and stormy night in Twilight Sparkle's library. (A+)

S01E09: "Bridle Gossip." Amy Keating Rogers. December 10, 2010. The residents of Ponyville assume the worst about a visiting zebra. (C+)

S01E10: "Swarm of the Century." M.A. Larson. December 17, 2010. Ponyville faces an ecological catastrophe on the eve of a visit by Princess Celestia. (B+)

S01E11: "Winter Wrap Up." Cindy Morrow. December 24, 2010. Twilight Sparkle struggles to fit in during Ponyville's annual cleaning of winter. (B)

S01E12: "Call of the Cutie." Meghan McCarthy. January 7, 2011. Apple Bloom sets out to find her Cutie Mark. (B)

S01E13: "Fall Weather Friends." Amy Keating Rogers. January 28, 2011. Rainbow Dash and Applejack compete to determine the better athlete. (C+)

S01E14: "Suited for Success." Charlotte Fullerton. February 4, 2011. Rarity struggles with her friends' tone-deaf demands when making their dresses for the Grand Galloping Gala. (A+)

S01E15: "Feeling Pinkie Keen." Dave Polsky. February 11, 2011. Rationalist Twilight Sparkle tries to quantify Pinkie Pie's seemingly impossible predictive spasms. (B)

S01E16: "Sonic Rainboom." M.A. Larson. February 18, 2011. Rainbow Dash's performance anxiety is exacerbated by Rarity's new wings. (B+)

S01E17: "Stare Master." Chris Savino. February 25, 2011. Fluttershy gets more than she bargained for after agreeing to babysit the Cutie Mark Crusaders. (B-)

S01E18: "The Show Stoppers." Cindy Morrow. March 4, 2011. The Crusaders attempt to get their Cutie Marks in music, with disastrous results. (A)

S01E19: "A Dog and Pony Show." Amy Keating Rogers. March 11, 2011. Rarity uses her wits to escape from the gem-obsessed Diamond Dogs. (A+)

S01E20: "Green Isn't Your Color." Meghan McCarthy. March 18, 2011. Rarity struggles with jealousy when Fluttershy unintentionally becomes a supermodel. (A-)

S01E21: "Over a Barrel." Dave Polsky. March 25, 2011. The Mane Six become involved in a land dispute between settler ponies and indigenous buffalo. (C+)

S01E22: "A Bird in the Hoof." Charlotte Fullerton. April 8, 2011. Fluttershy kidnaps Princess Celestia's ailing pet bird Philomena to nurse her back to health. (B-)

S01E23: "The Cutie Mark Chronicles." M.A. Larson. April 15, 2011. The Crusaders learn how the Mane Six got their Cutie Marks. (A+)

S01E24: "Owl's Well that Ends Well." Cindy Morrow. April 22, 2011. Spike becomes jealous of Twilight Sparkle's new nighttime assistant Owloysius. (C)

S01E25: "Party of One." Meghan McCarthy. April 29, 2011. Pinkie Pie suffers an emotional breakdown when she believes her friends have rejected her. (A+)

S01E26: "The Best Night Ever." Amy Keating Rogers. May 6, 2011. The Mane Six experience disappointment and heartbreak at the Grand Galloping Gala. (A+)

Season 2

S02E01: "The Return of Harmony, Part 1." M.A. Larson. September 17, 2011. Princess Celestia's ancient nemesis Discord, an embodiment of disharmony, splinters the Mane Six. (B)

S02E02: "The Return of Harmony, Part 2." M.A. Larson. September 24, 2011. The Mane Six regroup and defeat Discord. (B)

S02E03: "Lesson Zero." Meghan McCarthy. October 15, 2011. Twilight Sparkle drives herself to the point of madness with anxiety. (A+)

S02E04: "Luna Eclipsed." M.A. Larson. October 22, 2011. Princess Luna finds it difficult to move beyond her reputation as Nightmare Moon. (B)

S02E05: "Sisterhooves Social." Cindy Morrow. November 5, 2011. Sweetie Belle defects to the Apple Family after fighting with Rarity. (B+)

S02E06: "The Cutie Pox." Amy Keating Rogers. November 12, 2011. Apple Bloom's drive to find her Cutie Mark results in an ancient and possibly incurable disease. (B)

S02E07: "May the Best Pet Win!" Charlotte Fullerton. November 19, 2011. Rainbow Dash holds a competition to find a worthy pet. (A-)

S02E08: "The Mysterious Mare Do Well." Merriwether Williams. November 26, 2011. Rainbow Dash's boastful feats of bravery are overshadowed by a masked vigilante. (C-)

S02E09: "Sweet and Elite." Meghan McCarthy. December 3, 2011. Rarity forsakes her friends to climb the social ladder in Canterlot. (B+)

S02E10: "Secret of My Excess." M.A. Larson. December 10, 2011. Spike experiences growth spurts that make him greedy and dumb. (C+)

S02E11: "Hearth's Warming Eve." Merriwether Williams. December 17, 2011. The story of Equestria's founding is told through an annual winter pageant. (A)

S02E12: "Family Appreciation Day." Cindy Morrow. January 7, 2012. The Cutie Mark Crusaders try to stop Granny Smith from speaking at the school. (B-)

S02E13: "Baby Cakes." Charlotte Fullerton. January 14, 2012. Pinkie Pie gets in over her head when she babysits month-old twins. (B)

S02E14: "The Last Roundup." Amy Keating Rogers. January 21, 2012. Applejack leaves Ponyville, and her friends are determined to find out why. (D)

S02E15: "The Super Speedy Cider Squeezy 6000." M.A. Larson. January 28, 2012. Traveling hucksters Flim and Flam challenge the Apple Family's apple business. (A)

S02E16: "Read It and Weep." Cindy Morrow. February 4, 2012. A hospitalized Rainbow Dash discovers the awesomeness of reading via a pulp adventure novel. (B-)

S02E17: "Hearts and Hooves Day." Meghan McCarthy. February 11, 2012. The Cutie Mark Crusaders go to dangerous lengths to set up Cheerilee with Big Macintosh. (B)

S02E18: "A Friend in Deed." Meghan McCarthy. February 18, 2012. Pinkie Pie is determined to befriend an antisocial donkey, whether he wants her to or not. (C)

S02E19: "Putting Your Hoof Down." Merriwether Williams and Charlotte Fullerton. March 3, 2012. Fluttershy takes an assertiveness-training course, which works too well. (A+)

S02E20: "It's About Time." M.A. Larson. March 10, 2012. Twilight Sparkle assumes the worst after receiving an incomplete message from her future self. (A)

S02E21: "Dragon Quest." Merriwether Williams. March 17, 2012. Spike joins a migration of dragons to learn out more about his species. (B)

S02E22: "Hurricane Fluttershy." Cindy Morrow. March 24, 2012. Fluttershy faces her fears of failure when she participates in the creation of a tornado. (B+)

S02E23: "Ponyville Confidential." M.A. Larson. March 31, 2012. The Cutie Mark Crusaders write a gossip column for the school newspaper. (B for content, A+ for the title)

S02E24: "MMMystery on the Friendship Express." Amy Keating Rogers. April 7, 2012. Pinkie Pie and Twilight Sparkle investigate a dessert crime on the trans-Equestrian railroad. (B+)

S02E25: "A Canterlot Wedding, Part 1." Meghan McCarthy. April 21, 2012. Twilight Sparkle suspects her brother's fiancé is evil. (B+)

S02E26: "A Canterlot Wedding, Part 2." Meghan McCarthy. April 21, 2012. The Mane Six battle the Changeling Queen for the fate of Equestria. (B)

Season 3 and My Little Pony: Equestria Girls

S03E01: "The Crystal Empire, Part 1." Meghan McCarthy. November 10, 2012. The long-lost Crystal Empire reappears, as does its evil ruler Sombra. (C)

S03E02: "The Crystal Empire, Part 2." Meghan McCarthy. November 10, 2012. Twilight Sparkle and Spike search for the Crystal Heart to defeat Sombra. (C+)

S03E03: "Too Many Pinkie Pies." Meghan McCarthy. November 17, 2012. Pinkie Pie clones herself, and her clones get the same idea. (B)

S03E04: "One Bad Apple." Cindy Morrow. November 24, 2012. The Cutie Mark Crusaders are shocked to discover Apple Bloom's cousin Babs is a bully. (C)

S03E05: "Magic Duel." M.A. Larson. December 1, 2012. The showboating Great and Powerful Trixie returns to seek vengeance on Twilight Sparkle. (B)

S03E06: "Sleepless in Ponyville." Corey Powell. December 8, 2012. Princess Luna helps Scootaloo work through her fears in a dream. (B-)

S03E07: "Wonderbolts Academy." Merriwether Williams. December 15, 2012. Rainbow Dash discovers Wonderbolt Academy isn't all it's cracked up to be. (C+)

S03E08: "Apple Family Reunion." Cindy Morrow. December 22, 2012. Applejack micromanages her family reunion. (C)

S03E09: "Spike at Your Service." Merriwether Williams. December 29, 2012. After his life is saved by Applejack, Spike decides it belongs to her. (C)

S03E10: "Keep Calm and Flutter On." Dave Polsky. January 19, 2013. Princess Celestia returns Discord to Ponyville to be rehabilitated by the Mane Six. (B)

S03E11: "Just for Sidekicks." Corey Powell. January 26, 2013. While the Mane Six are on a business trip to the Crystal Empire, Spike attempts to watch their pets. (B)

S03E12: "Games Ponies Play." Dave Polsky. February 9, 2013. In the Crystal Empire, the Mane Six woo a pony they mistakenly believe is an Inspector from the Equestria Games. (A)

S03E13: "Magical Mystery Cure." M.A. Larson. February 16, 2013. After finishing an ancient spell believed to be unfinishable, Twilight Sparkle evolves into an Alicorn Princess. (A-)

My Little Pony: Equestria Girls. Meghan McCarthy. June 16, 2013. To retrieve her Element of Harmony from the renegade Sunset Shimmer, Princess Twilight travels through a mirror to Canterlot High, finding herself transformed into a biped, and surrounded by biped versions of her friends and neighbors. (B-)

Season 4 and My Little Pony: Equestria Girls—Rainbow Rocks

S04E01: "Princess Twilight Sparkle, Part 1." Meghan McCarthy. November 23, 2013. When Celestia and Luna vanish, Twilight finds herself the lone Princess in Equestria. (B-)

S04E02: "Princess Twilight Sparkle, Part 2." Meghan McCarthy. November 23, 2013. The Mane Six return the Elements of Harmony to their source, the Tree of Harmony. (C)

S04E03: "Castle Mane-ia." Josh Haber. November 30, 2013. The Mane Six spend an evening inadvertently scaring each other in the ancient Castle of the Two Sisters. (B+)

S04E04: "Daring Don't." Dave Polsky. December 7, 2013. Rainbow Dash discovers that the author of her favorite adventure novels lives those adventures in real life. (D)

S04E05: "Flight to the Finish." Ed Valentine. December 14, 2013. Scootaloo spirals into shame and self-doubt as the Crusaders practice a routine for the Equestria Games. (A)

S04E06: "Power Ponies." Meghan McCarthy, Charlotte Fullerton, and Betsy McGowen. December 21, 2013. The Mane Six and Spike are magically transported into a comic book. (C-)

S04E07: "Bats!" Merriwether Williams. December 28, 2013. Princess Twilight's attempts to rid Applejack's farm of vampire fruit bats accidentally turns Fluttershy into one. (B)

S04E08: "Rarity Takes Manehattan." Dave Polsky. January 4, 2014. Rarity's generosity is tested when she encounters duplicity and backstabbing during Fashion Week in Manehattan. (B+)

S04E09: "Pinkie Apple Pie." Natasha Levinger. January 11, 2014. Pinkie Pie joins the Apples on a road trip to determine whether they're distant cousins. (B-)

S04E10: "Rainbow Falls." Corey Powell. January 18, 2014. Rainbow Dash is tempted into disloyalty toward her friends while training for the Equestria Games. (B+)

S04E11: "Three's a Crowd." Meghan McCarthy and Ed Valentine. January 25, 2014. Discord crashes and monopolizes Princesses Twilight and Cadance's day together. (C-)

S04E12: "Pinkie Pride." Amy Keating Rogers. February 1, 2014. Pinkie Pie finds her status as Ponyville's party impresario threatened by newcomer Cheese Sandwich. (B+)

S04E13: "Simple Ways." Josh Haber. February 8, 2014. Rarity is infatuated with visiting travel writer Trenderhoof, who only has eyes for the disinterested Appleack. (A-)

S04E14: "Filli Vanilli." Josh Haber. February 15, 2014. Fluttershy provides the voice of a lip-syncing Big Macintosh in Rarity's *a capella* group the Pony-Tones. (D-)

S04E15: "Twilight Time." Dave Polsky. February 22, 2014. The Cutie Mark Crusaders use their friendship with Princess Twilight to curry favor at school. (A+)

S04E16: "It Ain't Easy Being Breezies." Natasha Levinger. March 1, 2014. A fairy-like species called the Breezies is briefly stranded in Ponyville, then decides to stay. (B-)

S04E17: "Somepony to Watch Over Me." Scott Sonneborn. March 8, 2014. Applejack declares Apple Bloom mature enough to stay home by herself, but can't bring herself to believe it. (B-)

S04E18: "Maud Pie." Noelle Benvenuti. March 15, 2014. Pinkie Pie's sister Maud visits Ponyville, and proves to be very different from Pinkie. (A-)

S04E19: "For Whom the Sweetie Belle Toils." Dave Polsky. March 22, 2014. Sweetie Belle struggles with being in her sister Rarity's shadow, with an assist from Princess Luna. (A)

S04E20: "Leap of Faith." Josh Haber. March 29, 2014. Flim and Flam return to town selling a fake miracle tonic that Granny Smith wholly believes in. (B)

S04E21: "Testing Testing 1, 2, 3." Amy Keating Rogers. April 5, 2014. The Mane Six, and eventually all of Ponyville, try to help Rainbow Dash study for a Wonderbolts history test. (B+)

S04E22: "Trade Ya!" Scott Sonneborn. April 19, 2014. The Mane Six visit the annual Traders Exchange in Rainbow Falls. (B+)

S04E23: "Inspiration Manifestation." Corey Powell and Meghan McCarthy. April 26, 2014. Rarity discovers a spell that brings whatever she can imagine to life. (D)

S04E24: "Equestria Games." Dave Polsky. May 3, 2014. Spike's fame in the Crystal Empire gets him in over his head during the Equestria Games. (B)

S04E25: "Twilight's Kingdom, Part 1." Meghan McCarthy. May 10, 2014. The demonic centaur Tirek steals magic throughout Equestria. (B)

S04E26: "Twilight's Kingdom, Part 2." Meghan McCarthy. May 10, 2014. Twilight acquires the magic of the other Alicorn Princesses to hide it from Tirek. (A)

My Little Pony: Equestria Girls—Rainbow Rocks Prequel Shorts. Cindy Morrow, Amy Keating Rogers, Daniel Ingram, Josh Haber, and Natasha Levinger. March–June 2014, April 2015. Canterlot High's Mane Six counterparts each acquire their instruments for their new band, the Rainbooms, and discover that Equestrian magic still lingers in their world. "Music to My Ears" (A+); "Guitar Centered" (B); "Hamstocalypse Now" (B-); "Pinkie on the One" (A); "Player Piano" (A+); "A Case for the Bass" (B-); "Shake Your Tail!" (C); "Perfect Day for Fun" (C).

My Little Pony: Equestria Girls—Rainbow Rocks. Meghan McCarthy. September 27, 2014. Princess Twilight returns to the biped world to help the Rainbooms and a reformed Sunset Shimmer battle Equestrian creatures known as the Sirens. (A+)

My Little Pony: Equestria Girls—Rainbow Rocks Encore Shorts. Jayson Thiessen, Katrina Hadley, Brian Lenard, Daniel Ingram & Michael Vogel. April 2015. "My Past Is Not Today" (A+); "Friendship Through the Ages" (A+); "Life Is a Runway" (A).

Season 5 and My Little Pony: Equestria Girls—Friendship Games

S05E01: "The Cutie Map, Part 1." Scott Sonneborn and M.A. Larson. April 4, 2015. A map in Princess Twilight's new castle leads the Mane Six to a village whose residents have renounced their Cutie Marks. (B)

S05E02: "The Cutie Map, Part 2." Scott Sonneborn and M.A. Larson. April 4, 2015. The Mane Six struggle to retrieve their Cutie Marks from cult leader Starlight Glimmer. (B)

S05E03: "Castle Sweet Castle." Joanna Lewis and Kristine Songco. April 11, 2015. Princess Twilight's friends decorate her castle, badly. (C+)

S05E04: "Bloom & Gloom." Josh Haber. April 18, 2015. Apple Bloom wrestles with her fear of getting a Cutie Mark she doesn't like. (B+)

S05E05: "Tanks for the Memories." Cindy Morrow. April 25, 2015. Terrified of being alone, Rainbow Dash takes extreme measures to prevent her pet tortoise from hibernating for the winter. (A-)

S05E06: "Appleoosa's Most Wanted." Dave Polsky. May 2, 2015. The Cutie Mark Crusaders befriend a notorious outlaw. (C+)

S05E07: "Make New Friends but Keep Discord." Nicole Wang and Sabrina

Alberghetti. May 16, 2015. Discord discovers the downside of friendship: jealousy. (B)

S05E08: "The Lost Treasure of Griffonstone." Amy Keating Rogers. May 23, 2015. Rainbow Dash and Pinkie Pie travel to Gilda the Griffon's blighted homeland. (B-)

S05E09: "Slice of Life." M.A. Larson. June 13, 2015. To quote Miss Cheerilee in *My Little Pony: Equestria Girls*: "No. Just, no." (F)

S05E10: "Princess Spike." Neal Dusedau. June 20, 2015. Spike makes decisions by proxy for a sleeping Princess Twilight. (B+)

S05E11: "Party Pooped." Nick Confalone. June 27, 2015. Pinkie Pie faces her greatest party-throwing challenge yet: a visiting delegation of yaks from Yakyakistan. (B)

S05E12: "Amending Fences." M.A. Larson. July 4, 2015. Princess Twilight reckons with the emotional damage she caused to her old Canterlot friend Moondancer. (A+)

S05E13: "Do Princesses Dream of Magic Sheep?" Scott Sonneborn. July 11, 2015. A monster from Princess Luna's dreams threatens to consume the waking world. (B+)

S05E14: "Canterlot Boutique." Amy Keating Rogers. September 12, 2015. Finally opening a shop in Canterlot, Rarity clashes with her business partner. (B)

S05E15: "Rarity Investigates!" Joanna Lewis and Kristine Songco. September 19, 2015. Rarity emulates her literary hero Shadow Spade when Rainbow Dash is accused of sabotage. (A)

S05E16: "Made in Manehattan." Natasha Levinger. July 11, 2015. Applejack faces her fear of the city as she and Rarity work to rebuild a community theater. (B)

S05E17: "Brotherhooves Social." Dave Polsky. October 3, 2015. Big Macintosh adopts the persona of a female cousin to compete in the Sisterhooves Social with Apple Bloom. (C+)

S05E18: "Crusaders of the Lost Mark." Amy Keating Rogers. October 10, 2015. The Cutie Mark Crusaders discover their purpose in life. (A+)

S05E19: "The One Where Pinkie Pie Knows." Gillian M. Berrow. October 17, 2015. Pinkie Pie has to keep a big secret: Princess Cadance is pregnant. (C)

S05E20: "Hearthbreakers." Nick Confalone. October 24, 2015. Spending Hearth's Warming Eve together, the Apples discover Pinkie Pie's family has very different holiday traditions. (B)

S05E21: "Scare Master." Natasha Levinger. October 31, 2015. Fluttershy attempts to get into the Nightmare Night spirit. (B)

S05E22: "What About Discord?" Neal Dusedau. November 7, 2015. Princess

Twilight struggles with regret and loneliness when her friends spend a fun weekend with Discord. (B+)

S05E23: "The Hooffields and McColts." Joanna Lewis and Kristine Songco. November 14, 2015. Princess Twilight and Fluttershy attempt to broker a peace between warring clans. (C-)

S05E24: "The Mane Attraction." Amy Keating Rogers. November 21, 2015. Applejack discovers a childhood friend has become a flashy pop superstar. (B)

S05E25: "The Cutie Re-Mark, Part 1." Josh Haber. November 28, 2015. Starlight Glimmer returns, seeking vengeance on Princess Twilight. (B+)

S05E26: "The Cutie Re-Mark, Part 2." Josh Haber. November 28, 2015. Princess Twilight and Spike ricochet between timelines in hopes of stopping Starlight Glimmer. (B-)

My Little Pony: Equestria Girls—Friendship Games Animated Shorts. Brian Lenard, Natasha Levinger, Ishi Rudell, and Jayson Thiessen. August 2015. Canterlot High prepares for the upcoming Friendship Games competition against Crystal Prep. "The Science of Magic" (A+); "Pinkie Spy" (B); "All's Fair in Love and Friendship Games" (C+); "Photo Finished" (B); "A Banner Day" (B).

My Little Pony: Equestria Girls—Friendship Games. Josh Haber. September 26, 2015. The biped world's Twilight Sparkle investigates the Equestrian magic at Canterlot High during the varsity Friendship Games. (A+)

Part 4

The Foal Free Press
(2010–2015)

Ultra-Feminine Yet Vinegary Ponies

Also published by McFarland, your source for fine scholarly books about cartoons, David Perlmutter's 2014 *America Toons In: A History of Television Animation* devoted a single paragraph to *My Little Pony 'n' Friends*. Perlmutter referred to its "toy synergy" as "no less disturbing" than that of the militaristic *G.I. Joe*, though he admitted that *Pony* "was milder in tone and intent."[1] He also referred to the 1992 followup series *My Little Pony Tales* not by name, but as "new episodes" which "further entrenched the sticky sweet ambience of the project."[2] That last statement linked to an endnote, which constituted *America Toons In*'s only reference to *Friendship Is Magic*:

> 121. In the early 2010s, Hasbro revived the project under the title *My Little Pony: Friendship Is Magic*. While the ultra-feminine Ponyland setting and characters were retained, the writing and characterization brought a shade more vinegar into the sweetness, in the fashion of later productions such as *The Powerpuff Girls*. This was no accident when you consider that this *Pony* had as its executive producer Lauren Faust, a veteran *Powerpuff Girls* writer (and the wife of *Powerpuff* creator Craig McCracken, to boot).[3]

Buried in the endnotes, this off-hand mention kept *Friendship Is Magic* from being listed in the index, while to say Hasbro "revived the project" suggested the show is a continuation of either of the previous series, which it is not.[4] *Friendship Is Magic* is set in the sovereign nation of Equestria and centers on the rural town of Ponyville, not the "ultra-feminine" Ponyland of the 1986 series, and while its main cast is female and it portrays a matriarchy—without being oppressive to other genders in the manner of patriarchies in our world—one would be hard-pressed to describe Rainbow Dash, Applejack, or Twilight Sparkle as ultra-feminine, and aside from certain names and physical traits, the characters are not "retained" from *My Little Pony 'n' Friends* and/or *My Little Pony Tales*.[5]

Friendship Is Magic's writing and characterization bringing "a shade more vinegar into the sweetness" *is* an excellent way to describe the show's relationship to its forebears, though it's closer to being a light meal than just vinegar-shaded candy. The reference to *The Powerpuff Girls* was also apt, though *Magic* creator Lauren Faust not only had writing credit on two *Powerpuff* episodes but was also the storyboard artist for six, and the director of 29 altogether.[6] But like the Cartoon Brew picture caption from 2009, to imply that Faust being married to *Powerpuff* creator Craig McCracken—and to again specify her as being his wife, which, though accurate, is a semantic choice which places her in a subordinate position to McCracken—is at all responsible for either specific *Powerpuff*-like qualities of *Friendship Is Magic* or any degree of the show's success is to denigrate the talent of not only Faust but the entire production staff, some of whom also worked on *The Powerpuff Girls* without being married to its creator. It's a pity that the digression takes up 10 of the 89 words in that paragraph (or that discussing it takes up half a paragraph in this book, space that could have been better served by something more important, like working in another reference to how Rarity is the best).

Is this degree of nitpicking necessary for something as frivolous as My Little Pony cartoons? Considering that the official description of *America Toons In* says the book "[discusses] the ways in which the genre has often been unfairly marginalized by critics," and takes pride in "taking seriously something often thought to be frivolous," then yes, *Friendship Is Magic* and *Equestria Girls* deserve to be taken seriously.[7]

Ponies: Harbingers of Even More Doom

"Friendship Is Magic, Part 1" (S01E01) faced the same problem as all pilot episodes, particularly two-parters which aren't broadcast back-to-back: the need to tell an exciting, plot-driven story which makes viewers want more, often at the expense of establishing the characters beyond rudimentary sketches. In fairness, the producers aren't yet sure who the characters are by this point, either. *Star Trek: The Next Generation* encountered that problem with its two-part pilot "Encounter at Farpoint," and though both parts premiered on the same night, it was a clunky episode that only became more disappointing in retrospect. Taken as a whole, "Friendship Is Magic, Parts 1 & 2" (S01E01-2) is a fair shake better than "Encounter at Farpoint"—a low bar, admittedly—and while they do not represent what the series would be at its best, they're not without thematic depth.

Every work of art, every book, movie, television show, or doodle on a notepad is a reflection of its era, and like the *Battlestar Galactica* reboot before it, *My Little Pony: Friendship Is Magic* reflects the tenor of its time. In the 1978 *Galactica*, the Cylons were an external threat, reptilian aliens who hated the freedom and independence the warm-blooded mammals cherished, so they created robots to kill all humans. Similarly in *My Little Pony 'n' Friends*, the villains were often outsiders with no motivation other than hating ponies for the goodness they represented (not unlike the show's critics, though most hid behind outrage about the merchandising aspect).

In the 2003 *Galactica* series, the Cylons were robot slaves created by humanity who rebelled, disappeared for a few decades, then returned in human form seeking revenge for their past mistreatment. It was not an external villain, but rather humanity's past sins catching up with them, and taking a form which allowed them to blend in with the populace. (And where they were called the Cylon Empire in the original series, in the re-imagined series they're far less organized, and are making it up as they go along just as much as the humans.) *Friendship Is Magic*'s Nightmare Moon is not a witch or other foul creature who hates the ponies for the sake of being evil; she was a former ruler who felt marginalized by her older sister, and allowed her jealousy and rage to overwhelm her.

As a result, both the re-imagined Cylons and Nightmare Moon are products of an America facing not a well-defined threat like the Soviet Union (which President Reagan would refer to as "an evil empire" well after the original *Galactica* went off the air, but around the time that the My Little Pony dolls first hit the market), but of a society that's learned the hard way that its actions have consequences, and sometimes the threats come from the inside.[8] This is *not* to suggest *Friendship Is Magic* is also a 9/11 allegory, or that such things were consciously on the writers' minds when developing the show (in Canada, no less), but merely that even several years down the line, it was the product of a country forever changed by its brush with terrorism, and one whose young children—even little girls, whose intelligence will be frequently disrespected if not disregarded altogether by critics going forward—are now able to deal with villains who offer a degree of moral ambiguity. After all, did Princess Celestia do *everything* she could to rehabilitate her sister? Was it necessary to leave Luna stranded in the moon for a thousand years? Was Nightmare Moon's rage perhaps justified? It would prove to be debatable as the series progressed.

* * *

The first significant post-premiere backlash occurred between "Friendship Is Magic, Part 1" on October 10, 2010, and "Friendship Is Magic, Part 2"

(S01E02) on October 22, the first regularly scheduled series broadcast. In his October 18 Cartoon Brew article titled "The End of the Creator-Driven Era in TV Animation," Amid Amidi declared that both the debut of the Hub and the presence of former Hanna-Barbera Vice President and Marvel Productions CEO Margaret Loesch as the new network's CEO signaled an unavoidable return to cartoons being a toy promotion, and therefore a decline in the kind of work made by producers such as *The Simpsons'* Matt Groening, *Beavis and Butt-head's* Mike Judge, the *Powerpuff Girls'* oft-mentioned Craig McCracken, and *South Park's* Trey Parker and Matt Stone.[9] (All of those shows spawned vast quantities of merchandise now residing in landfills, and all but *Powerpuff* have made their creators multi-millionaires, but none carry My Little Pony's Original Sin.) Though *Friendship Is Magic* was not the only Hub show mentioned, Amidi did single out its creative steward and her story editor:

> Watching names like Rob Renzetti and Lauren Faust pop up in the credits of a toy-based animated series like *My Little Pony* is an admission of defeat for the entire movement, a white flag-waving moment for the TV animation industry.[10]

Television animation: it's a movement! After suggesting other outlets for more "serious" animators, such as the Internet (okay!) or as a background for live performances (sure, why not?), Amidi concluded that "TV animation isn't going anywhere, and future Margaret Loesches will still find plenty of willing peons to fulfill their orders for extended toy commercials," implying that Faust and her story editor Renzetti were the current peons.[11] On the plus side, he didn't arbitrarily pluralize "My Little Pony" like before.

This was not the first time My Little Pony had been described as the antithesis of cartoons which are "creator-driven," and thus "good." In a 2001 *Orange County Register* article, Stephen Lynch had traced the creator-driven phenomenon back to Ralph Bakshi's short-lived *Mighty Mouse* series for CBS, describing the late 1980s landscape as such: "It was 1987, and Saturday mornings were filled with 'The Smurfs' and 'My Little Pony,' the tedious and the toy commercials."[12] (That *My Little Pony 'n' Friends* was never a Saturday morning show hardly seems worth revisiting, for the legend is bigger than the truth will ever be.) Though Amidi predicted that the number of "holdouts and idealists" will "continue to shrink in the coming years," the existence a half-decade later of shows like Rebecca Sugar's *Steven Universe*, Dan Harmon and Justin Roiland's *Rick and Morty*, Alex Hirsch's *Gravity Falls*, and Raphael Bob-Waksberg's *BoJack Horseman* suggest that Amidi's funeral for creator-driven animation was premature.

An unintended consequence of "The End of the Creator-Driven Era in TV Animation" was to bring *Friendship Is Magic* to the attention of the image website 4chan's comics and cartoons board /co/, where the Brony fandom was spawned.[13] By mid–July 2015, there were 363 comments on the Cartoon Brew article, many of which were from long after the 2010 publication date and had a "neener-neener!" tone, such as A Madman With a Box's comment in May 2013: "Wow … I wonder how it feels to write an article opposing a cartoon and have it backfire so terribly. Terrible article, thanks for creating bronies!"[14]

The word Brony is believed to have originated as a shortening of "pony-bro" on October 25, 2010, on /co/, and a screenshot on the Reddonychan Daily Wiki would appear to confirm this.[15] It was submitted to the crowd-sourced reference site Urban Dictionary on December 23 by a user named DavidDavidsonic, who defined it as "people who take pride in watching My Little Pony."[16] The most accepted etymology of the word is as a portmanteau of "pony" and "bro"—itself short for "brother," though an August 2011 episode of the more-reliable-than-not webseries *Know Your Meme* suggested that the "b" was in fact a reference to 4chan's notorious board /b/.[17] The word Pegasister was posted to Urban Dictionary by user PegasisterDDZ on July 27, 2011, defined as "the name for the older, adult female fans of My Little Pony: Friendship Is Magic."[18] (Just like how not all fans of any age or gender identify as Bronies, as an older, adult female fan of *Friendship Is Magic* and *Equestria Girls*, I do not identify as a Pegasister, either.)

The word "bro" had already been a root for neologisms before Brony; the most famous, "bromance," was first submitted by Pedro Calhoun to Urban Dictionary on January 13, 2004, defined as "an emotional attachment between bros."[19] Nor was DavidDavidsonic's entry the first definition of "Brony" on Urban Dictionary; on April 15, 2008, user Everar defined Bronies as "special brownies handed out at clandestine fraternity shindigs,"[20] which one can only hope is not as rapey as it sounds. On February 25, 2010, G. Ferro defined the word as "a bro-phony; people who are incapable of every being bros but try. Also known as broser."[21] If they were ever in use beyond the people who submitted them to Urban Dictionary, these unpleasant definitions are now archaic, and good riddance to them.

Judging a Pony by Her Corporate Website

Though *My Little Pony: Friendship Is Magic* began hitting stride by its third episode, "The Ticket Master" (S01E03)—which ignored the mythological elements introduced in the first episodes and focused on the Mane Six as individual characters with hopes, dreams, and glaring flaws—the first truly great episode was "Look Before You Sleep" (S01E08). Belying the standard description of the show as being about ponies going on wondrous adventures and solving problems with the power of friendship, "Sleep" was instead what's called a "bottle show," which typically take place on existing sets and don't have any guest stars or other costly elements. Traditionally they're done to free up the season's budget for other, more expensive episodes, but that doesn't make them a bad thing; two of the best episodes of the best live-action dramas of that same year, *Breaking Bad*'s "Fly" and *Mad Men*'s "The Suitcase," focused on a pair of characters in a single location. "Look Before You Sleep" found Rarity and Applejack at odds while waiting out a storm in Twilight Sparkle's library, their always-present animosity toward each other boiling over; fitting for a story which could be performed on stage, it's also the talkiest episode to date, but every word counts as Rarity and Applejack verbally slash at each other like characters in a Eugene O'Neill play.

It was in the week between the original broadcasts of "Look Before You Sleep" (S01E08) and "Bridle Gossip" (S01E09) that the second major criticism against *My Little Pony: Friendship Is Magic* occurred. On her Sociological Images blog, Occidental College Professor of Sociology Lisa Wade, Ph.D, had been writing a series of posts on the sexualized makeovers of girls' toy characters such as Dora the Explorer and Strawberry Shortcake, and on December 7, 2010, she considered My Little Pony, Rainbow Brite, and Candy Land.[22] Wade compared a single image of the G1 pony Snuzzle, which she described as "chubby and adorable," to G4's Pinkie Pie and Twilight Sparkle, whom she described as "thinner, with an open mouth, more provocative stances and more responsive positions."[23] (Unlike Jesse Rutherford's 2007 *Bitch* article, Wade did not further speculate on how an enterprising sleaze merchant might use them in a "stop-animation pedophilic porn flick."[24])

The article was also published on the *Ms.* magazine blog, the third of Wade's Sociological Images articles to be cross-posted, and it garnered two comments that day.[25] It might have ended there, except a *Ms.* magazine intern named Kathleen Richter fact-checked the article, which led her to investigating *My Little Pony: Friendship Is Magic* on the Hasbro site, which led to her posting an article on the *Ms.* blog on December 9 titled "My Little Homophobic, Racist, Smart-Shaming Pony," which led to all hell breaking loose.[26]

Richter wrote that the first image she saw of the Mane Six was in the same pose as they appear at the end of the opening credits, though she does not identify it as being from the opening credits, as she makes it clear that she did not watch any episodes[27]:

I was immediately concerned that the only pony that looked slightly angry or tomboyish was the rainbow pony. Since there's a false stereotype that all feminists are angry, tomboyish lesbians, it was disconcerting to think that a kid's TV show would uphold this. I watched the video clip and, indeed, the rainbow pony stands out as having a perpetually maniacal expression while the others are cute and cuddly.[28]

She dove further into the character of Rainbow Dash via Hasbro's "Meet the Ponies" page, and while she admitted to some relief that the description of the Pegasus as capable, bold, and athletic was a positive portrayal (without mentioning that Rainbow's expression on that page was pleasant and non-maniacal), a fellow intern brought to her attention the lack of black ponies.[29] Richter said she'd "originally assumed that the purple ponies were supposed to represent black ponies," but after seeing the gray-colored guards at the foot of Princess Celestia's throne, she then assumed that "the only black ponies in the TV show My Little Pony are slave ponies to the white pony overlord! How can we expect kids to grow up rejecting racism when they watch shows like this?"[30]

After reading Hasbro's tone-deaf description of *Friendship Is Magic*, which described Celestia as ordering Twilight Sparkle to "get your muzzle out of those books and make some friends!"[31] (which is not how it's phrased on the show), Richter next assumed that "Ponyville seems to be a culture that dismisses girls who prefer reading books to playing dress-up and looking beautiful (and sparkling, of course)."[32] In actuality, nothing on that page nor in the profiles of the Mane Six on the "Meet the Ponies" page prioritized dressing up, beauty, and/or sparkling over reading books; the only use of the word "sparkle" was in the name of the character whose love of reading provided the key to defeating the villain in the pilot, and the only reference to dressing up or looking beautiful was in the profile of Rarity, which emphasized that her beauty is matched by her generosity and work ethic.[33] (It didn't flat-out state that Rarity is the best, but it was implied.) Richter concluded, sight unseen, that the television series *My Little Pony: Friendship Is Magic* taught these lessons:

• Magical white ponies are suited for leadership; black ponies are suited to be servants.
• Stop learning! You will overcome any obstacle by resorting to strength in numbers (of friends).
• Girls that wear rainbows are butch.
• You need the government (ideally a monarch invested with supreme ultimate power and a phallic symbol strapped to her forehead) to tell you what to do with your life.[34]

Like Wade's previous article, there were only a handful of comments over the next few days. On December 15, *Friendship Is Magic* creator Lauren Faust commented on the article, expressing her disappointment that *Ms.* "would post an article that is so clearly under researched and approached with wild pre-conceived notions and an extremely closed mind," and that she fought as a feminist to make positive entertainment for girls in an industry "that disrespects their intelligence, reinforces old fashioned and limiting expectations on them, and severely under-represents them."[35] On December 24, she wrote in her DeviantArt journal that she'd been contacted by an editor of the *Ms.* blog who "graciously apologized that the post had not been more closely vetted," and offered to let her post a rebuttal.[36] Faust also linked to both the original post and that rebuttal, asking her DeviantArt followers to please leave a comment on *Ms.* if they liked either the post or the show. The cult of personality that grows around the creators of properties with strong fanbases was already in full blossom, so they commented in droves.

Faust's 1,472-word response, "My Little NON-Homophobic, NON-Racist, NON-Smart-Shaming Pony: A Rebuttal," was posted that same day on the *Ms.* blog, and it remains required reading for anypony interested in *My Little Pony: Friendship Is Magic*, or who are inclined to criticize the show sight unseen by virtue of it being an entertainment designed for young girls and/or preceded by a toy range.[37] As we will see, it went unread by the latter group. (Authorial intent is often the least important lens through which to view a work, but it can sometimes be crucial when discussing *Friendship Is Magic* and *Equestria Girls*, given the franchise's controversial reputation.) It can be regarded as Lauren Faust's mission statement, including her feelings about shows made for girls up to that time, noting that even as production values had increased, "the female characters have been so homogenized with old-fashioned 'niceness' that they have no flaws and are unrelatable. They are so pretty, polite and perfect; there is no legitimate conflict and nothing exciting ever happens. In short, animated shows for little girls come across as boring, Stupid, Lame."[38] She parried Richter's points, and laid out what messages she hoped to impart with *Friendship Is Magic*, including this key statement:

> Cartoons for girls don't have to be a puddle of smooshy, cutesy-wootsy, goody-two-shoeness. Girls like stories with real conflict; girls are smart enough to understand complex plots; girls aren't as easily frightened as everyone seems to think. Girls are complex human beings, and they can be brave, strong, kind and independent–but they can also be uncertain, awkward, silly, arrogant or stubborn. They shouldn't have to succumb to pressure to be perfect.[39]

She acknowledged that it had been "a challenge to balance my personal ideals with my bosses' needs for toy sales and good ratings," and that when she took the job, "I braced myself for criticism, expecting many people—without even watching the show—to instantly label it girly, stupid, cheap, for babies or an evil corporate commercial."[40] Those expectations were soon fulfilled, and her oft-stated disappointment with *My Little Pony 'n' Friends* also cleared the path for many Bronies to throw the 1980s series under the bus, and to disassociate from the franchise's history altogether.

Several months later, the founder of the Brony fansite Equestria Daily (which would not be launched until a month after the *Ms.* article appeared) described the show as having "accidentally targeted internet culture."[41] It was an apt description, and though Richter was neither the most vitriolic nor the most ill-informed, she was one of the first cultural critics to learn that it was no longer safe to criticize My Little Pony in a public forum with impunity. Since her article was written before the show's demographic-deying fanbase became known outside 4chan and certain gaming forums, it was also one of the last to only focus on the (presumed) content of the show and its potential impact on its target audience of young girls, an angle which faded as the media zeroed in on Bronies. The first appearance of the word "Brony" in the comments of Richter's article was on January 1, 2011, by user "L'il Brony," a little over a week after the Pony-related definition of the word appeared on Urban Dictionary; in their comment, L'il Brony wrote that "apparently, you haven't actually watched the show," or the recipient would have noticed that "the 'token black' pony is actually Zecora, who first appeared in episode 9."[42] It's unclear whether the comment was directed at Richter or at a different commenter, but there were many comments which accused Richter of ignorance for not having mentioned Zecora, even though the article was posted *before* the zebra was introduced. There was plenty of ignorance—or, to be charitable, poor attention to detail—on both sides of the discussion, because that's how discourse on the Internet works.

The 106th and final comment on the article was posted on February 6, 2011, again taking Richter to task for not having mentioned Zecora, and comments were closed shortly thereafter.[43] (Coincidentally or not, Richter seemed to disappear from the Internet around that same time.) As of mid–July 2015, comments remained open on Lauren Faust's article; posted on June 6, the 689th comment criticized Faust for the racial undertones of the episode "Daring Don't" (S04E04), which was produced long after she ceased having anything to do with the show.[44] That is also how discourse on the Internet works, which why Faust went on to post to Twitter every so often: "Periodical friendly reminder: I haven't worked on MLP:FiM since Season 2. Please direct comments on new episodes to current show staff. Thx!" It did not quite work.[45]

Yes, Really, Bronies Exist. Seriously.

Friendship Is Magic's first season concluded on May 6, 2011, with "The Best Night Ever" (S01E26), which along with "Party of One" (S01E25) and "The Cutie Mark Chronicles" (S01E023), constituted the series' strongest run of episodes. (Also in there was "Owl's Well That Ends Well" [S01E24], an adequate episode which suffered by comparison, and which would have felt more organic earlier in the season.) "The Best Night Ever" is a bruising experience for the Mane Six, as their individual aspirations for the annual Grand Galloping Gala first introduced back in "The Ticket Master" (S01E03) are ignored by a world which is not required to conform to their expectations. It's also something of a one-two punch for Pinkie Pie, who in the preceding "Party of One" suffers a nervous breakdown, and the subjective journey into her damaged psyche alone would have made it the best episode of the season if not for "The Best Night Ever." "The Cutie Mark Chronicles," meanwhile, was one of the series' most complex and carefully constructed stories, working with what we'd learned about the characters thus far while expanding both their backstories and the show's world. It was self-aware without being distractingly so, functioning as a commentary on how the show's critics will find the series too earnest, unironic, or (the greatest crime of all) feminine, while earning its sentimental ending in a way "Friendship Is Magic, Part 2" (S01E02) failed to.

Lauren Faust thanked the fans of the show—including "the kids, the parents, and all you bronies!!"—on her DeviantArt journal on May 8, two days after the broadcast of "The Best Night Ever," in a post in which she also announced that she would no longer be the show's executive producer.[46] The first major incursion of the word "Brony" into the mainstream would occur a month later in a June 9 *Wired* article by Angela Watercutter titled "My Little Pony Corrals Unlikely Fanboys Known as Bronies," in which she referred to the Bronies' love of the show as "internet neo-sincerity at its best."[47] She had defined "neo-sincerity" in a June 2010 article about fans of the series *Glee* as enjoying something without a sense of irony or detachment—in other words, to just enjoy something for what it is.[48] Her evidence for neo-sincerity among the Bronies was that "in addition to watching the show, these teenage, twenty- and thirtysomething guys are creating pony art, posting fan videos on YouTube and feeding threads on 4chan (and their own chan, Ponychan)."[49]

There was also a bit of hopefulness when she observed that "aside from a few brony-haters, blessedly very little (negative) hay seems to get made over dudes liking something that's 'supposed to be for girls' (like, for example, the way girls would be side-eyed for liking Transformers in years past)."[50]

From her lips to Princess Celestia's ears, but that blessing would not last, and the *Wired* article set the tone for later media coverage, particularly in its use of the word "unlikely" in the headline. Much like past articles which poked at G1-G3 collectors with a stick to get them to explain their "obsession" to the writers' satisfaction (an impossible goal), stories about Bronies would try to find reasons *why* adult and/or male fans like the show, never settling for or seemingly even considering the simplest explanation: That it's a good show, and worthy of being liked.

Later that day on Cartoon Brew, Amid Amidi wrote a post titled "My Little Bronies" which consisted of two paragraphs. The first was a context-free quote from an interviewee in the *Wired* article:

> "As a person with Asperger syndrome, I learned more about theory of mind, friendships and social interactions from this season [of *My Little Pony: Friendship Is Magic*] than I had in the previous 31 years of life."[51]

The second paragraph was Amidi giving context for the quote, and addressing what he figured his readers must have been thinking:

> That's a quote from [the *Wired* article] about the popularity of the Hub's *My Little Pony* series with adult men, who call themselves "Bronies." And no, it's not an article from *The Onion*.[52]

Oooh, snap! And with that virtual mic-drop, all was well—except for the commenters who pointed out how tasteless his joke was, resulting in a third paragraph added the next day:

> My comments were interpreted by some readers as making fun of people with Asperger's. That was never my intention. I wanted to point out that adult men were interested in the series, which is what I wrote, but my careless use of that quote caused confusion. I apologize to readers for the misunderstanding.[53]

Well, sure. Because he wanted to point out that adult men were interested in the series, and the most efficient way to get that simple idea across was to quote the final sentence of the third-to-last paragraph of *Wired*'s over 1,600-word article—the one that allowed him to make a hilarious joke about the improbability of such a thing as a man with a pervasive developmental disorder discovering that a certain work of fiction helps him relate to the world, a notion so absurd that it could only be from the *Onion*, right? As if it weren't bad enough that there would be no more creator-driven cartoons because of

Friendship Is Magic, it was now getting to the point where a grown man who wrote about cartoons for a living couldn't take a mickey on a second grown man who liked a cartoon that the first man did not care for! We all felt Mr. Amidi's pain that day.

An August 2011 *Wall Street Journal* article about the current crop of remakes of 1980s cartoons didn't share *Wired*'s Angela Watercutter's view of the Brony fandom as being sincere, neo- or otherwise, describing Bronies as "men with an affection for the show that may or may not be ironic."[54] Similarly, a *Los Angeles Times* review of a Katy Perry concert earlier that week described her current pop persona as lying "somewhere between the pinups painted on WWII-era fighter planes and a knowing cute-overload culture in which grown men can watch "My Little Pony: Friendship Is Magic" without ending up in a police database."[55]

Like the Spice Girls before her, this was not the first time Katy Perry was associated with the franchise. In an August 2010 *Guardian* article, Perry had referred to her *Teenage Dream* album, each physical copy of which was scented like candyfloss, as smelling "a bit like My Little Pony."[56] She clarified that to be a good thing, since "it smells of your childhood, which is always endearing."[57] The most overt connection between the two was the Hub's "Equestria Girls" promo, which was not related to the eventual *Equestria Girls* movies but instead a parody of Perry's hit "California Gurls," sung by Shannon Chan-Kent in the voice of Pinkie Pie. A 30-second version appeared on the Hub's website on May 24, 2011,[58] with a 90-second version released directly to Equestria Daily on May 27; this extended version included the word "Bronies," and the Hub described the song as having "some special lines in tribute to our favorite Pony fans."[59]

Some articles discussed the show's positive qualities, but always with a degree of detachment. An August 2011 *National Post* article by Joshua Ostroff described shows like *Yo Gabba Gabba!* and *Friendship Is Magic* as targeting "hipster" parents, without defining what distinguishes a hipster parent from a non-hipster parent.[60] He wondered who the shows were aimed at, describing *Friendship Is Magic* as not being "a long-term Hasbro toy ad," but rather a show that focuses on "smart storytelling, well-drawn characters, pop culture references (dating back as far as Benny Hill) and adorably gorgeous anime-inspired visuals—all intended to appeal to parents nostalgic for the nowhere-near-as-good original."[61] In fact, the smart storytelling, well-drawn characters, and adorably gorgeous anime-inspired visuals were also intended to appeal to children, girls in particular; as Lauren Faust pointed out in her *Ms.* blog post, and as anypony who has spent time with young girls knows, they like stories with real conflict, and are smart enough to understand complex plots.[62]

While Ostroff did not say any of those things, he did describe the Brony fandom thusly:

> Pony's cool cred has even led to its own adult-fuelled Internet subculture—tens of thousands of pieces of fan art, chiptune songs and videos mashing up pastel Pony scenes with movie trailer audio from The Dark Knight, The Watchmen and Inglourious Basterds—and sparked a surprising male following known as "bronies." Yes, really. According to Wired magazine, the Brony website Equestria Daily gets 175,000 page views per day.[63]

It would seem Ostroff felt the "Yes, really" was necessary because "surprising" was not enough, and his readers might think he was pulling their leg. "Surprising," "unlikely," and "unexpected" are recurring words in Brony coverage; Laurent Malaquais's sympathetic yet exploitative 2012 documentary *Bronies: The Extremely Unexpected Adult Fans of My Little Pony* included an adverb in its title in case the adjective didn't get the point across. (Also, Bronies are not fans of the overall My Little Pony franchise, but the *Friendship Is Magic* series in particular, but that sort of distinction doesn't get clicks or sell tickets.) How unexpected were these adult fans of My Little Pony? *Extremely* unexpected, that's how unexpected.

Except that beyond the breaking of the cultural taboo of boys enjoying things aimed toward girls, there was nothing unprecedented about the older and/or male *Friendship Is Magic* fandom. For example, the mashing up of elements from different properties can be traced at least as far back as the original *Star Trek* fanzines: the cover of *Plak-Tow* #6, published a week after the end of *Trek*'s second season in April 1968, featured an illustration of Leonard Nimoy as Spock standing next to Diana Rigg as Emma Peel from the popular BBC series *The Avengers* (no relation to the Marvel comics or movies),[64] while Jonathan Frid's Barnabas Collins from the soap opera *Dark Shadows* appeared in the *Enterprise*'s Transporter Room on the cover of *Plak-Tow* #8 that August,[65] and another drawing of Spock and Emma Peel appeared in the *Avengers*-oriented fanzine *En Garde* around that same time.[66]

That some (but by no means all) *Friendship Is Magic* fans adopted a collective name was also nothing new; *Star Trek* fans are often referred to as Trekkies or Trekkers, fans of the HBO series *Deadwood* called themselves Fucknuts while the show was in production,[67] and the term Whovian can be traced back to at least 1985 during the 22nd season of the original run of *Doctor Who*, and may go back further.[68] For that matter, the inaugural issue of the *Trek* fanzine *Enterprise* in 1984 featured a cover illustration of Spock mind-melding with the Doctor from *Doctor Who*.[69] The issue included a fan-fiction story titled "The Doctor and the *Enterprise*," with accompanying illustrations of the Doctor on the bridge; elsewhere in the issue were comic strips of various pop-culture figures such as Garfield the cat and the Three Stooges on the ship.[70]

So fandoms adopting collective names and the cross-pollination of various properties via amateur works had been going on for decades, but in the case of *Friendship Is Magic* it was treated as new, unprecedented, and confusing. Indeed, who could have expected that fans of one show would do what fans of other shows had been doing for more than forty years? Nopony, that's who.

Phantom Tea Parties, and Selling Toys to Young Girls Is Bad...

As the media came to delight in pointing out, many things regarding *My Little Pony: Friendship Is Magic* were surprising, unlikely, and unexpected, and sometimes those unlikely things even *extremely* surprisingly unexpected. However, *MacLean's* associate editor Jaime Weinman may well have been expecting to get a lot of traffic with his September 7, 2011, article "Men Who Love My Little Pony: Don't Mess with Guys Who Want to Talk About Pinkie Pie and Pretty Pony Tea Parties."[71] The first two lines of the article were pure Original Sin, trafficking in all the stereotypes and fears of femininity the franchise had been saddled with since the 1980s—including specifying that the characters are female—and the third line implied that any adult with their priorities straight was up in arms about the show, much like how the *Sunday Mirror's* Teena Lyons had told her readers to "prepare to froth at the mouth" with anger about Generation 2[72]:

> *My Little Pony: Friendship is Magic* seems to confirm adults' worst fears about kids' cartoons. The show, about female ponies with names like Twilight Sparkle and Pinkie Pie, is produced by Hasbro to convince kids to buy the line of toys it's based on, just like the company's *Strawberry Shortcake* and *Rainbow Brite* cartoons. But some adults don't have time to object to *Friendship is Magic*: they're too busy watching it and writing pony fan fiction.[73]

There's so much to unpack, just starting with the title. The article appeared four months after the end of the *Friendship Is Magic's* first season, during which there were only two references to tea parties; one was mentioned but not seen, while the other was an offhand suggestion by Fluttershy which was ignored, and there would be no more references to tea parties until the Season 4 finale. (In her *Ms.* blog post, Lauren Faust had listed the "endless tea parties" among the things she didn't like about *My Little Pony 'n' Friends*.[74]) The word "pretty" was most often used in Season 1 as an adverb, such as "pretty good" or "pretty cold," and the only reference to a "pretty pony" was in Pinkie Pie's mania about the Grand Galloping Gala in "The Best Night Ever" (S01E26). Weinman's title phrase "pretty pony tea parties" was also used in the body of the article:

4Chan, a website known for flooding the Internet with nasty jokes, erupted in a "civil war" when a moderator tried to ban pony discussion; eventually the site gave up and had to allow its members to talk about Princess Celestia and the pretty pony tea parties. "4chan once took on the FBI and won," a Brony told the *New York Observer*, "so you might say that *My Little Pony* is more powerful than the FBI."[75]

The source for the 4chan "civil war" quote was the referenced *New York Observer* article from August 3, 2011, and the Brony did not mention either Celestia or tea parties, but Weinman seemed to have been bolstering his attempt to gender-shame male viewers of the show by upping the femininity, and what can be more girly—and thus bad—than a "pretty pony tea party?"[76] It was a wonder he didn't include a "Yeee-uk!" or "Yeccch!" exclamation of the sort used by previous journalists to make it clear that they wanted none of that girly frou-frou nonsense.

His reference to Hasbro's equally fearful "Strawberry Shortcake and Rainbow Brite cartoons" was also poorly researched.[77] While *Strawberry Shortcake's Berry Bitty Adventures* did debut immediately after *My Little Pony: Friendship Is Magic* on October 10, 2010, there was no new Rainbow Brite series to be found on the Hub or elsewhere.[78] This is because that character was owned by Hallmark, not Hasbro, and the first Rainbow Brite animation since the 1986 movie *Rainbow Brite and the Star Stealer* would not appear until a new series debuted on Hallmark's Feeln streaming video service in 2014.[79] How *Friendship Is Magic* "confirms adults' worst fears about kids' cartoons" was also left unexplained, other than the fact that it features "female ponies with names like Twilight Sparkle and Pinkie Pie," and is based on an existing franchise, and thus has no purpose other to "convince" kids to buy the toys.[80] But My Little Pony had always been synonymous for cultural critics with the worst kind of crass commercialism no matter the actual content, and would continue to be in the years to come, sometimes from the Bronies themselves.

There were many other debatable points in Weinman's 2011 article about *Friendship Is Magic*, such as his claim that the new show's animation was "as limited in movement" as *My Little Pony 'n' Friends* (which is untrue), or that *Friendship Is Magic* lacked pop-culture references and overall "makes almost no concessions" to grown-up fans, or most alarmingly, that the show's success "is giving new credibility to the strategy of building cartoons around toys."[81] He backed up that assertion by quoting Cartoon Brew's Amid Amidi contending that the real goal of a show like *Friendship Is Magic* "'is to get viewers to hand over their money.'"[82]

An accomplished author, Amidi provided the text for two books about Pixar, 2009's *The Art of Pixar Short Films* and 2011's *The Art of Pixar*.[83] Speaking of getting viewers to hand over their money, though it is seldom criticized as such, Pixar's first feature film *Toy Story* in 1995 was overtly about both existing toy ranges and ones created for the film and then sold in the real world, and thus qualifies for feature-length commercial status. Among those existing toys was the Hasbro character Mr. Potato Head, first introduced in 1952 and legendary as the first toy to be advertised on television.[84] The last time Mr. Potato Head and his token wife Mrs. Potato Head had been animated prior to *Toy Story* was the Potato Head Kids segments of *My Little Pony 'n' Friends*, and it's an interesting thought experiment to speculate whether the *Toy Story* films would be so lionized by male critics if the owner of the toys had been a little girl rather than a little boy, and her toys had included My Little Pony or the Care Bears.[85]

Both *The Art of Pixar Short Films* and *The Art of Pixar* are fine books, and the work of Pixar is exemplary, but their parent company Disney is not a charity. Not only are their films only legally available if the viewer "hands over their money" in exchange for a movie ticket, Blu-ray purchase, streaming subscription, or any of the other ways studios monetize their catalogs, in July 2015 there were 84 *Toy Story* items available on the Disney Store,[86] 78 items for *Cars*,[87] 42 for *Monsters, Inc.*,[88] and 36 for *Finding Nemo*,[89] to name but a few examples. To clarify, those were just the items available online via the Disney Store, and not a comprehensive overview of all the products intended to get Pixar viewers to hand over their money.

Though the consensus remains fuzzy on whether the My Little Pony range went on sale in 1982 or 1983, let's err on the side of both the haters and even numbers and say it was 1982. The first television special premiered in April 1984, and it is because of that two-year gap that any further My Little Pony animation is reflexively denounced as being a commercial and nothing besides. With each passing year, the percentage of the lifespan of the franchise in which it was a toy without a cartoon grows smaller; by the time in 2011 when Amidi said the sole purpose of *Friendship Is Magic* was to get viewers to hand over their money, My Little Pony animation had existed for 27 out of the franchise's 29 years, or approximately 93% of its lifespan. It was sporadic because the longest sustained cartoon production would not begin until *Friendship Is Magic* in 2010, but the criticism always boiled down to the toys having existed *before* the cartoons, and thus in perpetuity the latter must exist for no other purpose than to sell the former, and whatever merits the cartoons might have as their own works are irrelevant. It is in that first 7% of its lifespan—now down to 6% at the time of this writing, and to have declined further when this book is published—in which My Little Pony's immutable Original Sin lies, world without end amen. It would eventually hit *Equestria Girls* even harder than *Friendship Is Magic*, due to the more overt femininity of *Equestria Girls*.

The Transformers was already a bestselling toy range before the premiere of the television series in September 1984[90] (and, as previously established, was even more successful at getting viewers to hand over their money than My Little Pony that year,[91] as well as in 1985[92] and 1987[93]), yet Cartoon Brew raised no alarms about the Hub's new *Transformers: Prime* series the way they had about *Friendship Is Magic*. On March 28, 2011, Cartoon Brew contributor Chris Arrant reprinted a recent Hub press release which referred to the new series *Transformers: Rescue Bots* as "inspired by the iconic 'Transformers' brand."[94] There was no editorializing on the toy-based origins of that "iconic brand" or whatever deleterious effects it may have on television animation, and the only authorial intrusion was an italicized and bracketed note from Arrant disclaiming that the press release had been edited down to include only the new shows. The ages-old practice of news outlets reprinting press releases verbatim is an ethical debate far outside of the scope of this book, but it does serve as another example of how My Little Pony is singled out in ways that masculine toy brands are not. In Amidi's Cartoon Brew coverage of 2014's *The Lego Movie*, a wildly overpraised male power fantasy which in its third act became an outright commercial for how swell it is for fathers and sons to play with a certain brand of interlocking plastic bricks—and how *girls ruin everything* when allowed to participate—he referred to Legos as a "unique source material," and only referenced its "toy-based origins" as one of many elements that other studios would likely use to replicate that film's success.[95]

The same day as his 2011 *Maclean's* article "Men Who Love My Little Pony: Don't Mess with Guys Who Want to Talk About Pinkie Pie and Pretty Pony Tea Parties," Jaime Weinman posted a follow-up titled "Ponies Do Sondheim" in which he thanked the first article's commenters for clearing up some issues, including the meaningless statistic of the recent number of hits received by Equestria Daily.[96] He reluctantly agreed that *Friendship Is Magic* had more pop-culture references than he'd given it credit for, noting the Stephen Sondheim-influenced song "The Art of the Dress" from "Suited for Success" (S01E14), and stated that "I think adults and kids do enjoy the show on somewhat different levels, but they enjoy it on similar terms."[97] To that end, he quoted a commenter on the original article who "explained the show's popularity from the point of view of its fans"[98]:

> As for why adults like it, let's play spot the influence…
> Good classic storytelling and likable but deceptively complex characters—Pixar
> Well animated with a fairly unique, highly expressive style—Powerpuff Girls/Samurai Jack
> Breaks with standard kids' show irony/hipness—(classic Disney/Pixar—agree with author's point)

Fairly deep world mixing high magic and daily concerns—Harry Potter
Good, creative slapstick bits—classic Warner Brothers/Looney Tunes
Suitably monstrous villains—Dungeons & Dragons, classic mythology

Again, this was Weinman quoting a commenter from the original post, and setting aside that Season 1 had few "villains," suitably monstrous or otherwise—Nightmare Moon from the pilot is the only character who comes close to being a monstrous villain—this speaks to a burden that *Friendship Is Magic* faced from the start: the need to explain "why adults like it" by comparing it to other, accepted properties, rather than it just being good on its own terms. (It's also endemic of how the Bronies often tended to regard the show in terms of what it could be compared to and combined with in art, fiction, and remixes.) Indeed, "Good classic storytelling and likable but deceptively complex characters" is a standard which to many scripted series should be held, whether or not they can also be compared to Pixar. Of course there's little in pop culture that's truly original or unlike anything that preceded it, and things that can't be readily compared to previous works, even on a subconscious level, seldom achieve widespread popularity; they're often pejoratively described as "arty," and there's a reason why directors like George Lucas, Alfred Hitchcock, and Steven Spielberg are household names, while Stan Brakhage, Peter Greenaway, and Guy Maddin are not. But there's an inherent defensiveness in defining why something is good because it's like *other* things that are good, and it prevents the work from becoming more than the sum of its parts. It's also possible for a series to have all the above attributes—to have "suitably monstrous villains" or "good, creative slapstick"—without gaining such a devoted fanbase, and it almost certainly wouldn't demand as much justification as *My Little Pony: Friendship Is Magic*.

But more often going forward, the comparisons would be to the many oranges that the apple of *Friendship Is Magic* paled next to; in her September 2014 Jezebel article "I Was the Weirdest Person at BronyCon 2014," Madeleine Davies wrote that after a Brony told her that *Friendship Is Magic* was just "a really good show," and that "the characters are good, the art is good and the stories are good and that's why we like it," she had to resist the temptation to reply, "Yeah, but have you ever seen an episode of *Mad Men*?"[99] (The author of the book you are currently reading can speak of the virtues of both *Mad Men* and *My Little Pony: Friendship Is Magic* at length if prompted.) In Sam Theilman's post-mortem of the Hub for *Adweek* in February 2015, he wrote that the Hub "had awesome content, including Transformers: Prime, which won nine Daytime Emmy Awards over three seasons, as well as a breakout hit in the creepily beloved My Little Pony Friendship Is Magic (It's good! It's just not The Brothers Karamazov! Don't hurt us, Bronies!) and a stylish G.I.

Joe cartoon." Neither *Transformers: Prime* nor the "stylish" *G. I. Joe: Renegades* were *The Brothers Karamazov*, either, but only *Friendship Is Magic* gets compared unfavorably with a classic of Russian literature.

Jamie Weinman also described "Swarm of the Century" (S01E10) as a "tribute" and "stock parody" of the *Star Trek* episode "The Trouble with Tribbles," though "Swarm" writer M.A. Larson would later say that the movie *Gremlins* was a stronger influence and that he'd never seen "Tribbles,"[100] while producer Lauren Faust wrote on her DeviantArt blog the day after "Swarm" was broadcast that the *Trek* parallels didn't occur to them until after they'd started developing a story about a locust-like plague.[101] It would not be fair to fault Weinman for being unaware of these behind-the-scenes details, but it still speaks to the unfortunate tendency to not allow a given story to stand on its own due to it sharing themes or elements with a previous story, as all stories must. Except for the destruction wrought by the parasprites, and the extent to which the main characters are distracted by the creatures' cuteness before grasping the environmental impact, "Swarm of the Century" shares no other story beats with "The Trouble with Tribbles," and may as well be a "tribute" to Exodus 10:1–20.

According to his book about the making of that *Star Trek* episode, scriptwriter David Gerrold was himself inspired by the true story of rabbits overrunning Australia in the 19th century, and it wasn't until after he wrote the script that it was brought to his attention that Tribbles were similar to the Martian flat cats in Robert A. Heinlein's novel *The Rolling Stones*.[102] The *Star Trek* producers sent the "Tribbles" script to Heinlein, who responded that "the analogy to my flat cats was mild enough to be of no importance."[103] As Gerrold put it: "Look, ideas are common. What counts is what different writers do with them. 'The Trouble with Tribbles' is NOT *The Rolling Stones*."[104]

And, by extension, "Swarm of the Century" is NOT "The Trouble with Tribbles." Unlike the "Tribbles" angle, however, the Stephen Sondheim connection is real; the song "The Art of the Dress" from "Suited for Success" (S01E14) was indeed inspired by "Putting It Together" from Sondheim's *Sunday in the Park with George*, and would be Season 1's best song if "The Pony Pokey" from "The Best Night Ever" (S01E26) didn't exist.[105] Where "The Pony Pokey" is a sad song about the disappointments faced by the Mane Six at the Gala (and also the first true diegetic song of the series, as Pinkie Pie is backed by the Gala's house quartet of piano, cello, sousaphone, and harp), the first-act showstopper "At the Gala" is again inspired by the work of Sondheim, in this case *Into the Woods*.[106]

Sondheim himself has always been open about the influence of the composer Steve Reich on *Sunday in the Park with George*,[107] and in a 1997 *Paris Review* interview, Sondheim said that particular musical was also inspired by the works of Benjamin Britten, and that in general he was influenced by composers such as Maurice Ravel, George Gershwin, and Harold Arlen ("A lot of Arlen").[108] Indeed, portions of the music in Sondheim's "I'm Still Here" from *Follies* are homages to Arlen,[109] while Bob Dylan wrote in his memoir *Chronicles: Volume One*[110] how he himself "could never escape from the bittersweet, intense lonely world of Harold Arlen." Nopony works in a vacuum, and all art is inspired by something that came before it.

    Friendship Is Magic's fondness for the body of 20th century music called the Great American Songbook would continue well into Season 2, often voiced by Pinkie Pie. In "A Friend in Deed" (S02E18), when Pinkie first meets the antisocial Cranky Doodle Donkey—or, more to the point, harasses him into telling her his full name—she launches into a version of the "Yankee Doodle Dandy" nursery rhyme, incorporating both his and her names. That song, which dates back to the Revolutionary War, is a standard which has long been in the public domain, and a piano rendition is played over the credits.[111] As Pinkie Pie leaves Matilda and Cranky to enjoy each other's company in peace and quiet, however, she sings a few revised lines from George M. Cohan's "Yankee Doodle Boy," which first appeared in the stage musical *Little Johnny Jones* in 1904, and the most famous rendition of which is by James Cagney in the 1942 biopic *Yankee Doodle Dandy*.[112] The Cohan song is a charter member of the Great American Songbook, marking Pinkie's brief song as *Friendship Is Magic*'s oldest pop-culture reference.[113] (And both songs mention ponies!) Later, in "MMMystery on the Friendship Express" (S02E24), Pinkie describes the cake known as the Marzipan Mascarpone Meringue Madness in an alliterative string of D-words which reference Cole Porter's "It's De-Lovely," which first debuted in the Broadway musical *Red, Hot and Blue!* in 1937.[114]

    Weinman ended "Ponies Do Sondheim" by doing something which may well be a first by any male critic in a public forum: praising *My Little Pony 'n' Friends*.

> I also have to give the show one more thing: as a child, I really liked the "My Little Pony" cartoon of the '80s, but having watched a couple of episodes of it again, the endings seem to be really lame, something Lauren Faust herself has mentioned trying to avoid. (There is one episode where they literally just defeat a horrifying villain by singing about love. That's it.) The plotting on the current cartoon is much better.[115]

That's true, but it's still backhanded praise, and Season 1 of *Friendship Is Magic* had its share of whiffed endings ("Dragonshy" [S01E07] and "Bridle Gossip" [S01E09] in particular both go for the Everypony Laughs ending). For the record, there's also an episode of the lauded *Powerpuff Girls* ("Mime for a Change") in which the villain is defeated by the heroes singing a song about love.[116] That's it—but it's not what is done, it's *how* it is done.

...Unless They're Toys from Boy-Friendly Franchises

Anypony interested in delving deeper into the history of children's television and its intersection with merchandising would do well to read *Street Gang: The Complete History of Sesame Street* by Michael Davis. Debuting in 1969 (the same year as *Hot Wheels*), *Sesame Street* has long been considered the pinnacle of educational programming for preschoolers, but funding was tricky in the early years, as the Nixon Administration was hostile toward the Public Broadcasting System and the very concept of federally-funded programing.[117] The Children's Television Workshop, later the Sesame Workshop, stayed afloat thanks to several millions of dollars in annual revenue generated from licensing and merchandising fees for products bearing their characters' likenesses; that they were doing good work is undeniable, but good work is not enough. Case in point is *Sesame Street*'s sister show, *The Electric Company*, which debuted in 1971 and was aimed at seven-to-nine-year-olds with a sketch-comedy format that emphasized reading.[118] Though Davis in *Street Gang* described *The Electric Company* as probably having had "as much or even more of an impact on children in its day than *Sesame Street*," there were no characters among its biped cast who could be printed on bedsheets or turned into dolls, and the show ended its run in 1977 due to a lack of funding.[119]

This is not to imply that any of the My Little Pony cartoons aspired to be as educational as *Sesame Street* or *The Electric Company*, but rather that merchandising is a reality in children's television, and worthy shows have been canceled when they haven't been able to, as the saying goes, get viewers to hand over their money. In August 2015, the *Wall Street Journal* announced that the Sesame Workshop had signed a deal with HBO to run new *Sesame Street* episodes on the premium-cable channel and its streaming services first, and then on PBS nine months later.[120] In the 2013 fiscal year, the Workshop's programming expenses were $96.1M while the revenue was only $30.9M, and only 10% of that revenue came from PBS; the majority instead came from licensing and DVD sales, but even those had been declining as more children used online platforms.[121] If not for the merchandising revenue, *Sesame Street* would have long since shut down. (At the Subcommittee on Telecommunications and Finance hearing on the commercialization of children's television in 1987, ACT founder Peggy Charren exonerated *Sesame Street*, saying that the point of the show is not to sell Big Birds, and that "one major difference with Sesame Street and everything else we have talked about here is that they don't even advertise it on television."[122] Charren's research failed her in this instance, as there were commercials for the Big Bird Story Magic talking doll running in 1986.[123])

But if Hasbro is demonized for trying too hard to sell toys to girls—and, as we've seen, it takes little more than to launch the third television show in as many decades based on a 28-year-old brand to destroy all that's good and decent in the world—they've also been called out for not trying hard *enough* to sell toys to girls. On April 28, 2015, three days before the release of the superhero film *Avengers: Age of Ultron*, Hulk actor Mark Ruffalo Tweeted this:

> @Marvel we need more #BlackWidow merchandise for my daughters and nieces. Pretty please.[124]

This was not the first time the paucity of merchandise featuring Scarlett Johansson's character had been noted. Since a few months after the first *Avengers* film was released in 2012, a Tumblr site called …But Not Black Widow had been documenting Black Widow–free Avengers merchandise.[125] Many entertainment news blogs covered the issue, including an anonymous post on the Mary Sue on April 7, 2015, by a person claiming to be a former Marvel employee, explaining the math behind why Black Widow as well as the 2014 film *Guardians of the Galaxy*'s lone female hero Gamora were marginalized by manufacturers.[126] The gist: Disney bought Marvel to access its male demographic, and felt no need to cater to female fans of Marvel properties or proportionately represent the female characters, having already cornered what they considered to be the separate girls' market with their Disney Princesses.[127]

But now the issue became a *cause célèbre*, more so as other celebrities joined the cause. On May 3, Clark Gregg (who portrayed Agent Phil Coulson in the first *Avengers* film and the concurrent *Agents of S.H.I.E.L.D.* television series, though he did not appear in *Age of Ultron*) Tweeted a hashtag and a link:

> #WheresNatasha? http://fb.me/3KWxPd3Pc[128]

The link was to a Change.org petition by Patricia V. Davis titled "Add Black Widow to the AVENGERS action figure pack," and read in part:

> Girls need strong and capable female role models. Please sign my petition asking HASBRO to add more of the female AVENGER movable action figures to the boxes of pre-packaged action figures for the growing number of girls for whom just dressing up a fashion doll

doesn't cut it anymore. Please promote the female action figure along with the other four Avenger action figures.[129]

There are a number of thorny representational issues regarding Natasha "Black Widow" Romanoff which must be set aside for now, such as the existing gender imbalance within the Avengers (which the text of the petition does address[130]); how her superhero name has a connotation of being predatory toward men; that she was enslaved as a child by the KGB and bred to be an assassin, including a forced sterilization, meaning that she lacks the agency afforded her male counterparts, all of whom chose their paths in life in ways that she could not[131]; or that the films frequently sexualize her and reduce her to a damsel in distress. *Guardians of the Galaxy*'s Gamora had a similar backstory, having been kidnapped as a child and turned into a killer without her consent.[132]

Having set those issues aside, the problem with the petition was that it created a dichotomy where none needed to exist. That girls need strong and capable female role models is unquestionable, but the reference to "the growing number of girls for whom just dressing up a fashion doll doesn't cut it anymore" was a reductive view of the toy options available to the young female population of 2015.[133] Fashion dolls were still being marketed to girls—including but not limited to the *Equestria Girls* range—but the argument would have been just as strong without propping up traditionally feminine toys as the enemy.

The petition also ignored one of the other positive benefits of making Black Widow available in the group packages: because then young *boys* would also be able to play with her character, reinforcing that she is an equal member of the Avengers alongside Iron Man or the Hulk, and that's it every bit as okay for boys to play with girl characters as it is for girls to play with boy characters. Ideally, this sort of blurring and eventual elimination of boundaries in terms of toys and children's entertainment may lead to the widespread recognition that the gender binary is a social construct, and that gender is a far more fluid and personal matter than whatever the doctor declares after looking between a newborn's legs. And it's a state of affairs which My Little Pony, with its popularity across age and existing gender lines, may in some small way help to us to achieve.

Are You Now or Have You Ever Been a Brony?

Not all male and/or adult fans of *My Little Pony: Friendship Is Magic* were Bronies, but the concept that being a Brony was a *sine qua non* for anypony who liked or even displayed the most basic knowledge of My Little Pony was birthed on June 24, 2011, when former President Bill Clinton, drumming up publicity for his Clinton Global Initiative's upcoming conference on job creation and economic growth, was asked three questions about *Friendship Is Magic* on the NPR game show *Wait Wait … Don't Tell Me!*[134] Part of a regular segment called "Not My Job" in which guests are asked questions outside of their usual field of knowledge, host Peter Sagal explained that the topic was chosen because it was something they could be sure a Rhodes Scholar and all-around well-informed person like President Clinton would know nothing about.[135] The three questions were presented in a multiple choice format, seemingly based on a cursory viewing of "Friendship Is Magic, Parts 1 & 2" (S01E01–2), and Clinton answered all three correctly.

The first question was "What is [Rarity's] particular enthusiasm?" The options were "she loves her little line of toys called My Even Tinier Ponies," "giving other ponies makeovers," or "eating paste."[136] It's true that Rarity enjoys giving makeovers, and does indeed insist on making over Twilight Sparkle (against Twilight's will) in "Part 1" in anticipation of the Summer Sun Celebration, but it's not Rarity's "particular enthusiasm" by any stretch—but it sure sounds exceedingly girly, thus making it even funnier that a grown-up adult man would even be asked such things, and of course it was all greeted with riotous laughter from the audience. The second question involved what the ponies earn when they discover their true talent in life: "a tattoo on their flank, known as a cutie mark," "a title, such as Fluttershy the Inventive," or "the right to mate." The third question, regarding the identity of "the ponies' most powerful enemy," again implied that the show's researchers hadn't made it past the pilot episodes: "Krastos the Glue Maker," "the evil pony Nightmare Moon," "or the cynical grownup, Chester." Nightmare Moon was defeated in "Friendship Is Magic, Part 2," which Sagal did acknowledge: "Nightmare Moon is released in the opening episode from the prison where she's been held for a thousand years, and is only defeated by the ponies working together, and then they have a party."[137] The basic framework of a villain returning from exile who can only be defeated by a group of disparate characters banding together for a common cause who subsequently celebrate their victory has been used in adventure stories for centuries—the post-victory celebration in the 2003 Best Picture winner *The Lord of the Rings: Return of the King* was what *Village Voice* film editor Alan Scherstuhl aptly described as "a tickle party," and was far more twee than the party in "Friendship Is Magic, Part 2"—but here it got a big laugh because isn't My Little Pony just so silly?[138]

Wait Wait … Don't Tell Me! is intended to be funny; NPR lists it as a comedy show, and invites viewers to "have a laugh and test your news knowledge while figuring out what's real and what we've made up."[139] Though Clinton knew it was a lark (when "Not My Job" began, he asked, "This is part where you make me look like a fool, right?"), the fact that he got three out of three answers correct in a multiple choice quiz designed to be silly is no great surprise.[140] The villain on a children's show about ponies is unlikely to be as dark as a glue maker, "the right to mate" would be far too sexual, and considering that his daughter Chelsea was in G1's target demographic while growing up in the 1980s, he may well have heard the phrase "Cutie Mark."[141] When the episode transcript was posted on npr.org, the very first comment read: "So, is President Clinton now a 'bronie'? Just asking."[142]

In addition to being one of the earliest instances of intentionally misspelling and scare-quoting the word Brony as "bronie"—spelling the word that way makes as much sense as spelling the singular of pony as ponie, which is not a thing anypony does—the answer from the rest of the media was "yes." Two days later, *Time*'s Newsfeed blog ran a piece titled "Guess Who's a Fan? Former President Bill Clinton Is a 'Brony,'" citing the proof as the "stumper of question on the Little Pony Rarity's favorite pastime. (Spoiler alert: It's giving makeovers!)"[143] Which it is not, and again, the word Brony was never spoken or even hinted at in the *Wait Wait … Don't Tell Me!* episode.

The same day as the *Time* piece, a Huffington Post article asked, "Bill Clinton a Brony?," answered the question in the final paragraph: "With three correct answers, Clinton is definitely a Brony."[144] Which is not how math works; had Clinton guessed at random, he would have had a 1 in 27 chance of getting all three answers correct. However, since he was making educated guesses, and two of the three options for each question were intended to be funny and obviously fake, his chances of getting all three correct were 1 in 8. He also implied during the game that he had never seen *Friendship Is Magic*; upon hearing "Krastos, the Glue Maker" as one of the options for the ponies' most powerful enemy, Clinton laughed and quipped, "If he's not, he ought to be," which is not what somepony who is "definitely a Brony" would say. Similarly, the "prize" for winning the quiz was one of the announcers recording an answering machine message for one of their listeners, and when Clinton was told the name of the listener he'd be playing for was Dave, he replied, "Poor Dave"—a reasonable reaction when he's about to be asked questions about a show he's never watched.[145]

As *Time* had, the Huffington Post also began with a dismissive callback to an earlier article: "Previously we told you about Bronies, a growing subculture of men who, for whatever reason, really like the 'My Little Pony' cartoon."[146] The questionable math of getting three multiple-choice questions (each with three possible answers, two of which are known to have been made up for comedy purposes) equaling being a Brony continued with the Mary Sue's headline "Former President Bill Clinton Knows Everything About My Little Pony," though they were one of the only outlets to put it into some perspective and acknowledge that, yes, the whole affair was very silly indeed.

> With no grandchildren to speak of who might watch the show, there are only three logical answers to this mystery that we can think of: 1) Chelsea Clinton was a big fan of the original MLP back in the day, 2) The former president is secretly a Brony (what else is there to do once your tenure in office is up?), or 3) He made some lucky guesses. The last one probably has the highest chance of being true, but we're gonna go with #2, as it's the most entertaining answer.[147]

Like the only other living Democratic former president before him, Jimmy Carter, Bill Clinton had been keeping himself occupied doing humanitarian work, hence him being on *Wait Wait ... Don't Tell Me!* to promote the Clinton Global Initiative. What's more troubling is the inclusion of the word "secret," a shaming term: he's not just a Brony (which he was not), but a secret Brony (which he was not, either), because if he *was* a Brony, it's something he would want to keep secret.

Getting three multiple-choice answers correct does not a Brony make, but that didn't keep the *Wait Wait ... Don't Tell Me!* episode from becoming a touchstone. In April 2012, William Harvey wrote in the *Tampa Bay Times*, "Anyone having difficulty believing Bronies aren't all freaks will have to tell that to Bill Clinton. The former president donned his own pair of horseshoes by accurately sharing his knowledge of the My Little Pony series on one of NPR's Wait, Wait, Don't Tell Me 'Not My Job' segments."[148] A few weeks later, T.L. Stanley wrote in the *Los Angeles Times* that "'MLP' and its loyalists have become so well known that gossip blog Gawker has written about them, Stephen Colbert has given two shout-outs to bronies on 'The Colbert Report' and NPR quizzed former President Bill Clinton on 'Pony' trivia for its show, 'Wait, Wait ... Don't Tell Me.' (He aced all questions, solidifying his brony cred.)"[149] Again, getting three multiple choice questions correct in a comedy quiz show no more solidifies somepony's "brony cred" than it confirms that they are "definitely a Brony."

The Gawker article referenced by T.L. Stanley was posted on the Gawker-owned blog Jezebel on August 4, written by Margaret Hartmann and titled "The Unlikely Origins of the Brony, or Bros Who Like 'My Little Pony.'"[150] In addition to sharing the *Wired* headline's use of "unlikely," the word is used twice in the first two paragraphs: the show "developed an unlikely fanbase," and that "the *New York Observer* tells the unlikely tale of how the charming 4chan cesspool inspired a legion of men to begin following the adventures of characters like Twilight Sparkle and Rainbow Dash."[151] She also quoted the "surprising" mantra of the Bronies: "I'm gonna love and tolerate the shit outta you." As things that are surprising go, we're to understand, men following the adventures of "characters like Twilight Sparkle and Rainbow Dash" is high up on the list. The shame-based phrasing continued until the final two lines: "With such high praise for the show, you might want to check out the first episode for yourself on YouTube. After all, even Ryan Gosling is a closet Brony."[152] Not just a Brony, but a *closet* Brony!

And like Bill Clinton, not a Brony at all, at least not based on the presented evidence: Hartmann linked to a YouTube clip from earlier that year in which Ryan Gosling, during a press junket for the movie *Blue Valentine*, was asked by interviewer Peter Travers to sing a few bars of whatever was in his head at the moment.[153] A good sport, Gosling said that his six-year-old *Valentine* co-star Faith Wladyka had been singing "this My Little Pony song" all day, and after disclaiming that "I always get it wrong—she's going to be so mad," he proceeded to approximate a few lines of "Good Morning, Ponyville" from *The World's Biggest Tea Party*.[154] It's very charming, particularly since it demonstrates the extent to which Gosling continued to bond with his young co-star long after the film was shot, but it doesn't make him a Brony by any possible definition, except that it was now considered hilarious to call any man who possessed (or gave the erroneous appearance of possessing) the slightest amount of knowledge of My Little Pony a secret/closet Brony.

Sometimes all it took was to express interest in seeing a documentary on the subject three years later at the film festival you founded. Covering the kickoff lunch for the Tribeca Film Festival in April 2014, Indiewire reported that Brent Hodge's documentary *A Brony Tale* had become "something of a joke"[155]:

> Tribeca Enterprises honcho Geoff Gilmore gave the movie a shout-out during his remarks; when the programmers and executive staff of the festival were asked what they were most looking forward to over the course of the festival, even Robert De Niro said "A Brony Tale." Of course, if you look at the words "A Brony Tale" too quickly they look like "A Bronx Tale," so it may have been that De Niro was feeling nostalgic for his brief days as a director. On the other hand, maybe one more Brony just came out of the closet.[156]

The following week, a *Vancouver Sun* article about the festival continued the joke that had never been funny in the first place:

> Is Robert De Niro secretly a "brony?" Does the veteran film star, producer and Tribeca Film Festival founder have a special place in his heart for friendship and magic? For rainbows and pixie dust and all things related to animated television hit My Little Pony?[157]

Setting aside that pixie dust and *Friendship Is Magic* are in no way related, the article went on to ruminate that "Vancouver filmmaker Brent Hodge can certainly wonder" about De Niro's possible secret Bronyhood, since De Niro "admittedly has a soft spot for the film," which by that point had an official tagline of "A Film About Men…. Who Love My Little Pony."[158] For some reason, the writer did not follow up by suggesting Hodge was a closet Brony for having made the film in the first place, or that famed documentarian Morgan Spurlock couldn't *not* be a Brony for making a deal with Hodge to distribute the film in North America, or even Tribeca Film Festival director Geoffrey Gilmore, who was surely more involved in the selection of the film than was De Niro and thus was mathematically certain to be a Brony.[159] So many potential secret closeted Bronies in all directions!

The "lol you're a secret [whatever group is being shamed]" joke isn't new or only about Bronies, and it's sometimes made by people who should know better. On March 3, 2011, the eve of the mainstream media becoming aware of Bronies, transgender activist Kate Bornstein was interviewed by Steve Scher on the talk show *Weekday* on KUOW 94.9FM in Puget Sound. Despite her best efforts, the conversation kept returning to Bornstein's BDSM activities[160]; Scher asked her to explain the concept of "ownership" in a master/slave relationship, and mostly keeping her exasperation in check, she replied, "Well, like I was saying, sexual orientation doesn't necessarily depend on the gender of your partner. It can depend more on, what is it you like to do? For example, furries. Do you know … oh, good!"[161] Bornstein paused, and if you listen to the podcast, and you can all but hear her eyes widening in feigned delight. "Steve, you're a closet furry! Oh, look at your bushy tail!"[162]

Sounding unsure as to why giving a non-verbal acknowledgment of being aware of the existence of a thing translated into him *being* that thing, let alone a "closet" version of it, Schur chuckled gamely and replied, "I have to admit I saw a *CSI* episode which introduced me to a concept I had never known before."[163] They shared a laugh over the imagined image of people cuddling while dressed as woodland creatures before moving on to other topics. That particular exchange took sixty seconds out of the 40-minute program, the first 20 minutes of which was an interview with John Vaillant, author of a book titled *The Tiger*; when archived, the *Weekday* episode was titled "Tigers and Furries."[164] Considering how much Bornstein has promoted openness, diversity, and the need to live an uncloseted life throughout her career in both word and deed, her mocking of Furries was peculiar at best. But even when it's done as a light-hearted joke, shaming can have a dangerous impact on the wider culture.

An April 3, 2014, *Vancouver Sun* article about *A Brony Tale* closing out the DOXA Documentary Film Festival a few weeks before it played Tribeca declared that "from Trekkies to Buffy singalongs to Twilight fan fiction, pop culture has spawned a lot of strange phenomena over the decades. But perhaps none is quite as strange as the bronies."[165] Indeed, what could be stranger than males liking something originally made for females? A more general article in the April 9 *Bristol Post* about a local Brony club described them as "just one branch of a global fan base of mainly adult men who share a strange and unlikely fascination with the My Little Pony: Friendship Is Magic TV series."[166] To the article's credit, not only was it one of the few to specify that the Brony fandom is for *Friendship Is Magic* in particular and not My Little Pony overall, the friendly headline of the print version acknowledged the female Bronies: "Meet the Bronies: The Men (and Women) Who Love My Little Pony."[167] The headline of the online version had no time for such namby-pamby nuance, however: "Bristol Bronies: The Men Who Love My Little Pony."[168]

On April 14, a *Financial Times* preview of the Tribeca Film Festival described *A Brony Tale* as the "strangest in show,"[169] and later in the month, the *New York Daily News* referred to the film as "a doc on the bizarre phenomenon of men obsessed with the Hasbro entertainment franchise."[170] The word "obsess" is never used in any form in *A Brony Tale*, and only three times in *Extremely Unexpected*, but in an echo of G3, it had been a go-to from the start of the media coverage of the Bronies, including in Una LaMarche's August 2011 *New York Observer* article which referred to *Friendship Is Magic* as having "amassed a legion of fanboys between the ages of 18 and 35 who obsess over" the characters,[171] and several others that followed.

A few days after Hasbro's April 21 announcement that the Girls category had grown 21% in the first quarter of 2014, *Washington Post* writer Caitlin Dewey posted, "Don't Laugh, But Bronies May Be Propping Up One of America's Favorite Companies." She first acknowledged that the "peculiar Internet phenomenon called brony has received its share of derision over the years," and then indulged in that derision by asking her readers to "hold your repugnance," because those repugnant "adult male fans of Hasbro's girliest product" may have been the reason for Hasbro's recent financial success.[172] Throughout it all, Dewey adopted the sort of "this is all an unfathomable mystery which is far too mysterious to even attempt to fathom" tone which may have made a modicum of sense for a *New York Post* writer in 2012, but not a *Washington Post* writer in mid–2014:

> Anyway, leaving aside the big questions of why bronies exist and what fandom means, this still leaves the curious case of Hasbro's recent resurgence. Did My Little Pony's popularity spark the birth of bronies, or did bronies push a retro toy back into the spotlight? Alternately did both things spring from a third event entirely—namely, Hasbro's 2010 relaunch of the My Little Pony line?[173]

Even the most rudimentary research into Bronies or My Little Pony would have revealed that the answers to those three questions were, in order: "Yes, though not My Little Pony as a whole but rather the *Friendship Is Magic* series"; "No, the retro toy had already been back in the spotlight for several years by then," and "Yes, though less because of the toys and much more because of the endless remixing possibilities of *Friendship Is Magic*." But even at this late date many journalists were indulging in a kind of willful ignorance, perhaps out of fear of being called a "closet Brony" by other journalists for having too much knowledge about such things.

On April 30, Karen Kemmerle interviewed *A Brony Tale* director Brent Hodge on the Tribeca Film Festival's website.[174] It began with the standard, unexamined acknowledgment of just how strange and off-putting it all is, thus reminding the reader how lucky they are that it didn't happen to them:

> One might be hesitant to explore the strange and close-knit world of the Bronies, but not Brent Hodge. He had the perfect "in" to this community, given his friendship with Ashleigh Ball, one of the voice actresses on *My Little Pony: Friendship is Magic*. What started out as a film to explore Ashleigh Ball's relationship with her Brony fans became so much more.[175]

Hodge described how "the minute" Ball told him about the Bronies, "I asked her start forwarding their emails," because "the notion of grown men identifying themselves as 'Bronies' seemed so odd to me that I knew it would make an interesting subject for a documentary."[176] As we've seen, *Friendship Is Magic* itself was always a minor detail in most media coverage of the Bronies, and not without reason to an extent; as Hodge put it: "Perhaps the most interesting thing I learned was that Bronies are not so much about the show, but about the community. They are interested in friendship and in finding common ground within a group."[177] As we'll see in "Battles of the Brand," the show as it exists is often the least of their interests.

Another minor detail which tended to be ignored for the purposes of a juicier story is the fact that not all adult *Friendship Is Magic* fans are Bronies or male, though both media and the Bronies have tended to perpetuate that narrative. Pointing out that other than Ball, only two women were interviewed for the documentary, Kemmerle asked, "Is there a female presence in the My Little Pony fandom? Are lady fans under-represented in light of the Bronies?" Hodge replied:

> Female fans are called Pegasisters. That's the term. I shied away from them a little because I wanted to focus on the guys. There's nothing really off the wall about a ton of girls liking *My Little Pony*. I mean, they grew up with them. They got them in their Happy Meals. Plus, Ashleigh was always my leading lady.[178]

That this makes sense on a marketing level makes it no less problematic. The media had certainly found women who were still interested in My Little Pony to be "off the wall" in the coverage of the G3 conventions, while female fans of *Friendship Is Magic* are only called Pegasisters in the contexts in which male fans are called Bronies, and even then, there are many women who embrace the term Brony. More troubling is the fact that the decision to "shy away" from the women and present Brony fandom—and by extension *Friendship Is Magic* fandom—as being a guy-centric thing only served to further bolster the notion of it being "strange" and "unexpected" in a way that would not have been the case had the truly age-and-gender-spanning viewership been represented. Also, just because Ashleigh Ball was his leading lady doesn't mean there wasn't room for other women, as though they're tokens who reach capacity much faster than men.

The snickering about Robert De Niro being "a closet Brony" and the continued bafflement about just how *strange* it all was in April 2014 alone came on the heels of two high-profile cases of young boys being bullied for openly liking My Little Pony. On January 23, an 11-year-old boy who had been relentlessly bullied and called "gay" for identifying as a Brony, and for liking Pinkie Pie in particular, attempted suicide.[179] Eleven weeks later, on the same day the *Financial Times* called *A Brony Tale* "strangest in show" at Tribeca,[180] it was reported that he remained in a persistent vegetative state.[181] A less tragic story which also received national attention came in March, as a 9-year-old boy who got bullied for his Rainbow Dash backpack—including getting punched and pushed to the ground—was victim-blamed by the school, which asked him to leave the backpack at home because it was a "trigger for bullying."[182] After a week and a half of very bad press and an outpouring of support for the boy's right to choose his preferred luggage, the school reversed their decision and allowed him to bring the backpack.[183] It is not insignificant that the backpack was blue, the accepted color of boyhood in America for over a century, and that its other distinguishing features were just Dash's eyes, ears, mouth and an orange-and-yellow tuft of her mane, not even her full rainbow; appropriately enough for the rough-and-tumble tomboy character, there's nothing about the (admittedly atrocious) backpack that is coded as overtly feminine in the way that a Pinkie Pie backpack might have been.[184]

Bullying had been an important issue since long before *Friendship Is Magic* debuted, let alone the bullying of boys who dare to violate the strict confines of gender, and it would be unrealistic at best to suggest that these bullies had personally read many of the horrible things that had been written about Bronies. For example, the boys who pushed and punched the 9-year-old for wearing a Rainbow Dash backpack probably did not read Matt Labash's *Weekly Standard* essay "The Dread Pony" the previous August, in which

Labash wrote, "to defuse a few common Brony stereotypes straightaway, despite their fascination with pastel talking ponies, there's no evidence that Bronies are mostly gay or pedophiles"—the kind of "common Brony stereotypes" which can be traced back to articles such as "The Dread Pony."[185] Labash also stated that "children of the eighties will recall the original My Little Pony (MLP) franchise from the Technicolor ponies in their little sisters' toy chests," because of course all children of the eighties are male by default.[186] (In fairness, according to the *Weekly Standard*'s 2013 media kit, three-quarters of their online and print readership were male, a statistic which speaks highly of American women.[187])

The bullies most likely were unaware that by the premiere of Season 2 on September 18, 2011, the Brony-happy media coverage of *Friendship Is Magic* tended to ignore that the show was also popular with all genders in all age groups, and that it was a top-rated show not just on the Hub in the United States, but also on the Treehouse channel in Canada, and Cartoon Network's UK Boomerang channel.[188] (Treehouse worked with Kidomo and Play-Doh to put on a "30-minute live, interactive, musical adventure" which toured Canada through the summer and fall of 2011, the first traveling My Little Pony live show since *The World's Biggest Tea Party* ended in 2009.[189]) *Friendship Is Magic* was also available on the Okto channel in Singapore, where it developed its own localized Brony fandom, and there's little chance that the bullies had read Natasha Ann Zachariah's article "Pony Posse" in the October 30, 2011, *Straits Times*.[190] It hit what were by then all the standard beats, many of which were in the opening line: "Sparkles, pink ponies and cutesy names such as Twilight Sparkle are things little girls' dreams are made of."[191] The distancing mechanism of "cutesy names such as" was already a common tool for discussing the show, i.e., "female ponies with names like Twilight Sparkle and Pinkie Pie" in Jaime Weinman's *Maclean's* article,[192] "characters with names like Twilight Sparkle, Rainbow Dash, Applejack and Pinkie Pie" in Una LaMarche's August *New York Observer* article,[193] "a small gaggle of ponies with names like Twilight Sparkle, Fluttershy and Rainbow Dash" in Angela Watercutter's *Wired* article,[194] and "the latest shenanigans of Ponies with names like Twilight Sparkle and Fluttershy" in a *Wall Street Journal* article that November by Vauhini Vara.[95]

Along with referring to the local Brony community as "the unlikeliest fans" and describing their fandom as an "obsession," Zachariah's *Straits Times* article addressed the "flak and nasty comments" that many of them received, "with some even calling them 'gay' or 'weird.'"[196] In a sidebar to the main article titled "Bonding Over Magical Ponies"—which covered much of the same ground as the main article in a third as many words—she described the characters of the show as being "on a mission to spread love and tolerance."[197] (The Mane Six do often *learn* about love and tolerance as a happenstance, but they just as often do not, and they never set out to spread it until the introduction of the Cutie Map and its mandate to solve friendship problems in Season 5, four years after this article.) As the show gained more press attention, and that press attention was due to the "extremely" "unlikely" older and/or male segment of the fans who identified as Bronies, there were few attempts to engage with the text of the show; a victim of its own success in terms of media coverage, *My Little Pony: Friendship Is Magic* was painted as being far less complicated and character-driven than it was. "Bonding Over Magical Ponies" was also one of the first articles to use the word Pegasister, which had otherwise been absent from the coverage.[198]

Even being a national publication, odds are slim that any of the bullies had read "Hey, Bro, That's My Little Pony" in the *Wall Street Journal* that November, an article which at the time was the most mainstream United States news outlet yet to delve into (to coin a phrase) the psychology of the Brony.[199] In addition to being the second article to mention Pegasisters, defining the word as "what the small minority of female bronies sometimes call themselves in this male-dominated world," the article quoted BronyCon organizer Jessica Blank about what the readers no doubt wanted to know most of all about Bronies: "Actually, the overwhelming majority are straight."[200] The quote ended there, so it's unknown whether Blank went on to point out that the sexual orientation of a given Brony is neither relevant nor anypony else's damn business. That the "Ha ha they must be gay!" phenomenon—and that the reaction was a defensive "No we are not!" rather than "It's doesn't matter either way!"—was happening at a time when great strides in civil rights were being made for queer people, and overt homophobia was becoming less culturally acceptable, makes this aspect of the coverage all the more retrograde and distasteful.

Were one to ask the bullies, it is unlikely they were aware of how Reed Tucker used the word "pretty" in his January 2012 *New York Post* article about the third biannual BronyCon, which he described as "a much stranger, more dilapidated Comic Con where pony nerds gather to buy merchandise, meet talent associated with the show or just hang with like-minded equestrian lovers."[201] But it was his description of the show that went straight for the gender jugular:

> "My Little Pony: Friendship Is Magic" launched in 2010 and is an update of the 1980s toy and animation franchise that was built around plastic horses with pretty, pretty tails that little girls could brush. It features colorful characters such as Rainbow Dash and Applejack.[202]

Much like Bronies being "extremely" unexpected, only doubling up on the word "pretty" could express Tucker's disdain in a way that just "plastic horses with tails that little girls could brush" would not,[203] while also echoing Jaime Weinman's "pretty pony tea parties."[204] And while Tucker started out straightforward about character names, he hit a wall when writing of "a 20-year-old from Texas who came dressed as something called Pinkie Pie."[205] It's odd that Tucker learned that Rainbow Dash and Applejack were character names but not Pinkie Pie, and he could not deduce from the fact that he was reporting from a *Friendship Is Magic* Brony fan convention that the young Texan was a dressed as a *Friendship Is Magic* character. (Then again, he was writing for the *New York Post*, which has never been known as a brain trust.)

Sometimes the baggage of the My Little Pony brand, or the notion of the series being a cartoon created for young girls, was stripped down to the culturally-accepted canard that only those girls can express any interest in ponies, period. Surely unread by the bullies, Rob Wennemer's June 2012 *Pittsburgh Post-Gazette* article "Beer, Women and … My Little Pony? Men Profess Newest Love" began by describing "a group of mostly young Pittsburgh men" who gather weekly to "enthusiastically [debate] their favorite TV episodes and the most captivating ponies."[206]

Anticipating that the reader was slapping their forehead in disbelief, Wennemer began the next paragraph with the shocking truth: "Ponies? Yes ponies."[207]

Men talking about ponies? You've never seen such goings-on!

The article went deep into the now-standard "So are they gay, or what?" question, quoting a survey by Wofford College which found that out of 5,200 Bronies aged 14 to 57, 84% described themselves as heterosexual.[208] He also paraphrased a statement by a Carnegie Mellon University statistics major, who was quoted as saying the show has "actual drama" to appeal to older audiences, and that it "is not just for little kids"; Wennemer rephrased this as the show presenting some comedy and dialog "that cannot be understood by young girls."[209] Lest we forget, young girls—the ones who are *supposed* to like ponies, unlike men—are not intelligent.

So, no. The bullies didn't read those articles, but nopony, not even schoolyard bullies, exists in a vacuum. They were still immersed in a media ecology which had done nothing but point and laugh at Bronies, calling them strange and weird and reinforcing the very basic notion that boys cannot like things for girls, period. It's impossible to say whether those two boys in particular would have been bullied without two and a half years of the media (and thus the culture) shaming Bronies, but the constant reinforcement that it's strange and weird for boys to like My Little Pony could not have helped—

and without it, the 11-year-old Pinkie Pie fan may not have been compelled to try to take his own life to make the harassment stop.

Not that there was any sign that the laugh riot about Bronies would stop anytime soon. In a June 2015 interview with the UK fetish magazine *Bizarre* (appropriately enough), *Extremely Unexpected* director Laurent Malaquais described the show as "being about friendship, getting along with other people, and creating a community," which is true on a macro scale, but in the very next sentence he misrepresented the storytelling, suggesting a formula that does not exist: "In every episode there's a situation that divides or challenges the ponies, but by the end they all reunite harmoniously."[210] There are indeed situations that challenge the ponies, as there must be with characters of *any* species to create drama in storytelling, and some of the best episodes from Season 1 of the show are about interpony conflict, such as "The Ticket Master" (S01E03), "Look Before You Sleep" (S01E08), and "Party of One" (S01E25). Episodes in which the ponies are not divided or challenged in a way that requires them to "reunite harmoniously" at the end include but are not limited to "Applebuck Season" (S01E04), "Dragonshy" (S01E07), "Swarm of the Century" (S01E10), "Call of the Cutie" (S01E12), "Stare Master" (S01E17), "The Show Stoppers" (S01E18), "The Cutie Mark Chronicles" (S01E23), and "Owl's Well that Ends Well" (S01E24). To state that every episode is about the importance of getting along sells *Friendship Is Magic* short, but it does help to perpetuate the narrative that it's too simplistic and juvenile a show for grown-ups, and the selling of both *Extremely Unexpected* and *A Brony Tale* depended on shifting the focus from "this is a show which appeals to grown-ups" to "what's wrong with these grown-ups that they like this show?"

The second to last question in the *Bizarre* interview was, "Does the media still ridicule the fandom?"[211] Malaquais replied that he thought his film "has answered a lot of questions and taken the Bronies out of this dark, weird area," and that while he didn't think the Bronies will get "less trolls or negative stigma," at least now their parents can see that it's "just a bunch of people hanging out because they love this cartoon."[212] Then, in an example of the media still ridiculing the Brony fandom, the interviewer asked, "Did you end up becoming a Brony yourself?"

> During the making of the film I had to really hold myself back from getting too sucked in, because I would have lost my objectivity as a documentary film-maker. Now that the film is done, I can admit that during the film-making process I did begin to feel like a Brony...[213]

Not even the director of the film can avoid getting snarky about it, but it is the ellipsis—no doubt an editorial choice on the part of the magazine—that drives home the terror of Malaquais "admitting" that he did "begin to feel" like a Brony…. A horrible fate, and there but for the grace of God go *you*, dear reader…

Hasbro Catches Up

It took Hasbro a while to openly acknowledge and embrace the "extremely" "unexpected" demographics of My Little Pony's modern fanbase, whether self-identified Bronies or not. On their November 9, 2010, Investor Day webcast, a month after the broadcast premiere of *My Little Pony: Friendship Is Magic*, Hasbro's Chief Marketing Officer John Frascotti said the strategy behind the new series and brand relaunch was to create a new core cast that would allow "the My Little Pony girl, that four to six-year-old girl, to get to know the ponies better and to really identify with the ponies."[214]

A few days after the *Wired* article about Bronies in June 2011, a Hasbro press release about the "branded lifestyle goods" featured at the International Licensing Expo included the "General Motors BUMBLEBEE Camaro that may be Dad's pride and joy," and that "little guys can mimic Dad and cruise on a BUMBLEBEE electric ride-on car" while "girls may opt to ride with their favorite pony friends on a MY LITTLE PONY ride-on."[215] (One can hardly blame them for opting out of the Bumblebee car, considering how much the modern *Transformers* films hate girls.) The next month, Hasbro announced a range of products to be sold exclusively in Target stores and focusing on the Equestria capital, using the e'er-controversial S-word in their description of "a dedicated display that is designed to share the magic and sparkle of CANTER-LOT with young girls."[216] Hasbro's October announcement listing their new holiday toys was divided by gender, and because each half was alphabetized, the Boys list started off with the violent-sounding Beyblade: Metal Masters Triple Battle Set, while the Girls list began with an upgrading of the perennial Easy-Bake Oven, now called the Easy-Bake Ultimate Oven due to having "a larger cooking chamber and bigger baking pan," and thus it could cook more junk food at a time.[217] The Pony presence on the list was in the form of Rarity's Carousel Boutique Playset, promising that "girls will be enchanted" as the carousel "'comes to life' with playful sounds, spinning round and round."[218] This is another example of the disconnect between *Friendship Is Magic* and the Generation 4 merchandise: though the commercials used repurposed animation from the show, the Carousel Boutique on *Friendship* is Rarity's home and business, and it is not a merry-go-round.[219] In keeping with the junk food theme, the press release described her as serving French Fries and popcorn in the "concession stand," foods that the show's Rarity would consider déclassé,[220]

Hasbro's February 2012 press release about the upcoming American International Toy Fair described the My Little Pony brand as "eager to take girls on magical journeys of friendship and fun," and that those girls "will adore discovering the whimsical world of pony friends, and watching their adventures unfold in the 'My Little Pony: Friendship is Magic' animated series."[221] By June Hasbro began to openly acknowledge that things had changed, announcing that My Little Pony "continues to be a worldwide favorite with fans of all ages, largely fueled by the global popularity of the MY LITTLE PONY: FRIENDSHIP IS MAGIC animated series."[222] But it was their July 9 release about the 2012 San Diego Comic-Con in which Hasbro further acknowledged what their thirty-year-old brand had become, calling it a "pop-culture phenomenon," and describing *Friendship Is Magic* as having "amassed a fan following as varied as the ponies of Ponyville."[223] In 373 words about both the brand and the show's presence at Comic-Con, at no point are age, gender, target demographics, or Bronies mentioned, instead only ever referring to the fans as "fans."[224] Similarly, a Hasbro press release later that week about the launch of *Friendship Is Magic* comic books by IDW Publishing never used the word "young" or "girl," instead referring to the show's "all-ages appeal" and referring to "fans of all ages" as well as the brand "having brought fun, friendship & joy to millions of kids of all ages around the globe" since the 2003 re-launch, while also referring to *Friendship Is Magic* as having gained "much acclaim due to its brilliantly written plot lines" and "high quality graphics"—marking both one of the first times Hasbro acknowledged the quality of the show, and one of the last times they would reference Generation 3.[225]

The Season 3 premiere was at a "Playdate Premiere Party" in New York City on November 10, 2012, and Hasbro described the attendees as simply "kids and their families."[226] B-roll footage of the event shot by Premiere TV shows a mix of boys and girls, and host Melissa Joan Hart tells an interviewer that she was a My Little Pony fan as a child, and she's glad that her sons now watch *Friendship Is Magic* because it's a show about "friendship and values."[227] A few days later, Hasbro announced their new products for the 2012 holiday season; the list was alphabetized but not divided by gender like the 2011 press release, landing the My Little Pony Pony Princess Wedding Castle Playset between the Monopoly Millionaire Game and Nerf N-Strike Hail-Fire Blaster.[228] Though the descriptions for Littlest Pet Shop, Furreal Friends, and Twister all specified that they were for girls, the My Little Pony item did not, in spite of it being about a pony princess getting married, which according to most stereotypes is the perfect storm of femininity.[229]

The Season 3 finale "Magical Mystery Cure" (S03E13) was celebrated on February 12, 2013, with a "Coronation Concert" in Los Angeles, hosted by the recently crowned Miss America, Mallory Hagan.[230] The Hub held a sweepstakes to allow a fan to attend, and Hasbro's press release buried the gender lede: "a 10-year-old fan from Buncombe, IL won a trip for four to the coronation concert with his family."[231] Hasbro would continue to be gender-neutral in press releases intended to be picked up by news outlets read by the general public, such as their March announcement about Pinkie Pie and Rainbow Dash becoming available at Build-a-Bear Workshops, which referred to the fans as capital-G "Guests," as in "Guests can take a pony personality quiz, recite the pony promise, and learn how to style their pony's hair with a special hair care brochure."[232] The Workshop founder was quoted as saying that "We know our Guests, from all generations, love the MY LITTLE PONY characters" and that mothers who grew up with the brand "can share the nostalgia, friendship, and fun with their own kids."[233] (This is in contrast with Hasbro's 2005 announcement about the "build-your-own MY LITTLE PONY" display at the Once Upon a Toy store in Walt Disney World, which used the phrase "little girls" three times.[234]) Industry-oriented press releases still reflected the categorization in their internal ledgers, such as a June 19 release which promised licensees that the brand will "touch every major category immersing girls in entertaining, inventive, stylish, and fun MY LITTLE PONY lifestyle experiences," and that the "explosive growth" of the brand will extend "engagement in new and meaningful ways for millions of young girls around the globe."[235]

A common sign of encroaching gender equality is men complaining about being underrepresented in ways that they almost never did about women being underrepresented, hence an analyst during Hasbro's Investor Day webcast on September 10, 2013, asking a question which would have been unthinkable just three years earlier: "Is there some reason why none of the main characters in Pony are male?"[236] He phrased it in terms of whether or not adding male characters would increase sales, to which Hasbro's Head of Girls and New Brands Samantha Lomow responded that while they're not part of what she still referred to as the Core 6, "there are plenty of male ponies in the lore," pointing out that Princess Cadance's marriage to Shining Armor was "just to kind of reinforce our male pony heritage."[237]

Hasbro embraced the diversity of the My Little Pony fanbase by mid–2014, and without reducing it to just those who identify as Bronies. In a July 21 press release, they announced a partnership with the 3D-printing company Shapeways to launch the website SuperFanArt, in which fans could create and sell customized 3D models of the characters without getting dinged for violating copyright. A number of fan artists were mentioned by name, such as Brandon Lee Johnson, "a student, 3D artist and longtime MY LITTLE PONY fan," and Melinda Rose, "a lifelong MY LITTLE PONY fan and an accomplished 3D designer."[238] Most importantly, though Hasbro had been referring to the franchise for the past few years as "a pop-culture phenomenon" and as having become "a significant part of pop culture transcending both age and gender,"[239] it was no longer just for little children or a passing fad, but something for all to enjoy, if they wanted to—though many would only enjoy it if it conformed to certain narrow expectations.

PART 5

Battles of the Brand
(2012–2016)

World War Derp, Part I: The Eyes of the Gray Mare

In an interview on the podcast *James Bonding* in 2013, comedian Ben Blacker described the nature of how he and his similarly-named comedy partner Ben Acker became James Bond fans at Syracuse University in the early 1990s: "The thing that we were into was the James Bond fandom, the James Bond *thing*," and that they were into "the trappings of James Bond, way more than any individual movies."[1] The same holds true for much of the Brony fandom, many of whom are less interested in *Friendship Is Magic* as a series of 22-minute character-driven stories with a beginning, middle, and end than with the trappings of the fandom—the fan art, the remixes, the social aspect, and a cult that grew around a certain gray mare.

There is what appears to be an animation glitch in "Friendship Is Magic, Part 1" (S01E01). This is nothing unheard of for the first episode of a series, let alone one with as many moving parts as *Friendship Is Magic*, but one particular glitch got picked up on by those studying the show closely at the time: a gray mare with a blond mane in the background of a single shot, her right eye pointing upward while her left eye pointed forward, giving her a look similar to a meme known as "derp face."[2] Know Your Meme, which catalogs internet trends, defines "derp" like so:

> Derp is an expression associated with stupidity, much like the earlier forms of interjections like "duh" and "dur." In image macros, the subject is typically portrayed with eyes that are pointed to each side and a caption that reads "DERP."[3]

In the comments to a post on the Ponychan imageboard in March 2011, supervising director Jayson Thiessen explained that the eyes had been misaligned by "some cheeky animator," and Thiessen kept it in both because he found it funny, and because Hasbro didn't catch it.[4] In the week between the broadcasts of "Friendship Is Magic, Part 2" (S01E02) and "The Ticket Master" (S01E03) in October 2010, 4chan user Dr. Foreigner dubbed the pony "Derpy Hooves."[5] (One may wonder why "hooves" when it was her eyes which were misaligned, but one would be thinking too hard.) The gray mare appeared again as an unnamed character with non-glitchy eyes in "The Ticket Master" and "Applebuck Season" (S01E04); in the latter episode, broadcast on November 5, 2010, she's one of a group of ponies who are excited by the promise of freshly baked muffins. Both she and an aquamarine-colored pony mouth the word "Muffin!" at the same time, though one voice is heard saying the word in sync with the mouth movements, and it could just as easily be parsed as having come from the aquamarine mare. For that matter, there were other ponies in the shot who were more visibly excited about the muffins than the gray mare—one pony who would later be named Bon Bon is licking her lips, and another is rather grossly salivating—but nopony on the Internet was bending over backwards to build up a legend around any of *them* at the time. It should be restated that the young gray mare's eyes in that scene ain't what they used to be, which is to say that they were correctly aligned and not at all glitchy, but it was decided all the same that she had a muffin fixation. (Ignored was the fact that the payoff to the gag was that they all got food poisoning from the muffins, an experience which might lead a pony to swearing off the baked good altogether.) This became a part of the lore in the countless artworks and stories and video remixes which were posted in the ensuing months, as did the even more arbitrary decision that she was a mail carrier. Published to the "Doctor Who + My Little Pony Crossover" category of the website FanFiction.net on January 30, 2011, between the broadcasts of "Fall Weather Friends" (S01E13) and "Suited for Success" (S01E14), Victorian R. Hellsly's "My Little Time Lord" was one of the earliest stories to depict her as a mail carrier; she's also paired up with another background pony, a brown stallion with an hourglass Cutie Mark whom the Bronies had dubbed Dr. Whooves.[6] In "My Little Time Lord," the gray mare's given name is Ditzy Doo, but everypony calls her Derpy Hooves, much to her chagrin.[7] (For better or worse, they would be paired up officially on the show in the Brony-inspired Season 5 episode "Slice of Life" [S05E09].)

The gray mare appeared in the background of most of the next several episodes after "Applebuck Season," including "Winter Wrap Up" (S01E11), in which a reference is made to an unseen character named Ditzy Doo having accidentally gone north to retrieve the southern birds. With "Feeling Pinkie Keen" (S01E15), broadcast on February 11, 2011—four months and a day after the premiere of the show—the feedback loop between the Bronies and the producers came full circle, as the gray mare's misaligned eyes returned. She also interacted with the plot of the episode for the first time, dropping a pile of increasingly heavy objects on Twilight Sparkle's head in a *Looney Tunes*–style escalation gag, which is also considered by many Bronies to be the inspiration for declaring her to be a mail carrier.[8] Jayson Thiessen confirmed in the March Ponychan thread that her misaligned eyes in "Feeling Pinkie Keen" was a direct result of the Brony reaction to the background gag in the pilot episode.

> We loved the response so much that when we were finalizing the episodes, whenever we would catch the grey pony in the BG I'd call for a revision on her eyes to make them DERP. thats why you don't see them crossed again until several episodes in … we had finished a bunch before she was born. we did it without Lauren's blessing actually and i was a bit apprehensive how she would react. but she loved it and Derpy remains.[9]

Lauren Faust's approval was demonstrated not only by the fact that she allowed the character to exist with the misaligned eyes from "Feeling Pinkie Keen" onward, but that as part of an auction to raise money for the Japanese earthquake and tsunami relief earlier that month, she'd offered not only original sketches of Twilight Sparkle and Applejack from the 2008 *Friendship Is Magic* pitch bible, but a new drawing of the gray mare, noting that it was "the first time I've ever drawn this character."[10] The illustration went for $2,151 on eBay.[11] (Not that it's a competition, but your humble author was running a *Mystery Science Theater 3000*–style live movie-riffing show called Bad Movie Night at the time, and we devoted the proceeds of our March 13 show to the Red Cross. And at $163, it was only $1,988 less than the drawing of the gray mare!)

This was not the first time that a show's producers altered a character or otherwise changed the direction of the show based on feedback from the fans. During the first season of *The X-Files* in 1993, negative fan reaction to the skepticism of Dana Scully resulted in the writers having her change her mind about the paranormal much earlier in the season than originally intended; according to writer James Wong, who interacted with fans on chat rooms, "there weren't really trolls back then, but everyone felt like Scully was being a dick."[12] (By the time of the gray mare brouhaha two decades later, many trolls would be indistinguishable from the fans.) Nor was "Feeling Pinkie Keen" the first instance of an Internet fan creation being acknowledged in an official product; the 2006 film *X-Men: The Last Stand* incorporated a meme of the character of Juggernaut.[13] In 2007, fans of the Vocaloid Hatsune Miku (the avatar of a certain kind of voice synthesizer software) created a blank-eyed, leek-waving, and very silly derivative version which they called Hachune Miku.[14] In 2010 she was incorporated into the official video game

Hatsune Miku Project Diva 2nd,[15] and more significantly, original illustrator KEI drew Hachune alongside Hatsune in his 2012 collection *Mikucolor: KEI's Hatsune Miku Illustration Works*,[16] an acknowledgement from on high akin to Lauren Faust drawing the gray mare.

Intentionally misaligned though her eyes were, the mare was not yet internally called Derpy while "Feeling Pinkie Keen" was being produced. Staff writer Amy Keating Rogers later confirmed that while the mare's name wasn't mentioned in the episode, the inept furniture mover in "Keen" was considered by the producers to be the Ditzy Doo referenced in "Winter Wrap Up," and was so named because they thought of her "as being a bit dingy."[17] Lauren Faust wrote on Twitter that she'd considered canonically naming the gray mare Ditzy,[18] but by then the Bronies had named her Derpy and she didn't want to step on that.[19]

Her eyes crossed, the gray mare next appeared as a background (and occasional extreme foreground) character in "Sonic Rainboom" (S01E16), twice in "Green Isn't Your Color" (S01E20), and without her misaligned eyes in "The Cutie Mark Chronicles" (S01E23). She was visible with her misaligned eyes in the Season 2 premiere "The Return of Harmony, Part 1" (S02E01), fighting with the Mayor over Twilight's enchanted doll in "Lesson Zero" (S02E03), bobbing for apples unsuccessfully in "Luna Eclipsed" (S02E04), and elsewhere in "May the Best Pet Win!" (S02E07), "The Mysterious Mare Do Well" (S02E08), "Sweet and Elite" (S02E09), and "Hearth's Warming Eve" (S02E11). But it wasn't until "The Last Roundup" (S02E14) that she was not only referred to in dialog as Derpy (not Derpy *Hooves*, perhaps because of how thuddingly unimaginative that was), but also got to speak. The character's name was Ditzy in the first draft, and for the second draft, writer Amy Keating Rogers was asked to change the name to Derpy as a "'tip of the hat' to the fans," herself unaware of the word having any meaning beyond "klutzy and clumsy."[20]

The scene in which the gray mare accidentally destroys City Hall while helping Rainbow Dash decorate the building is fifty-three seconds of quality slapstick, and the best part of what is otherwise the weakest episode of *My Little Pony: Friendship Is Magic* thus far. "The Last Roundup" is an Applejack story, and like "Applebuck Season" (S01E04), it's mostly just a series of gags relating to Applejack's stubborn pride before slamming to a close at the end of the second act. Some of those gags are very good, and some are very bad, such as *Friendship Is Magic*'s first potty joke, which would have dragged down even a much stronger episode. Indeed, "The Last Roundup" *was* followed by a much stronger Applejack-centric episode with much better gags, "The Super Speedy Cider Squeezy 6000" (S02E15).

But the gray mare's tide raised the leaky boat that was "The Last Roundup" for the Bronies, and to put it indelicately, they lost their shit. It can be witnessed being lost in real time in a video posted to YouTube later that day titled "MLP FiM—Chat Reactions to Derpy in 'The Last Roundup,'" a recording of the Brony fan site Bronystate's chatroom's reaction to the original broadcast of the episode.[21] An Equestria Daily post titled "DERPY DERPY DERPY DERPY DERPY DERPY" was timestamped at 8:40 a.m., and the 1,428 comments it garnered by midnight—finally topping out at 1,573— also make a strong case that the Bronies were very pleased with both the episode and themselves.[22] There were a few commenters who realized that the episode itself was not so good, such as Ponyceum, who wrote that they were "disappointed of every brony" because "the episode was dedicated to APPLEJACK, and everyone is wet because Derpy spoke,"[23] and that "Im just sad that one of main characters is less popular than background pony. I hope someday AJ will get her own (for real) great episode like 'Party of One' or 'Lesson Zero.'"[24] There were also discussions about how this impacted the reams of Brony fan fiction that had already been written about the gray mare, collectively known as "fanon," particularly the fiction in which her name was Ditzy rather than Derpy. Another relevant term is "headcanon," which refers to how the individual viewer fills in the blanks of the characters and details that aren't specified in the canon of the show; user Tora helpfully distinguished the three levels of canon in a wistful way:

> I have enough love and tolerance in my heart for canon Derpy, the various fanon Derpy and my own headcanon Derpy. Thank you The Hub/Studio B(DHX)/Top Draw/Hasbro for giving the Bronies love and tolerance.[25]

Love and tolerance would be in short supply in the weeks to come, and there was already a dearth of such things in the comments, such as a debate over whether or not the gray mare sounded "retarded." The word appears over five dozen times in the thread, with many references to the phrase "full retard" from the R-rated Hollywood satire *Tropic Thunder*.

In 1992, an attorney who specialized in disability rights and legislation told the *Washington Post* that thanks to the disability rights movement gaining political power since the 1970s, the words "retard" and "invalid" were now considered "first-class insults."[26] So "retard" was known to be a slur by the time *Tropic Thunder* was released in 2008—that the characters were tossing around the word in so cavalier a manner was in fact the point, working as a commentary on how shallow and out-of-touch pampered Hollywood stars can become—and it was certainly known by the time "The Last Roundup" was broadcast in 2012. But nopony in the "DERPY DERPY DERPY DERPY DERPY DERPY" thread objected to the use of the outdated and offensive word, just whether or not it applied to the gray mare. Commenter sUiCiDaLn00b wrote at 12:42 p.m. that they "did not much like her voice and they made her seem too full retard,"[27] Vulcan539 wrote a few minutes later that they "would like a less retarded sounding voice, but thats the only problem I have at the moment,"[28] followed by GumballCrash, who lamented, "The voice wasn't the best, the role was a bit over-retard, and frankly there was a lot more going on there than needed to be happening," before getting to the heart of the matter: "BUT I DON'T GIVE A BUCK. DERPY IS CANON. WE ARE THE WIN."[29] A few hours and several hundred comments later, Senior Waffles told the people who thought the gray mare's voice might be offensive that they were wrong: "Whoa there people, Derpy is not offensive. Her voice isn't 'retarded' sounding."[30] Commander Hurricane also tried to clear things up: "Okay, after watching it like 20, maybe 30 times now, I don't think Derpy sounds retarded either, she is clumsy and not the brightest pony in Equestria, but def. not retarded."[31] But it took user hyreia to take the people who felt differently than themself to task, while adding a *soupçon* of homophobia by equating lesbianism with developmental disabilities:

> Who says Derpy was retarded? Just because she's clusmy and doesn't have a "pretty" voice? Shame on you haters. That's like claiming Rainbow Dash is a lesbian just because she's a tomboy and likes rainbows. People complaining about our beloved Derpy getting a scene and a voice just prove that there ARE people you can't please and who will never be satisfied.[32]

At a quarter past nine that evening, after there'd been more than a thousand comments on the page, user ThinLine_3RX reported that a backlash had begun: "Why is nobody talking about the whole Anti-Derpy hooves movement? There's a petition to change her look and Name or something it's stupid, and probably going to die since only two people have signed but still it's crazy. He demands an official apology for Derpy by the creators."[33]

The petition to which ThinLine_3RX referred was titled "Make Amends for Hurtful Ableist Stereotype in My Little Pony," posted by Jenna Pitman to Change.org shortly after the initial broadcast of "The Last Roundup," and directed to Hasbro.[34] The letter described the episode as allowing "a very hurtful, pro-bullying message to be aired" in an attempt to "reach out to the increasing number of childless adults who have started watching."[35] The petitioner also wrote that the pony is "given a voice similar to that of Lennie Small from Of Mice and Men, that slow, loopy and lispy drawl we have all heard others use as an insult for a person or a subject"—which is debatable at best; indeed, when the voice was eventually re-recorded with a more classically female voice, the *rhythm* remained the same.[36] She also noted that "the show's creators were made aware months ago of the hurtful nature of that name and yet they used it anyway," though how and when they were made aware is unclear.[37]

A creator who had not been made aware was episode writer Amy Keating Rogers, who didn't watch the episode until after its original broadcast on January 21, 2012, and then only because she was getting emails about the portrayal of the mare: about 200 positive messages thanking her, and 10 negative messages from offended viewers, some of whom called her an "ableist" and accused her of being insensitive to disabled people.[38] It was then that she did deeper research into the word "derpy" and discovered that it could not only mean "embarrassing" or "awkward," but also "retarded."[39]

> Now, you have to realize that reading that made my heart sink. My son Soren (of Soarin' fame) is severely disabled. We do not use the word "retarded" in our house because it really has become an offensive slur. And while I knew that it was only a minority of people that defined "derpy" this way, it still upset me that I was the writer that put that name out there. It was painfully ironic and goes against the fact that I'm an advocate for the disabled.[40]

Voice actor Tabitha St. Germain (who also received hate mail) was unaware of the Brony cult that had grown up around the mare, nor had she been informed prior to the recording session that the character was female, so she based the voice on the klutzy son of a neighbor.[41] But it wasn't just the writers and the talent who were receiving both positive and negative feedback; Hasbro and the Hub were also under fire. According to Rogers, she met with the Hub, and they narrowed their course of action to four options:

1. Do nothing.
2. Cut Rainbow saying "Derpy" but keep Derpy's voice.
3. Cut Rainbow saying "Derpy" and change Derpy's voice.
4. Find a creative way to change Derpy's name in a future episode.[42]

As that decision was being pondered, the Brony fandom noticed by January 30 that the episode had been removed from iTunes (but was still available to stream on the Hub's website).[43] The new version of the episode was released on iTunes on February 24, though the DVD compilation *The Friendship Express* released the following week retained the original cut.[44] (Considering that it was the first *My Little Pony: Friendship Is Magic* DVD release, it's a shame such a mediocre episode was included at all.)

The comments on the original "DERPY DERPY DERPY DERPY DERPY DERPY" post on January 21 slowed down in the days following the broadcast, though there was still discussion about the backlash. The following day, user Prophet of Ponies predicted that "several stay-at-home moms will complain to Hasbro that Derpy deeply offends their retarded sons. And then Derpy will be removed."[45] The baseline misogyny of that comment went uncommented upon, and mothers raising their children (such as episode writer Amy Keating Rogers, who had both a successful television career and a developmentally disabled son) would go on to be one of the main scapegoats. On January 23, user Ragemoar had this to say to the people who objected to the portrayal: "She's most likely just clumsy and very unlucky. And yeah her name is Derpy. Get over it. Stop complaining seriously."[46]

"Get over it" was the tenor shared by one of the two pro–Derpy petitions which appeared on Change.org by February 2, when Equestria Daily also reported that merchandise from the online store We Love Fine—which had begun selling licensed My Little Pony shirts and other items the previous summer—was being renamed on the site "to everything from Ditzy to nothing at all."[47] A petition credited to "Jakep Chellen" and titled "Keep Derpy Named Derpy" was not what one might call an exemplar of the love and tolerance which Bronies claimed to promulgate, and also failed to grasp that the point of a petition is to request an action, and not simply to grouse about another petition you don't like:

> I saw a petition that wanted to change Derpy's name back to Ditzy because it is "offensive" to the disabled. I think that naming this pony Derpy (which is a named that was created by the community) has helped unite the audience and the maker's of My Little Pony in an unique way. Derpy's name has no association with the mentally disabled and is just meant to be silly and fun, not insulting. Just relax and unclench your butthole people, jeese.[48]

The day's other petition, Andrew Holt's "Hasbro Studios/The Hub: Do not change Derpy's name" was closer to what a petition is supposed to be, and certainly less sphincter-oriented:

> "Derp" is not a slur against mentally disabled people. Derp is a word expressing messing something up, regardless of mental ability. There is absolutely nothing offensive about it, especially when Derpy was created by an error, or a "derp." Her character evolved entirely around that, making her a very ditzy pony, but NOT disabled.
>
> I am not offended by Derpy, and believe the name absolutely must stay. The voice was great for her as well, and should also stay. Keep the name![49]

The petition by "Jakep Chellen" was soon abandoned, capping out at 3,384 supporters, but Andrew Holt's continued to be updated. On February 4, he wrote that he'd emailed "Hasbro's PR asking for official clarification on the entire Derpy issue," but hadn't heard back yet.[50] In an update a few days later after a somewhat vague message from Hasbro which was relayed secondhand to Equestria Daily (and had nothing to do with the mare as such),[51] Holt wrote that he was shutting down the petition because "Derpy is safe, regardless of if it's because of us or not."[52] The next day, he reopened the petition, citing that many people were concerned about the petition being closed without any direct acknowledgment from Hasbro regarding the mare; he declared that he'd keep it going until they heard something, adding, "Please Hasbro, keep Derpy! With over 26,000 people supporting her, I think it's quite evident that we love her."[53]

Twenty-six thousand people is a statistical anomaly at best by corporate standards; in their Q4 2011 Earnings Conference Call earlier that month, Hasbro reported that while the Girls category didn't grow overall, My Little Pony had posted year-over-year gains—as did Baby Alive, which did not also have an "extremely unexpected" fanbase.[54] This is why it shouldn't have been too much of a surprise when Equestria Daily reported on February 24 that "The Last Roundup" had reappeared on iTunes with the young gray mare's voice changed, her eyes both facing forward, and Rainbow Dash no longer referring to her by any name.[55]

Regarding the changes, Amy Keating Rogers would later write:

> In the end, Derpy's voice was re-voiced to be more ditzy. And while, again, I had nothing to do with the casting, this is closer to the voice that was in my head. And as for cutting her name, if it truly can be defined as "retarded," then I am personally glad that name is gone. I wouldn't want my writing to perpetuate children—our target audience—to call other children "derpy" with that meaning behind it.[56]

On February 24, *Friendship Is Magic* animator Kreoss posted a plea for civility on his DeviantArt journal, in which he asked the Bronies to stop "pointing fingers and throwing hate around," and to try to show some respect and humility[57]:

> Oh I also want to address on a artist name Yamino. I've heard that she has been garnered a lot of hate by the Brony Community due to her not liking Derpy's portrayal. Let it be known, that she had NOTHING to do with the sudden change. She expressed an opinion on Derpy. That is all. She did not ask me to do this or anyone on the staff. I had to say this because the hate she's been receiving is unnecessary. So leave her be.[58]

It didn't work, and there may be no greater example of the tension between positivity and negativity on the Internet that while the January 21 Equestria Daily post about the gray mare speaking and being given an official name on the show received 1,573 comments, the February 24 post about her voice, name and eyes having been modified received 2,254 comments. Among the approximately 100,000 words in those comments were a great deal of anger toward Hasbro and iTunes, dire predictions of the end of the Brony fandom, a mere 46 uses of the word "retard," and many people blaming Yamino, even though all she did was state her negative opinion about the character beginning several months before the episode aired.[59] She received a number of death threats,[60] and later that year a Brony rapper scheduled to perform at a convention wrote a song in which he described murdering her in vivid detail.[61] But there was only one comparison to Hitler in the February 24 Equestria Daily thread, which is a low number by Internet argument standards:

If she did come across as "special" to you, the changes to make her appear more normal should be even more offensive, as it teaches that it is ok to hide or even get rid of "special" people. Go down that road long enough and what Hitler did, begins to seem less and less terrible, maybe even correct.[62]

User Dsludge evoked the Cold War rather than World War II, as well as the tyranny of the minority:

They didn't make it less offensive. It was never offensive to begin with. But by going in and revise everything Soviet style because of a very loud minority in the name of the Holy Political Correctness, THAT action was in itself very offensive.[63]

User Mystic described it as "chasing political correctness to pander to the minority,"[64] and keneticpest referred to their adversaries as "a minority of overly PC trolls."[65] References to the strawman of political correctness by other commenters included, "Another disgusting victory for over the top political correctness,"[66] "I'm merely disappointed that a potentially unique and sympathetic character was weakened because of PC douche-nags,"[67] "This edit is the epitome of what is wrong with this PC bullshit,"[68] and "I'm guessing the rage that's going to (or already has?) result from this change will make the original handful complaints from 'political correctness' fags seem like a speck of dust in comparison,"[69] to quote just a few of dozens, some of which were far more vulgar. Mothers who not only devoted their time to raising their children but possibly transported them to and from intramural sports events were also singled out, such as "god damn soccer moms,"[70] "We can't let soccer moms step on our right to express ourselves,"[71] "All this because some fucktard soccermoms could be offended?"[72] "the collective will of soccer mom's everywhere is hard to fight,"[73] and "To all the soccormothers of America, F*** YOU PARENTS!"[74]

Much of the controversy in the media over the very concept of Bronies stemmed from the narrative that the vast majority of *Friendship Is Magic* fans were grown-up adult men, a narrative that was never true but far easier to exploit—e.g., Brent Hodge marginalizing the presence of women in *A Brony Tale* because "there's nothing really off the wall about a ton of girls liking My Little Pony"—but this anger toward parents, and mothers in particular, suggests the presence of high school and college-age boys who were still far from anything approaching maturity.[75]

That the Bronies had asked for a thing to happen and yet it did *not* happen was also a cause of some consternation in the February 24 Equestria Daily thread; user Shine asked, "What about the petitions? Hasbro listens to a handful of trolls but ignores thousands of fans?"[76] Perhaps not aware of the already-extant petitions, Thecrazyrabbidfangirl spelled out the sense of entitlement that many Bronies were displaying: "We need to start a petition or something to get Hasbro's attention. I mean we're a better part of the fanbase than the intended audience. Even from a corporate stand point, who has more disposable income? Little girls or bronies?"[77] Though the official target demographic of My Little Pony has always been in flux, let's say that the intended audience is girls under 10 years old. According to the United States Census Bureau's *Population By Age and Sex: 2012* chart, there were 19,826,000 civilian, noninstitutionalized girls under the age of 10 that year.[78] Meanwhile, Andrew Holt's petition topped out at 44,395 signatures.[79] Now let's consider some hypotheticals: if only one out of every four people who identified as a Brony decided to take the three minutes out of their day to sign Holt's petition during the several weeks it was open, that would mean there were approximately 117,580 Bronies in early 2012. If only one out of ten girls under the age of 10 in the United States liked My Little Pony enough to convince their parents to shell out $5 at Walgreens for a doll, that would still be 1,982,600 little girls. In that respect, the original inclusion of Derpy in the episode can be viewed as "pandering to the minority," as Mystic put it, since the Bronies who were upset by no means constituted a majority of My Little Pony fans in 2012; at best they were, to use Shine's description of the opposition, a very loud minority.

For his part, Andrew Holt was flustered by the inefficacy of his petition, and pondered in the Equestria Daily comments:

> This is seriously not okay. The voice change is fine, but I feel like our petition did absolutely nothing to change their minds on the meaning of the word "Derp." Clearly, they still decided it was offensive. It was a beautiful name, and a beautiful shoutout to us, and now it's been taken away. My rage is pretty well eternal right now.[80]

Eternal though his rage may have been, he kept it in check in his February 25 update to his petition, in which he reminded everypony to "always be civil with Hasbro," and wrote that he'd be "taking a more personal approach to this," that he was going to "stand up and speak for the community, rather than letting the community's signatures speak for themselves," and most importantly, "We WILL be heard."[81] He was of course not the only Brony perplexed by the failure of the petitions to get them what they wanted; one of a handful of users who made rape comparisons on the Equestria Daily thread, GuerreroPerdido wrote, "After that huge petition? Really Hasbro? I don't care for the new voice. What I hate is that fact that they took away what they've given us as a gift. I feel violated."[82] Kyli Rouge was at least half-correct when they wrote, "This PROVES that the majority and petitions mean nothing."[83]

That same day, the creators of the "Make Amends for Hurtful Ableist Stereotype in My Little Pony" petition (which collected 136 signatures) declared themselves the ones who'd been heard, with an update titled "Hasbro and Studio B Heard Our Cries!"[84] They praised the fact that the "hateful name" had been removed and the voice re-recorded, but also admitted that they were ambivalent about the mare's eyes being straightened—further evidence that Equestria Daily commenter hyreia was right about one thing: It's impossible to please everypony.[85]

The following day, Andrew Holt changed the title of the petition from "Hasbro Studios/The Hub: Do not change Derpy's name" to "Return Derpy's scene in The Last Roundup to normal," and added three new paragraphs to the text of the petition, including that "we as a community feel as though our strongest connection to the creators of the show has been ripped apart," and that the edit "portrays a very negative message of 'you have to be perfect or you're not allowed to be seen.' A message, I might add, that feels completely against what the show normally teaches."[86] In an update to the petition's supporters, Holt acknowledged that altering the petition might prove controversial:

> I'm assuming I'll have no objections, but since changing a petition someone's already signed after it being signed has the slight potential to ruffle feathers, if I get even one message that someone's upset by the new title and message, I'll change it back.[87]

The petition remained unchanged and was closed the following month, so it's safe to assume that no feathers were ruffled, but it's worth noting that he was prepared to pander to a minority, even if it was a minority of one. It is far more consideration than was given to those who might have taken genuine offense at the portrayal of the gray mare and were dismissed by many as a minority of overly-PC soccer moms.

The battle between the minority and the majority was also a theme in a new petition by Andrew Shen directed to Hasbro Studios and the Hub, titled "Save Derpy (and Hasbro's creative process)."[88] In addition to requesting that the original cut of "The Last Roundup" be released, Shen also swore the allegiance of the Bronies in future battles:

> We will not tolerate the tyranny of the angered minority that believes it has the right to enact changes that affect the majority without consent. This leads us to our third point: if and when people attack you for your creations, we will defend you. We will fight on your behalf, doing whatever it takes to preserve the vision behind My Little Pony: Friendship is Magic. No matter how strong the opposition to your work, we will stand by you.
>
> We sincerely hope you understand the weight of that last point especially. Your fan base is willing to do so much to protect your creations. Our attachment to and love for My Little Pony: Friendship is Magic is too strong to allow the voices of the minority dictate the future of the show. While not all of us will like the result of your creative process, we fully support the process itself and the staff behind it.[89]

(Unless the staff is working on *My Little Pony: Equestria Girls*, in which case it would prove to be open season for attacks.) Furthering the notion that the

Bronies who were upset constituted a "majority," he signed the petition as "The collective viewership of My Little Pony: Friendship is Magic," which was presumptuous at best. He was speaking for a particular segment of the show's viewership, but hardly the entirety, or even a majority; between the broadcast of "The Last Roundup" and the posting of Shen's petition, "Hearts and Hooves Day" (S02E17) became *Friendship Is Magic's* highest-rated episode to date, with Nielsen reporting an audience of 316,000 children from 2–11 years of age.[90] Though not all Bronies were upset about the change to the gray mare, those who were did not qualify as the "collective viewership," and even if they had constituted over 50% of the viewers, that did not mean that the production of *Friendship Is Magic* was a direct democracy in which all of their hoof-stamping demands were required to be met.

But whether in spite of or due to the veiled threat to dogpile onto any-pony with differing opinions from themselves—particularly if they were perceived as a "minority"—Shen's petition gained 9,542 signatures.[91] It also had the benefit of being far more professional than the five new petitions which sprang into existence around that time: Justin Jurek's "Change Derpy Back" (40 signatures total),[92] Daniel Reinert's "Return Derpy Hooves! Name, voice, and eyes!" (69 signatures),[93] Kylen Taskovic's "WE WANT DERPY HOOVES'S NAME BACK!" (39 signatures),[94] Sarah Patterson's "No money for Hasbro until Derpy Hooves's name, voice and eyes are restored!" (575 signatures),[95] and Charles "Shuttershade" Rhue's "Do not alter Derpy in 'The Last Roundup,'" which garnered all of 7 signatures, and consisted of a single line: "Because the fandom is pissed and something needs to be done."[96] It should be reiterated that while all this was happening, it was known that the *Friendship Express* DVD due to be released a few days later—a physical piece of media which by definition had more permanence than an iTunes download—would contain the original version of the episode.[97] On the day the DVD was released, Gawker ran an article about the whole affair which included a quote from a Hasbro spokesperson:

> "The 'My Little Pony Friendship is Magic' series has always been about acceptance and inclusion, and the series strives to convey that through the playful antics of a diverse cast of characters," Hasbro spokeswoman Nicole Angello told us over email. "Some viewers felt that aspects of the episode 'The Last Roundup' did not stay true to the core message of friendship which is the heart and soul of the series. Hasbro Studios decided to make slight audio alterations to this single episode."[98]

That slightly altered version was the one released on the *My Little Pony: Friendship Is Magic Season 2* DVD in May 2013. Though there was some debate in the comments on Equestria Daily leading up to the release about whether or not buying the set amounted to supporting censorship, the furor had by and large died down in the intervening year.[99] The extent to which the war was fading into the mists of history made was clear in a post by Equestria Daily contributor Calpain the day before the DVD was released, titled "An Appeal to the Fandom: Keep Calm and Trot On."[100] The opening paragraph gave an overview of the Brony fandom's many and varied dramas over the years:

> Our fandom has seen its share of upheaval and drama this past half year or so with the coming of alicorn Twilight and the reveal of Equestria Girls. Not since the departure of Lauren Faust as executive producer back in the first season have I seen such unrest in the community, but unlike those times the way the fandom has handled this news has at times been not exactly ideal. We have spewed some vitriolic things at Hasbro for sure, but we have also done the same to the people who brought us ponies and made them what they are: the good folks at DHX.

For perspective, Lauren Faust left the show in 2011, and Twilight becoming an Alicorn in "Magical Mystery Cure" (S03E13) and the introduction of *Equestria Girls* both occurred in 2013. (And ours was not the only universe in which Twilight Sparkle evolving into an Alicorn was controversial; in the March 17 edition of the comic strip *Phoebe and Her Unicorn*, the young female protagonist Phoebe is troubled by the fact that the character of Boysenberry Swirl from her favorite television show *Pastel Unicorns* has now grown wings, which leads to her having to decide whether she wants to get an updated Boysenberry doll, further leading to her realizing that "Capitalism is weird."[101] The strip was later reprinted in the 2015 collection *Unicorn on a Roll*, for which Lauren Faust wrote the introduction.[102]) The gray mare drama of 2012 wasn't referenced until Calpain's second paragraph, and then only parenthetically as part of a larger point establishing the Bronies as the reason the show was being produced, and suggesting they would not enjoy the show as much if not for the shout-outs to that segment of the viewers:

> These folks for going on three years now have not only done the impossible and made those who would scoff at the MLP name ardent fans but have also shared in our enthusiasm and become part of the community in their own wonderful way. Never before have I seen such tight connections between the creators and the fans, a connection I fear without would have lessened many of our experiences (Derpy anyone?). This connection has been a feedback loop that fuels our passions as well as their own, making them work long into the nights on both weekdays and weekends to make the best things they can because they love what they do and they love seeing us react.[103]

Describing the hope of getting a positive reaction from the same Bronies who had "spewed some vitriolic things" as the primary reason the animators worked long hours, and not just because high-quality animation requires long hours, demonstrates the degree of entitlement many felt toward the show, though the overall point of the post was asking readers to cool off on their backlash against the production studio for the movie *My Little Pony: Equestria Girls*, which had not yet been released.

The only post–"Feeling Pinkie Keen" appearance of the gray mare to be altered was the iTunes and subsequent Season 2 DVD release of "The Last Roundup." She continued to appear, neither speaking nor spoken to but with her eyes misaligned to the Bronies' expectation, throughout the remainder of Season 2 after "The Last Roundup" in the far superior "The Super Speedy Cider Squeezy 6000" (S02E15), "Hearts and Hooves Day" (S02E17), "A Friend in Deed" (S02E18), "Putting Your Hoof Down" (S02E19), "Hurricane Flutter-shy" (S02E22), and "A Canterlot Wedding, Part 2" (S02E26). In June 2012, Hasbro announced the Special Edition Pony for the upcoming San Diego–Comic Con (a tradition dating back to the Pony Project during G3), describing her as "sure to be a fan favorite: Inspired by the animated series 'My Little Pony Friendship is Magic,' this gray, Pegasus pony features rooted blonde hair and a cluster of bubbles for a cutie mark."[104] For all of the stomping of hoof, gnashing of teeth, and reckless petitioning by a vocal minority of Bronies about the injustice of Hasbro making minor alterations to the iTunes version of "The Last Roundup," it is not insignificant that not only was the controversial gray mare that year's Special Edition Pony, but she was the *first* G4 Special Edition Pony.[105] The 2011 Special Edition Pony, though released after the completion of Season 1 of *Friendship Is Magic*, was a G3-style pony.[106] (Poor G3.5, overshadowed in both directions.) As had been the case with the press release, the gray mare was not given a name on her box; it was instead festooned with illustrations of muffins, which would continue to be used in lieu of the D-bomb in much of the officially licensed merchandise going forward.[107] Continuing the Equestria Daily trend of good news getting far less attention than bad, a May 28 article which reported the still-unconfirmed rumor of the gray mare being that year's exclusive received a mere 197 comments,[108] and a May 30 article confirming the rumor only received 306 comments, though contributor Cereal Velocity did ask in appropriate wonder, "We just totally made a toy, didn't we?"[109]

World War Derp, Part II: Muffins Triumphant

The production of the Special Edition gray mare doll marked a significant turning point for My Little Pony: it was no longer accurate to describe *Friendship Is Magic* as a show based on a toy. It never had been, as the original characters were conceived for the television show and the dolls were made from those models, but Original Sin had been too strong for the show to catch a break. Now, there was a toy which was incontrovertibly based on a character from the show, and not vice versa. This would not change the public perception, but there was now at least one case in which the show well and truly came before the toy horse.

The 13-episode Season 3 premiered on November 10, 2012, and she appeared in three of the first five episodes: "The Crystal Empire, Part 2" (S03E02), "Too Many Pinkie Pies" (S03E03), and "Magic Duel" (S03E305). She didn't appear in the next seven episodes, which was just enough time for yet another petition: Travis Tucker's "Return Derpy Hooves in season 4 of MLP: FiM," which was posted in the weeks between "Just for Sidekicks" (S03E11) and "Games Ponies Play" (S03E12), and garnered 2,396 supporters.[110] "Just for Sidekicks" and "Games Ponies Play" are the high point of the otherwise rocky Season 3, an interesting experiment in story structure in that the episodes take place at the same time: S03E12 picks up not where not where S03E11 left off, but at the end of that episode's first act, using 25 seconds of footage from S03E11 before diverging to tell its own story. There's no "Previously on My Little Pony" recap as in past two-parters, nor is it even labeled as a two-parter, there's no effort made in S03E12 to ground the viewer who may not have seen S03E11, and while the parallel plotlines intersect at the end of the S03E12, the full conclusion to *both* stories had already occurred in S03E11. It was a brave choice in a season that hadn't taken as many narrative chances as the previous two, but also not as important in some circles as what Tucker's petition referred to as "their disappointment of not seeing their favorite Easter Egg mare in the background of episodes."[111]

My Little Pony: Friendship Is Magic was not the only cartoon in which (certain) fans tended to focus on minutiae rather than what was actually happening on screen, nor was it the only show in which much of that was deliberate on the part of the producers. *Gravity Falls* completed its first season in August 2013, and creator Alex Hirsch has said that from the beginning he filled it with "crazy backwards messages and secret codes and puzzles" that he figured very few viewers would catch, but they did indeed: "Fans are a million times smarter than I am. I have learned that the hard way."[112] Dan Harmon and Justin Roiland's *Rick and Morty* debuted that December, and Harmon later explained that the producers had decided that there would be "a secret we keep from the audience forever"—and then, halfway through the first season, a fan on Reddit figured out what that secret was.[113] (Notably, neither Hirsch nor Harmon reported the audience getting angry because of them not putting in the Easter Eggs some fans demanded.)

The gray mare appeared in the controversial *Friendship Is Magic* Season 3 finale "Magical Mystery Cure" (S03E13) in which Twilight Sparkle evolves into a winged Alicorn Princess, and next in biped form in the even-more-controversial movie *My Little Pony: Equestria Girls*, in which the newly crowned Princess Twilight travels through a magic mirror and finds herself transformed into a biped, and surrounded by human versions of her friends and neighbors. In addition to being in the background of a few shots, the gray biped appeared at the end of the closing credits, swaying back and forth while holding a muffin. (At the *Equestria Girls* screening I caught, a nighttime showing mostly attended by families, a Brony in a gray hoodie stood and exhorted the audience to "clap if Derpy is your favorite!" Nopony but him clapped.) However, her presence in that episode and movie did nothing to allay the Brony outrage about the fact that either "Magical Mystery Cure" or *Equestria Girls* happened at all; in a "Worst Pony Drama So Far This Year?" poll on Equestria Daily that June, that episode and the movie received approximately 2,700 votes each, though they paled in comparison to the 6,568 votes for Hasbro's lawyers sending a cease-and-desist letter to the creators of a *Friendship Is Magic*–themed video game called *Fighting Is Magic*.[114] (The project was later revived under the name *Them's Fighting Herds*, with new, non–Pony-related art and characters provided by Lauren Faust.[115])

The gray mare didn't appear in Season 4 until "Rainbow Falls" (S04E10), in which she has a prominent role in the story and spends a fair amount of screentime alongside the Mane Six, though she still neither speaks nor is spoken to by name. The day of the broadcast, supervising director Jim Miller wrote on Twitter, "We avoided hiding that certain pony in any episodes before her return today to keep it more of a surprise."[116] She continued to appear sporadically throughout the rest of Season 4, including a significant role in the "Rainbow Falls" followup "Equestria Games" (S04E24), and her biped equivalent also had increased screentime in the second *Equestria Girls* film, *My Little Pony: Equestria Girls—Rainbow Rocks*. After appearing in a handful of episodes during the first third of Season 5, the gray mare finally spoke again in "Slice of Life" (S05E09). It was the 100th episode of *My Little Pony: Friendship Is Magic*, a remarkable achievement for any television series; of the other shows to premiere on the Hub's "Sneak Peek Sunday" on October 10, 2010, only *Strawberry Shortcake's Berry Bitty Adventures* lasted as long, but due to its abbreviated seasons and a far more erratic schedule including a hiatus between May 2013 and June 2014, that series only topped out at 65 episodes by the end of its fourth season, which ran concurrent with *Friendship Is Magic*'s fifth season.[117] *Transformers: Prime*, the extensive program-length commercial history of which was ignored by outlets like the *Wall Street Journal* and Cartoon Brew in favor of raising an alarm about a new culture-ruining My Little Pony series, was canceled after three seasons.[118] In the negative column, "Slice of Life" was not good.

It's a solid concept, focusing on the background characters in preparation for a wedding between two other background characters, but it doesn't feel like a *Friendship Is Magic* episode, and with good reason. On a panel at the MLP-MSP convention immediately after the broadcast of the episode on June 13, 2015, writer M.A. Larson described how "Slice of Life" came to be. Assigned to write the episode, originally conceived as Princess Twilight taking somepony on a tour of Ponyville and/or Equestria, Larson said that he didn't want to do it, because as far as he was concerned there *were* no background characters.[119] As he told the assembled Bronies, "They're not characters, they're designs—to you guys, they're characters, but to us, Lyra is just a green pony.... Background Pony #2, that's who she is to me."[120] Unable to break the story on an organic level, Larson said he finally realized when he was far behind schedule that "this is clearly a Brony episode, there's no way around that, so let's just go for it—do a Brony episode and put in every single character" created by the Bronies.[121] It is significant that for as much as some Bronies tended to act like the show revolved around them and what *they* wanted it to be, it was desperation that resulted in Larson using their ideas. Earlier that week, Larson had Tweeted that "shipping," in which viewers imagine fictional characters in a show as being in a relationship, "is a FAN thing. None of us care about it."[122] Supervising director Jim Miller chimed in later that morning: "I have ZERO interest in fan ships. The show isn't about who should be with whom."[123] This is not to suggest that Larson, Miller, and other producers of the show didn't have a strong relationship with the Bronies—again, Larson was on a panel at a convention immediately after the broadcast of the episode, and the cast and crew regularly interacted with them on social media and elsewhere—but it also demonstrated that the Bronies may not have had as much influence as some chose to believe.

The net result is that "Slice of Life" feels like Brony fan-fiction, and for those who find such things unreadable, it can render the episode well-nigh unwatchable. But only one unwatchable episode out of 100 is not a bad ratio, and it never crossed my mind to harass the production staff because this particular episode was not what this particular viewer wanted the show to be.

The entirety of "Slice of Life" was fanservice to the Bronies, and the gray mare was involved in the plot and had plenty of dialog—though Tabitha St. Germain's high-pitched, childish voice for the character would have been more appropriate for *My Little Pony 'n' Friends* than *Friendship Is Magic*—but there was still backlash about her being referred to in the closing credits as Muffins, not Derpy. Not even the fact that "Muffins" came from the Bronies' decision to give her a muffin fixation eased the blow. (For some, being a fan means never having to compromise.) Equestria Daily commenter CMC_Scootaloo blamed their arch-nemeses the soccer moms, while making up a rule on the spot which proved that just because Muffins was the gray mare's name on screen, that didn't make it real[124]:

> Her official name is still "Derpy," not "Muffins." That they replaced her name with "Muffins" is just censoring from Hasbro's side because it is anxious over using the name after the pressure the soccer moms put on it during Season 2. And a placeholder name invented out of censorship can and is never be official.[125]

(By that logic, the name of the video game *Pac-Man* is an unofficial placeholder, since it was changed in the United States from its original Japanese title *Puck-Man* because "puck" was too close to "fuck."[126]) One Brony on Twitter railed against the "executive meddling" which they were sure was responsible for the gray mare's name being Muffins,[127] and episode director Jim Miller responded:

> She's been that name on products for a couple years now. Also, legal reasons that I don't understand.[128] And just because YOU don't like or understand why a decision was made, doesn't mean it was executive 'meddling.'[129]

When the Brony accused Miller of the unethical debate practice of "goalpost moving,"[130] Miller became the new hero of this book:

> Seriously? You think that's what this is? Gimme a break. You asked if you needed to worry about "executive meddling." Based on[131] my ACTUAL EXPERIENCE WORKING ON THE SHOW, there was NO executive meddling.[132]

Her name had indeed been Muffins on products for a couple years by then, pictographically or otherwise. Similar to how her Special Edition Pony for the 2012 San Diego Comic-Con box was festooned with muffins, in September 2013 a Soaring Pegasus Set went on sale at Kmart which included her, Fluttershy, and Thunderlane, a male pony who'd had a few lines in "Hurricane Fluttershy" (S02E22).[133] Fluttershy and Thunderlane were listed by name on the front of the box, the gray mare was again represented by a muffin, and the product description sidestepped the issue: "This 3-character set includes Fluttershy and Thunderlane figures for fast-trotting fun, and another pony figure."[134] A trucker hat with her face listed as "My Little Pony Muffins" appeared on Amazon in August 2014,[135] as did a My Little Pony–branded version of the Game of Life with her on the cover, the product description of which said it had "4 colorful collectible ponies: Dr. Hooves, Twilight Sparkle, Muffins, DJ Pon-3."[136] She even got a possessive credit when Muffins' Blueberry Muffin Flavored Lip Balm went on sale in January 2015.[137] (To quote Glenn Lovell: Yeee-uk!)

The Bronies treated the name "Muffins" the way much of the media continued to treat the word "Brony," as something inexplicable and without precedent in scare quotes that didn't fit into their worldview and needed to be poked at with a stick because what does that word even *mean*, anyway? When the UK Build-a-Bear website announced in August 2015 that Muffins was available as an online exclusive, Equestria Daily's headline was "Derpy Hooves Hits Build a Bear Site as Web Exclusive—Vinyl Scratch 'Coming Soon.'"[138] Though the Build-a-Bear graphic embedded in the post described her as "MY LITTLE PONY MUFFINS—a fan favourite!," Equestria Daily founder Sethisto was not fooled:

> Build a Bear fans finally have a Derpy to acquire. "Muffins" has officially hit their online store.[139]

Commenter CMC_Scootaloo, still smarting from the forces of darkness (a.k.a. the soccer moms) having forced the gray mare's name to be Muffins in "Slice of Life" two months earlier, shared their own ongoing trauma:

> I makes me incredibly sour to see the name "Muffins" for Derpy officially pop up in merchandise now. Every time I see it, it gives a stab in my heart, giving me the feeling that those senseless haters and overprotective moms from three years ago have won a partial victory. That they stripped Derpy off of her name.
>
> All these years and yet this cowardry by Hasbro, giving in to a literal number of 10 or 20 haters, as opposed to hundreds of supporters of Derpy, of her name and everything that has to do with her, is still there.[140]

So much pain, and for a Build-a-Bear doll which would not bear *either* name. If one were to take the built doll and show it to somepony who was neither one of the "10 or 20 haters" or "hundreds of supporters"—a modest estimate, quite a bit down from the tens of thousands cited by Bronies in the past to posit themselves as the righteous majority—but rather a member of the vast public who neither knows nor cares anything about *Friendship is Magic* or the attendant dramas and told them the pony's name was Derpy *or* Muffins, they would most likely shrug and roll with it either way.

The most graceful way to react to the Build-a-Bear announcement would have been to remember what Cereal Velocity had said when it was confirmed that there would be any merchandise of the gray mare at all: "We just totally made a toy, didn't we?"[141] But it was rare for the response to be one of grace or gratitude—instead, it was often anger because things were not exactly how the Bronies wanted them to be.

The gray mare affair was by no means the first time that a fandom, or at least a segment thereof, had reacted in a way that could be seen as inconsistent with the core values of the property they love. In 1995, the *Star Trek: Deep Space Nine* episode "Rejoined" featured a kiss between two women; to be precise, they were members of an alien species called the Trill who, for complicated science fiction reasons, had been husband and wife in past lives. That they were now both women, or at least occupying cisgender female bodies, was not a problem for their species, and never addressed in the context of the story. However, it was a problem for many of the *homo sapiens* watching the show; as executive producer Ira Steven Behr is reported to have told *Star Trek: Deep Space Nine—The Official Poster Magazine*:

> I know they [Paramount Pictures] got a lot of negative feedback, which only goes to prove a point I always believed in, which is that science fiction fans and *Star Trek* fans are much more conservative than people want to believe, and this whole Gene Roddenberry liberal Humanistic vision is truly not shared by a significant portion of them.[142]

Working together, fans of a pop culture franchise can accomplish good things. Brony conventions tend to be non-profit organizations with a strong charity aspect; the 2012 Everfree Northwest convention's charity auction raised $13,535 for the Seattle Children's Hospital,[143] for example, and the BronyCon 2015 auction brought in $30,645 for CureSearch, a charity dedicated to curing children's cancer.[144] In July 2011, less than two months after the end of Season 1, users on Ponychan decided to find a charity to support.[145] This led to the formation of Bronies for Good, which organized a blood drive that September,[146] and as of early 2016 continues to facilitate donations to worthy causes.[147] (Because it was on the Internet, there was still a political argument in the initial Ponychan thread that resulted in one Brony telling another to go fuck themselves.[148])

But a television series cannot change human nature, nor does it only attract those who share its politics or worldview. It can have a positive influence on individuals, such as the gentleman with Aspergers whose testimonial in the *Wired* article Amid Amidi had found so hilarious and *Onion*-y, but when coupled with the anonymity of the Internet and the impetuousness of so many (mostly) young (mostly) men, it can result in a culture in which death threats get tossed around like they're no big deal.

In a way, the whole sorry affair can be viewed as a definitive refutation of the fears stoked by the December 1984 *New York Times* article "Toy Makers Frolic in Fantasy Land," and its dire warnings that pre-packaged backstories for toys might weaken the imagination.[149] The gray mare alternatively known as either Ditzy, Derpy, or Muffins was a creation of the collective Brony imagination, and though they tended to be teenagers and older, they still grew up in the backstory era, though many likely played with (as Craig McCracken put it) Star Wars junk rather than My Little Pony junk, since most Bronies made their disdain for all pre–G4 Pony graphically clear. (And imagination doesn't become any less important as a grown-up; if it did, then there wouldn't be millennia of fiction written by adults.) The danger instead becomes not that the end user won't be able to use their imagination to create new stories and characters, but that they will instead get angry when, on the off-chance that their creations are acknowledged by the producers and incorporated into the work, the representation is not exactly how they had imagined it to be. Not that they're any happier when the franchise goes in a new direction that they have nothing to do with.

No (Equestria) Girls Allowed, Part I: Two-Legged Terror, and Daily v. Girls, Round 1

The law of pop-culture thermodynamics which states that My Little Pony cannot exist, or be announced to soon exist, without somepony being angry about the fact of its existence was demonstrated once again in mid–2013 with the introduction of *Equestria Girls*. It was also the first time that a significant portion of those waiting with knives out was a segment of the existing fanbase.

The first inkling that a storm was coming occurred in December 2012, when Hasbro registered two trademarks for "Equestria Girls": serial number #85804403, for "Toy ponies and accessories for use therewith"[150]; and serial number #85805634 for both "Entertainment services, namely an on-going animated television series for children," and "Dolls, doll clothing and doll accessories."[151] That March, a *New York Times* article about classic toy ranges being redesigned to appeal to modern youth (a theme that was also popular a decade prior around the launch of Generation 3) described Hasbro as having revamped My Little Pony as "a lifestyle brand, with 200 licenses in 15 categories, including publishing, apparel, bedding and digital gaming" as a response to the rise of the Bronies.[152] In addition to not being true, this demonstrates the extent to which the media insisted on conflating the Bronies with the larger customer base or the show's very existence. Hasbro had been referring to My Little Pony as a "lifestyle" brand since G3, and three days before the premiere of *Friendship Is Magic* the company boasted of already having "nearly 150 licensees onboard in 2010 to bring MY LITTLE PONY-branded products to the global marketplace ranging from apparel to publishing, arts & crafts, school supplies, domestics, and collectibles,"[153] all back when the most recent definition of "Brony" on Urban Dictionary was a "brophony."[154]

The *Times* article was also one of the first references in the media to *Equestria Girls*: "To celebrate the brand's 30th anniversary this year, the company plans to introduce a new extension this fall called Equestria Girls."[155]

(In fact, there wound up being very little attention paid to the 30th anniversary; perhaps because it was so soon after The My Little Pony Project: 25 Ponies for 25 Years, Hasbro focused on the 30th anniversary of Transformers instead.[156]) The article also included one of the first publicly released *Equestria Girls* images: the Mane Six standing next to humanized versions of each of themselves, the bipeds sporting pony ears, long, mane-like hair, and in the case of Fluttershy, Rainbow Dash, and Princess Twilight, wings. Twilight had achieved her wings in the Season 3 finale "Magical Mystery Cure" (S03E13) the month before, though the pony lacked them in the *Times* picture, which was clip art from Season 1. The illustrations of the bipeds—hereafter referred to as the Rainbooms, the name of their band in *My Little Pony: Equestria Girls—Rainbow Rocks*—were far more detailed and fashion-oriented than they would appear in the *My Little Pony: Equestria Girls* movie that summer; in addition to having their Cutie Marks on their cheeks, they appear to be wearing makeup—most noticeable is the lipstick on Rainboom Applejack, which pony Applejack would find abhorrent. (Onscreen, Rainboom Applejack's disdain for fashion or even caring about how she's dressed is equal to her Mane Six counterpart, and will reach a boiling point in *Rainbow Rocks*, which puts her and the fashion-minded Rarity at odds to an extent not seen since their pony counterparts in "Look Before You Sleep" [S01E08].)

Those illustrations would be used on the backs of the boxes of the first set of *Equestria Girls* dolls, and the dolls themselves would look very little like the illustrations or the animated characters. This gulf between the appearance (and personality characteristics) of the dolls and the animated characters they represent has been present since the first wave of G4 / Year One (2010), such as the Fashion Style Applejack who "has found the perfect outfit to wear while apple picking" including "pretty barrettes and her favorite cowgirl hat."[157] The toy-universe characters had always been into fashion and general frivolity in a manner that was incongruous with the show-universe characters, but until *Equestria Girls*, they had never been presented in such a high-profile way that didn't make a distinction between the toys and the show, let alone in their initial announcement; the first images of *Friendship Is Magic* characters in *Advertising Age* in May 2010 had been of Twilight Sparkle and Pinkie Pie in Ponyville, with art taken directly from the show.[158] But nopony was paying close attention to such details in mid–2010, and details have always been of a secondary concern to critics of My Little Pony. Yet this disconnect between the show and the toys need not be considered a bad thing; Lauren Faust had rejected both the character descriptions on the boxes as well as the stories in *My Little Pony 'n' Friends* to imagine a whole new universe as a child, one which she later used as the basis of *Friendship Is Magic*.[159]

Those initial Rainboom illustrations were used again against a backdrop of Canterlot High in a May 12 *New York Times* piece dedicated to *Equestria Girls* titled "A New Direction for a Hasbro Stalwart," the online version of which also included the official trailer for the film, slated to be released "in more than 200 theaters nationwide."[160] The opening paragraph referred to it as Hasbro's "next summer blockbuster" after their recent *Transformers* and *G.I. Joe* movies, but even though the My Little Pony brand was more popular than ever, 200 theaters did not qualify as a blockbuster release pattern in 2013.[161] (The brand was also referred to as "a Hasbro staple for 30 years," which it hadn't been for 10 of those years.)[162] Like *A Very Minty Christmas* and its G3 followups, the theatrical release of *My Little Pony: Equestria Girls* was little more than a precursor to the subsequent DVD release and now Hub broadcast, though unlike the G3 films, *Equestria Girls* was not always booked to play for single matinee shows on Saturdays and Sundays throughout the month, or even consecutive weekends.

The movie would go on to play in ten theaters throughout the state of Tennessee on the weekends of June 22–23 and July 13–14, but in San Francisco it was only scheduled to play on Saturday, June 22, and Tuesday, June 25, at the small Balboa Theatre, and again at the AMC Metreon 16 multiplex on Saturday, July 13.[163] By July 1, new dates were added "due to the success of My Little Pony: Equestria Girls in theaters," including another showing at the Balboa on the evening of Tuesday, July 9, where I was finally able to see it.[164] Meanwhile, for reasons that surely made sense to the spreadsheets of distributor Screenvision, the picture received a traditional theatrical distribution in the Michigan towns of Birch Run, Canton, Novi, Rochester Hills, Royal Oak and Woodhaven, screening every day from June 16 to July 14.[165] Hasbro later confirmed that the film had a "theatrical launch on 360 screens," a figure which most likely included the July expansion.[166]

As was always the case with My Little Pony, debates were raging about this new iteration of the franchise well before it was released. The official My Little Pony account on Facebook linked to the *New York Times* article on May 12, using the same graphic.

> We are proud to introduce My Little Pony Equestria Girls! Learn all about the magical parallel universe with high schools instead of castles, where six pony friends become real girls with a love for fun and fashion in the The New York Times.[167]

However many people reading the Gray Lady's web presence who were at all emotionally invested in My Little Pony is impossible to gauge because the *Times* article wisely lacked a comment section, but far more of them must have seen the Facebook post, which received 1,094 mostly-negative comments in its first six hours. Both the *Times* article and the Facebook post failed to make the distinction between the dolls and the cartoon, and that this early description and images were representative of the ancillary *Equestria Girls* dolls, not of how they would appear or behave in the eventual movies. Also not clarified is that the Rainbooms would only appear in the spinoff movies, and not be integrated directly into *Friendship Is Magic*. But the reference to the setting being "a magical parallel universe" had less of an impact than the phrase "six pony friends become real girls with a love for fun and fashion."[168] Those became fighting words, the most inflammatory being that second F-bomb, to which Hannah F. commented, "No thank you. The last thing we need is another show that promotes unhealthy stereotypes for young girls. Then there's the implication that real girls have to have a love for fashion? Yeah. No."[169] Jade-Elise N. saw a dichotomy where none had been hinted at: "Passion for fashion instead of teaching girls morals and the value of friendship and being thoughtful of others. Bah!!! Modern society sucks."[170] (Rarity represents the Element of Generosity, which is the very definition of being thoughtful of others, and she has a passion for fashion and is also the best, but pick pick.) Maria C. wrote, "Hasbro, you pretty much just murdered the entire concept that made MLP:FiM so great in the first place. Congratulations."[171]

Many parents swore they would keep it from their children, and some conflated the Rainbooms with Furries, such as Rachel C., who wrote: "I liked My Little Pony because they weren't super skinny sexualized characters like so many other shows and toys aimed at girls. Way to ruin it not to mention fetishize it. Furries? Pony Girls? What are you thinking? I will not let my daughter watch any such version of MLP. This is such a disappointment."[172] Kama O. chimed in with, "Uhhh wow. Yeah sorry my husband and I are completely weirded out by this and no way are we letting our six year old watch it. WTH like you really needed to strengthen the ties with the Furry fetish people?!"[173] "I follow MLP because my 3 and 5 year old daughters like it. This is like a gross cross between Bratz and weird furry stuff," wrote Karen M.[174]

In fact, *Equestria Girls* was of no interest to the Furry fandom, which is an appreciation of *animals* behaving in human ways, not *humans* behaving in human ways. The "What Is Furry?" introductory brochure from the 2016 Anthrocon, the world's largest Furry convention, pointedly referenced one Pony universe but not the other:

The word "anthropomorphic" (literally "human-shaped") refers to animals or objects given human characteristics. Anthropomorphic animals include everything from the gods of ancient Egypt with their dog, cat, and crocodile heads, to the tool-using characters of the

Sonic the Hedgehog video games, to the talking ponies of the *My Little Pony: Friendship Is Magic* television series.[175]

Having attended the Furry convention Further Confusion in San Jose regularly in the early-to-mid 2010s, as well as the nightclub Frolic in San Francisco, I saw a great deal of *Friendship Is Magic* artwork and costuming—including full fursuits of Rainbow Dash and Muffins—but nothing from the *Equestria Girls* films after 2013, and I saw nopony else wearing replicas of the ears and tails that Rainboom Rarity had made for her fellow students during her Freshman year to show their Canterlot Wondercolt Pride.

Many others in the May 12 Facebook comments referenced Bratz, such as Kimberly K.: "Sweet valley high meets bratz dolls meets MLP? Say it ain't so! Granted, I have a toddler so we aren't the target audience at all, but no. Just no."[176] *Equestria Girls* was also accused of being not only a Bratz but also a Monster High clone, such as Mary C.'s statement, "This just seems like another 'Bratz' or 'Monster High' concept, and if that's the case, as much as I live MLP:FIM, this spinoff will not be welcome in my house,"[177] or Mario B.'s free-associative murmur, "My little girl loves ponies not this.... This is just a copy of monster high and brats.. and all others.. what makes MLP unique is that everypony loves it."[178] Monster High in particular would continue to be a lazy but persistent comparison to *Equestria Girls* long after the difference between the two had become clear.

My Little Pony: Friendship Is Magic story editor and *My Little Pony: Equestria Girls* screenwriter Meghan McCarthy was quoted in the May 12 *New York Times* article that "Our goal is to stay true to who those characters are," and that while the setting of a high school allowed for new storytelling possibilities, "it's still an extension of our mythology."[179] The expansion of storytelling possibilities would indeed flourish with the *Rainbow Rocks* and *Friendship Games* films, which would prove to surpass the *Friendship Is Magic* seasons that immediately preceded them.

It was also clarified that to "maintain continuity, Hasbro retained the same creative talent, animation style and message of friendship."[180] Most controversially, Hasbro's Chief Marketing Officer John Frascotti said that with the launch of *Equestria Girls*, "We are responding to the desire by our fans to experience the brand in more ways."[181] That statement was one of many things which angered many Bronies, who once again interpreted "fans" to mean "themselves" and nopony else. As user Benschachar reacted to Frascotti's statement when it was reposted on Equestria Daily, "Worst. Misunderstanding. Ever."[182] User Sweetiebot commented, "Show of hands. Who were the ones that 'desired'?"[183] Millstone attempted to bring some perspective: "Reminder: We are not the target demographic. Not with the show. Not with the books. Not with the c…. Okay, the comics are by bronies for bronies. Not with this movie either."[184] The horror of Bronies having to contend with increased femininity was invoked by Chimakara:

> Well ok. The animation, the writing, the music, and the characters we love will still be there in the movie. But ugh, I don't think that'll be enough for me to want to go anywhere near it. Judging from the trailer, the plot of the movie has a Sabrina the Teenage Witch kind of feel. All the characters are really feminized, and I wouldn't have become a brony if MLP:FiM was so overly girly in the first place.
>
> But hey, maybe this is just Hasbro's way of saying, "Yeah we know their's lots of grown adults that enjoy the show, but the target demographic, little girls, will always be our top priority."[185]

Dyxid, meanwhile, began to ponder whether the Cartoon Brew wag who may or may not have been the catalyst for Bronies existing had a point in the first place:

> I wonder if this would be an appropriate time for someone to make an "AMID AMIDI WAS RIGHT" button? Twilicorn was blatant enough, but it seems Equestria Girls is bound and determined to take MLP back to it's branlessly girly toy-pusher days.[186]

Regarding Twilight becoming an Alicorn as being a "blatant" move by Hasbro to take the franchise "back to it's branlessly girly toy-pusher days," the first toys of her with wings appeared during G4 / Year Four (2013) in the Princess Twilight Sparkle and Rainbow Dash set from the Crystal Princess Celebration line; it was a direct reference to the events of "Magical Mystery Cure" (S03E13), although the Crystal Empire didn't factor into that story.[187] There were several different toy variations on Twilight Sparkle up to that point, many of which were off-model from the character on *Friendship Is Magic*: the Riding Along with Twilight Sparkle figure from G4 / Year Two (2011) featured her on a scooter with a pet cat, neither of which were from the show[188]; Traveling Twilight Sparkle from G4 / Year Three (2012) included a pet dog, which, again, she does not have on *Friendship Is Magic* (and which bears no resemblance to Applejack's pet Winona, the only dog on the show)[189]; and also from G4 / Year Three was the Twilight Sparkle RC Car, which is described as a car used by Twilight to run errands for Princess Cadance and Shining Armor's wedding from "A Canterlot Wedding, Part 2" (S02E26), though internal combustion vehicles don't exist in Equestria, and in the episode itself she's too busy trying to save Equestria from a Changeling invasion to "pick up flowers or a cake for the wedding" as suggested by the product description.[190] And yet, both Twilight Sparkle becoming an Alicorn and the introduction of the spinoff were now regarded as the worst kind of moneymongering.

Two days later came Calpain's "Keep Calm and Trot On" post, in which they exhorted the Brony fandom to perhaps exhibit a little grace in their anger, particularly after it had been confirmed that *My Little Pony: Equestria Girls* was being produced by DHX, the studio that co-produced *Friendship Is Magic* along with Hasbro Studios:

> Word has been going around that since the trailer for Equestria Girls was released, and us learning that DHX was behind the movie, that attacks have been made on the competency, the commitment, and ability of the staff to pull this off. This wave of negativity, compounded surely by the months of them nervously waiting on our reactions, has apparently gotten more than a few members of DHX disheartened and possibly considering leaving the show (MLP or EqG). While I can understand that change is scary and that it can be easy to let emotions run high and say what comes to mind, the negativity has a real life impact, something I can relate to very much as of late.[191]

The post received 1,538 comments, the majority of which made it clear that no, they would *not* lay off the negativity about this movie that they knew little about and wouldn't see for another month—and in some cases, they stated that they would make a point of *not* seeing it, in order to express their displeasure at its existence. A sub-debate was the morality of sending death threats to the people working on *Equestria Girls*, Andrew Shen's promise that the Bronies would defend Hasbro Studios and fully support their creative process even if "not all of us will like the result of your creative process" being long forgotten.[192]

A particularly telling exchange started with user MoppyPuppy stating, "I'm not going to enjoy Equestria Girls simply because someone at DHX will cry if I don't."[193] User z55177 replied, not unreasonably: "You're not getting the point. You're not supposed to enjoy anything. Hate it all you want. Just don't send death-threats to people who work on the show and their families."[194] HMS_Celestia stepped in with a chilling but telling comment in which he defended sending death threats:

> True, true, but what then? Death threats never meant anything on the internet, they never amount to anything. Whoever sent them might have just been trying to make US look bad. I'm not going to care about this issue at all unless the staff is truly spooked, which they shouldn't be. They have to understand, there is a whole contingent of our fandom that freely and willingly talks about rape and murder in the pony/human mutliverse like it's practically nothing … there are bad parts, I don't know why it's suddenly an issue now that something happened that we knew was going to happen anyways.[195]

MrOptimist666 took a similar stance, both minimizing the possibility of death threats having been made in the first place, and shaming the victims for being troubled by having their life threatened:

> Is this supposed to make me feel guilty for hating EG? Because it isn't working. The people at DHX need to grow a spine if their gonna cry about this. I'm not trying to justify any death threats that they might have received (though I think you people are over exaggerating about that), but if you're an adult you shouldn't take that shit to heart (or seriously).

Thirteen months earlier, a man was sentenced to more than 10 years in prison for threatening the creators of *South Park* for an episode in which the prophet Muhammad (peace be upon him) was depicted as wearing a bear costume. *South Park's* creators could not have been surprised by the response to the episode; *Equestria Girls'* creators had every reason to be surprised.[196] "That's just how fans are, get over it" is not and never will be an acceptable excuse for threats of violence. Not all Bronies were so callous, of course, nor even necessarily a majority—indeed, it was almost certainly that dreaded "minority" of Bronies who were reacting in such a manner. But there were still enough, and doing so loudly enough, that Calpain's "Keep Calm and Trot On" post was necessary in the first place.

A debate also raged about whether or not *Equestria Girls* was canon, and how that would affect their feelings about DHX as well as Hasbro. There were many bursts of what can be best described as faux-magnanimity, such as RDisBestPony writing, "I'm just going to pretend it's a bad fanfic (which I can do so long as it never becomes canon). I completely forgive DHX, the voice actors, etc. because they are just doing what they are told to, but Hasbro forced the bad premise on them, so it's Hasbro's fault."[197] Squidward Tentacles wrote, "I'm willing to forgive Hasbro for Equestria Girls and pretend it never happened, but if this becomes cannon, and they put humans in Equestria for Season 4, I will go Apeshit."[198] (Except for the part about going apeshit, I do sympathize; I choose to believe that "Slice of Life" [S05E09] didn't happen.) The same user also weighed in on the death threats: "Wow Death threats is going too far. Just tell them that Equestria Girls is shit and don't watch their movie."[199] To restate, the movie for which they were recommending their fellow Bronies tell the production studio that also made their ostensible favorite television cartoon is "shit" and that they would not watch was something which would not be watchable for another month.

My Little Pony was not the last Hasbro property born in the 1980s for which the announcement of a feature film resulted in death threats from so-called fans; the day after his live-action adaptation of *Jem and the Holograms* was released in October 2015, director John M. Chu reported during a speech at the Film Independent Forum that "I get fans sending me hate mail, I get death threats, I get racist remarks."[200] As with *Equestria Girls*, it was for a film they hadn't yet seen—and, perhaps not coincidentally, a movie that was for and about young girls.

Lauren Faust, long separated from the production of the show, weighed in with her feelings about the *Equestria Girls* dolls with three Twitter posts on May 27. The first was an image of the dolls[201]; the second was 31 emoticons: ">:(>:(

>:(>:(>:(>:(>:(>:(>:(>:(>:("[202]; the third was a drawing of herself turning into the Incredible Hulk, i.e., getting very angry indeed.[203] Like the original, fashion-oriented images released by the *New York Times*, the first run of *Equestria Girls* dolls bore little resemblance to how the characters would appear in the film, and movie-accurate dolls which reflected the appearance and personalities of the individual characters would not become available for another two and a half years.[204]

On May 30, Hasbro released an official description of the film:

> When a crown is stolen from the Crystal Empire, Twilight Sparkle pursues the thief into an alternate world where she transforms into a teenage girl who must survive her biggest challenge yet ... high school. With help from her new friends who remind her of Ponyville's Applejack, Rarity, Rainbow Dash, Pinkie Pie and Fluttershy, she embarks upon a quest to find the crown and change the destiny of these two parallel worlds.[205]

It was one of the few descriptions of the film or the *Equestria Girls* brand overall which tried to make the distinction that other than Princess Twilight, the Rainbooms and the Mane Six were *not* the same individuals, and whose bodies had been transformed. However, the narrative of "the ponies have been turned into sexy teenagers" was already firmly entrenched, becoming the latest example My Little Pony destroying the culture, and the shapes of the characters having a deleterious effect on the current generation of young girls. Nicole Lyn Pesce's June 13 *New York Daily News* article quoted many mothers who were as angry about *Equestria Girls* as the commenters on Equestria Daily, providing a common enemy for Bronies and soccer moms to rally against, though the soccer moms likely made far fewer threats (death or otherwise) against the animators.[206]

The article described the G4 pony characters as being "flirtier foals with longer legs, oversized anime eyes and skinnier frames" compared to past iterations.[207] Hasbro's marketing director Donna Tobin explained that depicting the ponies as people would help kids "empathize with the characters," even as bipeds wearing in-vogue short skirts, but that "it's still all about the power of Pony, just now in a different form that allows them to do different things in this parallel universe that they can't do in Ponyville," and that parents "can feel assured that they can know and trust us."[208] Storytelling possibilities were of less importance to the critics than the appearance of the characters, though by this point the trailer and many images had been released showing that the Rainbooms appeared far less coquettish in the film than in the original images. A mother of a 4-year-old fan was quoted in the *New York Daily News* as saying, "I hope to God she never hears about this movie." Another mother, a collector of G1 ponies, argued that "they're not ponies anymore! So what's the appeal?" and that "these look more like Bratz dolls."[209] While the header image of the article was a still from the movie *My Little Pony: Equestria Girls*, it is likely that she was reacting to the dolls, not to how the characters appear in the film.

The bare-naveled, pouty-lipped and makeup-heavy Bratz dolls had been something of a foe since the G3 launch when Cheryl McCarthy, though not citing that doll range by name, had announced that new vision for My Little Pony was of a "magical and innocent world for young girls, with no makeup, no belly buttons, just My Little Pony."[210] As samey as the original *Equestria Girls* dolls had been, the only resemblance they bore to either the Bratz or the more recent Monster High line was that they were dolls of teenage girls wearing brightly colored clothes, boots, and skirts which, yes, could stand to be longer. Unlike the Bratz dolls (which your author finds repulsive, and hopes she never has to look at again after writing this book), the *Equestria Girls* dolls do not have grotesquely oversized lips (seriously, the mouths of the Bratz dolls are nothing less than nauseating), their eye makeup is far subtler, and perhaps the most significant difference of all is that they are smiling. The *Equestria Girls* dolls look friendly in a way that the mean-girl Bratz and Monster High dolls do not, and had they been released without the baggage of the My Little Pony brand, it is unlikely they would have caused as much of an uproar. On the other hand, had they not been related to My Little Pony, the *Equestria Girls* dolls would not have featured pony ears, which would have been a shame.

On Slate, Amanda Marcotte went for the darker, you-know-you-were-thinking-it route in a June 13 article titled "Triumph of the Bronies: Hasbro Turning My Little Ponies into Sexy Human Characters. *Neigh*."[211] After describing *My Little Pony: Friendship Is Magic* as having "done really well for a kid's TV show established just to sell more plastic toys," and ruminating on the "baffling choice" to introduce yet another line of biped dolls into a market already full of them, she went in for the kill[212]:

> But what if the change wasn't about little girls at all? What if there was another audience—an older, male, and kind of off-putting audience—that also loves the Ponies and wants nothing more than imagery of them as humans to appeal to their less-than-innocent fantasies about really getting personal with their favorite toys? If there was such an audience, they have a little bit more disposable income than little girls, and selling to them, even if you alienate parents of little girls, might end up being quite profitable indeed.[213]

She went on to explain that "Bronies have expressed a strong interest in seeing the Ponies in sexy, humanized forms"—daring the reader to do a Google search for "my little pony porn" as proof, which belies the fact that Googling most anything along with the word "porn" will yield results, known in Internet parlance as Rule 34[214]—and that "Hasbro has given them exactly what they want," thus delaying any potential decline of the Brony fandom.[215] It is true that humanized ponies were a major subset of the Brony fan art from the beginning, to the extent that *Friendship Is Magic* animator Kreoss (who would later plead for civility among the Bronies during the gray mare kerfuffle) started posting a series of drawings to his DeviantArt page in December 2010.[216] In addition to the specious "disposable income" argument, this notion that the *Equestria Girls* line was sure-fire pandering to the sexual fantasies of the Bronies was a misreading of the situation, likely based on not having done any reading; about an hour on Equestria Daily would have made it clear that this segment of the fandom was feeling anything but catered to, and that *My Little Pony: Equestria Girls* was not what the Bronies wanted, at all.

For that matter, on the May 12 Facebook post Danny J. had commented, "I really wish they could have appealed more to the male side of the fanbase," and that *Equestria Girls* was turning *Friendship Is Magic*—which he described as "a television show for all ages" rather than a show for little girls—into "a human version of a stupid high school spinoff like bratz and monster high. Those are the REAL girly shows."[217] Logan H. had also spoken up for the male, anti-girly side of the fanbase: "I LIKED THE SHOW WHEN IT WASN'T GIRLY. How many times must we drill this into Hasbros head! Why must they ruin the integrity of the show by doing this!"[218] Though one who has actually watched the *Equestria Girls* films would be hard-pressed to describe them as "girly" beyond the main characters being girls, it was as true in 2013 has it had been at the dawn of My Little Pony in the early 1980s: girliness and integrity were diametrically opposed.

Interviewed by *Bitch*'s Melody Wilson at BronyCon in 2012 well before the *Equestria Girls* announcement, Lauren Faust said that she hoped that the growth of Bronies would signal wider acceptance of breaking gender barriers[219]:

> "It breaks my heart that the word 'girly' is synonymous with 'stupid,'" she says candidly. "I want so badly for that to change. If this is a start in the direction of maybe changing that, or at least making that better, I can die happy."[220]

This cultural bias against girliness is one of the more pernicious ways sexism and misogyny remain entrenched in the United States and is indeed something that needs to be changed, but there is no evidence that Bronies—or, at least, the first wave of Bronies—will have anything to do with that change occurring. This is not to meant to imply that Faust was a *de facto Equestria Girls* supporter, as she made her displeasure with the first set of dolls clear, but merely that the success of *Friendship Is Magic* among a particular demographic had not yet done anything to salvage the word's image.

Potentially adding insult to injury concerning which subset of fans Hasbro was catering to was a June 19 press release titled "Hasbro Builds on My Little Pony Brand Growth Catering to Fans Worldwide," concerning a "global licensing program" which would "touch every major category immersing girls in entertaining, inventive, stylish, and fun MY LITTLE PONY lifestyle experiences."[221] They also bragged that the brand was "experiencing explosive growth paving the way for highly thoughtful licensing programs that further extend the brand engagement in new and meaningful ways for millions of young girls around the globe," without so much of a hint about the Bronies, those fans who were feeling so insulted by both Twilight Sparkle becoming an Alicorn and the *Equestria Girls* spinoff, neither of which catered to *them*.[222] (Speaking to the *Wall Street Journal* later that year, Hasbro's Donna Tobin explained that in creating *Equestria Girls* they had instead "tapped the preferences of hundreds of girls from ages 6 to 10," showing them sketches and asking, "Do you recognize this girl? What do you think about her ears? How old do you think she is?"[223]) And because they did not want those changes, they must have been made for *no other conceivable* reason than to just make money, while the *status quo* they were now mourning was somehow above such petty considerations.

Equestria Daily contributor CouchCrusader's June 23 post titled "Movie Followup: 'Equestria Girls'" began with a very controversial statement: "It's good. No, guys! Seriously! You can put down the torches and pitchforks—or lower them a shade or two, please!"[224] They described the demographics of the screening's audience: "There were around thirty people sitting in on our showing, and the large majority of them were families with little children. The bronies I met there conducted themselves with style and I want to thank y'all for putting on a good face for the fandom."[225] CouchCrusader further acknowledged that the Bronies were not who the film and by extension *Friendship Is Magic* was aimed at, and tried to assuage their fears about the two dreaded F-words:

> And sure, if you're not part of the target audience there will be times when you might roll an eye. Do consider, however, that you also got through "Suited for Success." Once you get over the "fun and fashion" moments in the film—I'm real, guys; they're moments—you're going to see some incredible set pieces.[226]

The reference to "Suited for Success" (S01E14) as an episode that had to be "gotten through" demonstrated how easy a target fashion was for the Bronies, though it also suggests a selective memory. One of the best episodes of the middle third of Season 1, "Suited for Success" was indeed the most fashion-oriented episode, which makes sense considering that it was the first episode to focus on the fashion career of Rarity (who is also the best). But it was also the source of one of the most popular lines of dialog in the show, spoken by

Rainbow Dash (who is often the worst) during a reprise of the song "The Art of the Dress" regarding how much cooler percentage-wise a dress Rarity is making for her needs to be, and it was the origin of one of the first *Friendship Is Magic* shirts to be sold at Hot Topic in August 2011, a silhouette of Rainbow Dash with the words "This Shirt Just Got 20 Percent Cooler."[227] At the "Confound These Ponies—Rise of My Little Pony Fandom" panel at the July 2011 ConnectiCon convention, Otaku in Review's Scott Spaziani spent 10 minutes examining how "The Art of the Dress" both moves the story forward and gives a great deal of insight into Rarity's character; he played both halves of the song, and even though it's Rarity singing about the joy she finds in designing and making clothes, the Bronies in the audience can be heard singing along and having a grand old time, and of course loudly quoting Rainbow Dash's line.[228] (Spaziani also described the Sondheim connection to "The Art of the Dress" as something "12-year-old girls aren't going to get," which is an unfair singling out of 12-year-old girls, since the vast majority of 22-year-olds, 32-year-olds, or 42-year-olds of any gender in the United States wouldn't recognize such a deep Sondheim reference if it bit them.[229]) "Suited for Success" was also the first appearance of a Brony-favorite pony as a background DJ at Rarity's fashion show; a poll on Equestria Daily a few days after the broadcast decided that DJ PON-3 was her DJ name and Vinyl Scratch her "real" name.[230] But if one sets aside the two vital elements of the Brony fandom which came from that episode, then yes, "Suited for Success" was no doubt a painful memory because of all the fun and fashion (yeccch!).

After discussing the good and the bad of *My Little Pony: Equestria Girls*, and attempting to put it in some perspective with *Friendship Is Magic*, he spoke to the recent dramas:

> The hiatus until Season 4 airs has definitely been the most challenging to weather yet, so much in part to the natural divisions that will arise within a fanbase of our size. And I empathize with those who were disappointed to learn what Equestria Girls was going to do to best purplesmart pony. All I can say to that is to vote with your dollar, and let the the the staff and Hasbro know what you want to see from MLP in the future. I'm still holding out for Film 2: The Epic Crossing of Equestria in Which Everypony Saves the World myself, but just remember that ponies pulled us in for what it was and not what we wanted it to be.[231]

Although he got to the heart of the matter—that My Little Pony "pulled us in for what it was and not what we wanted it to be"—his plea for civility, like so many before, did not have a noticeable impact. Among the 664 comments was one from MrOptimist666, who the previous month had opined that the DHX staff needed to "grow a spine" regarding any death threats they might have received for producing *My Little Pony: Equestria Girls*, who now announced that "after I see this stupid fucking movie, I NEVER want to see or hear about it ever again, I'll share my thoughts on it then I want to forget it ever existed."[232] Equestria Daily was accused, not for the first time, of being shills for Hasbro ("This entire post reads like a desperate PR piece. You guys may not be Hasbro shills, but holy shit you sure write like you are"[233]) or, put more colloquially, "Hasdrones" ("When i read comments about good music, plot or villain i lose faith in this fandom. I don't wanna say that you are hasdrones, but you are frikkin hasdrones"[234]). User Silver_Smoulder objected to CouchCrusader even expressing an opinion about *My Little Pony: Equestria Girls* without getting the majority's consent, for fear that Hasbro might get the wrong idea:

> I'd also like to accuse CouchCrusader of violating journalistic integrity. The way you present the article makes it look like you speak for the majority of the fandom. You don't. You can't make a blanket statement of "It's good." That's BAD JOURNALISM.
>
> Did you do polls? Did you do random interviews? Did you ask the people on the various pony communities what they thought? I did not think so. You base this on personal experience, which means that the marketing people at Hasbro will assume that the fandom as a whole is good and that we want more Equestria Girls, which may or may not be true—we don't have the data.
>
> If you would be kind enough to post an edit at the top saying that this represents only your OPINION rather than stating it as fact. That'd be nice.[235]

Caving in to pressure from a loud minority, the title of CouchCrusader's article was changed to "Movie Followup/Editorial/Opinion Piece: Equestria Girls" less than eight hours later, and by February 2014 it was removed from the site.[236] The day after the movie followup was first posted, Equestria Daily founder Sethisto wrote a followup to the followup, titled "Editorial: Hype. Equestria Girls, EqD, Episode Followups, and Twilight Sparkle."[237] He addressed many of the issues swirling around the movie and Equestria Daily's controversial reaction to it:

> Let's start off strong and answer the big question people keep posing in the comments: Does EQD have anything to do with Hasbro? We don't, actually. In fact, I haven't talked to anyone from Hasbro in almost a year and a half. We do talk with DHX and Hub people occasionally, but they aren't the ones that decided to release a humanized pony toyline, and they definitely don't pay us. The only thing EQD runs off of is the Google Ads you see at the top, and they have nothing to do with pony.[238]

In this and the other threads, many Bronies announced that they weren't going to see it in the theater even if they could as a way of expressing their displeasure at its existence, and several YouTube links to bootleg videos of the film were posted. For her part, Phoebe from the comic strip *Phoebe and Her Unicorn* was no happier about her universe's equivalent of the *Equestria Girls* announcement, in which the characters of her favorite show become humans and enroll in Popular High School in a film titled *Pastel Unicorns:*

Skinny Pretty Non-Unicorns—all for the purposes, she realizes, of getting her parents to have to buy her an entirely new set of toys.[239]

The official theatrical premiere date of ~~Pastel Unicorns: Skinny Pretty Non-Unicorns~~ *My Little Pony: Equestria Girls* was June 16, 2013—this writer's 40th birthday, which was not a bad coincidental birthday present—while the world premiere screening was at the Los Angeles Film Festival the night before.[240] Because I had recapped the first two seasons of *Friendship Is Magic* for *SF Weekly*, I was invited but was not able to attend. (Yes, it *does* still sting a little, thank you for asking.) The embedded graphic of the Rainbooms used their appearance from the movie rather than the more stylized versions from the *New York Times* articles—Applejack in particular looked far more like herself, standing up straight and clutching a backpack strap rather than her coquettish pose from the original images—while the main text on the graphic was a misrepresentation of the film which echoed the May 12 Facebook post:

> You and your young guest are cordially invited to a purple carpet event celebrating the world premiere of *My Little Pony: Equestria Girls*, a full-length animated adventure where six beloved pony friends become real girls with a love for fun and fashion![241]

Though the dreaded, culture-destroying words "fun and fashion" were still present, the phrase "purple carpet" represented a subtle shift in the identity of the franchise. Purple carpet is of course a play on red carpet, but since the early years of Generation 3, the phrase had been *pink* carpet, more often than not with one or both words in quotes. The second announcement for the November 2004 screenings of *Dancing in the Clouds* was titled "Hasbro's MY LITTLE PONY and the Starlight Starbright Children's Foundation Roll out the 'Pink' Carpet for Hundreds of Kids," and promised that at the event, "Starlight Starbright children will parade down a pink carpet."[242] In March 2007, a press release for *My Little Pony Live!: The World's Biggest Tea Party* promised journalists photo opportunities a-plenty since "Celebrities and their families have been invited to a 'Pink Carpet' event," and that there would be "'Pink Carpet' Interview Opportunities."[243] (Pictures taken at the event show a carpet that was more of a russet or ochre than pink, however.[244]) Later in summer 2007, the first press release for what would become Generation 3.1 announced that "long-time licensees such as HarperCollins, American Greetings, General Mills, Hemma, Redan, Smith and Brooks and Carel are already onboard to roll out the pink carpet for the updated line."[245] Like so many other things, that carpet soon got yanked out from under G3.1, as a press release in February 2008 announced that as part of the 25th anniversary events that would occur that year, a "'pink carpet'" event would mark the New York City premiere of *The World's Biggest Tea Party*.[246] But for *Equestria*

Girls in 2013 the carpet was being described as purple, and indeed, photos from the Los Angeles Film Festival premiere show a lush purple carpet.[247]

Taking *My Little Pony: Equestria Girls* on its own merits, CouchCrusader was right: it's good. (Note to Hasbro: this is being stated as a fact in a work of scholarly nonfiction. Please use it as an excuse to make more *Equestria Girls* films.) The film picks up where the Season 3 finale "Magical Mystery Cure" (S03E13) left off, with Princess Twilight stressing out about becoming royalty and still trying to adjust to her new wings. Physical bodies are tricky things to contend with under normal circumstances, more so when traumatic changes happen, and even ostensibly positive ones like gaining wings can make it difficult to do things as simple as getting comfortable in bed. Princess Twilight grappling with this body-horror will be an ongoing theme in the film; where Spike takes his transformation from a dragon into a dog in stride because dogs exist in Equestria, her immediate reaction when emerging as a biped on the other side of the mirror is to scream in terror, since she lacks a frame of reference for what she is.

Equestria Girls wisely lingers on her transition, spending three minutes of its 73-minute running time following her trying to make sense of her New Flesh, of how to do such unnatural things as standing upright on two legs, let alone walking on them without collapsing. Back in Equestria she's still getting used to having wings, and now she has to start all over. (When I was five years old, I had surgery on my legs to correct a birth condition called Internal Tibial Torsion, and after several months in casts and a wheelchair, I had to learn to walk from scratch. It ain't easy.) The film's first post-credits song, "Strange New World," is set to a montage of Princess Twilight trying to figure out the customs and mores of this alien place; it's the weakest song of the film, so much so that it was left off the official five-song soundtrack EP, but it also demonstrates how difficult and confusing this experience is for her, and that the movie is taking its premise seriously. It's a testament to *Equestria Girls*'s world-building that when Princess Twilight looks into a (non-magical) mirror in a moment of indecision at 49 minutes into the movie and imagines seeing a reflection of her pony self, it's almost jarring, since she'd become a complete character as a biped.

This metaphor for adolescence ties into the setting of *Equestria Girls*, Canterlot High. A high school isn't a perfect analog for Ponyville or Equestria, and there are any number of disconnects, particularly in that the Mane Six tended to be portrayed as college-age at the least on *Friendship Is Magic*. They work, are concerned about money (both Rarity and Applejack have businesses to keep afloat) and in general they tend to have grown-up responsibilities. But parallel-universe stories always have to take a number of logistical shortcuts to work, though the need to establish this world of 2013-vintage cell phones and computers results in a rather overwritten film, as though the producers had more ideas to include than the running time could comfortably accommodate. (It stands to reason, because screenwriter Meghan McCarthy confirmed in the *Rainbow Rocks* audio commentary that when writing *My Little Pony: Equestria Girls*, she wasn't expecting there to be a second film.[248]) One subplot involving Princess Twilight being framed for vandalism is introduced and resolved in under two minutes, though it does serve to further establish the new character of Flash Sentry, on whom Twilight develops a mutual crush. As a female pony, she's never shown romantic interest in a boy, but as an adolescent biped girl, it's another unexpected consequence of her New Flesh.

The speediness of that subplot does allow more breathing room for a more interesting arc: whereas the rest of the Mane Six were already friends when Twilight Sparkle arrived in Ponyville in "Friendship Is Magic, Parts 1 & 2" (S01E01–2), the Rainbooms have since fallen out with each other, which gives them more to do as characters than the Mane Six were afforded those episodes. Notably, the only two Rainbooms who are still friends are Applejack and Pinkie Pie, who in Equestria are the Earth ponies.

My Little Pony: Equestria Girls rewards repeat viewings, setting the stage for the far superior *Rainbow Rocks* and *Friendship Games*, and those films' redemption arc for the villain Sunset Shimmer, who would go on to become one of the franchise's most emotionally complex characters. *Equestria Girls* also does good character work with Twilight Sparkle at the end regarding her still-new status as a Princess, and except for elements of the Season 4 premiere "Princess Twilight Sparkle, Parts 1 & 2" (S04E01–2), it would be the last time Twilight openly struggles with these changes in her life until "Twilight Time" (S04E15), which is also the first great episode of that season. Though the series picks up the thread again in the season's final three episodes, both *Equestria Girls* and *Rainbow Rocks* offer more insight into the emotional impact of her Princesshood than anything on *Friendship Is Magic*.

No (Equestria) Girls Allowed, Part II: Sunset Rising

In spite of the scattered release and the immediate and continued backlash from Bronies and civilians alike, Hasbro announced during their Investor Day on September 10, 2013, that they'd already made back more than their initial investment on *My Little Pony: Equestria Girls*, which had "exceeded expectations with packed houses and numerous sellouts by exhibitors in major markets," and that in addition to strong sales of the DVD release, as of the previous week the picture had been the top seller in the Kids category and number 20 overall in movies on iTunes.[249] According to the marketing research company NPD, the *Equestria Girls* range was the top-selling fashion-themed doll during the week of Christmas that year,[250] which may well have been because of the scarcity of the other, more established brands by that point (much like how the G1 dolls tended to sell out in the mid–1980s), and by July 2014, it was back down to number five on the list.[251]

Domestic grosses are difficult to come by, but according to Box Office Mojo the film did well in Latin America, particularly in Peru, grossing $314,194 from September 3 to September 29, compared to a $20,341 gross August 22 through September 8 in Chile, or $82,134 from September 13 to November 3 in Colombia.[252] Further evidence of Peru's love for the spinoff came in October when Animanía Show, an organization in Lima which provided live Spanish-language versions of popular children's properties such as Sesame Street, Marvel superheroes, and Disney Princesses for birthdays and similar events, added *Show Infantil Equestria Girls* to their slate.[253] Perhaps for budgetary reasons, the only characters featured in the original lineup were Princess Twilight Sparkle, Pinkie Pie, Rainbow Dash, and Applejack, with Fluttershy and Rarity namechecked in the rewrite of "Equestria Girls (Cafeteria Song)" that served as the troupe's theme song but otherwise not appearing in the production.[254] But there's never a good reason to shut out Rarity, and by February 2015 the lineup had been expanded to include all five Rainbooms in faithful recreations of Princess Twilight meeting them in the first film, complete with Rainbow Dash holding a soccer ball.[255] (She's introduced playing soccer in *Equestria Girls*, and carries a soccer ball with her for much of the first half of *Rainbow Rocks*. Though the films studiously avoid any mention of parents, it does raise the question: would Rainbow's mother be a soccer mom?)

After eight prequel shorts were released to YouTube between March and June of 2014 ("Music to my Ears," "Guitar Centered," "Hamstocalypse Now," "Pinkie on the One," "Player Piano," "A Case for the Bass," "Shake Your Tail!," and "Perfect Day for Fun"), and Season 4 of *Friendship Is Magic* concluded with "Twilight's Kingdom, Parts 1–2" (S04E25–26) in May, *My Little Pony: Equestria Girls—Rainbow Rocks* premiered in United States theaters on Saturday, September 27, 2014, including a special screening that afternoon at the TCL Chinese 6 Theater in Hollywood. The text of the email sent to invited press promised "a magical afternoon full of fun and fashion," as though the copywriter either didn't know or didn't care about the outrage that phrase had stirred the year before.[256] The embedded graphic used the same stylized illustrations of the Rainbooms as had appeared on the cover of Perdita Finn's novelization of the *Rainbow Rocks* prequel shorts published that April,[257] based on the template from the original *New York Times* announcement, and the invitation once again described the screening as a "'Purple Carpet' event," one which would feature a "'Ponyfication Station' fashion experience."[258] (No, I was not able to attend *that* premiere, either. Please stop asking.)

My Little Pony: Equestria Girls came after the shortened, 13-episode Season 3 of *Friendship Is Magic*, but *My Little Pony: Equestria Girls—Rainbow Rocks* followed the full, 26-episode Season 4. The season had no shortage of high concepts and trotted all over the wide, wide world of Equestria, but *Friendship Is Magic* is always at its best when it keeps the focus on the characters without distracting gimmicks. There had been only two character-driven stories confined to Ponyville until "Twilight Time" (S04E15), and the season tended to focus more on character than spectacle from that point, including a terrific run about sisterhood: Applejack and Apple Bloom in "Somepony to Watch Over Me" (S04E17), Pinkie Pie and her heretofore unmentioned sister Maud in "Maud Pie" (S04E18), and Rarity and Sweetie Belle in "For Whom the Sweetie Belle Toils" (S04E19). "Toils" is also notable for the parallels it draws between Sweetie Belle's jealousy of her older sister Rarity and the jealousy that turned Princess Luna into Nightmare Moon, the ancient conflict which kicked off the series (and was briefly revisited during a flashback in the season opener "Princess Twilight Sparkle, Parts 1 & 2" [S04E01–2]), but which had never been addressed until now. Luna tacitly admits that she still struggles with that jealousy toward her sister Celestia, a struggle that may never end; the mortal Sweetie Belle will continue to grow and find her own identity, and may even someday outshine Rarity (who, lest we forget, is the best), but the immortal Luna will forever be in Celestia's shadow.

It's a theme that is reflected between Sunset Shimmer and Princess Twilight in *Rainbow Rocks*. Though Sunset is older (established by her having been Celestia's student prior to Twilight), like Luna she let her darkness overwhelm her, and will pay the price for the rest of her life. It's possible that if Sunset had stayed on the straight and narrow in Equestria, she might have ascended to Alicorn status, but now she'll never know. It's probably one of the reasons why she chooses to remain in the biped world.

The emotional crux of *Rainbow Rocks,* and all My Little Pony up to this point, is a simple conversation between Twilight and Sunset late at night after a slumber party at Pinkie Pie's well-appointed home. Unable to sleep after the others have gone to bed, Princess Twilight adjourns to the kitchen to continue working on the counter-spell she believes is needed to defeat the

Sirens; the establishing shot of her hunched over the kitchen island in darkness, with only a single key light from above, is one of the loveliest images in a franchise which has never lacked for loveliness. Because she isn't being observed, she writes with the pen in her mouth and her still-alien hands clenched like hooves; earlier, she had volunteered to sing for the Rainbooms for fear that it would take too long to learn to play an instrument with her unfamiliar hands, and when she's stressed out and/or in deep thought, she holds those hands in hoof-like fists. Even well into the second film, this is still not her world, and not her true body.

She's joined by Sunset Shimmer, and in the night kitchen they open up to each other about their vulnerabilities: Twilight is feeling pressured to save the day, a pressure she's always felt but which is much heavier now that she's a Princess and is expected to have all the answers, while Sunset faces the Sisyphean task of redemption, well aware that the others are expecting her to screw up and *ruin* the day. Each carries a heavy burden, and they share a bonding moment when they realize that they're in the same emotional place. An offhand comment by Sunset that writing a song is probably simple compared to the duties of Equestrian royalty almost gives the recently crowned Princess of Friendship the courage to embrace that thing which she is the Princess *of*, to admit that she's in over her head and ask her former enemy for help ... but she can't. It's a heartbreaking moment, heightened by a rare extreme close-up of Twilight's face as she tries and fails to do the right thing, as she has so many times before and no doubt will again in the future. Perdita Finn's novelization twists the knife deeper, suggesting that Twilight is so despondent, she may not be able to face returning to Equestria as a Princess if she can't solve this simple problem.[259]

Rainbow Rocks is as stressful an experience for her as "The Best Night Ever" (S01E26), "Lesson Zero" (S02E03), or "It's About Time" (S02E20), and she gets her emotional teeth kicked further in by her second encounter with Flash Sentry, deep under the Sirens' influence like all the Canterlot High students: he first ignores her, and then accuses her of returning just to defeat him in the Battle of the Bands. Flash acts as the barometer of the Sirens' influence, as he's his usual adorable self before they arrive, then can only talk about his band in his first, post–Siren conversation with Twilight, and is now outwardly hostile toward her. Harshest is a mickey-take that cuts deeper than he could know, as he accuses her of not having the slightest idea what she's even doing—which she doesn't, and the fate of this world hangs in the balance, and now her crush has turned on her and it's all too much for her to handle, Alicorn Princess or not.

* * *

That *Rainbow Rocks* had resulted in the best 72 consecutive minutes of My Little Pony thus far did little to rehabilitate *Equestria Girls'* public image. *New York Times* and the Awl contributor Mario Bustillos had a major bone to pick with *Equestria Girls*, and she picked it in a 3,706-word blog post in January 2015 on the content aggregation site Longreads titled "Friendship Is Complicated: Art, Commerce, and the Battle for the Soul of My Little Pony."[260] A fact-checker was credited, which was somewhat hilarious considering how many facts about both the show and the movies the article got wrong.

She described *Friendship Is Magic* as "infectious, beautifully produced, with fine original music and inventive, striking animation," and said that "it had transcended its toy origins, and it became a work of art on its own," though her characterization of the storytelling was typically reductive: "The episodes are generally about discovering how we can befriend and help those different from ourselves, despite the frustrations those differences may cause us at first."[261] Though the article was written in the hiatus between Seasons 4 and 5, in two of the first six episodes of Season 1, "Griffon the Brush Off" (S01E05) and "Boast Busters" (S01E06), outsiders come in to Ponyville, cause trouble, reject the efforts of certain characters to befriend them, and leave without having learned any lessons at all.

Ruminating on why so many boys and young men respond to the show, she described the Mane Six as "[combining] to form a larger, more powerful entity, in a manner similar to the 'boys' shows' Voltron and Power Rangers."[262] This was presumably a reference to the Elements of Harmony, during the use of which the ponies do briefly glow, levitate, and are linked by magical rainbows emanating from their individual Elements, beams which then combine to vanquish whatever foe requires vanquishing. But they do not create a new robot or creature along the lines of the Zords in *Mighty Morphin Power Rangers* or the giant robot in the *Voltron* series. It is a fact which would have been easy to check, considering that by the time the article was written the Elements had only been used twice, in "Friendship Is Magic, Part 2" (S01E02)," and "The Return of Harmony, Part 2" (S02E02), and then retired altogether in "Princess Twilight Sparkle, Part 2" (S0402), all of which were the second parts of the more blockbuster-oriented season premieres; the Elements of Harmony were not referenced outside of the two-part season premieres or finales until "Keep Calm and Flutter On" (S03E10) in Season 3. Bustillos also stated that "nearly all the stories in the show are adventure stories, unconcerned with romance or dating," which is half true: romance and dating are themes of Rarity's subplot in the episodes "The Ticket Master" (S01E02) and

"The Best Night Ever" (S01E26), and they're an explicit theme in "Hearts and Hooves Day" (S02E17), "A Canterlot Wedding, Parts 1 & 2" (S02E25–26), and "Simple Ways" (S04E13), but are otherwise unexplored on the show. However, nowhere close to "nearly all" the episodes are adventure stories; Season 1 episodes which cannot reasonably be called adventures include "The Ticket Master" (S01E03), "Applebuck Season" (S01E04), "Griffon the Brush Off" (S01E05), "Look Before You Sleep" (S01E08), "Winter Wrap Up" (S01E11), "Call of the Cutie" (S01E12), "Suited for Success" (S01E14), "The Show Stoppers" (S01E18), "Green Isn't Your Color" (S01E20), "A Bird in the Hoof" (S01E22), "Party of One" (S01E25), and "The Best Night Ever" (S01E26). Those are just from Season 1, and the article was written in the hiatus between Seasons 4 and 5, by which time 91 episodes had been produced. Season 4 episodes which lack adventure elements include "Rarity Takes Manehattan" (S04E08), "Pinkie Pride" (S04E12), "Twilight Time" (S04E15), "Maud Pie" (S04E18), "For Whom the Sweetie Belle Toils" (S04E19), "Testing Testing 1, 2, 3" (S04E21), "Trade Ya!" (S04E22), and "Inspiration Manifestation" (S04E23).

However unchecked the facts, the praise she lavished on the show was refreshing, even if it was done primarily by comparing it to boys' adventure shows, suggesting that masculine-leaning entertainments have more inherent integrity than those which are feminine. (It is very similar to the approach Hal Erickson took 20 years earlier when he considered whether or not selling toy horses to girls was "in the best interest of sexual equality."[263]) There are often adventure elements to the show, but Bustillos emphasized that word in order to further set up her adversary to be knocked down[264]:

> Despite the runaway success of *My Little Pony: Friendship is Magic*, Faust left the show before its third season, for reasons neither the studio nor the artist herself have cared to elaborate on in public. The likely causes of a split aren't difficult to surmise—particularly in view of the 2013 spin-off, *Equestria Girls*, which turned the adventurers of *My Little Pony* into ultra-skinny, status-obsessed high-school girls who are one thousand percent about combing hair and changing clothes. In order to effect this transformation, the ponies leap through a mirror into an alternate universe. (As, perhaps, does the viewer.)[265]

All of which sounds like a terrible fate for our adventurers! But in the plus column, none of it is accurate. Working backwards, the ponies (plural) do not leap through a mirror to effect the transformation; only Princess Twilight and Spike the Dragon do. After being transformed into a human and a dog respectively, they go on to encounter the Rainbooms, while the Mane Six stay behind in Equestria and are seen at the end of the film, nervously awaiting Princess Twilight and Spike's return. The Rainbooms, though indeed saddled with the bobblehead-like craniums that were the trend for female characters in children's cartoons, are not "one thousand percent about combing hair and changing clothes."[266] Even if one were to dial down the hyperbole to mathematically correct levels, the Rainbooms cannot be described as being one hundred percent into grooming or costume changing, or even 10 percent. As has always been the case, only Rarity has an active interest in fashion, and the first change of clothes for any character doesn't occur until Princess Twilight's second day in the human world at 33 minutes into the 73-minute film, when Rarity somewhat nonconsensually puts Twilight into an unspeakable green dress and blond wig to hide her from the student body. It's Rarity's first appearance, but we do see that Pinkie Pie, Applejack, Fluttershy, and Sunset Shimmer are wearing the same clothes as when they were introduced the previous day, and within a few minutes Princess Twilight is back in the rather smart blouse, skirt, and boots the portal had been kind enough to provide her with during her transformation.

The first significant clothing change of any kind doesn't occur until 43 minutes, and then it's just the Rainbooms wearing long-sleeved Canterlot High sweaters, pony ears, and tails over their street clothes. They then remove the sweaters, and after a scene set at a clothing boutique at 48 minutes, none of them can be said to do any true changing of clothes until a montage at 54 minutes of the Rainbooms trying on different dresses and hairstyles in preparation for the Fall Formal that evening—no doubt one of the "fun and fashion" moments that CouchCrusader had assured the Bronies that they were strong enough to get over. This montage also includes the only instances of hairgrooming: Pinkie Pie poking at her hair with a pick, Fluttershy brushing her own hair, and Princess Twilight combing Rainbow Dash's hair. Rainbow looks like she's in pain, suggesting Twilight is combing out the tangles that an eternal tomboy like Rainbow might not have attended to on her own, being not even one percent about combing hair; it's a subtle, purely visual touch that doesn't draw attention to itself, the sort of show-don't-tell character detail both *Friendship Is Magic* and *Equestria Girls* excel at. And the Rainbooms are never shown as obsessed with status, or at all concerned with it; the only status-obsessed character is the villain, Sunset Shimmer. The villains of *Rainbow Rocks*, the Sirens, are also the closest any of the *Equestria Girls* films get to Monster High–type characters in appearance—and even then, head Siren Adagio is more reminiscent of Mackenzie Hollister, the mean girl in Rachel Renee Russell's *Dork Diaries* book series.[267] But just because either the *Equestria Girls* films or the *Dork Diaries* books feature teenage girls with big hair in high school doesn't make them in any way like Monster High as Bustillos and others have contended.

After describing *My Little Pony: Equestria Girls* in a manner that suggests that her research on the film extended no further than the original "fun and fashion" announcement eighteen months prior, she went in for the kill:

> The contrast between these two children's shows provides a literal illustration of certain eternal tensions, not only in children's entertainment but in literature and in American culture in general: Innocence vs. Experience, Nerds vs. Normies, Individualism vs. Conformity, Gender-Neutral Egalitarianism vs. Explicitly Heteronormative Sexuality—and maybe most strikingly, Art vs. Commerce.[268]

When "Friendship Is Complicated: Art, Commerce, and the Battle for the Soul of My Little Pony" was posted in January 2015, the entirety of *Equestria Girls* animated product was two feature films and eight shorts totaling two hours and forty-five minutes of content, or roughly the running time of seven and a half episodes of *Friendship Is Magic*. Though the films were indeed broadcast on the Hub after their theatrical and DVD debuts, and the shorts were posted to YouTube, there was never an *Equestria Girls* television series, yet throughout the article Bustillos refers to it as a "show" in the same vein as *Friendship Is Magic*. It's an important distinction to make, primarily because the *Equestria Girls* films at 73 minutes long necessarily have a very different storytelling rhythm than 22-minute *Friendship Is Magic* episodes, and because it's another example of a critic of My Little Pony not having properly researched what they're discussing. Such details should matter when building an argument, but criticizing My Little Pony has always been more of an art than a science.

Her overall point, which had been made by many others within minutes of the first announcement in May 2013, was that the *Equestria Girls* spinoff was a cold cash-grab compared to *Friendship Is Magic*, which was now posited as flawless and humane—and if the television series also happened to be profit-making venture, that was excusable in a way that it wasn't for *Equestria Girls*. Indeed, in many circles, *Equestria Girls* absolved *Friendship Is Magic* of its Original Sin; as Bustillos put it, the series "transcended its toy origins, and it became a work of art on its own."[269] But none of that goodwill was transferred to the spinoff, which from the briefest of glances was nothing more than a toy commercial modeled after *Monster High* (which she also described as being a "series" in spite of it having been an unserialized mélange of webisodes, TV specials, and direct-to-DVD movies).

Though enough time had passed by January 2015 for the differences between them to be clear, Bustillos wrote that *Equestria Girls* "hews very closely" to the "unequivocally sexy" *Monster High* formula in which "girl characters compete for the boys' attention and try to look as cool as they can, showing off their dance moves, cell phones, clothes and boots and so on," and that those clothes "are super-revealing—skin-tight nightclub gear really."[270] True though it may be for *Monster High*, none of that applies to *Equestria Girls*, though her cited example attempted to prove otherwise:

> Here a mini-skirted, platform-shod Twilight Sparkle acquires a crush almost immediately: blue-haired Flash Sentry, who manages to recall both Robert Pattinson and Sonic the Hedgehog. (But, horrors! He is the ex-boyfriend of the wicked Sunset Shimmer!)[271]

Princess Twilight's skirt does indeed stop above her knee, as do the skirts of the rest of the Rainbooms, but this does not a miniskirt make, and though the Rainbooms' skirts are not uniforms, they have similar proportions to many school uniform skirts in the real world. None of the clothes worn by any of the *Equestria Girls* characters are "super-revealing" or "skin-tight night-club gear really," not even the dresses they wear to the climactic Fall Formal. Except for the fact that it doesn't go all the way to the ground, Twilight's peplum-and-front-bow dress would also be suitable for a Quinceanera—appropriately enough, considering the popularity of *Equestria Girls* in Latin America—but it wouldn't get her into a nightclub. She does have a meet-cute with Flash Sentry straight out of the romantic comedy rulebook at 12 minutes in after having bumped into his pony equivalent within the first two minutes in Equestria, but doesn't encounter him again until 40 minutes. Her crush is in bloom, but at no point in the film does she allow herself to become distracted from her mission, not even deigning to dance with Flash until after Sunset Shimmer has been vanquished. And until then, Princess Twilight and the Rainbooms had all been dancing with each other, paying no mind to any of the boys other than Twilight briefly waving to Flash as he plays onstage with his band, and the Rainbooms certainly do not "compete for the boys' attention and try to look as cool as they can, showing off their dance moves, cell phones, clothes and boots and so on," as a "close hewing" to the *Monster High* formula that Bustillos described would require. Quite the opposite: when Twilight finally dances with Flash it's only after he reminds her, and displaying a laudable lack of self-consciousness, Twilight gets on all fours and busts out the helpless dance moves that first horrified the attendees of the Canterlot garden party in "Sweet and Elite" (S02E09)—and after a moment, Flash joins in. He's a sweet kid, and there is nothing problematic about the Flash Sentry subplot—and it *is* a subplot, and a minor one at that—unless one considers any hint of romance to be problematic. Teenage girls get crushes, as do teenage boys, as do people of all ages and genders well into their 40s and beyond (and I am totally not speaking from personal experience here).

Bustillos was not alone in her distaste for the notion of Twilight Sparkle experiencing those emotions as a consequence of her New Flesh; it was a major sticking point for many of the Bronies, resulting in Flash Sentry becoming as hated as the gray mare was loved. At the MLP-MSP panel after the broadcast of "Slice of Life" (S05E09), episode writer M.A. Larson revealed that he'd originally intended for the pony version of Flash to appear in the episode, to which the assembled Bronies booed and hissed in response; they then cheered and applauded when they learned that Flash's cameo would have had him wondering aloud why nopony likes him.[272] (For voice actor Vincent Tong's sake, it's just as well that gag fell through.) And as for Bustillos' snark about Flash "being the ex-boyfriend of the wicked Sunset Shimmer" (horrors!), the penitent Sunset Shimmer confirms in *Rainbow Rocks* that the only reason she'd been with Flash was to be popular—to confer the status that she, and *only* she, was obsessed with in the first film.[273]

Regarding the always-controversial issue of how a property geared toward young girls and featuring teenage protagonists represents aspirations and budding sexuality, Bustillos wrote:

> Weirdly, on this score I find *My Little Pony: Friendship is Magic* quite a bit more grownup than either *Monster High* or *Equestria Girls*, because the latter, with their very narrow-minded, totally heteronormative, totally body-dysmorphic, materialistic and shallow understanding of sexuality really are so retrograde. And maybe even somewhat harmful?? Because only the impossibly skinniest, most fashionable girls are presented as admirable or even acceptable in these shows. No character without these very specific, fantastical physical attributes is considered worthy of the remotest interest.[274]

Again, though this may hold true for *Monster High*, it does not apply to *Equestria Girls*; tomboys Rainbow Dash and Applejack do somewhat incongruously wear skirts, but they have the same take-it-or-leave-it attitude toward fashion as their Mane Six counterparts, and yet are afforded plenty of interest. (The *Equestria Girls* Minis Dolls released in January 2016 finally put soccer aficionado Rainbow Dash in character-appropriate athletic shorts.[275]) As previously mentioned, Rainboom Applejack's utter lack of interest in dressing up even while on stage, and her frustration that Rarity does care about such things, is a major source of conflict between them in *Rainbow Rocks*.

And not all the female characters wear skirts or dresses; Principal Celestia and Vice Principal Luna both wear trousers, Scootaloo is in cargo shorts, and Apple Bloom wears jeans, all of which are appropriate for their characters. Many of the unnamed female background Wondercolts who are closer to the Rainbooms' age are seen wearing pants, and others are wearing long skirts. (The Great and Powerful Trixie's daily ensemble, which includes a zip-up hoodie, is totes adorbs but in no way sexualized.) Most of the Wondercolts are more overtly fashionable than any of the Rainbooms, and yet are not "considered worthy of the remotest interest," because the story isn't about them.

The hyper-sexualized homogeneity described by Bustillos, and the marginalization of those who do not conform to it, simply does not exist in *Equestria Girls*. Indeed, there is a great deal more diversity in character shapes and sizes in *Equestria Girls* than in *Friendship Is Magic*, and while in both cases there's more variety in the men than the women, that's an unfortunate trend which has also been observed in the respectable Disney and Pixar movies.[276]

But such details are less important than whether or not a "getting viewers to hand over their money"-type reduction can be applied:

> *Equestria Girls*, though just a little less "knowing," is hitting all the same marks as *Monster High* with respect to swooning high-school crushes, scheming Mean Girls, provocative clothes and stick-thin body imaging ... and not by mistake. Even if these shows aren't very good, so long as they produce merchandise sales—even just as a viable alternative for girls who may tire of their *Monster High* toys—the project will be counted a success where it matters most: in earnings per share.

As it happens, earnings per share is where the success of *Friendship Is Magic* matters most as well, at least for it to continue on as a series. Though Bustillos argued that the series had become capital-A "Art" thanks to it boy-friendly adventure elements and the devotion of the Bronies—while suggesting that *Equestria Girls* has an Artistically invalid "merch-first strategy" because she quotes Hasbro's Girls category as having grown by 26% in 2013, and that My Little Pony represented $650M of the net revenue of $4.08B—the reality is that even though the G4 toys were based on *Friendship Is Magic* and not the other way around, the series would not have continued had the merchandise not been profitable. Hasbro reported that the Girls category grew another 21% in the first quarter of 2014, and that "MY LITTLE PONY, MY LITTLE PONY EQUESTRIA GIRLS and NERF REBELLE contributed to the continued strong growth in the category."[277] Whether Bustillos considered the Nerf Rebelle line of archery toys to be pure Art like *Friendship Is Magic,* or pure Commerce like *Equestria Girls,* is unknown.

She also took time out to praise *Magic* creator Lauren Faust, as well as to speak highly of Bronies she'd met in person, describing them as "sharing an effortless camaraderie" and as being "twenty-somethings with the simple, unaffected friendliness of 5-year-olds." (There's no way of telling whether any of them were the same Bronies who under the cover of Internet anonymity had railed against "fucktard soccermoms" and "'political correctness' fags" or harassed DHX employees for making *Equestria Girls*—almost as though Bronies are a group of diverse humans who have varying personalities, and cannot be reduced to a single type for the purposes of whatever political point a given writer is making, whether her initials are S.C. or M.B.) Maria Bustillos also wrote about attending the Grand Galloping Gala costume dance at Knott's Berry Farm in November 2014, which she described not unkindly as taking place in a "single featureless, glaringly-lit hotel meeting room haphazardly decorated with streamers, a mirror ball, a few merchandise tables and a dance floor in the center, the whole producing an atmosphere reminiscent of a middle-school dance." It all sounds very charming indeed, and she was particularly taken by the "kids"(her word) jumping and chanting "Friendship!"—which she later presented as article-concluding proof that *Friendship Is Magic* had become capital-A Art—and so much the better for a section which focused on the positive impact of the series on the Bronies, not dragging *Equestria Girls* into it until the last paragraph:

> [The Grand Galloping Gala] was about as far away from the world of *Equestria Girls* as could be. Improvisational, random, low-budget, the opposite of glossy or corporatized. The imagination of Lauren Faust and her brave and gentle characters may have inspired these kids to come together so improbably in this Knott's Berry Farm Resort Hotel meeting room, but really, they were here for each other.[278]

It also sounds not unlike the Fall Formal at the end of *My Little Pony: Equestria Girls*, which takes place in the Canterlot High gymnasium decorated with streamers and a mirror ball—though it lacked the multiple merchandise tables she described in the Anaheim ballroom, or any other signs of Commerce. It is also notable that the high school gymnasium was decorated by the entire student body, considering themselves the Canterlot Wondercolts regardless of their social status; a running theme of all three films is bringing the myriad groups and cliques of the school together after having been torn asunder by Sunset Shimmer. The brave and gentle Wondercolts may have been present because they're expected to participate in the ritual of dancing and the selection of the Fall Formal Princess, but really, there were there for each other.

*   *   *

Confirmation came two and a half weeks after "Friendship Is Complicated" was published that *Equestria Girls* was indeed producing merchandise sales and was a success in earnings per share, and thus could be considered pure Commerce, unlike the Art of *Friendship Is Magic:* during Hasbro's Annual Investor Meeting at the American International Toy Fair, John Frascotti announced that 2014 was "the best year ever for My Little Pony."[279] Recently promoted from chief marketing officer to president of Hasbro Brands in spite of having angered so many Bronies by describing *Equestria Girls* as being a response to the desires of the fans, he reported that the brand was growing revenue "in every major geography around the world" with more than half of that business occurring outside the United States, and that it all resulted in My Little Pony becoming Hasbro's "newest $1 billion at retail brand."[280] He also confirmed that part of the reason for the global growth was *Equestria Girls*, and that the *Rainbow Rocks* movie helped the brand to "grow significantly" in 2014, all of which would seem to confirm the suspicions of critics that *Equestria Girls* was nothing but soulless "merch-first" strategizing—except for this statement:

> Now what is driving our growth is our top-rated Friendship is Magic television show from Hasbro Studios. It is now being broadcast on over 24 networks in 180 territories around the world and it is also streamed on multiple digital platforms. It is fair to say that the popularity and reach of this show has exceeded everyone's expectations. It is consistently a top-rated show globally and importantly, it continues to attract a very broad and growing audience. It is no longer a show adored only by young girls. In fact, its passionate and diverse audience spans age and gender with moms co-viewing with children and people of all ages enjoying the show.
>
> So we are now into our fifth season. Our theme this year is Cutie Mark Magic and we will bring this theme across the entire blueprint.[281]

There was no specific mention of the patrons of the Arts known as Bronies, and "people of all ages enjoying the show" notably came after "moms co-viewing with children," some of whom might have been *soccer* moms. Frascotti defined the "blueprint" as "the strategy we employ to drive the profitable long-term growth of Hasbro through innovation and storytelling," and "Cutie Mark Magic" was indeed the theme for much of the *Friendship Is Magic* merchandise sold in 2015—though not for *Equestria Girls*. Frascotti said that Hasbro was "going to continue to grow our *Equestria Girls* brands," and that "the growing popularity of *Equestria Girls* demonstrates how we are using compelling storytelling to build a brand franchise."[282] That compelling storytelling was promised to continue with *My Little Pony: Equestria Girls— Friendship Games*, which he said would debut in theaters that fall.[283]

But a theatrical release in the United States was not to be, as Screenvision put their "Event Cinema" programming on hold later that year due to a merger with KAOS Connect,[284] though the film did open at the Vue Cinemas chain in the UK on October 23.[285] To promote the film on their Facebook page, Vue held a contest to give away a few sets of *Friendship Games* dolls, and it was aimed at both adults and children of all genders: "If you were an Equestria girl or boy, what would your Cutie Mark be? If you're entering for your kids, tells us what their Cutie Mark would be."[286] Several hundred people replied, most of whom did so on behalf of children, and about three dozen referenced sons, grandsons, or nephews; one of the two official winners was a boy, as was one of the four runners-up.[287] Perhaps owing to the fact that the Vue post had addressed both boys and girls equally and without implied judgment, there was only one parent who felt the need to suggest a problem where none existed, saying her son "loves my little pony I think that makes him a brony lol some people think it's girly but who cares that's what he likes."[288] Nopony but her cared.

Season 5 premiered on the rebranded Discovery Family Channel on April 4, 2015, with "The Cutie Map, Parts 1 & 2" (S05E01–2), kicking off a season which had an unusually heavy emphasis on and reference to Cutie Marks (the aforementioned season premiere, as well as "Bloom & Gloom" [S05E04], "Appleoosa's Most Wanted" [S05E06], "The Lost Treasure of Griffonstone" [S05E08], "Made in Manehattan" [S05E15], "Crusaders of the Lost Mark" [S05E18], "The Hooffields and the McColts" [S05E23], "The Mane Attraction" [S05E24], and "The Cutie Re-Mark, Parts 1 & 2" [S05E25–26]). This did not make them bad episodes—"Crusaders of the Lost Mark" was the emotional high point of the season, and nearly as much of a change to the *status quo* as "Magical Mystery Cure" (S03E13)—but it does suggest that the Art of *Friendship Is Magic* had not transcended its toy origins enough to be untouched by the Commerce of the "Cutie Mark Magic" theme which Hasbro was bringing across the entire brand blueprint.

Season 5 was also the first season of *Friendship Is Magic* to premiere in the spring rather than the fall, and it was preceded by three new musical *Rainbow Rocks* encore shorts posted to YouTube in April: "Friendship Through the Ages," "Life Is a Runway," and "My Past Is Not Today." Perhaps owing to the fact that the film itself was so music-driven, Daniel Ingram's songs for *Rainbow Rocks* had been among his best work for the franchise and could be the subject of a book in Bloomsbury's *33 1/3* series, with "Under Our Spell," "Welcome to the Show," and particularly "Shine Like Rainbows" up there with "The Art of the Dress" and "The Pony Pokey" from Season 1, as well as the Daytime Emmy–nominated "May the Best Pet Win" and "Becoming Popular" from Season 2.[289] Indeed, while only "Equestria Girls (Cafeteria Song)" from the first film holds up, the songs from *Rainbow Rocks* were the most essential music from Season 4, and while it doesn't have as many songs, "CHS Pep Rally" and the latter third of "Unleash the Magic" (Twilight's verse, and the counterpoints from Luna and Cadance) from *Friendship Games* are better than any individual songs in Season 5.

The three *Rainbow Rocks* encore shorts continued that film's musical high standards; the transition from Rainbow Dash's electric guitar-based verse to Applejack's gentler acoustic verse in "Friendship Through the Ages" raises goosebumps, as does the key change halfway through "Life Is a Runway" as it picks up steam. Lyrically, the ensemble piece "Friendship Through the Ages" and Sunset Shimmer's solo "My Past Is Not Today" respectively concern her continuing to learn to embrace friendship, and forgive herself for her past misdeeds. In many ways, Sunset Shimmer in the *Equestria Girls* films fulfills the promise of Twilight Sparkle's arc in Season 1 of *Friendship Is Magic*. Princess Celestia sent Twilight to Ponyville in the first episode to make friends and learn how to be a social creature, and by the third episode she'd largely gotten the hang of it. This not to say that Twilight Sparkle didn't grow and evolve, but the episodic, largely un-serialized nature of the show combined with the time devoted to the character development of the Mane Six and the Cutie Mark Crusaders didn't allow much space for that subplot. This is not a bad thing, as it actually made Twilight a more well-rounded character than if she were just an antisocial bookworm who needed to be actively taught a lesson in every story: indeed, one of the great storytelling strengths of *Friendship Is Magic* is that Twilight doesn't have to be the protagonist, that not every episode is about her embarking on "wondrous adventures" with her pals, or fixing their problems. It's also why her becoming an Alicorn Princess at the end of Season 3, and being given the title of Princess of Friendship at the end of Season 4, was such a boon to the show's storytelling possibilities, as they put a whole new set of pressures on her.

"Friendship Through the Ages" is not a historical review of friendship as the title might suggest, but rather an examination of how it can transcend differences in lives and personalities, as well as the inevitable fact of impermanence and change—and, by extension, changes such as a Unicorn becoming an Alicorn, or the discovery of a parallel universe inhabited by biped equivalents, both of which caused so much knee-jerk outrage among the Bronies and some members of the general public because it was different. The song may be the purest expression of the themes of My Little Pony, and was further evidence that *Equestria Girls* was operating on the same level as *Friendship Is Magic*.

The Rarity solo number "Life Is a Runway" can also be viewed as a rebuttal to everypony who got up in arms about the words "fun and fashion," being a joyous and unapologetic paean to the transformative power of fashion and the personal fulfillment that comes from a girl dressing up and looking sharp if she wants to. The song does not use the word "fun," though "fun and fashion" was referenced in Hasbro's July 8 press release about their Special Edition *Equestria Girls* Doll for the 2015 San Diego Comic-Con, which promised that "fans can discover more fun and fashion digitally within the all new EQUESTRIA GIRLS app."[290] The doll itself was of "Sci-Twi," the version of Twilight Sparkle native to the biped world; though she's never identified as Sci-Twi in the films, she'll be referred to as such going forward in this book for clarity's sake. The press release was also one of the better descriptions of the multiple universes of the films:

It's the moment we've all been waiting for—meet TWILIGHT SPARKLE from CRYSTAL PREP! First seen at the end of the "My Little Pony Equestria Girls Rainbow Rocks" animated film, this TWILIGHT SPARKLE has always lived in the EQUESTRIA GIRLS world—she just attends another school! The special edition studious SCI-TWI doll is dressed for any science experiment, dressed in a chic lab coat over a turtleneck sweater dress with circuit board patterned tights, knee-high boots and her signature glasses.[291]

(Nothing says "super-revealing skin-tight nightclub gear" like a turtleneck sweater dress and a lab coat.) Five *Friendship Games* prequel shorts were released in August: "The Science of Magic," "Pinkie Spy," "All's Fair in Love and Friendship Games," "Photo Finished," and "A Banner Day." While nine out of the ten *Rainbow Rocks* shorts focused on Sunset Shimmer or the Rainbooms, three of the five *Friendship Games* shorts were about supporting characters—including Flash Sentry in "A Banner Day," who continued to exist in spite of how much the Bronies hated him.

The film's lone theatrical screening in the United States was at the Angelika Film Center in New York on September 17, and it was again described as a "Purple Carpet" event, complete with quotes around the phrase.[292] While *Equestria Girls* and *Rainbow Rocks* had both been released after the ends of Seasons 3 and 4, due to Season 5 not beginning until the spring of 2015 and taking a two-month hiatus in the summer, *Friendship Games* premiered on Discovery Family on September 26 halfway through Season 5, the same day as "Made in Manehattan" (S05E16). It was also the first film to feature no scenes set in Equestria, and Princess Twilight doesn't appear until the final scene, when she confirms that the movie takes place during the events of the Season 5 finale "The Cutie Re-Mark, Parts 1 & 2" (S05E25–26), which would not be broadcast for another nine weeks. However, this unusual scheduling didn't impact the story as much as it would have if *Equestria Girls* or *Rainbow Rocks* premiered during rather than after their respective seasons. Where those first two films had been directly informed by the increasing burdens put on Twilight Sparkle from becoming a Princess, *Friendship Games* found Sunset Shimmer having to learn to stand on her own without Twilight's help, while still struggling with her own guilt and shame over the chaos she's wrought. Indeed, *Friendship Games* confirms that Sunset Shimmer is the true emotional core of these films, and appropriately enough, Sunset voice actress Rebecca Shoichet gets second billing after Sci-Twi's Tara Strong after Shoichet had been relegated to the supporting cast in the first two films.

As of "Friendship Through the Ages," Sunset is also the first of the *Equestria Girls* characters—who, by some estimates, are "one thousand percent about combing hair and changing clothes"—to change her clothes for good, replacing her orange-and-yellow ensemble from the first two films with a light blue dress. It's significant on two levels. In the first film and again in flashback in "My Past Is Not Today," we see pictures of her being crowned as the Princess of the previous three Fall Formals: in the first photograph, she's wearing a white dress with a yellow sash, and has an innocent look on her face; in the second her dress is two-toned with light and dark purples, and she has a more sinister countenance; in the third and final picture she's laughing like the cartoon villain she's become, and more importantly, the top of her gown is purple and the skirt is orange with purple and yellow stripes, matching the color scheme of her street clothes in the first two films. In the pictures from the past Formals she'd also worn earrings of her Cutie Mark, and it was in the center of her purple blouse from those films, but her new look lacks it. As a pony, it had been an indelible part of her body since she was a foal, but as a biped, she's rejected her Cutie Mark altogether, representing the new path she's chosen in this world. None of this is referenced in dialog; as they always had on *Friendship Is Magic*, the producers of the *Equestria Girls* films make full use of the visual language of cinema to express character details. It also bucks the "Cutie Mark Magic" theme which was being brought across the entire blueprint—except in the case of the second most important character in the franchise. (The most important character is Princess Twilight, and of course Rarity remains the *best*, but that's not the same as *important* in this context.)

Rainbow Rocks began Sunset's struggle for redemption, and while she achieved it to an extent at the end of that film, the past is always knocking at her door: she's all too aware that she's the root of everything bad that's happened to Canterlot High, and the fabric of spacetime is breaking down in *Friendship Games* because Sci-Twi is unintentionally stirring up the Equestrian magic Sunset brought to this world but can't control (and, as established in the short "The Science of Magic," cannot truly comprehend). Princess Twilight and the Rainbooms have forgiven her, as have the the rest of the Canterlot Wondercolts, but she still hasn't forgiven herself for her sins. The literalized magic of friendship seems benign on paper, but it's only served to make the biped world of the *Equestria Girls* films a more dangerous place, as she is constantly being reminded. The way the Season 5 finale "The Cutie Re-Mark, Part 2" (S05E26) sets up villain Starlight Glimmer for a redemption arc similar to Sunset Shimmer's also suggests the producers had realized that they'd hit upon something special with the *Equestria Girls* films, and were looking to replicate that character dynamic on *Friendship Is Magic*.

Whatever the reasons for the delay in the broadcast of Season 5, it may have benefited from *Friendship Games* having premiered not after the season but in the middle, with nine *Friendship Is Magic* episodes broadcast afterward.

Watched back-to-back, it becomes clear that "The Cutie Re-Mark, Parts 1 & 2" is as plot-driven as *Friendship Games* is character-driven, particularly in the case of the final confrontations with the villains. Starlight Glimmer in "Re-Mark" is seeking vengeance against Princess Twilight for having defeated her in "The Cutie Map, Parts 1 & 2" (S05E01–2), while the shy and awkward Sci-Twi only becomes the villain in *Friendship Games* due to a combination of her natural curiosity and emotional manipulation by Crystal Prep's evil Principal Cinch. "The Cutie Re-Mark, Parts 1 & 2" is a thrilling adventure that rewards faithful viewers of the show, leaning heavily on knowledge of "The Cutie Mark Chronicles" (S01E23) as well as previous two-part season premieres and/or finales, but it's also oddly mechanical. Even the attempt to explain Starlight's behavior via last-minute backstory lacks a moment as emotionally charged as Sci-Twi's Spike catching her eye during the climax of *Friendship Games*.

In the commentary on the Blu-ray, art director Rebecca Dart relates that somepony on the production staff objected to the magically-created outfit which character designer Kora Kosicka designed for Sunset Shimmer, and which she wears for all of seventy seconds of screen time, because it included the "so girly" color of pink—to which Dart replied that there's no reason why pink can't be a powerful color.[293] And so the color remained, and a small victory was made in the rehabilitation of the word "girly."

* * *

In July 2015, during the two-month hiatus between the broadcasts of "Do Princesses Dream of Magic Sheep?" (S05E14) and "Canterlot Boutique" (S05E15), creative director Armando Reyes of Tycoon Gou Producciones in Mexico announced auditions for a stage show called *My Little Pony y Equestria Girls: El Show en Vivo.*[294] *Show Infantil Equestria Girls* was still going strong 4,200 miles south in Peru, no doubt thanks in part to Rarity having been added to the cast, and by September the show had been upgraded from *My Little Pony: Equestria Girls* to the superior *Rainbow Rocks.*[295] But where *Show Infantil Equestria Girls* was a necessarily intimate production intended to be performed in small spaces, *My Little Pony y Equestria Girls: El Show en Vivo* was a 90-minute stage extravaganza with 17 songs, a dozen characters and 13 scene changes, beginning in Equestria with the Mane Six in pony form.[296] (And if the Rainbooms were supposed to be ultra-skinny, Reyes did not get that memo, for his cast cannot be described as ultra-skinny, super-skinny, or even just plain ol' skinny.)

The show combined elements of both *Equestria Girls* and *Rainbow Rocks,* changing the narrative as necessary for a stage production; most notably,

Sunset Shimmer is a sympathetic character from the start, replacing Princess Twilight as the rallying subject of "Equestria Girls (Cafeteria Song)," as well as taking lead vocals for the Rainbooms during both halves of "Welcome to the Show." *My Little Pony y Equestria Girls: El Show en Vivo* premiered the weekend of October 31 (the same week that *Friendship Games* was playing in the Vue Cinemas in the UK) at the 2,200-seat Cultural Center #1 in Mexico City, and played there again on the weekends of November 21 and 28 before moving on to dates in Xalapa, Veracruz, Puebla, Oaxaca, and Querétaro through December.[297] Due to the success of the original run, the show returned to Mexico City for the last two weekends in January, then toured throughout the rest of Mexico in February and March, played for a weekend in Panama City, Panama in April, and made its way through Colombia in May and June before converging with *Show Infantil Equestria Girls* in Lima, Peru, in July.[298]

My Little Pony y Equestria Girls: El Show en Vivo was a terrific, high-energy show which captured the spirit of the first two movies.[299] The libretto used all of Daniel Ingram's songs from those movies except "Tricks Up My Sleeve" from *Rainbow Rocks* and "Opening Titles (Remix)" from *Equestria Girls*, and breathed new life into many of them: the otherwise slight "Strange New World" particularly pops in Spanish, the performance of "Awesome as I Want to Be" has an unhinged quality lacking from the original, and Sunset's solo lines during the Rainbooms' second verse in "Welcome to the Show," already one of the musical high points of the franchise, are just chilling. The show also incorporated the extended version of "Make a Wish" from "Pinkie Pride" (S04E12), not coincidentally the best song from Season 4 of *Friendship Is Magic*.[300]

As much as the media fascination with Bronies had created the false but very marketable impression that modern My Little Pony fandom was primarily 1) men 2) in the United States, as of February 2015 *Friendship Is Magic* was being broadcast on over 24 networks in 180 territories, and *Equestria Girls* was as much of a global phenomenon with all ages and genders as *Friendship Is Magic* whether the Bronies cared for it or not—but there was a particular age and gender considered most troublesome.

No (Equestria) Girls Allowed, Part III: Daily v. Girls, Round 2

On September 29, 2015, a few days after the premiere of *Friendship Games* on Discovery Family and a month before it played the Vue Cinemas in the UK and *My Little Pony y Equestria Girls: El Show en Vivo* premiered in Mexico, some United States men had their say via an Equestria Daily essay by founder Sethisto titled, "Is Equestria Girls a Bad Thing for Pony?"[301]

The essay echoed many criticisms of My Little Pony that had been leveled over the decades at the franchise; the text of *Friendship Is Magic* and *Equestria Girls* is largely ignored, with more of a focus on how the latter affects the Bronies by not catering to them as much as they expected. The distrust of young girls throughout and reduction of *Equestria Girls* to nothing but a toy commercial resemble Hal Erickson's entry on *My Little Pony 'n' Friends* and *My Little Pony Tales* in *Television Cartoon Shows: An Illustrated Encyclopedia, 1949–1993,* particularly his reference to the "several otherwise rational high school and college-age young ladies" he knew in 1994 who had not only collected G1 My Little Pony dolls, but persisted in not getting rid of them in adolescence.

The first two paragraphs set the tone:

> We now officially have a third Equestria Girls movie under our belt, and after two and a half years of melding oddly colored humans with candy colored equines, people are still wondering what kind of impact having this extra side-canon has on Friendship is Magic as a whole. Rumors and conspiracies are everywhere surrounding the rise of the Equestria Girl.
> Why does something so off-base to what brought us all here in the first place exist, and why is it seemingly so popular? Is the "High School Musical" alternate dimension version of what many of us consider to be a an incredibly well-created pony world a bad thing?[302]

The phrase "rumors and conspiracies" gives *Equestria Girls* a dark bent, not unlike when the *New York Times* referred to Hasbro as My Little Pony's "perpetrators" in 1989, while what is and is not canon had always been a major concern of the Bronies.[303] *Equestria Girls* may have been a spinoff consisting of movies and shorts comprising roughly four hours and twenty minutes of content by September 2015, but it was no less canonical than its parent series; the first thirty seconds of *My Little Pony: Equestria Girls* established that, picking up directly from where "Magical Mystery Cure" (S03E13) left off. But only the things the Bronies liked—"what brought us all here"—were considered real, and the rest was "extra side-canon."

He harkened back to mid 2013, when "people were rightfully wary of the direction the show was going":

> Not only was our favorite unicorn booknerd becoming a princess, but ALL the ponies were being tossed into the most obvious "SELL MORE TOYS!" plan ever in the form of humanization and high school. The core reason why Friendship is Magic is so successful is because they kept the product placement to a minimum, avoiding the "toy commercial" vibe that earlier incarnations of My Little Pony suffered from. The brony fandom was understandably wary, and in some cases downright angry.

Exactly how biped versions of the ponies qualifies as "the most obvious 'SELL MORE TOYS!' plan ever" was left unexplained, and makes less sense considering that a high school populated by humans—and not even *magical* humans, except in very limited circumstances, the hows and whys of those circumstances driving much of the story in the second and third films— doesn't offer nearly as many possibilities as anthropomorphic ponies in a fantasy land not strictly beholden to the rules of the human world.

As we've seen, the criticism of My Little Pony cartoons as being nothing but venal toy commercials has always been held to be self-evident, such as Jaime Weinman feeling no need to clarify why *Friendship Is Magic* "seems to confirm adults' worst fears about kids' cartoons" in 2011, other than describing it as being produced by Hasbro to "convince kids to buy the line of toys it's based on," and quoting Amid Amidi that it only exists to "get viewers to hand over their money."[304] For Equestria Daily to describe keeping "product place-ment to a minimum" as *the* core reason for *Friendship Is Magic's* success is unfair to the many talented people who've worked hard to create a show that is a satisfying experience on every level—and those same people worked on *Equestria Girls* (only some of whom received death threats from angry Bronies). It also ignores the existence of "Power Ponies" (S04E06), broadcast six months after the premiere of *Equestria Girls* during the wildly uneven first half of Season 4, in which the Mane Six and Spike become comic-book superheroes for reasons that are never properly explained. They embraced that episode, and Equestria Daily ran polls to decide which pony had the best powers and costume.[305] (Rarity won by a landslide for best costume, so never let it be said the Bronies and I can't agree on anything.) The episode was of course heavily merchandised, including the Special Edition Pony for the 2014 San Diego Comic-Con being the "Power Ponies" villain in both pony and biped form,[306] and the Mane Six in their superhero costumes were also released as products which Equestria Daily reported on with excitement.[307]

One of the suggested answers in an essay section titled "Why is Equestria Girls a Thing?" (besides "the obvious attack on the ridiculously successful Monster High line of dolls," the eternal millstone) was the humanized Brony fan art which had existed from the beginning, which he used to compare Bronies to a resource being exploited by Hasbro[308]:

> There is no doubt that Hasbro does, in fact, keep an eye on the brony fandom. They may not admit it often, but if you have seen the leaks over the years, they data mine us like it's the gold rush era and we are California. We've had entire packs of Doctor Whoof and Derpy resources materials come in, leaked from DHX, Hasbro, and Top Draw, as far back as 2013. Creating something that little girls will gobble up, while a portion of the "brony" fans might enjoy probably sounded like a good idea.[309]

Describing it in terms of "data mining" and leaks of materials based on Brony-created characters continued to make Hasbro seem all the more monolithic and overreaching, as though they were actively engaging in an invasion of the privacy of these consumers, a loaded implication in an era in which high-profile data breaches involving Julian Assange, Edward Snowden, and Chelsea Manning are big news with wide-reaching implications. But unmentioned is that the mined data in question was posted in droves to public sites such as DeviantArt and Equestria Daily, and all manner of social media—as he pointed out elsewhere in the article, there was once "a period of time where you couldn't go 10 links on the internet without running into at least one pony avatar"—and among the results were those characters being featured on the show to the great delight of the Bronies, and being made into toys which they gobbled up no less so than the little girls who were regarded with such contempt throughout the article.[310] But Cereal Velocity's joyful "We just totally made a toy, didn't we?" response to the gray mare being announced as the Special Edition Pony for the 2012 San Diego-Comic Con was now a dim memory.[311]

Although he referred to employees at DHX Media who had said that "switching to humans for a bit was a breath of fresh air" after working on *Friendship Is Magic* for years, the notion that *Equestria Girls* might have spawned from any kind of a creative impulse struck Sethisto as improbable, because "a project like Equestria Girls is something the higher ups at Hasbro would cook up." That's a reasonable conclusion, because *Friendship Is Magic* (i.e., "what brought us all here") was *also* cooked up by Hasbro's higher-ups.

As she related to Equestria Daily in 2011, series creator Lauren Faust had pitched "a micro-series pop opera" for her Milky Way and the Galaxy Girls dolls, and Hasbro's general manager of entertainment and licensing Lisa Licht instead asked if she had any ideas for a new My Little Pony series. Hasbro was already planning a reboot, and Licht "was really pushing to match the right talent with the right project," but had Faust not agreed to be the creative steward, it would have been somepony else.[312] In a 2013 Q&A session on 4chan's /mlp/ board, Faust confirmed that Milky Way and the Galaxy Girls was "designed to be a doll line," and that she "never wanted it to be a show, but the folks who make toys want shows before they invest."[313]

So, Faust had gone into Hasbro to pitch what would have been a program-length commercial whose primary purpose was to, as the saying goes, "SELL MORE (GALAXY GIRLS) TOYS!," and wound up developing a program-length commercial to "SELL MORE (MY LITTLE PONY) TOYS!" If *Friendship Is Magic* "transcended its toy-based origins," as Maria Bustillos put it, then so did *Equestria Girls*, at least in terms of how the movies and shorts stand on their own. But if one can only view them as a merchandising machine as so many critics have viewed every iteration of My Little Pony since time out of mind, then that is all it shall be—unless you like one of those particular iterations, in which case all those *other* iterations are Commerce, and the one *you* like is Art.

After ruminating about the extent to which the first film was responsible for people possibly getting "scared away and 'leaving the fandom'" in 2013 (a trend represented by a decline in comments on Equestria Daily), he did suggest that *Equestria Girls* "broadened the spectrum of potential fans" by bringing in people who "may have ignored the show if it was simply a cartoon about ponies," in that "the group out there collecting Monster High dolls or simply into High School Musical might give pony a shot after learning about Twilight and crew from watching the movies."[314] The third film in the *High School Musical* trilogy had been released seven years earlier, and thus hardly counted as a market to be tapped, while the suggestion that the girls who are (still) into that or Monster High or might somehow not already be aware of My Little Pony is ludicrous at best, but it supports the recurring narrative among Bronies that they are the only true fans of *Friendship Is Magic*, or at least the only fans who matter. It's also worth noting that Monster High has always had a higher key demographic than My Little Pony; when Monster High started to be unveiled in May 2010—around the same time that *Friendship Is Magic* was announced as the title of the new Pony series—a spokesperson told the *Los Angeles Business Journal* that they hoped to bring the characters to life "by developing a fantasy world that resonates with tween and young teen girls," typically defined as from 8 to 12 years old. But whether in 2010 when *Monster High* and *Friendship Is Magic* debuted, or 2013 with the advent of *Equestria Girls*, it is simply not feasible that a wide swath of young girls in the United States were unacquainted with My Little Pony. And while it's true that *Friendship Is Magic* breathed a new and unprecedented life into the franchise, to such an extent that Generations 3, 3.1 and 3.5 tend to be forgotten, the brand was not entirely moribund before Generation 4 the way it was before Generations 2 and 3. After all, when *Friendship Is Magic* was only halfway through Season 1 in January 2011, Ryan Gosling's 6-year-old co-star in *Blue Valentine* was still singing songs from the G3 show *The World's Biggest Tea Party*.[315]

There's also the implication that the setting and characters of the films (teenagers in a high school) gives them a narrower demographic appeal than that of the series (ponies in a fantasy land), when if *Friendship Is Magic* proved anything, it's that the setting and characters aren't nearly as important as what's done with them. People of all ages and genders can enjoy both *Friendship Is Magic* and *Equestria Girls*, if they're so inclined. The automatic dismissal of the high school setting, as though it could not possibly provide any opportunities for compelling stories or characters, is an echo of the AV Club's Todd VanDerWerff writing in April 2011 that the primary obstacle *Friendship Is Magic* had to overcome was that in addition to being "a show built to advertise a toy line," it was about "fucking cartoon ponies."[316] Though I do know of at least one case where the movies led somepony to the show: my grown-up friend KrOB agreed to see *My Little Pony: Equestria Girls—Rainbow Rocks* in the theater with me even though he'd never watched any My Little Pony, and enjoyed it enough to start watching *Friendship Is Magic*. (He's more fond of *Magic*, but isn't threatened by *Equestria Girls*, either.)

In a section of the post titled "Money Appeases the Hasbro Masters" (more about that title in a moment), Sethisto wrote that "there is no doubt that the show has a much higher budget than it originally did," and displaying the deep fear of change that has characterized the Brony attitude toward the show from the start, pondered whether that extra money may "have been better spent on simply expanding the already existing ponyland as opposed to a new, humanized side IP?"[317] He surmised, not altogether incorrectly, that it comes down to the merchandise, though the conclusion drawn is questionable at best:

> You can only sell so many variants on the mane 6 in horse form before people just stop buying them. Sure you have your die-hard collectors that need every possible variant on Twilight Sparkle's cutie mark placement or cheap plastic comb, but for most of us, and even little girls, our single Twilight from years ago is good enough.[318]

In addition to being the second of four increasingly dismissive references to little girls, it's somewhat disingenuous from the editor of a site which reports on every release, rumor, and conspiracy of new My Little Pony merchandise. The post immediately preceding "Is Equestria Girls a Bad Thing for Pony?" on September 29, 2015, was "My Little Pony Dog Tags Series 2 Announced!" by contributor Cups, and the first line was "Pony accessory junkies rejoice, because the second series of My Little Pony Dog Tags are on the way!"[319] In an August 17 post, Sethisto had written about the German candy company Kinder offering small dolls of Princess Twilight, Fluttershy, Pinkie Pie, and Rainbow Dash in both pony and Rainboom forms: "Each one is surprisingly well detailed, and makes me jealous that we can't get them over here!"[320] On October 4, less than a week after the "Is Equestria Girls a Bad Thing for Pony?" essay, he posted a picture showing the two different sizes of the pony Princess Twilight dolls from Kinder: "Color me impressed, these things are huge! I'll just be over here wishing the U.S. government would allow these things to be sold again…"[321] It was a discordant amount of enthusiasm about yet another Princess Twilight doll from somepony who had written five days earlier that "for most of us, and even little girls, our single Twilight from years ago is good enough."[322]

The thing about money is that it appeases *all* the masters, not just those at Hasbro. Whether that's good or bad is far beyond the scope of this book; it's just how the system is, at least in the United States in the early 21st century. Money appeases whoever provides the bandwidth for Equestria Daily, it makes the publication of this book possible, and it allows for such mediocre yet Brony-beloved episodes as "The Last Roundup" (S02E14) and "Slice of Life" (S05E09) to exist, as well as straight-up classics like "Party of One" (S01E25) and *Rainbow Rocks.* Even if we accept Bustillos's conclusion that Bronies in an Anaheim ballroom jumping up and down and shouting "Friendship!" is what proved the show was capital-A Art (as opposed to the merits of the show itself), for certain money is also why *Friendship Is Magic* was developed in the first place. Lisa Licht wouldn't have been looking for a creative steward to helm the reboot if she didn't think it could increase their profits, and the people who work on the show don't do it for free. (If so, there may well have been a mass exodus after the intense Brony backlash to the announcement of *Equestria Girls,* for it wouldn't have been worth it to continue doing something for such a mercurial and volatile fanbase). This doesn't mean there are no labors of love at all; running Equestria Daily is as much an expression of love for My Little Pony as the writing of *Ponyville Confidential,* no matter how different our opinions.

For better or worse, the profit motive applies across the board to any beloved franchise, whether My Little Pony or Doctor Who, Harry Potter or Star Wars. They would not exist without it, certainly not at their level of mainstream popularity, and it's playing dirty pool to selectively write off certain aspects because they can be linked to ancillary sales. After *Star Wars: The Force Awakens* was released in December 2015, I noticed that any elements somepony didn't like tended to be written off as just existing for the merchandise; a friend told me they loved the droid BB-8, but dismissed the alien-heavy scene in Maz Kanata's Castle as existing "just to sell Disney toys," when in fact BB-8 was at the forefront of the toy releases that began three months before the film was released.[323]

As for other ways the increased budget could have been spent on "simply expanding the already existing ponyland as opposed to a new, humanized side IP," these were Sethisto's suggestions:

> Could a lineup of an alternate mane 6 in another corner of ponyland been as successful for Hasbro's bottom line as breaking into the doll market? Would a perpetually drunk and jaded old Doctor Whoof teaming up with Derpy traveling the multiverse be a killer for an untapped segment of the potential adult market? Who knows! They went with the safe bet, focusing on the little girl market they already have all that doll-based research on, and it payed off.
>
> In the end, this means more pony for us, even if some of it goes to furthering Canterlot

High and humans instead of a side series exploring Luna's school of Witchcraft and Wizardry back in Equestria. (I want that so bad.)[324]

This once again reduces *Equestria Girls* to nothing but a carefully researched effort to market dolls to little girls, echoing Amid Amidi's April 2010 prediction that the new My Little Pony series would be nothing more than Lauren Faust being hired to "take this toy designed in a corporate boardroom and make a prettier version of it," while ignoring that *Friendship Is Magic* was also the result of "doll-based research" in the form of what Hasbro had learned since the launch of My Pretty Pony in 1981 leading into Generation 1, the scrubbed launch of Generation 2, and the success of Generation 3. The series was not created in a vacuum, independent of and unaffected by research and commerce. (Speaking as somepony who always checks the toy aisle at stores that have such things, *Friendship Is Magic* dolls, toys, and ancillary merchandise always outnumbered *Equestria Girls* dolls as of early 2016, and while I've been in many stores that carry both, I have yet to see *Equestria Girls* dolls being sold without *Friendship Is Magic* dolls nearby.) Sethisto also gives *Friendship Is Magic* a boost in "Is Equestria Girls a Bad Thing for Pony?" by described it in terms of its characters, while ignoring that *Equestria Girls* is no less character-based.

Even with the lingering magic and occasional pony-ups, neither of which are taken for granted in the movies, the more realistic milieu of *Friendship Games* in particular results in a more grounded, character-and-emotionally-driven story than *Friendship Is Magic* was able to produce on a regular basis during Season 5. Which is not to say there weren't any; "Tanks for the Memories" (S05E05), "Make New Friends but Keep Discord" (S05E07), and "Amending Fences" (S05E12) all go to some deep emotional places. But it's also why *Friendship Games* is so much more satisfying than the finale "The Cutie Re-Mark, Parts 1 & 2" (S05E25–26). There were still elements of magic and monsters in *Friendship Games*, but the movie came down to an examination of two damaged individuals: Sci-Twi, who has talent but no experience or wisdom, and Sunset Shimmer, whose ambition has always outstripped her talent and wisdom. The battle of wills between them, a battle that the sheltered and overwhelmed Sci-Twi barely realizes is being waged, creates some of the most compelling interpony conflict the franchise has yet produced. One of the ways this is expressed is in Sunset's and Sci-Twi's first head-to-head competition—not for boys' attention by trying to "look as cool as they can, showing off their dance moves, cell phones, clothes and boots and so on" as Bustillos suggested, but rather by racing to complete a geometry problem. (And not a simple one, either; in the Blu-ray commentary, art director Rebecca Dart says she found it by Googling "hardest geometry problem."[325]) Sci-Twi solves the problem correctly, but Sunset does not, her ambitions having always outstripped her talents. By comparison, Princess Twilight in "The Cutie Re-Mark" doesn't have much of an arc to speak of; it's a high-stakes situation, but she doesn't learn anything new or have to confront her weaknesses the way Sunset and Sci-Twi do. And, by the same token, the show's best finale ever—Season 1's "The Best Night Ever" (S01E26)—is entirely character-based, with no magic or adventure elements at all.

A month before *Friendship Games* and "Is Equestria Girls a Bad Thing for Pony?," Nima Nourizadeh's film *American Ultra* debuted in sixth place, and was considered a flop. Screenwriter Max Landis took to Twitter to wonder aloud about the future of films not based on existing intellectual properties; as he pointed out, his film—an original script that was not an adaptation of an IP—lost out to a sequel (*Mission Impossible: Rogue Nation*), a sequel reboot (*Hitman: Agent 47*), a biopic (*Straight Outta Compton*), another sequel (*Sinister 2*) and a reboot (*The Man from U.N.C.L.E.*).[326] It is then worth noting that of the three suggestions offered as alternatives to *Equestria Girls*, "a lineup of an alternate mane 6 in another corner of ponyland" is just more of the same, while the other two are the kind of combination of existing intellectual properties that drives so much fan-fiction (e.g., Victorian R. Hellsly's January 2011 "My Little Time Lord" on FanFiction.net, or going back further with a different franchise, Jean Airey's 1984 "The Doctor and the *Enterprise*" in the fanzine *Enterprise*) but would be prohibitively expensive just to license, let alone produce. What makes even less sense about the "[Princess] Luna's school of Witchcraft and Wizardry" spinoff that he "wants so bad" is that in addition to being a bald repurposing of Hogwarts School of Witchcraft and Wizardry from the Harry Potter series, "The Cutie Mark Chronicles" (S01E23) in Season 1 established that Princess *Celestia* already runs a school for Unicorns with strong magical gifts. So the show had already provided a location for a spinoff about a magical school without having to combine it with another intellectual property, but the actual text of *Friendship Is Magic* is as unimportant as the text of *Equestria Girls* when criticizing the latter. The text of the show is further disregarded in the description of Doctor Whoof (or Whooves, or Hooves, depending on where you look) as being "perpetually drunk and jaded," which is nothing like the way the character was portrayed in "Slice of Life" (S05E09), but instead sounds like the multiverse-hopping, perpetually drunk and jaded title character of Rick Sanchez on *Rick and Morty*, which is itself a broad parody of the main characters from *Back to the Future*. Even if Hasbro did indeed go with "the safe bet, focusing on the little girl market they already have all that doll-based research on," it's unrealistic to blame *Equestria Girls* for preventing a My Little Pony version of *Doctor Who* or *Rick and Morty* becoming an official series.

Whatever else you can say about *Equestria Girls*, it is at least an *original* idea. They may not approach Stan Brakhage's *Mothlight* or Michael Snow's *Wavelength* as wholly unique works of art with no true antecedent, but the fact that the *Equestria Girls* films are not the first pieces of fiction to focus on girls in high school does not mean they can be reduced to copies of *Monster High* or *High School Musical*—or the 1982 television series *Square Pegs* or the *Betty and Veronica* comics or Francine Pascal's *Sweet Valley High* books, to name other examples of the subgenre—and more importantly, they fulfilled Meghan McCarthy's stated goal in the May 2013 *New York Times* article of a new setting allowing for new storytelling, while staying true to who the characters are and extending the mythology.[327] The first film borrowed quite a lot from the pilot episodes "Friendship Is Magic, Parts 1 & 2" (S01E01–2) while establishing its strange-to-Princess-Twilight new world, but *Rainbow Rocks* and *Friendship Games* are stories that could not have been told on the *Friendship Is Magic* series.

In the next section, "Keeping It Separate Is Good," he again posits Bronies (and the volatility thereof) as being the reason for major creative decisions, while continuing to imply that *Equestria Girls* is not part of the *Friendship Is Magic* canon:

> Pony canon is important to most of us. We love this show, we love the world, we love the characters, and messing with that trifecta of fandom obsession is a dangerous game. With the third movie, it's pretty obvious that Hasbro got the hint that we want these things to be separate entities.[328]

Again, "Pony canon" here means "what the Bronies want *Friendship Is Magic* to be," and as we've seen, what they love is their collective interpretation of the show, the world, and the characters, and that it's a "dangerous game" to mess with those obsessions. (Points for owning both that and the word "obsession," at least.) But correlation is not causation, and to suggest that because *Friendship Games* has no scenes set in Equestria—or indeed any ponies at all, other than brief glimpses through the rips in spacetime caused by Sci-Twi—means that "Hasbro got the hint" about what Bronies want and acted on it is what people who like to drop fancy Latin phrases call a *post hoc, ergo propter hoc* fallacy ("After this, therefore because of this"). A far more likely reason based on the movie itself is that there was no *need* for any scenes in Equestria, as one of the themes in the film is Sunset Shimmer learning to solve problems without Princess Twilight's help. In the commentary on the *Friendship Games* Blu-ray, screenwriter Josh Haber relates that an early script ended with Principal Cinch winding up in Equestria transformed into a horrible monster, but they decided against it because it would be too dark, and he in no way implies that it was because they'd "gotten the hint" that the Bronies wanted to keep things separate.[329]

Indeed, after suggesting that the production team "understands" that many Bronies want nothing to do with *Equestria Girls*, Sethisto reinforceed the narrative that it's nothing but a toy commercial, while getting in yet another dig at those troublesome young girls:

> If nothing else good comes out of the idea of humanized ponies to you, at least you have a sacrificial lamb to keep the merchandising hammer away from Equestria. Even if Flash Sentry does find time to hook up with humanland Twilight for the sake of selling more toys to love-crazed little girls, our precious equine version will still be safe. Applejack's pink trunk never became a thing, and the only major product placement we have been bombarded with is Twilight's balloon.[330]

The phrase "love-crazed little girls" phrase is as reductive and misogynistic as Erickson's reference to the "otherwise rational" young women he knew who still had their My Little Pony dolls in their attics, but even if the character of Flash only existed to appeal to straight girls who are old enough to appreciate a kind and pretty teenage boy who also plays a mean guitar, it is not automatically a bad thing just because it's outside the comfort zone of the 16–35 male demographic that so many Bronies fall into. Indeed, even if the genesis of Flash was as crass as somepony blurting out "a cute boy to sell more toys to love-crazed little girls!" during a brainstorming session in the cold corporate boardroom that surely spawned *Equestria Girls* (but not *Friendship Is Magic* or Star Wars, both of which are pure works of Art above financial concerns), what matters is the end result. As Lauren Faust had written in her *Ms.* blog post five years earlier when she was still working on *Friendship Is Magic*, there was always a need to balance her ideals with her employers' requirements of toy sales and good ratings, as well as "a need to incorporate fashion play into the show, but only one character is interested in it and she is not a trend follower but a designer who sells her own creations from her own store."[331] That character is of course Rarity, who (to borrow a phrase) transcended her toy-based origins to become the best. By the same token, even if the true impetus of *Equestria Girls* was Hasbro looking to compete with Monster High like so many Bronies and other critics have suggested, that still takes nothing away from the artistic success the final product, Original Sin be damned.

Regarding Flash, the article also ignores his diminishing role in the films as a romantic interest of Princess Twilight, much like it ignores most everything that happens in the movies. For all intents and purposes, Flash and Princess Twilight's relationship arc was completed at the end of *Rainbow Rocks* when an impromptu victory hug results in them both blushing with embarrassment and pulling away from each other, another emotionally painful moment for Twilight in a film full of them. He's also noticeably absent from her goodbyes to the Rainbooms and Sunset Shimmer before Twilight re-enters the portal at the end of both *Equestria Girls* and *Rainbow Rocks*, he isn't present during her brief cameo at the end of *Friendship Games*, and when he crosses paths with Sci-Twi earlier in that film, she neither knows nor cares who he is. (Poor Flash. The kid can't catch a break.)

Meanwhile, the suggestion that the existence of *Equestria Girls* kept the "merchandising hammer" away from *Friendship Is Magic* doesn't hold up, even within the context of a franchise which has been denigrated from the start as nothing but a toy commercial—a narrative which some Bronies perpetuate when it suits their needs. "Twilight's balloon" refers to the hot air balloon seen in the opening titles of *Friendship Is Magic*, and later used in episodes including "Fall Weather Friends" (S01E13), "Sonic Rainboom" (S01E16), "The Return of Harmony, Part 2" (S02E02) and "Wonderbolts Academy" (S03E07). Lauren Faust did confirm that the balloon was based on a toy that was already being developed, and the implication here is that because the balloon is seen in the beginning of every episode and is also available as a toy, it qualifies as a "bombardment" of product placement.[332] If so, then other elements from the opening titles as of Season 5 which must also qualify as product placement include (in order of appearance) Princess Celestia's castle,[333] Applejack's barn,[334] the train they call the *Friendship Express*,[335] Fluttershy's cottage,[336] Princess Twilight's castle[337]—and, most significantly, almost all the characters who appear onscreen, though "products" in this context seems to refer to anything *other* than the character dolls. But if the balloon qualifies as a bombardment, then the full thirty-five seconds of the opening titles is akin to the firebombing of Dresden.

As stated in the beginning of "Is Equestria Girls a Bad Thing for Pony?," September 2015 marked approximately two and a half years of "melding oddly colored humans with candy colored equines."[338] (Candy colors are no less odd for ponies than they are for humans, but that's beside the point.) When *Equestria Girls* was introduced to great anger, derision, and probably not all *that* many death threats in May 2013, it was just over two and a half years after the October 2010 premiere of *Friendship Is Magic*. In addition to the many variations of the Mane Six and supporting characters, *Friendship Is Magic* products which were available by the time *Equestria Girls* was announced include but are not limited to the aforementioned playsets of Princess Celestia's castle and the *Friendship Express*, as well as Rarity's Carousel Boutique,[339] a Canterlot Wedding Toy & Playset,[340] the Ponyville Schoolhouse,[341] the Royal Ball at Canterlot Castle Playset,[342] Applejack's farm truck[343] (which may be the mysterious "pink trunk" referred to in the article), a Pinkie Pie RC car,[344] a Twilight Sparkle RC car,[345] and the scooter that came with the Riding Along with Twilight Sparkle figure, though those last four may not qualify as "product placement" in this context because they don't appear on the show, since (it bears repeating) internal combustion engines don't exist in Equestria.

But for *Equestria Girls* to have succeeded at "[taking] MLP back to it's branlessly girly toy-pusher days" as Equestria Daily commenter Dyxid so memorably predicted in May 2013, it would stand to reason that there would be at least as many toys and ancillary products created in the first two and a half years of *Equestria Girls* as there were in the first two and a half years of *Friendship Is Magic*. Just like with the ponies, there were many variations of the Rainbooms and other bipeds in doll form—though never Sunset Shimmer's previous Fall Formal looks as seen in the first film, which would seem to be an obvious choice for a series of movies which exist only to "SELL MORE TOYS!" to little girls—yet there were only four toys released that could qualify as a balloon-style product placement bombardment by virtue of both appearing in the films and also being available as toys: the Canterlot High Pep Rally playset,[346] the Mane Event Stage playset[347] and DJ Pon-3's Rockin Convertible[348] (both of which are based on items not seen until the second *Equestria Girls* film), and the Canterlot High School playset, another obvious choice which didn't appear until July 2015, a little over two years after the dawn of *Equestria Girls*.[349] (Also, like the gray mare, DJ Pon-3 was a background pony named by the Bronies who now so hated the films.[350])

Indeed, if *Equestria Girls* had just one job—to be the sacrificial lamb which diverted the blunt object of merchandising away from *Friendship Is Magic*—then it had failed long before "Is Equestria Girls a Bad Thing for Pony?" was posted. First announced at the New York Toy Fair in February 2015, Hasbro's *Friendship Is Magic* Collection mined the elements and settings of that show like (to borrow a simile) it was the gold rush era and *Friendship Is Magic* was California.[351] The first to be released was a collection of collectable figurines related to Applejack's farm, mining such deep veins as extended Apple Family members Peachy Sweet, Jonagold, and Apple Munchies, and others like them who have only appeared in the background of episodes without ever interacting with the story or even being given names—what M.A. Larson would describe at the MLP-MSP panel later that year as "not characters, they're designs," little more than Background Pony #2—as well as Flim and Flam from "The Super Speedy Cider Squeezy 6000" (S02E15) and "Leap of Faith" (S04E20), who are actually full-fledged characters. Sethisto approved of it all, writing in May that "Wow, these things look really good!"[352] and that "This set looks to be covering just about everything you'd expect from the Apple family. Hopefully you guys have some dedicated shelf space for it!"[353]

A week and a half before "Is Equestria Girls a Bad Thing for Pony?," he wrote in a post about a new *Friendship Is Magic* Collection set focusing on Pinkie Pie and her family, "We really need more Maud Pie in our lives," and "I wonder if they will go all out with a neat looking display similar to the Apple Family part?"[354]

Like the concurrent "Cutie Mark Magic" theme, this new line did not extend to the *Equestria Girls* dolls, and it was clear that the merchandising hammer was coming down on *Friendship Is Magic* harder than before. Sethisto's excitement about the new wave of toys from his favorite television cartoon was palpable, more than a little endearing, and forgotten altogether when he wrote in "Is Equestria Girls a Bad Thing for Pony?" that "we missed out on our brony bucks going toward more actual equine stuff" because of *Equestria Girls*.[355] Except for all the actual equine stuff continuing to be released along with and to greatly outnumber the biped stuff, which suggests My Little Pony merchandise is not a starvation economy, and the existence of *Equestria Girls* dolls and toys did not mean fewer *Friendship Is Magic* dolls and toys for the Bronies' bucks to go toward.

This writer's non–Brony bucks have gone more toward *Equestria Girls* stuff than actual equine stuff since 2013, and as may be apparent by now, she considers *Equestria Girls* to not be a bad thing for Pony, for it *is* Pony, and no less so than *Friendship Is Magic*. If all you want is more of the same—with elements from other existing IPs mixed in, however impractical that may be—then yes, *Equestria Girls* is bad for Pony. If you like the idea of the franchise's storytelling and character possibilities expanding, for the creators to be able to try new things, then *Equestria Girls* is a very good thing for Pony.

Though the first thirty seconds of *My Little Pony: Equestria Girls* established that the films are canon, the debate continued now after the third film in the comments as to *Equestria Girls'* canonicity, including Zer0C0re stating that "I detest these films," and that *Equestria Girls* is bad for "the main show" because "it may be a separate canon but if it's considered canon (which admittedly is vague on purpose) it could be a future potential threat to the storyline of the show and could drag the show's storyline in a direction the fandom doesn't want it to go."[356] What greater sin can *Equestria Girls* commit than to make *Friendship Is Magic* go in directions the Bronies don't want? Causing people to stop watching that show due to the wickedness of *Equestria Girls*, such as commenter paladin3210, who said "I stopped supporting MLP because of EG, I don't watch it since season 4 ended," and that while "I still enjoy seeing what the Fandom creates," the official Hasbro material "no longer exists for me."[357] Our old friend CMC_Scootaloo replied, "That's the most bad thing you can do now in that situation with EQG. I don't like EQG either, no, I hate it with all of my passion. But the last thing one who hates EQG should do is letting My Little Pony: Friendship is Magic suffer from it."[358] He assured them that "stronger support for My Little Pony: Friendship is Magic is the best way to oppose EQG," and that to "leave" Pony "will only harm it and achieve the opposite by literally playing into EQGs hands."[359] This portrayal of *Equestria Girls* as a devious enemy to be defeated complements Sethisto's statement that "rumors and conspiracies are everywhere surrounding the rise of the Equestria Girl," while also bringing to mind the famous 1943 American propaganda poster imploring citizens to join a car-sharing club, bearing the slogan "When you ride ALONE you ride with Hitler!"[360] In 2015, if you didn't ride with *Friendship Is Magic*, you were riding with *Equestria Girls*. Upon learning that paladin3210 was reluctant to discuss these things in public because of receiving "hate and vitriol" in the past,[361] including being told to kill himself,[362] CMC_Scootaloo promised that "I won't make any death threats."[363] As expressions of how the Capital-A Art of *Friendship Is Magic* has brought out the best in the Bronies, promising to *not* make death threats may not be on quite the same level as kids in an Anaheim ballroom jumping up and down and shouting "Friendship!"

The three *Equestria Girls* films are superior to *My Little Pony 'n' Friends*, *My Little Pony Tales*, and the G3, G3.1, and G3.5 cartoons in every way, and are no less of an expression of the vision Lauren Faust established in her December 2010 *Ms.* blog post than *Friendship Is Magic*, but they still bore the brunt of the sexist and hypocritical backlash that had dogged My Little Pony from the start. Much like how Erickson, Amidi, Beck, and so many others either excused or ignored the commercial aspects of the boy-oriented Transformers range while heavily criticizing My Little Pony for the same sins, here *Friendship Is Magic* got a pass while *Equestria Girls* was summarily condemned due to it being more and about teenage girls.

Two and a half weeks after "Is Equestria Girls a Bad Thing for Pony?"—and surely coincidental to it—Lauren Faust tweeted an article by Laura Moss on the Mother Nature Network titled "Why Must We Hate the Things Teen Girls Love?"[364] (More evidence that being a Brony does not mean a man is a feminist, or even a compassionate human being, is offered by the first reply to her tweet: "I <3 you Lauren but I don't believe in this war on women/girls that everyone keeps pushing. I'm sorry."[365]) Moss's article considered the negative reaction on the Internet to the release of a new book in Stephenie Meyer's *Twilight* series, as well as the harsh online response to teenage girls who were sad when a member of the band One Direction announced he was leaving, and the way that "mocking teenage girls and portraying their interest as worthless can further reinforce ideas that things created for women and by women are unimportant."[366] Moss also quoted feminist writer and activist Bailey Poland regarding how in modern criticism, the enthusiasm teenage girls show for the things they like is often described as "hysteria," a term that was in use in the 1800s and 1900s, and which speaks to "an underlying assumption that teen girls are not in control of their emotions or interests and become overly excited or upset for no reason." Echoing the controversies in the 1980s about girls bonding over a shared love of a given pop culture item, Poland is also quoted as saying "the reality is that teen girls are often very intentional about what they're interested in and aware of the social influences behind those media products, and they deliberately use excitement and passion as the foundation for community-building and empathetic development."[367] This echoes what Ellen Seiter wrote in *Sold Separately* in 1993 regarding merchandising, that it's a mistake "to see marketers as evil brainwashers and children as naïve innocents, as they are so often depicted in journalists' accounts of the toy industry," and that "children's desire for toys and media is more than the direct fulfillment of the designs of manufacturers and marketers, however attractive this notion may be in its simplicity."[368] In the case of *Equestria Girls* that simple notion was more attractive, hence Sethisto describing it as "focusing on the little girl market they already have all that doll-based research on," while also playing on the hysteria angle by reducing the young female audience to "love-crazed little girls."[369]

In April 2016, I attended a Hatsune Miku concert in San Francisco. Knowing that it would be a cosplay-heavy event, I wore my recreation of the Canterlot Wondercolt outfit from the cafeteria rally in the first *Equestria Girls* film: yellow pony ears, blue-and-yellow tail, a top with the Wondercolt logo, and a pleated skirt with Princess Twilight's Cutie Mark. I was working on this chapter at the time, and being mired in the hatred and anger from the Bronies and others toward *Equestria Girls*, I figured that nopony would recognize what I was wearing—or, perhaps, being a pop culture-savvy crowd, I would get the same dirty looks that Sunset Shimmer received in the Canterlot High gymnasium in her first scene in *Rainbow Rocks*. After all, Bronies are a majority, and *Equestria Girls* was not what they wanted.

Instead, a fifteen-year-old girl standing in line behind me recognized it immediately, and it made her very happy to see somepony repping the Wondercolts out in the world. It was not unlike how Ellen Seiter had described how children were likely to strike up a conversation in public with another child because they bore some representation of a mutually beloved pop culture item; in this case it was a teenager and a woman old enough to be her mother, but that's precisely the kind of cross-generational appeal that My Little Pony can have in all its forms.[370]

I was also reminded of a quote by Joel Hodgson, the creator of my favorite television show, *Mystery Science Theater 3000*: "We never say *who's* going to get this—we always say the *right* people will get this."[371]

Future Twilight

Where the franchise goes from here is impossible to predict, any more than the new life it found after the premiere of *Friendship Is Magic* could have been prophesized. My Little Pony is no more a principal source of income for Hasbro in the 2010s than Hal Erickson had claimed it had been in the mid–1980s; though the brand did have a record year with "more than $1 billion in global retail sales" according to Hasbro's *2014 Annual Report*, Pony was one of seven brands (the others being Littlest Pet Shop, Magic: The Gathering, Monopoly, Nerf, Play-Doh, and Transformers) which collectively brought in only 55% of their aggregate net revenues.[372] A significant portion of their overall business was also brought in by partnerships with Disney, Marvel, Sesame Street, Rovio, and that flower of integrity and an artist's creative vision, Star Wars.[373] Hasbro's 2015 *Annual Report* referred to My Little Pony as their "top licensed brand" and "billion dollar brand" for that year, though it was again just one of seven brands that totaled 52% of their aggregate net revenues; the Girls' category declined 22% from 2014, and while "core MY LITTLE PONY revenues increased but were, however, more than offset by lower net revenues from the MY LITTLE PONY EQUESTRIA GIRLS products."[374]

The great experiment in corporate synergy that was the Hub ended on September 25, 2014, with an announcement that it would be rebranded as Discovery Family Channel (not to be confused with Discovery Kids, its pre–Hub name), and that Hasbro's 50% stake in the channel would be reduced to 40%.[375] This did not impact the Pony franchise; on October 20, *Variety* announced that Hasbro greenlit a big-budget My Little Pony film to be produced by their in-house unit Allspark, and which Hasbro Studios president Stephen Davis hoped to release "on the broadest possible number of screens" in 2017, unlike the limited, scattershot distribution of the first two *Equestria Girls* films.[376] The *Hollywood Reporter*'s coverage of the Allspark movie announcement used a picture from Generation 3, and while they acknowledged that it had "already been the subject of animated TV series, including one currently airing on Discovery Family Channel (formerly The Hub)," they described the project as "an animated film about [Hasbro's] My Little Pony toy line."[377] Now and forever, a toy commercial is all My Little Pony cartoons shall be, and Discovery Communications announced in March 2015 that the one currently airing on Discovery Family Channel (formerly the Hub) would be returning for a sixth season.[378] That season of *My Little Pony: Friendship Is Magic* began in April 2016, while Hasbro announced earlier that year that *My Little Pony: Equestria Girls—Legend of Everfree* would debut that fall.[379]

Regarding the big-budget 2017 film, Hasbro's 2015 *Annual Report* described their Allspark Pictures label as working with Lionsgate "to bring MY LITTLE PONY to the big screen in our first animated feature film," which is not true even if you take the sporadic theatrical distribution of the first two *Equestria Girls* films out of the equation. (Just because nopony ever really liked you, 1986's *My Little Pony: The Movie*, that doesn't mean you didn't exist.) But for as much as it's branded as a retro toy commercial, My Little Pony has always had a way of moving forward and letting the past be the past.

The popularity of My Little Pony will wax and wane, as all franchises must; *Friendship Is Magic* will eventually be canceled and *Equestria Girls* films will no longer be made, and in time a new creative steward will revive it in a way that makes it as relevant to its decade as *Friendship* was to the 2010s. In the end it will be the work that lasts, not the controversies or the snark about the "extremely unexpected" fanbase of the Bronies or the toys having existed for upwards of 24 months before the first cartoon was produced or the Bronies getting angry because their demands aren't being catered to. Future bipeds watching the show on their brain implants will care not a whit about anything other than what's on their mind-screens, and whether the gray mare's name is Muffins or Derpy won't be an issue.

No iteration of My Little Pony will ever cure cancer, end wars, or reduce income inequality, but I do believe it will have a positive impact on the generation currently growing up with it. Much of this comes from observing children in my capacity as a librarian. The girls have a television and movie series which challenges them and never condescends to them or insults their intelligence, presenting female characters with depth and complexity who are never held back by their gender, and who demonstrate many of the countless ways to be a girl. The boys are also benefiting from these portrayals of complicated female characters—a nozzle though she may be, the popularity of Rainbow Dash among boys is a major step forward—and the growing acceptance of boys embracing My Little Pony may not only help to further dismantle the too-rigid gender lines in entertainment, but also help that generation of boys to grow up respecting women as equal human beings, and not as objects or the Other. This popularity of *Friendship Is Magic* across gender lines may also help those children who do not fit in to the gender binary to find the courage to be themselves at an early age.

Sexism, misogyny, and discrimination against queer people will not vanish overnight, or even within a generation; such things haven't even disappeared among Bronies. Violent male power fantasies like the Transformers range have always outgrossed My Little Pony and probably will continue to for years to come, and as I write, there's no shortage of problematic children's toys and entertainment that traffic in gender-role notions that are indeed outdated by early 2016, such as the deeply stereotypical Lego Friends range, which has all the pastels of My Little Pony with none of the complexity or depth.[380] And not all children of any gender enjoy the current incarnation of My Little Pony—and that's fine, because nopony should have to play with *any* toy or watch any show they don't want to, regardless of what society tells them is expected of their perceived gender—but some of those who do may grow into adults who help to make the world a better and more compassionate place.

Who knows? Someday, *Equestria Girls* may even receive the respect it deserves.

Chapter Notes

Introduction

1. Todd VanDerWerff, "My Little Pony Friendship Is Magic," *A.V. Club*, last modified April 29, 2011, http://www.avclub.com/tvclub/imy-little-pony-friendship-is-magici-55168.

2. *Ibid.*

3. *Ibid.*

4. Genevieve Koski, "Friendship Is Magic Pony-Creator Offers Endless Permutations of Cuteness," *A.V. Club*, last modified January 6, 2012, http://www.avclub.com/article/emfriendship-is-magicem-pony-creator-offers-endles-67298.

Part 1

1. Hal Erickson, *Television Cartoon Shows: An Illustrated Encyclopedia, 1949 Through 1993* (Jefferson, NC: McFarland, 1995), 350.

2. Bob Davis, "Tough Game," *Wall Street Journal*, December 13, 1984.

3. Marsha King, "Channeling the Wish Lists—Parents Need Strategy to Fight TV's Influence Over What Their Kids Request for Christmas," *Seattle Times*, December 3, 1985.

4. Joseph Pereira, "Toy Industry Faces a Lackluster Year—Absence of Runaway Hits Is a Major Factor," *Wall Street Journal*, July 27, 1987.

5. *Ibid.*, 248.

6. *Ibid.*, 247.

7. John Canemaker, "Fantasia in Eight Parts: 'The Pastoral Symphony,'" *The Walt Disney Family Museum*, http://www.waltdisney.org/blog/fantasia-eight-parts-pastoral-symphony.

8. Erickson, 350.

9. "ERA: History," *Equal Rights Amendment*, http://www.equalrightsamendment.org/history.htm.

10. Erickson, 350.

11. "Reagan's Nomination of O'Connor," *Center for Legislative Archives*, http://www.archives.gov/legislative/features/oconnor.html.

12. "Ferraro's Acceptance Speech, 1984," *CNN*, http://www.cnn.com/ALLPOLITICS/1996/conventions/chicago/facts/famous.speeches/ferraro.84.shtml.

13. Erickson, 350.

14. Ellen Seiter, *Sold Separately. Children and Parents in Consumer Culture* (New Brunswick, N.J.: Rutgers University Press, 1993), 145.

15. *Ibid.*

16. Tom Engelhardt, "The Shortcake Strategy," in *Watching Television*, ed. Tod Gitlin (New York: Pantheon Books, 1986), 97.

17. *Ibid.*, 158.

18. Erickson, 350.

19. Davis.

20. Beth Wolfensberger, "Trouble in Toyland," *New England Business* 12, no 9 (September 1990): 32.

21. Erickson, 248.

22. Hal Erickson, *Television Cartoon Shows: An Illustrated Encyclopedia, 1949 Through 2003* (Jefferson, N.C: McFarland, 2005), 576.

23. Lauren Faust (Fire_Flye), *Twitter* post, November 29, 2013, 4:31pm. https://twitter.com/Fyre_flye/status/406581132805689344.

24. "Lauren Faust," *Internet Movie Database*, http://www.imdb.com/name/nm0269260/reference.

25. Sidney Lohman, "News of TV and Radio: New Pre-School Age Show—Other Studio Items," *New York Times*, November 16, 1952.

26. Jack Gould, "Television in Review: 'Ding Dong School,' a Worthwhile Video Program Directed at Children, Stubs Toe on Commercialism," *New York Times*, April 1, 1953.

27. *Ibid.*

28. Pamela Colby, "From Hot Wheels to Teenage Mutant Ninja Turtles: The Evolution of the Definition of Program Length Commercials on Children's Television," (presentation,

Annual Meeting of the Broadcast Education Association, Las Vegas, NV, April 12–16, 1993).

29. Mitchell E Shapiro, *Television Network Weekend Programming, 1959–1990* (Jefferson, N.C: McFarland, 1992), 9.

30. Henry John Uscinski,"Comments Deregulating Commercial Television: Will the Marketplace Watch Out for Children?," *American University Law Review* no. 34 (1984). 141–173.

31. Bernard Nossiter, "Licenses to Coin Money: The FCC's Big Giveaway Show," *Nation*, October 26, 1985, 402.

32. *Ibid.*

33. Sydney Stern and Ted Schoenhaus, *Toyland: The High-stakes Game of the Toy Industry* (Chicago: Contemporary Books, 1990), 116–117.

34. "MLP Through the Years," *Hasbro*, n.d., https://web.archive.org/web/20120309232144/http://www.hasbro.com/mylittlepony/en_U.S./parents/through-the-years.cfm.

35. Bonnie D. Zacherle, Charles Muenchinger, and Steven D. D'Aguanno, "United States Patent: 269986—Toy Animal," August 2, 1983.

36. "Class D21: Games, Toys, and Sports Equipment," *United States Patent and Trademark Office*, n.d., http://www.uspto.gov/web/patents/classification/uspcd21/defsd21.htm.

37. LadyM, "Found an Interview with One of the MLP Creators!," *My Little Pony Trading Post*, last modified February 9, 2008, http://www.mlptp.net/index.php?threads/found-an-interview-with-one-of-the-mlp-creators.42431/.

38. *Ibid.*

39. *Ibid.*

40. Bryan Rourke, "A Pony Tale: 100 Million Sold and Climbing," *Providence Journal*, June 22, 2008.

41. *Hasbro.*

42. Advertisement, *The Los Angeles Times*, November 15, 1981: 8.

43. LadyM.

44. *Ibid.*

45. *My Little Pony Trading Post.*

46. "Hasbro Showcases Top Entertainment Properties at San Diego Comic-Con," Hasbro Inc. press release, July 16, 2009.

47. PixelKatties (M_A_Larson), Twitter post, September 4, 2015, 2:03pm. https://twitter.com/m_a_larson/status/639906683465035776.

48. Rebecca Tyrrel, "Pony Tale," *Sunday Telegraph Magazine*, December 19, 2004.

49. *Hasbro.*

50. "Category:Year One (1982–1983)," *My Little Wiki*, last modified April 16, 2012, http://mylittlewiki.org/wiki/Category:Year_One_%281982-1983%29.

51. Hasbro Inc., *2006 Annual Report*, n.d., p.

6, http://investor.hasbro.com/common/download/download.cfm?companyid=HAS&fileid=472634&filekey=A11B3D06-BE18–4782–94FC-3D97DE61D865&filename=2007AR.pdf.

52. *Hasbro.*

53. Advertisement, *Los Angeles Times*, December 18, 1982: 17.

54. Advertisement, *Los Angeles Times*, October 16, 1983: AC4.

55. "Year 1 (1982–1983)," *Dream Valley*, n.d., http://www.kimsites.net/dreamvalley/1st_edition.html.

56. Philip Dougherty, "BBDO Direct Is Picked for Hasbro Toy Work," *New York Times*, November 25, 1983.

57. "Matthew Weiner's No Madman," *Adweek*, July 30, 2007, http://www.adweek.com/news/advertising/matthew-weiners-no-madman-89728.

58. "Zayre: We're Sorry," *Evening News*, December 11, 1983.

59. Ted J. Rakstis. "1984: Another Year of Product Scarcity?" *Playthings* (March 1984): 32.

60. "Sporting Goods, Toy Sales Gain," *Discount Store News* (April 30, 1984): 1+.

61. Grimes LLC, "Chapter 1: The History of Licensing," n.d., http://www.gandb.com/documents/Chapter-1-Licensing-101-The-History-of-Merchandising-and-Licensing.pdf.

62. Ellen Shea, "Manufacturers Double As Licensors," *Playthings* (June 1984): 64+.

63. *Ibid.*

64. Kathleen Low, "'Dumping' Adds to Spotty Traffic at Volume Show," *Footwear News* (June 11, 1984): 21.

65. *Ibid.*

66. Gary Vineberg, "Gremlins Debuts in Theaters, Stores," *Footwear News* (June 11, 1984): 6.

67. Sethisto, "Lauren Faust Ponychan Q&A Compiled," *Equestria Daily*, last modified June 8, 2013, http://www.equestriadaily.com/2013/06/lauren-faust-ponychan-q-compiled.html.

68. "ApplejackBackcard.jpg," *My Little Wiki*, last modified March 25, 2010, http://mylittlewiki.org/wiki/File:ApplejackBackcard.jpg.

69. "TwilightBackcard.jpg," *My Little Wiki*, last modified March 24, 2010, http://mylittlewiki.org/wiki/File:TwilightBackcard.jpg.

70. Lauren Faust (Fire_Flye), Twitter post, November 29, 2013, 4:42pm. https://twitter.com/Fyre_flye/status/406583985846763520.

71. Lauren Faust (Fire_Flye), Twitter post, November 29, 2013, 4:33pm. https://twitter.com/Fyre_flye/status/406581739708882944.

72. Lauren Faust (Fire_Flye), Twitter post, November 29, 2013, 4:40pm. https://twitter.com/fyre_flye/status/406583490495279104.

73. Lauren Faust (Fire_Flye), Twitter post, November 29, 2013, 4:45pm. https://twitter.com/fyre_flye/status/406584676451487744.

74. Lauren Faust (Fire_Flye), Twitter post, November 29, 2013, 4:57pm. https://twitter.com/Fyre_flye/status/406587739211980801.

75. Philip S. Gutis, "Toy Makers Frolic in Fantasy Land," *New York Times*, December 23, 1984.

76. *Ibid.*

77. Richard Meyers, "The Selling of Star Wars," *Starlog*, August 1978, 56.

78. "Davy Crockett Collectibles," *Disney Memorabilia,* last modified March 5, 2007, http://disneymemorabilia.com/collectibles/davy-crockett-collectibles.

79. Ken Farrell, *Warman's Disney collectibles field guide: Values and identification* (Iola, WI: Krause Publications, 2006), 36.

80. Dale Kunkel, "From a Raised Eyebrow to a Turned Back: The FCC and Children's Product-related Programming," *Journal of Communication* 38, no. 4 (1998): 90.

81. John Rosemond, "Some Toy Makers Don't Turn Out Schlock, Some Do," *Wichita Eagle*, November 29, 1984.

82. Janet Sutter, "Kids Play Favorites as They Toy Around," *San Diego Union-Tribune*, December 3, 1984.

83. "Humbug! The London of 'A Christmas Carol' Has Gone Commercial," *Philadelphia Inquirer,* December 25, 1984.

84. "TV Listings," *Newburgh-Beacon Evening News*, March 31, 1984.

85. "Saturday," *Hour*, April 7, 1984.

86. "Weekly Specials," *Mohave Daily Miner*, April 6, 1984.

87. "Mon., April 9 Daytime Specials," *Daytona Beach Sunday News-Journal*, April 8, 1984.

88. "The Tube," *Baltimore Afro-American*, April 13, 1984.

89. "Specials," *Ellensburg Daily Record*, April 14, 1984.

90. fyre-flye, "Galaxy Girls, My little Pony and 2010," *DeviantArt*, last modified March 31, 2010, https://web.archive.org/web/20130825231559/http://fyre-flye.deviantart.com/journal/Galaxy-Girls-My-Little-Pony-and-2010–228911071?offset=20#comments.

91. *My Little Pony*, directed by John Gibbs. (1984; Stamford, CT: Children's Video Library, 1984), VHS.

92. Jonathan Takiff, "Plug into these Holiday Gifts," *Philadelphia Daily News*, December 19, 1984.

93. "Plenty of Programming on NATPE Display," *Broadcasting* 108, no. 2 (January 14, 1985): 90.

94. *Ibid.*, 82.

95. "Where the Action Was: Natpe's Programing Panoply," *Broadcasting* 108, no. 3 (January 21, 1985): 54.

96. "Monday," *Southeast Missourian*, March 24, 1985.

97. "Television Programs Today," *Hour*, April 4, 1985.

98. "He-Man and the Masters of the Universe." *Epguides,* last modified December 30, 2001, http://epguides.com/HeMan_1983/.

99. Charles Solomon, "Syndication Threat: Kidvid on the Way Out?," *Los Angeles Times,* Nov. 15, 1986.

100. Engelhardt, 76.

101. John Wile, Lois Therrien, and Amy Dunking, "Are the Programs Your Kids Watch Simply Commercials?," *Business Week*, March 1985, 53–54.

102. Kunkel, 92.

103. *Ibid.*, 98.

104. *Ibid.*, 94.

105. Kunkel, 103–104.

106. "Strike Two for FCC Order on Children's TV," *Broadcasting* 113, no. 14 (1987): 36.

107. Congress of the U.S., Washington, DC. House Committee on Energy and Commerce. *Commercialization of Children's Television. Hearings on H.R. 3288, H.R. 3966, and H.R. 4125: Bills To Require the FCC To Reinstate Restrictions on Advertising during Children's Television, To Enforce the Obligation of Broadcasters To Meet the Educational Needs of the Child Audience, and for Other Purposes, Before the Subcommittee on Telecommunications and Finance of the Committee on Energy and Commerce, House of Representatives,* One Hundredth Congress, 1988.

108. *Ibid.*

109. Advertisement, *Broadcasting* 114, no. 7 (February 15, 1988): 93.

110. *Ibid.*

111. Phil Phillips, *Turmoil in the Toybox* (Lancaster, PA: Starburst, 1986), 79.

112. *Ibid.*, iv.

113. *Ibid.*, 79.

114. *Ibid.*, 80.

115. "Vinyls: My Little Pony—Applejack," *Funko,* http://funko.com/products/vinyls-my-little-pony-applejack.

116. "FashionApplejackBackcard.jpg," *My Little Wiki*, last modified April 8, 2011, http://mylittlewiki.org/wiki/File:FashionApplejackBackcard.jpg.

117. *Ibid.*

118. King.

119. *Seattle Times.*

120. Pereira, 1987.

121. Glenn Lovell, "Super Star Summer Sequels, Sequels Kiddie Heroes and Space Cadets Are Back," *San Jose Mercury News*, May 18, 1986.

122. Glenn Lovell, "Taking a Careful Journey in Wonderland," *San Jose Mercury News*, August 7, 1987.

123. Nina Darnton, "My Little Pony Movie Review," *New York Times*, June 27, 1986.

124. *Ibid.*

125. Joe D'Angelo, "Billboard Sours On Prince's Musicology Experiment," *MTV*, last modified May 28, 2004, http://www.mtv.com/news/1488027/billboard-sours-on-princes-musicology-sales-experiment/.

126. *Ibid.*

127. Charles Solomon, "Movie Review: 'Pony' Has a Bad Case of the Cutes," *Los Angeles Times*, June 20, 1986.

128. *Ibid.*

129. Eleanor Ringel, "Movie Review—Toy-into-Tot-Movie Trend Gallops in 'My Little Pony,'" *Atlanta Journal-Constitution*, June 11, 1986.

130. *Ibid.*

131. Desmond Ryan, "Film: Tale of Fantasy for Kiddies," *Philadelphia Inquirer*, June 28, 1986.

132. Desmond Ryan, "Film: Disney Offering Has Artful Animation," *Philadelphia Inquirer*, July 2, 1986.

133. MyStuff, "The Great Mouse Detective," *Collector Stuff*, last modified November 16, 2011, http://bingksjunk.blogspot.com/2011/11/great-mouse-detective.html.

134. Mark Russell, "Uniting the Two Koreas, in Animated Films at Least," *New York Times*, August 31, 2005.

135. Jane Wollman Rusoff, "Bart Is Just One of Many Roles for Voice-Over Actress," *Columbus Dispatch*, June 29, 2000.

136. Richard Martin. "Movie Sure to Give Toy Sales a Boost," *Ottawa Citizen*, July 21, 1986.

137. *Ibid.*

138. *Ibid.*

139. *Ibid.*

140. *Ibid.*

141. John Hartl, "'My Little Pony' Is OK Matinee Fare," *Seattle Times*, June 23, 1986.

142. Elliot Krieger, "Movie Review: 'My Little Pony' Trots Out Some Fun," *Providence Journal-Bulletin*, June 24, 1986.

143. Bill Hagen, "Critic's 'Aides' Like Slimy Stuff, Call 'Pony' Kids' Film," *San Diego Union-Tribune*, June 24, 1986.

144. Norma Dyess, "Musical Score, Vivid Animation are Pony Highlights, *Advocate*, June 13, 1986.

145. Norma Dyess, "Recapping the Summer's Best, Worst, and in Between," *Advocate*, September 12, 1986.

146. Janet Maslin, "In Animation for Children, The Old Days Were Better," *New York Times*, January 18, 1987.

147. Ralph Novak, V.R. Peterson, Campbell Geeslin, Joanne Kaufman, and Kristin McMurran, "Picks And Pans Review: Snow White and the Seven Dwarfs," *People*, October 12, 1987.

148. Constance Dyckman, "Audiovisual Review: My Little Pony," *School Library Journal* 33, no. 8 (1987): 66–67.

149. Kathleen Brachmann, "*My Little Pony Under the Big Top!*" *School Library Journal* 33, no. 7 (1986): 153.

150. Scott Cain, "Video," *Atlanta Journal-Constitution*, November 8, 1986.

151. *Ibid.*

152. Scott Cain, "Movie Review—'Transformers' a Bleak Commercial Mutant," *Atlanta Journal-Constitution,* August 12, 1986.

153. Carrie Rickey, "Film: Autobots vs. Decepticons," *Philadelphia Inquirer*, August 8, 1986.

154. "Top 10 Money Makers," *San Francisco Chronicle*, June 25, 1986.

155. Neil Downing, "Hasbro Sees Record Sales and Profits," *Providence Journal*, May 21, 1987.

156. William K. Knoedelseder Jr., "De Laurentiis: Producer's Picture Darkens," *Los Angeles Times,* August 30, 1987.

157. "Jem and the Holograms," *Box Office Mojo*, n.d., http://www.boxofficemojo.com/movies/?id=jemandtheholograms.htm.

158. Sherilyn Connelly, "*Jem and the Holograms* Isn't Even Close to Being the Worst Movie Ever Made," *SF Weekly*, last modified October 27, 2015, http://www.sfweekly.com/exhibitionist/2015/10/27/jem-and-the-holograms-isnt-even-close-to-being-the-worst-movie-ever-made.

159. Scott Cain, "Movies—A G Rating the Kiss of Death?—Most Kiddie Films Are Taking a Beating at the Box Office," *Atlanta Journal-Constitution*, June 6, 1987.

160. "Parents Guide for *The Transformers: The Movie,*" *Internet Movie Database*, http://www.imdb.com/title/tt0092106/parentalguide.

161. Erickson, 1995, 536.

162. *Ibid.*

163. Leonard Maltin, *Leonard Maltin's TV Movies and Video Guide* (New York: New American Library, 1990), 1210.

164. Maltin, 792.

165. Abraham Reisman, "Do You Have 'The Touch'? Learn the Bizarre History of the Greatest Transformers Song Ever," *Vulture*, June 26, 2014, http://www.vulture.com/2014/06/transformers-

song-history-the-touch-stan-bush-mark-wahlberg-boogie-nights.html.

166. "Syndication Marketplace," *Broadcasting* 109, no. 20 (November 11, 1985): 60.

167. *Ibid.*

168. "Wall to Wall Television at NATPE," *Broadcasting* 110, no. 4 (January 27, 1986): 38.

169. *My Little Pony 'n Friends Intro,* YouTube video, 0:47, posted by "1337bonsly," April 8, 2007, https://www.youtube.com/watch?v=ub7bJj49j_U.

170. *My Little Pony 'n Friends (Moondreamers Version),* YouTube Video, 0:56, posted by "1337bonsly," June 4, 2009, https://www.youtube.com/watch?v=YpD40IYSqKc.

171. *My Little Pony 'n Friends (Glo Friends Version),* YouTube video, 0:57, posted by "1337bonsly," April 15, 2008, https://www.youtube.com/watch?v=-_JwhaCPkas.

172. *My Little Wiki.*

173. Ashley Terrill, "Ladies, Leading," *Elle,* n.d., http://www.elle.com/culture/movies-tv/g2297/ladies-leading-514518/?slide=4.

174. Eric Volmers, "Split with Charlie Sheen Was 'Heartbreaking', Producer Says; Chuck Lorre Receives Comedy Award at Banff Media Festival," *Vancouver Sun,* June 16, 2012.

175. Seiter, 165.

176. *Ibid.*

177. *Ibid.,* 7–8.

178. *Ibid.,* 9.

179. Margery Davies, "Never Too Young to Buy," *Women's Review of Books,* 11 no. 6 (Mar. 1994): 7.

180. *Ibid.*

181. Robert Ferrigno, "These Cartoons Are Not Just for Kids," *Orange County Register,* September 21, 1987.

182. *Ibid.*

183. Congress of the U.S., Washington, DC. House Committee on Energy and Commerce. *Commercialization of Children's Television.*

184. *Ibid.*

185. *Ibid.*

186. Peggy Charren, "FCC Should Ban These Half-hour Commercials," *USA Today,* October 8, 1987.

187. "Action for Children's Television," *Harvard Graduate School of Education,* https://www.gse.harvard.edu/library/collections/special/act.

188. Brian Lowry, "How Peggy Charren Outflanked the Children's TV Establishment," *Variety,* January 22, 2015, http://variety.com/2015/tv/columns/how-peggy-charren-outflanked-the-childrens-tv-establishment-1201412528/.

189. Eugene Gilligan, "Retailers to Rely on Tried and True Licenses for '88," *Playthings* (December 1987): 62.

190. "Outlook '88: Toy Manufacturers Search for New Masterpieces," *Playthings* (February 1988): 111.

191. *Ibid.*

192. "Hasbro, Inc." *Capital District Business Review* (November 12, 1990): 27.

193. Katherine Imbrie, "Holiday Gifts Rated: Love It or Loathe It," *Providence Journal,* January 25, 1989.

194. Imbrie.

195. Patricia Leigh Brown, "When Child's Play Is Collecting, It's Serious Stuff," *New York Times,* December 14, 1989.

196. Tom Gliatto, "My Little Obsession," *USA Today,* December 7, 1988.

197. Brown.

198. Neil Downing, "Guess Who? My Little Pony Trots into Soviet Toy Market," *Providence Journal,* December 23, 1989.

199. David Gerrie, "Turtle Hero Worship," *Marketing* (June 14, 1990): 28.

200. Wolfensberger.

201. Matthew Grimm, "Toys Are No Fun in a Flat Year," *Adweek* 41, no. 39 (September 23, 1991): S117.

202. Nancy White, "Annie's as Good as It Gets for Kids," *Toronto Star,* March 25, 1990.

203. *Ibid.*

204. *Ibid.*

205. Val Ross, "Striking a Chord," *Globe and Mail,* May 18, 1991.

206. Christine Donahue, "A Limit on Children's Advertising?" *Adweek's Marketing Week* 30, no. 29 (July 17, 1989): 2.

207. "1983 Sayles Film Is Finally Released," *Philadelphia Inquirer,* September 14, 1989.

208. "'Milagro Beanfield War' and a Fantasy with Aliens," *Philadelphia Inquirer,* September 15, 1988.

209. Congress of the U.S., Washington, DC. House Committee on Energy and Commerce. *Bill Summary & Status, 101st Congress (1989–1990), H.R.1677, All Information,* 101st Congress.

210. David Lauter, "Children's TV Bill Will Become Law Without Bush's Signature," *Los Angeles Times,* October 8, 1990.

211. Edmund L. Andrews, "F.C.C Adopts Limits on TV Ads Aimed at Children," *New York Times,* April 10, 1991.

212. *Ibid.*

213. Colby.

214. "My Little Pony Tales," *My Little Wiki,* last modified April 4, 2015, http://mylittlewiki.org/wiki/Category:My_Little_Pony_Tales.

215. *My Little Pony Tales,* "The Great Lemonade Stand Wars," written by George A. Bloom, DVD (1992; USA: Shout! Factory, 2015).

216. "Cathy Weseluck," *Internet Movie Database*, http://www.imdb.com/name/nm0921699/reference#musicX20department.

217. "Friday," *Ocala Star-Banner*, February 18, 1995.

218. "New for NATPE in a Nutshell," *Broadcasting* 123, no. 1 (January 4, 1993): 34.

219. Caroline Dunphy, "Magic Fable Eco-Dazzles," *Toronto Star*, April 16, 1992.

220. Ray Richmond, "Ren Breaks Cartoon Mold," *Austin American Statesman*, May 17, 1992.

221. John Davis, "Acoustic Alchemy," *Austin American Statesman*, November 19, 1992.

222. Tim Carter, "If You're into Physical Violence, This Is a Hard Target to Miss," *Ottawa Citizen*, August 26, 1993.

223. Joel Stice, "Jean-Claude Van Damme Is Now Kicking Ass with My Little Pony," *CollegeHumor*, last modified March 3, 2015, http://www.collegehumor.com/post/7013462/heres-the-jean-claude-van-dammemy-little-pony-mash-up-youve-been-waiting-for.

224. David Kiley, "Mobilizing Mom and Dad for the War on Kids' TV," *Adweek's Marketing Week* 32, no. 36 (September 2, 1991): 4.

225. Elaine Dutka, "The Brains Behind 'Beauty,'" *San Francisco Chronicle*, January 20, 1992.

226. Kathleen Moloney, "Close Up," *Los Angeles Times*, March 15, 1992.

227. John Douglas, "Impotence Killed the Cat, and Mouse," *Grand Rapids Press*, August 1, 1993.

228. Alex Strachan, "Teletoons Animate Ratings," *Vancouver Sun*, June 13, 1998.

229. Booth Moore, "Saturday Cartoons: Taking the Good with the Bad," *Los Angeles Times*, January 6, 1999.

230. Timothy Burke and Kevin Burke, *Saturday Morning Fever: Growing Up with Cartoon Culture* (New York: St. Martin's Griffin, 1999), 79.

231. *Ibid.*, 161–165.

232. *Ibid.*, 57.

233. Anne Sherber, "Toy Fair Provides Video Inspirations," *Billboard* 111, no. 10 (March 6, 1999): 85.

234. Seiter, 156.

235. "Morning," *New York Times*, September 16, 1986.

236. "Morning," *Los Angeles Times*, February 20, 1987.

237. "Monday Television," *Sarasota Herald-Tribune*, October 6, 1986.

238. "Thursday—Sign on to 5 p.m.," *Milwaukee Journal*, October 8, 1986.

239. *My Little Pony Friendship Is Magic*, Youtube Video, 0:20, posted by "Hub Network," December 22, 2010, https://www.youtube.com/watch?v=8iLFjT_h64I.

240. James Turner, "Is TV Paying Too Much Attention To Fans?" *Christian Science Monitor*, March 20, 2012.

241. Harlene Ellin, "Leafing Through the New Fall Shows for Kids," *Chicago Tribune*, September 6, 1998.

242. *Ibid.*

243. "Powerpuff Girls," narrated by Madeleine Brand, *Morning Edition*, NPR, November 15, 2000, http://www.npr.org/templates/story/story.php?storyId=1114006.

244. *Ibid.*

245. Drew Jubera, "Watching TV: Cartoon Network Exec Loves to Show His Daffy Side," *Atlanta Journal*, February 18, 2001.

246. Raoul V. Mowatt, "Improved `He-Man' series heads to Cartoon Network," *Chicago Tribune*, August 16, 2002.

247. "Q3 2011 Hasbro Inc Earnings Conference Call," Hasbro Inc. press release, October 17, 2011.

248. Constance Rosenblum, "Eerie Metamorphosis Is Turning Girls into Turtles," *New York Times*, October 31, 1991.

249. *Ibid.*

250. Mark Patinkin, "Let's Remember the Victim and Forget the Killer," *Providence Journal-Bulletin*, January 28, 1996.

251. Brian Hall, "Lauren Burleson Wins Horsemanship Honors," *Orange County Register*, March 7, 1996.

252. Sasha Whyte, "Children's Express: Girl Talk Unplugged; Everything from Sex to Barbie to Toys," *New York Amsterdam News*, March 23, 1996.

253. Monica Soto, "One Reporter's Foray into the ABCs of Football," *Santa Fe New Mexican*, August 30, 1997.

254. Olivia Hawkinson, "In Sci-Fi's Mostly Male Realm, `Star Wars' Blasts Gender Lines," *Orange County Register*, January 29, 1999.

255. Eric Kurhi, "Cupertino Couple Rides to Raise Funds to Fight Rare Disease That Struck Daughter," *San Mateo County Times*, October 5, 2013.

256. John Diamond, "Advice to the Lovelorn: Don't Ask; Private Life," *Times*, July 16, 1992.

257. Suzanne Moore, "Clash of Symbols," *Times*, April 11, 1993.

258. Tony Thorne, *Fads, Fashions & Cults* (London: Bloomsbury, 1993), 166.

259. Andrew Lauren, "The Oldest Case of Disco Fever," *New York Magazine*, January 14, 1991.

260. Thorne, 219.

261. Alan Jackson, "This Little Pony," *Guardian*, November 21, 1993.

262. *Ibid.*

263. William Cook, "Aladdin Working," *Guardian*, December 21, 1993.

264. Marianne MacDonald, "Time of Freedom Tempered by an Adult 'Conspiracy' Over Finances," *Independent*, August 24, 1994.

265. Catherine Bennett, "Inside Story: Private," *Guardian*, June 3, 1995.

266. Richard Holledge, "An Independent Week," *Independent*, November 27, 1995.

267. Mary Riddell, "An Outsider Who Took the Hot Seat; Profile; Pat Roberts Cairns," *Times*, January 1, 1996.

268. Marianna McDonald, "Interview: Demi Moore: Twice the Woman She Used to Be," *Observer*, October 12, 1997.

269. Katharine Viner, "Women: Sidelines," *Guardian*, February 4, 1997.

270. Shawn Meghan Burn, A. Kathleen O'Neil, and Shirley Nederend, "Childhood Tomboyism and Adult Androgyny," *Sex Roles* 34, no. 5–6 (1996): 425.

271. Simon Hoggart, "Simon Hoggart's Week: Royals, Gazza, Spice et Moi," *Guardian*, October 26, 1996.

272. Bernice Harrison, "Spice Girls Set the Tone," *Irish Times*, November 23, 1996.

273. Susannah Frankel, "Ready to Wear," *Independent*, August 7, 2006.

274. Glenn Whipp, "If You Pick One Movie to Miss, Make It 'Spice World,'" *Los Angeles Daily News*, January 23, 1998.

275. Jay Boyar, "Tell You What We Want, What We Really, Really Want: A Good Movie," *Orlando Sentinel*, January 23, 1998.

276. Hoggart.

277. Whipp.

278. Nicole Lyn Pesce, "Gen X Moms Fear New 'My Little Pony' Feature Film Horses Are Too Hot to Trot," *New York Daily News*, June 13, 2013.

Part 2

1. Teena Lyons, "Why Size Isn't Everything," *Sunday Mirror*, January 18, 1998.

2. *Ibid.*

3. Bill Mouland, "My Little Comeback; Comeback Internet Petition Gives 1980s Toy New Lease of Life," *Daily Mail*, January 30, 1998.

4. *Ibid.*

5. *Ibid.*

6. "Hasbro Unveils a World of Fun at American International Toy Fair," Hasbro Inc. press release, February 6, 1998.

7. *Ibid.*

8. Summer Hayes, *The My Little Pony G2 Collector's Inventory* (Denville, N.J.: Priced Nostalgia Press, 2010), 7.

9. "Hasbro Interactive Brings Kid's Favorite Toys and Games to Life in Three New CD-ROM Games, My Little Pony, Operation and Candy Land," Hasbro Inc. press release, October 6, 1998.

10. "Reviews," *FamilyPC* 6, no. 4 (April 1999): 104.

11. *Ibid.*

12. "Welcome," *Dream Valley*, n.d., http://www.kimsites.net/dreamvalley/index.html.

13. T.L. Stanley and Karen Benezra, "Amid Takeover Buzz, Toy Schleppers Brace for Godzilla, Teletubbies and McD's Happy Meal Girl," *Brandweek* 39 no. 7 (Februay 16, 1998): 9.

14. *Ibid.*

15. Simon Ellery, "Analysis: Toy Revivals Must Look Beyond Adult Nostalgia," *PR Week (UK)*, August 15, 2003.

16. Hasbro Inc., *2000 Annual Report*, n.d., p. 1, http://files.shareholder.com/downloads/HAS/1221912837x0x456758/1BF7BB27-F652-4BD9-8263-8D0890E2B8FE/2000AR.pdf.

17. "Hasbro Forms Business Sector Designed to Leverage Company's Intellectual Properties," Hasbro Inc. press release, September 30, 1999.

18. *Ibid.*

19. Hasbro Inc., *2002 Annual Report*, n.d., p. 7, http://ccbn18.mobular.net/ccbn/7/182/190/.

20. Katherine M. Franke, "Theorizing Yes: An Essay of Feminism, Law, and Desire," *Columbia Law Review* 101, no. 1 (2001): 192.

21. Simon Marquis, "The Young Ones," *Marketing* (March 10, 1994): 22.

22. *Ibid.*

23. "An In Depth Look at the My Little Pony Relaunch," *Mason Williams*, July 2011, http://www.mason-williams.co.uk/case-studies/my-little-pony-relaunch-2003-2/.

24. Joyceann Cooney, "My New Little Pony," *License!* 5, no. 12 (January 2003): 44.

25. *Ibid.*

26. *Ibid.*

27. *Ibid.*

28. "Hasbro Revamps My Little Pony to Draw Younger Girls," *Marketing Week* 28, no. 26 (July 10, 2003): 9.

29. Ellen Creager, "Barbie Bares Her Belly to Compete with Bratz," *Detroit Free Press*, November 27, 2002.

30. Cooney.

31. Karen Raugust, "Talking Trends," *Publishers Weekly* 247, no. 23 (June 5, 2000): 24.

32. Cooney.

33. *Ibid.*

34. *Ibid.*

35. *Ibid.*

36. "MY LITTLE PONY Holiday Film to Premier at Special Family Matinees Nationwide," Hasbro Inc. press release, September 29, 2005.

37. Carl DiOrio, "Fat Rock Tooning Up Toy-Based Pix," *Daily Variety* 277, no. 54 (December 19, 2002): 5.

38. *Ibid.*

39. "Theater Screenings Promote DVD Release," *Entertainment Marketing Letter*, July 1, 2005, 7.

40. Cooney.

41. Hasbro Inc., September 29, 2005.

42. Janet Hetherington, "Just Hit Play: Toy Brand Animated DVDs," *ANIMATIONWorld*, last modified, March 30, 2007, http://www.awn.com/animationworld/just-hit-play-toy-brand-animated-dvds.

43. "MY LITTLE PONY Makes Its Highly Anticipated Return; Hasbro Celebrates Cherished Brand with Worldwide Launch in 2003," Hasbro Inc. press release, February 10, 2003.

44. *Ibid.*

45. T.L. Stanley, "Toying Around with Stardom on Video," *Video Business* 23, no. 25 (June 23, 2003): 10.

46. Hasbro Inc. press release, February 10, 2003.

47. "Hasbro Properties Group Creates 'Lifestyles' Based on the World's Most Entertaining Toy and Game," Hasbro Inc. press release, June 9, 2003.

48. "Hasbro Campaign Will Push My Little Pony's Comeback, *PR Week (UK)*, June 27, 2003.

49. *Ibid.*

50. *Mason Williams.*

51. *Ibid.*

52. Donna Werbner, "Campaign: Second Opinion," *PR Week (UK)*, September 10, 2004, http://www.prweek.com/article/221752/campaign-second-opinion.

53. Jonathan Thompson, "My Little What?," *Independent on Sunday*, July 20, 2003.

54. *Ibid.*

55. *Ibid.*

56. *Ibid.*

57. *Ibid.*

58. *Ibid.*

59. *Ibid.*

60. *Ibid.*

61. *Ibid.*

62. *Ibid.*

63. "Rehash of Classic Properties Dominates Apparel Programs," *DSN Retailing Today* 42, no. 11 (June 9, 2003): 35.

64. T.L. Stanley, "Irony Giants," *Brandweek* 44, no. 23 (June 9, 2003): 42.

65. *Ibid.*

66. Peter Hartlaub, "Deadly Alliance Revives Kombat," *San Francisco Chronicle*, January 7, 2003.

67. *Ibid.*

68. "CORRECTING and REPLACING It's Time to Celebrate! Hasbro's MY LITTLE PONY Brand Makes Its Long Anticipated Return; MY LITTLE PONY Now Available Nationwide," Hasbro Inc. press release, September 19, 2003.

69. *Ibid.*

70. Thompson.

71. Hasbro Inc. press release, June 9, 2003.

72. *Ibid.*

73. "Selected 1980s Relaunches: Here Are Some of the Licensed Properties that are Being Reintroduced," *Publishers Weekly* 250, no. 33 (August 18, 2003): 32.

74. *Ibid.*

75. Karen Raugust, "What's Old Is New Again," *Publishers Weekly* 250, no. 33 (August 18, 2003): 30.

76. *Ibid.*

77. *Ibid.*

78. "My Little Pony Books Hit 3.5 Million Unit Mark for Harper Collins Children's Books," HarperCollins Publishers press release, November 22, 2004.

79. *Ibid.*

80. *Ibid.*

81. *Marketing Week.*

82. *Mason Williams.*

83. "Q3 2003 Hasbro Inc Earnings Conference Call," Hasbro Inc. press release, October 20, 2003.

84. *Ibid.*

85. Mercedes M. Cardona, "Toy Story: Nostalgia Sells Big," *Advertising Age* 74, no. 48 (December 1, 2003): 4.

86. Paul Bond, "DVD Players Pack Santa's Sleigh," *Hollywood Reporter* 381, no. 25 (December 1, 2003): 22.

87. Donna Werbner, "Campaign: Hasbro resurrects My Little Pony brand—Consumer PR," *PR Week (UK)*, September 10, 2004, http://www.prweek.com/article/221751/campaign-hasbro-resurrects-little-pony-brand—-consumer-pr.

88. "Hasbro's My Little Pony and the Starlight Starbright Children's Foundation Roll Out the "Pink" Carpet for Hundreds of Kids," Hasbro Inc. press release, November 9, 2004.

89. *Ibid.*

90. My Little Pony, *Friendship Songs*, Compact Disc, Genius Entertainment, 32072, 2004.

91. My Little Pony, *Pony Party Favorites*, Compact Disc, Genius Entertainment, 32082, 2004.

92. My Little Pony, *Musical Treasures*, Compact Disc, Genius Entertainment, 32132, 2004.

93. My Little Pony, *Sweet Classics in Ponyland*, Compact Disc, Genius Entertainment, 32122, 2004.

94. "Federal Judge Rules 'Happy Birthday' Is in the Public Domain," narrated by Laura Sydell, *NPR News*, NPR, September 23, 2015, http://www.npr.org/2015/09/23/442907049/federal-judge-rules-happy-birthday-is-in-the-public-domain.

95. My Little Pony, *Pony Party Favorites*.

96. "Fluttershy," *Strawberry Reef*, n.d., http://www.strawberryreef.com/Index/Name/fluttershy.html.

97. "*My Little Pony: Musical Treasures My Little Pony Sweet Classics in Ponyland*," WorldCat, n.d., http://www.worldcat.org/title/my-little-pony-musical-treasures-my-little-pony-sweet-classics-in-ponyland/oclc/61690487.

98. Johnny Loftus, "*My Little Pony: Friendship Songs*," *Allmusic*, n.d., http://www.allmusic.com/album/my-little-pony-friendship-songs-mw0001375227.

99. MacKenzie Wilson, "*My Little Pony: Musical Treasures*," *Allmusic*, n.d., http://www.allmusic.com/album/my-little-pony-musical-treasures-mw0000450550.

100. "Atari Ships Three New Games Based on Blockbuster Children's Brands," Atari Inc. press release, October 19, 2004.

101. *Ibid.*

102. Warren Buckleitner, "Teacher's Picks [Best New Tech]," *Scholastic Parent & Child* 12, no. 2 (October 2004): 20.

103. Scott Colvey, "My Little Pony: Best Friends Ball," *Computer Act!ve*, November 23, 2006.

104. "MY LITTLE PONY Meets the Art World with the Unveiling of the Pony Project," Hasbro Inc. press release, October 21, 2005.

105. *Ibid.*

106. "The Pony Project," *Pony Project*, n.d., https://web.archive.org/web/20050804003809/http://www.theponyproject.com/.

107. Lucas Conley, "A Craving for Cool," *Fast Company*, last modified July 1, 2006, http://www.fastcompany.com/57129/craving-cool.

108. *Ibid.*

109. "Pony Project: White," *Strawberry Reef*, n.d., http://www.strawberryreef.com/Index/Name/ponyprojectwhite.html.

110. "Rare Ponies," *Strawberry Reef*, n.d., http://www.strawberryreef.com/Topics/rare.html.

111. "My Little Pony Collectors' Convention," *mylittleponyconvention.com*, last modified October 20, 2004, https://web.archive.org/web/20041210121905/http://www.mylittleponyconvention.com/.

112. Tyrrel.

113. *Mason Williams.*

114. Tyrrel.

115. *Ibid.*

116. Claire Morrall, "It's Pony Mane-ia; Fans Flock All the Way from Texas for Toy Show," *Sunday Mercury*, October 29, 2006.

117. Cole Moreton, "Scientist? Banker? My Little Pony Fanatic?," *Independent on Sunday*, October 12, 2008.

118. *Ibid.*

119. Tyrrel.

120. *Ibid.*

121. "Lorna Dounaeva," *Amazon*, n.d. http://www.amazon.com/Lorna-Dounaeva/e/B00BSQL9YG.

122. *Ibid.*

123. Morrall.

124. Pamela Perkins, "Saddle Up Memphis: My Little Pony Fair Hitches Up Downtown," *Memphis Commercial Appeal*, July 29, 2007.

125. "MLPFAIR in VIVA LAS VEGAS, just around the corner!!," *My Little Pony Arena*, last modified May 28, 2004, http://www.mlparena.com/archive/Forums/viewtopic/p=63856.html.

126. Jon Tevlin, "My Little Pony Tales, the (Sweet, Happy) Collector's Edition," *Minneapolis Star Tribune*, August 4, 2005.

127. "Fans of My Little Pony Can Now Create Their Own Play Experience—Hasbro and Disney Create a Build-Your-Own Program at Downtown Disney," Hasbro Inc. press release, March 7, 2005.

128. Rourke, 2008.

129. *Ibid.*

130. *Ibid.*

131. *The Making of Me: John Barrowman (complete)*, YouTube video, 58;55, posted by "N. Lion-Storm," https://www.youtube.com/watch?v=dq6aRrFehgE.

132. *Ibid.*

133. *Ibid.*

134. Suzanne Moore, "Dessie … Great Horse but Still JUST a Horse," *Mail on Sunday*, November 19, 2006.

135. "Vintage Barbie White Hanky," *Fashion Doll Guide*, n.d., http://www.fashion-doll-guide.com/Vintage-Barbie-White-Hanky.html.

136. Jesse Rutherford, "My Little Calliponian," *Bitch Magazine*, Spring 2007, 19.

137. Natalie Corinne Hansen, "Queering the Horse-Crazy Girl: Part II," (presentation, Annual Thinking Gender Confernce, UCLA Center for the Study of Women, February 1, 2008).

138. *Ibid.*

139. *Ibid.*

140. *Ibid.*

141. MoondancerMLP, "Princess Promenade in WA Theater!," *My Little Pony Trading Post*, last modified January 21, 2006, http://www.mlptp.net/index.php?threads/princess-promenade-in-wa-theater.11981/.

142. "The Hasbro Properties Group and VEE Corporation to Bring My Little Pony Live 'The World's Biggest Tea Party' to Venues across the U.S. This Fall," Hasbro Inc. press release, June 16, 2006.

143. "For Drug Chains, Category Has Lots of Untapped Potential," *Chain Drug Review* 28, no. 20 (November 20, 2006): 36.

144. "My Little Pony Holiday Film Climbs to Top of Billboard Charts," Hasbro Inc. press release, November 22, 2005.

145. Geoff Boucher, "VHS Era Is Winding Down," *Los Angeles Times*, December 22, 2008.

146. Tekaramity.

147. *Ibid.*

148. "mylittlepony-video_rainbow," *Hasbro*, https://web.archive.org/web/20060811181434/http://www.hasbro.com/mylittlepony/default.cfm?page=video_rainbow.

149. "My Little Pony: The Runaway Rainbow," *Amazon*, n.d., http://www.amazon.com/My-Little-Pony-Game-Boy-Advance/dp/B000FNY4SG/.

150. "Capsule Reviews," *Hartford Courant*, January 4, 2007.

151. "Top Kid DVD," *Billboard* 119, no. 9 (March 3, 2007): 64.

152. "Movie Clock," *New York Times*, November 13, 2009.

153. "Media Relations: Two Minutes—Jen Barker, Editor, My Little Pony," PR Week (UK), June 23, 2006.

154. Karen Raugust, "Hasbro: A Toy Story," *Publishers Weekly* 253, no. 37 (September 18, 2006): 10.

155. Raugust, 2006.

156. "Hasbro Properties Group Strikes Licensing Deals That Elevate Core Toy and Game Properties to New Levels of Global Brand Extension," Hasbro Inc. press release, June 20, 2006.

157. *Ibid.*

158. "Mini-trend: Horses Run Wild," *Licensing Letter*, July 3, 2006.

159. *Ibid.*

160. "Editorial: A Reconsideration," *Baltimore Sun*, November 4, 2007, http://articles.baltimoresun.com/2007-11-04/news/0711040177_1_pony-cuteness-parents.

161. *Ibid.*

162. Bryan Rourke, "The Mane Event for Little Ones," *Providence Journal*, November 19, 2006.

163. *Ibid.*

164. *Shadow and Wolfy rage at My Little Pony: The World's Biggest Tea Party Live*, YouTube video, 1:15:04, posted by "TheInvertedShadow," March 18, 2013, https://www.youtube.com/watch?v=KdItJEWHyBk.

165. "Tour Dates," *My Little Pony Live*, last modified January 12, 2008, https://web.archive.org/web/20080113225437/http://mylittleponylive.net/tourdates.asp.

166. Michael Ray, "Tea Party Movement," *Encyclopedia Britannica*, last modified June 11, 2014, http://www.britannica.com/EBchecked/topic/1673405/Tea-Party-movement.

167. "Q3 2006 Hasbro, Inc. Earnings Conference Call," Hasbro Inc. press release, October 23, 2006.

168. "Hasbro Continues to Build Global Lifestyle Brands Bringing Innovative Products to Market that Touch Every Aspect of Consumers' Lives," Hasbro Inc. press release, June 19, 2007.

169. Tina Benitez-Eves, "Buzz Report: Licensing Show 2007," *Gifts & Dec*, last modified June 21, 2007, http://www.giftsanddec.com/article/429753-buzz-report-licensing-show-2007.

170. *Ibid.*

171. Raugust, 2003.

172. PoniesYeah, "Doing my pony duty. A tiny preview from the toy show!" *My Little Pony Arena*, n.d., http://www.mlparena.com/archive/Forums//viewtopic/t=117990/.

173. RobynGraves, June 2007, comment on ilfiorelaluna, "Licensing Show News—Core Seven Ponies," *My Little Pony Arena*, June 2007, http://www.mlparena.com/archive/Forums//viewtopic/t=117990/.

174. Firebyrd, June 25, 2007 (6:22pm), comment on ilfiorelaluna, "Report from Licensing Show 'Core Seven' BAD NEWS FOR MLP," My Little Pony Trading Post, last modified June 25 2007, http://www.mlptp.net/index.php?threads/report-from-licensing-show-core-seven-bad-news-for-mlp.31962/.

175. Archer06, September 6, 2008 (7:40pm), comment on midnightthunder, "Core 7?" *My Little Pony Trading Post*, last modified September 6,

2008, http://www.mlptp.net/index.php?threads/core-7.52123/.

176. Summer Hayes, *The My Little Pony 2007–2008 Collector's Inventory* (Denville, N.J.: Priced Nostalgia Press, 2009), v.

177. "Hasbro's My Little Pony Brand Celebrates 25 Years of Magic and Imagination with a Year-Long Global Celebration," Hasbro Inc. press release, February 14, 2008.

178. *Ibid.*

179. "Hasbro Unveils 'The My Little Pony Project: 25 Ponies for 25 Years' Collection," Hasbro Inc. press release, September 10, 2008.

180. "My Little Pony: Pinkie Pie's Party Parade—PC," *Amazon*, n.d., http://www.amazon.com/My-Little-Pony-Pinkie-Party-Parade/dp/B000VRH6TK/.

181. "My Little Pony: Short Features," *Hasbro*, https://web.archive.org/web/200807120 15458/http://www.hasbro.com/mylittlepony/default.cfm?page=Entertainment/Videos/ShortFeatures.

182. Hayes, *The My Little Pony 2007–2008 Collector's Inventory,* 45.

183. "Hasbro Accelerates the Leveraging of Company's Vast Global Brand Portfolio Through Entertainment and Licensing," Hasbro Inc. press release, June 2, 2009.

184. "Hasbro Delivers Wide Range of Entertainment Experiences This Holiday Season," Hasbro Inc. press release, September 30, 2009.

185. "My Little Pony Newborn Cuties Family Convertible with DVD," *Amazon.co.uk.*, n.d., http://www.amazon.co.uk/Little-Newborn-Cuties-Family-Convertible/dp/B0031U1SPW.

186. "Videos," *Hasbro*, last modified March 4, 2010, https://web.archive.org/web/20100304160520/http://www.hasbro.com/mylittlepony/en_U.S./play/videos.cfm.

187. "MY LITTLE PONY: Twinkle Wish Adventure in Theaters in November," *Hasbro*, last modified November 14, 2009, https://web.archive.org/web/20091114121329/http://www.hasbro.com/mylittlepony/en_U.S./discover/MY-LITTLE-PONY-Twinkle-Wish-Adventure-in-Theaters-in-November.cfm.

188. "SBpamphlet 0001.jpg," *My Little Wiki*, last modified May 26, 2010, http://mylittlewiki.org/wiki/File:SBpamphlet_0001.jpg.

189. "Event Brief of Hasbro and Discovery Communications Announce Joint Venture," Hasbro Inc. press release, April 30, 2009.

190. *Ibid.*

191. *Ibid.*

192. Sam Schechner and Joseph Pereira, "Hasbro and Discovery Form Children's TV Network—Toy Maker Says Deal Reflects Its Shift into Entertainment; Consumer Groups Fear Shows Will Be Long-Playing Ads," *Wall Street Journal*, May 1, 2009.

193. *Ibid.*

194. Erickson, 1995, 868–870.

195. "Fall 2009 Investor Day," Hasbro Inc. press release, November 5, 2009.

196. *Ibid.*

197. "Introducing the Hub—Discovery Communications and Hasbro Officially Unveil Children's Network Brand:—New Joint Venture Children's Network to Launch in Fall 2010," Discovery Communications press release, January 14, 2010.

198. Lisa Johnston, "*The Animated Movie Guide,*" *Booklist* 102, no. 12 (February 15, 2006): 125.

199. Jerry Beck, *Animated Movie Guide* (Chicago: Chicago Review, 2005), xii.

200. *Ibid.*, 176.

201. *Ibid.*, 175.

202. *Ibid.*, 289.

203. Jerry Beck, "Day One: CTN-Expo Is a Hit!," *Cartoon Brew*, last modified November 21, 2009, http://www.cartoonbrew.com/events/day-one-ctn-expo-is-a-hit-18381.html.

204. *Ibid.*

205. Jerry Beck, "New from McCracken and Faust," *Cartoon Brew*, last modified January 20, 2010, http://www.cartoonbrew.com/animators/new-from-mccracken-and-faust-19994.html.

206. Horatio, January 20, 2010 (7:29 p.m.), comment on Jerry Beck, "New from McCracken and Faust," *Cartoon Brew*, last modified January 20, 2010, http://www.cartoonbrew.com/animators/new-from-mccracken-and-faust-19994.html.

207. *Ibid.*

208. Amid Amidi, "Ruby-Spears and Sid and Marty Krofft Team Up," *Cartoon Brew*, last modified April 13, 2010, http://www.cartoonbrew.com/bad-ideas/ruby-spears-and-sid-and-marty-krofft-team-up-22390.html.

209. "About Me," *Chris Battle Art & Stuff*, n.d., http://chrisbattleart.tumblr.com/about_me.

210. Chris Battle, April 13, 2010 (1:19 p.m.), comment on Amid Amidi, "Ruby-Spears and Sid and Marty Krofft Team Up," *Cartoon Brew*, last modified April 13, 2010, http://www.cartoonbrew.com/bad-ideas/ruby-spears-and-sid-and-marty-krofft-team-up-22390.html.

211. *Ibid.*

212. Amid Amidi, April 13, 2010 (1:57 p.m.), comment on Amid Amidi.

213. Dale Pollock, *Skywalking: The Life and Films of George Lucas* (New York: Harmony Books, 1983), 194.

214. *Ibid.*

215. Anthony Ramirez, "Tonka Accepts Offer from Hasbro," *New York Times*, February 1, 1991.

216. *Ibid.*, 193.

217. Lauren Faust, April 13, 2010 (2:09 p.m.), comment on Amid Amidi.

218. CMcC, April 13, 2010 (3:18 p.m.), comment on Amid Amidi.

219. *Ibid.*

220. Amid Amidi, April 13, 2010 (11:12 p.m.), comment on Amid Amidi.

221. *Ibid.*

222. Joe Flint and Dawn Chmielewski, "Toys and TV: A Winning Pair?," *Los Angeles Times*, October 5, 2010.

223. Ann Zimmerman and Sam Schechner, "Toys Take a Star Turn," *Wall Street Journal*, October 6, 2010.

224. Flint and Chmielewski.

225. *Ibid.*

226. "Hasbro Continues to Expand Its Immersive Global Brand Experiences Through Entertainment and Lifestyle Licensing," Hasbro Inc. press release, June 7, 2010.

227. "The Hub," *Advertising Age*, May 3, 2010, http://brandedcontent.adage.com/cable guide10/network.php?id=16.

228. "Hasbro Delivers Innovative Products and Brand Experiences This Holiday Season," Hasbro Inc. press release, September 28, 2010.

229. "Hasbro's Iconic My Little Pony Brand Excites a New Generation of Girls with Its Message of Friendship and Adventure," Hasbro Inc. press release, October 7, 2010.

230. Hasbro Inc. press release, September 28, 2010.

231. Hasbro Inc. press release, October 7, 2010.

232. Gweiswasser, "The Hub Arrives 10.10.10," *Discovery Blog*, October 8, 2010, https://corporate.discovery.com/blog/2010/10/08/the-hub-arrives-10–10-10/.

Part 4

1. David Perlmutter, *America Toons In: A History of Television Animation* (Jefferson, N.C: McFarland,2014), 219.

2. *Ibid.*

3. *Ibid.*, 385.

4. Tekaramity, "Exclusive Season 1 Retrospective Interview with Lauren Faust," *Equestria Daily*, September 6, 2011, http://www.equestria daily.com/2011/09/exclusive-season-1-retro spective.html.

5. Perlmutter.

6. "The Powerpuff Girls (1998–2005)," *Internet Movie Database*, http://www.imdb.com/title/tt0175058/fullcredits.

7. Perlmutter.

8. "'Evil Empire' Speech," *Miller Center*, http://millercenter.org/president/speeches/speech-3409.

9. Amid Amidi, "The End of the Creator-Driven Era in TV Animation," *Cartoon Brew*, last modified October 18, 2010, http://www.cartoonbrew.com/ideas-commentary/the-end-of-the-creator-driven-era-29614.html.

10. *Ibid.*

11. *Ibid.*

12. Stephen Lynch, "Re-Animated Television Cartoons, for So Long Moronic and Mundane, Are Cool Again Thanks to the Return of Creator-driven Animation," *Orange County Register*, March 23, 2001.

13. *Confound These Ponies—Rise of My Little Pony Fandom—Connecticon 2011*, YouTube video, 54:39, posted by "Scott Spaziani," July 18, 2011, https://www.youtube.com/watch?t=475&v=-0V5CCCT2Yc.

14. A Madman with a Box, May 8, 2013 (3:33 a.m.), comment on Amid Amidi, "The End of the Creator-Driven Era in TV Animation," *Cartoon Brew*, last modified October 18, 2010, http://www.cartoonbrew.com/ideas-commentary/the-end-of-the-creator-driven-era-29614.html.

15. "History of 'Bronies'," *Reddonychan Daily Wiki*, n.d., http://reddonychandaily.wikia.com/wiki/History_of_%22Bronies%22.

16. DavidDavidsonic, "Brony," *Urban Dictionary*, last modified December 23, 2010, http://www.urbandictionary.com/define.php?term=Brony&defid=5460072.

17. *Know Your Meme: My Little Pony*, YouTube Video, 7:26, posted by "KnowYourMeme," August 10, 2011, https://www.youtube.com/watch?v=ol LDrvclqt4.

18. PegasisterDDZ, "Pegasister," *Urban Dictionary*, last modified July 27, 2011, http://www.urbandictionary.com/define.php?term=Pegasister&defid=5979315.

19. Pedro Calhoun, "Bromance," *Urban Dictionary*, last modified January 13, 2004, http://www.urbandictionary.com/define.php?term=Bromance&defid=444973.

20. Everar, "bronies," *Urban Dictionary*, last modified April 15, 2008, http://www.urban dictionary.com/define.php?term=Brony&defid=3009740.

21. G. Ferro, "Brony," *Urban Dictionary*, last modified February 25, 2010, https://web.archive.org/web/20110603082349/http://www.urban dictionary.com/author.php?author=G.+Ferro.

22. Lisa Wade, "More Sexy Toy Makeovers: My Little Pony, Rainbow Brite, and Candy Land," *Sociological Images*, last modified December 7, 2010, http://thesocietypages.org/socimages/2010/12/07/more-sexy-toy-makeovers-my-little-pony-rainbow-brite-and-candy-land/.

23. *Ibid.*

24. Rutherford.

25. Lisa Wade, "More Sexy Toy Makeovers: My Little Pony, Rainbow Brite, and Candy Land," *Ms.*, last modified December 7, 2010, http://msmagazine.com/blog/2010/12/07/more-sexy-toy-makeovers-my-little-pony-rainbow-brite-and-candy-land/.

26. Kathleen Richter, "My Little Homophobic, Racist, Smart-Shaming Pony," *Ms.* last modified December 9, 2010, http://msmagazine.com/blog/2010/12/09/my-little-homophobic-racist-smarts-shaming-pony/.

27. *Ibid.*

28. *Ibid.*

29. *Ibid.*

30. *Ibid.*

31. "MY LITTLE PONY Is now on TV," *Hasbro*, last modified September 27, 2010, https://web.archive.org/web/20101012212441/http://www.hasbro.com/mylittlepony/en_U.S./discover/MY-LITTLE-PONY-is-now-on-TV.cfm.

32. *Ibid.*

33. "MY LITTLE PONY—Meet the Ponies," *Hasbro*, https://web.archive.org/web/20101002222511/http://www.hasbro.com/mylittlepony/en_U.S./play/details.cfm?guid=1b03b79b-19b9-f369-10e8-d2d56966309c.

34. *Ibid.*

35. Lauren, December 15, 2010 (9:36 a.m.), comment on Kathleen Richter, "My Little Homophobic, Racist, Smart-Shaming Pony," *Ms.*, last modified December 9, 2010, http://msmagazine.com/blog/2010/12/09/my-little-homophobic-racist-smarts-shaming-pony/.

36. fyre-flye, "Ms. and MLP," *DeviantArt,* last modified December 24, 2010, http://fyre-flye.deviantart.com/journal/Ms-and-MLP-222240234.

37. Lauren Faust, "My Little NON-Homophobic, NON-Racist, NON-Smart-Shaming Pony: A Rebuttal," *Ms.*, last modified December 24, 2010, http://msmagazine.com/blog/2010/12/24/my-little-non-homophobic-non-racist-non-smart-shaming-pony-a-rebuttal/.

38. *Ibid.*

39. *Ibid.*

40. *Ibid.*

41. Jaime Weinman, "Men Who Love My Little Pony: Don't Mess with Guys Who Want to Talk About Pinkie Pie and Pretty Pony Tea Parties," *Maclean's*, September 7, 2011, http://www.macleans.ca/culture/television/men-who-love-my-little-pony/.

42. L'il Brony, January 1, 2011 (9:37 a.m.), comment on Ricther.

43. Gravy, February 6, 2011 (5:54 a.m.), comment on Ricther.

44. Something, June 6, 2015 (1:09 a.m.), comment on Lauren Faust, "My Little NON-Homophobic, NON-Racist, NON-Smart-Shaming Pony: A Rebuttal," *Ms.*, last modified December 24, 2010, http://msmagazine.com/blog/2010/12/24/my-little-non-homophobic-non-racist-non-smart-shaming-pony-a-rebuttal/.

45. Lauren Faust (Fire_Flye), *Twitter* post, September 12, 2015, 10:15am. https://twitter.com/Fyre_flye/status/642748283253714944.

46. fyre-flye, "THANK YOU!!!," *DeviantArt*, last modified May 8, 2011, http://fyre-flye.deviantart.com/journal/?catpath=%2F&offset=40.

47. Angela Watercutter, "My Little Pony Corrals Unlikely Fanboys Known as 'Bronies,'" *Wired*, last modified June 9, 2011, http://www.wired.com/2011/06/bronies-my-little-ponys/.

48. Angela Watercutter, "Sincerely Ours: *Glee*'s Success Cements Age of Geeky 'New Sincerity,'" *Wired*, last modified September 21, 1010, http://www.wired.com/2010/09/new-sincerity/.

49. Watercutter, 2011.

50. *Ibid.*

51. Amid Amidi, "My Little Bronies," *Cartoon Brew*, last modified June 10, 2011, http://www.cartoonbrew.com/cartoon-culture/my-little-bronies-44016.html.

52. *Ibid.*

53. *Ibid.*

54. Monika Anderson, "Never Too Old for *Thundercats*?" *Wall Street Journal*, August 12, 2011.

55. August Brown, "Pop Music Review; Pure Confection from Katy Perry; The Singer Brings Sugary Pop Savvy to Her Three-Night Nokia Theatre Stand," *Los Angeles Times*, August 8, 2011.

56. Tom Shone, "Katy Perry: 'You Have to Bust Your Ass at This,'" *Guardian*, August 7, 2010.

57. *Ibid.*

58. Sethisto, "Equestria Girls: Official Song by Pinkie Pie," *Equestria Daily*, last modified May 24, 2011, http://www.equestriadaily.com/2011/05/equestria-girls-song-by-pinkie-pie.html.

59. Sethisto, "Premiere: Extended Equestria Girls," *Equestria Daily,* last modified May 27,

2011, http://www.equestriadaily.com/2011/05/extended-equestria-girls.html.

60. Joshua Ostroff, "All-Ages Show; Mom and Dad Hipsters Are Just as All Right with the Indie-Infused Children's Programming of Today," *National Post*, August 4, 2011.

61. Ostroff.

62. Faust, December 24, 2010.

63. Ostroff.

64. "Plak-Tow (Star Trek: TOS newsletter edited by Shirley M.)," *Fanlore*, last modified November 3, 2013, http://fanlore.org/wiki/Plak-Tow_%28Star_Trek:_TOS_newsletter_edited_by_Shirley_M.%29.

65. *Ibid.*

66. "En Garde," *Fanlore*, last modified May 25, 2012, http://fanlore.org/wiki/En_Garde.

67. Station Manager Ken, "Seven Minutes in Deadwood," *WFMU's Beware of the Blog*, last modified May 20, 2005, http://blog.wfmu.org/freeform/2005/05/seven_minutes_i.html.

68. Geoff Gehman, "Dr. Who, That's Who," *Morning Call*, October 19, 1985.

69. "Enterprise (Star Trek: TOS zine published in 1984)," *Fanlore*, last modified March 11, 2013, http://fanlore.org/wiki/Enterprise_%28Star_Trek:_TOS_zine_published_in_1984%29.

70. *Ibid.*

71. Weinman.

72. Lyons.

73. Weinman.

74. Faust.

75. *Ibid.*

76. Una LaMarche, "Pony Up Haters: How 4chan Gave Birth to the Bronies," *New York Observer*, August 3, 2011, http://observer.com/2011/08/pony-up-haters-how-4chan-gave-birth-to-the-bronies/.

77. Weinman.

78. Gweisswasser.

79. Chris Harnick, "Rainbow Brite Rides Again! The Iconic '80s Character Gets New Cartoon," E! Online, October 14, 2014, http://www.eonline.com/news/588229/rainbow-brite-rides-again-the-iconic-80s-character-gets-new-cartoon.

80. Weinman.

81. *Ibid.*.

82. *Ibid.*

83. "Amid Amidi," *Amazon*, n.d., http://www.amazon.com/Amid-Amidi/e/B001JS6FGK/ref=sr_tc_2_0?qid=1436054748&sr=8-2-ent.

84. "Hasbro's Iconic POTATO HEAD Character Celebrates 60th Birthday," Hasbro Inc. press release, February 14, 2012.

85. Erickson, 1995, 351.

86. "Toy Story," *Disney Store*, n.d. http://www.disneystore.com/toy-story/mn/1000055/.

87. "Cars," *Disney Store*, n.d., http://www.disneystore.com/cars/mn/1000012/.

88. "Monsters," *Disney Store*, n.d., http://www.disneystore.com/monsters/mn/1000035/.

89. "Finding Nemo." *Disney Store*. n.d. http://www.disneystore.com/finding-nemo/mn/1000020/.

90. "Hasbro Says Profit in Fiscal 1st Quarter Nearly Quadrupled," *Wall Street Journal*, April 20, 1984.

91. Davis, 1984.

92. King.

93. Pereira, 1987.

94. Chris Arrant, "The Hub Announces 2011–2012 Program Line-Up, Including a Warren Buffet Animated Series," *Cartoon Brew*, last modified March 28, 2011. http://www.cartoonbrew.com/biz/the-hub-announces-2011-2012-program-line-up-including-a-warren-buffet-animated-series-39441.html.

95. Amid Amidi, "Let's Talk About the Animation in 'The Lego Movie,'" *Cartoon Brew*, last modified February 5, 2014. http://www.cartoonbrew.com/ideas-commentary/lets-talk-about-the-animation-in-the-lego-movie-95781.html.

96. Jaime Weinman, "Ponies Do Sondheim," *Maclean's*, September 7, 2011, http://www.macleans.ca/authors/jaime-weinman/ponies-do-sondheim/.

97. *Ibid.*

98. *Ibid.*

99. Madeleine Davies, "I Was the Weirdest Person at Bronycon 2014," *Jezebel*, last modified September 2, 2014, http://jezebel.com/i-was-the-weirdest-person-at-bronycon-2014-1616532065.

100. *Interview with M.A. Larson*, YouTube video, 1:30:40, posted by "CelestiaRadio" January 27, 2013, https://www.youtube.com/watch?v=DyhFKhu7GhM&.

101. fyre-flye, "Comment on fyre-flye's profile," *DeviantArt*, last modified December 18, 2010, http://comments.deviantart.com/4/1603670/1787126283.

102. David Gerrold, *The Trouble with Tribbles* (New York: Ballantine Books, 1973), 253.

103. *Ibid.*

104. *Ibid.*

105. *BroNYCon Winter 2012—Daniel Ingram Skype Interview—High Quality Audio*, YouTube video, 54:31, posted by "Everfree Network" January 11, 2012, https://www.youtube.com/watch?v=4jAua6QpX6w.

106. Kevin Rutherford, "Behind the Music

of Pop Culture Smash 'My Little Pony: Friendship Is Magic,'" *Rolling Stone*, last modified April 20, 2012, http://www.rollingstone.com/music/news/behind-the-music-of-pop-culture-smash-my-little-pony-friendship-is-magic-20120420.

107. Stephen Holden, "Melodist and Minimalist in Harmony," *New York Times*, February 1, 2015.

108. James Lipton, "Stephen Sondheim, The Art of the Musical," *Paris Review*, Spring 1997, http://www.theparisreview.org/interviews/1283/the-art-of-the-musical-stephen-sondheim.

109. Samuel G. Freedman, "The Words and Music of Stephen Sondheim," *New York Times*, April 1, 1984.

110. Bob Dylan, *Chronicles: Volume One* (New York: Simon & Schuster, 2004), 49.

111. "Yankee Doodle," *Library of Congress*, n.d., http://www.loc.gov/teachers/lyrical/songs/yankee_doodle.html.

112. "The Yankee Doodle Boy," *Library of Congress*, last modified December 10, 2014, http://lcweb2.loc.gov/diglib/ihas/loc.natlib.ihas.200000020/default.html.

113. Cleve Callison, "Great American Songbook Memorial Day Special," *WHQR*, last updated May 22, 2015, http://whqr.org/post/great-american-songbook-memorial-day-special.

114. Charles Schwartz, *Cole Porter: A Biography* (New York: De Capo, 1992): 167–168.

115. *Ibid.*

116. *Mime for a Change | The Powerpuff Girls Moment #9 | Cartoon Network*, YouTube Video, 3:17, posted by "Cartoon Network," January 13, 2014, https://www.youtube.com/watch?v=y6iROyn5MjE.

117. Michael Davis, *Street Gang: The Complete History of Sesame Street* (New York: Viking, 2008): 218.

118. *Ibid.*, 217.

119. *Ibid.*, 325.

120. Joe Flint, "Sesame Street's Favorite New Letters: HBO," *Wall Street Journal*, August 13, 2015.

121. *Ibid.*

122. Congress of the U.S., Washington, DC. House Committee on Energy and Commerce. *Commercialization of Children's Television.*

123. *Commercial—Ideal Big Bird Story Magic*, YouTube video, 0:30, posted by "TVRetroQc," September 2, 2012, https://www.youtube.com/watch?v=7unOrpcrfs8.

124. Mark Ruffalo (MarkRuffalo), *Twitter* post, April 28, 2015, 6:16pm. https://twitter.com/MarkRuffalo/status/593222325325209601.

125. Butnotblackwidow, "Reason for the Blog," *But Not Black Widow*, last modified Sep-

tember 12, 2012, http://butnotblackwidow.tumblr.com/post/31547288566/reason-for-the-blog/.

126. Annie N. Mouse, "Invisible Women: Why Marvel's Gamora & Black Widow Were Missing from Merchandise, And What We Can Do About It," *Mary Sue*, last modified April 7, 2015, http://www.themarysue.com/invisible-women/.

127. *Ibid.*

128. Clark Gregg (ClarkGregg), *Twitter* post, May 3, 2015, 12:10pm. https://twitter.com/clarkgregg/status/594942140045754369.

129. Patricia V. Davis, "Add Black Widow to the Avengers Action Figure Pack," *Change.org*, last modified May 2, 2015, https://www.change.org/p/hasbro-add-more-female-superhero-merc-add-black-widow-to-the-avengers-action-figure-pack.

130. *Ibid.*

131. "Black Widow," *Marvel Cinematic Universe Wiki*, n.d., http://marvelcinematicuniverse.wikia.com/wiki/Black_Widow.

132. "Gamora," *Marvel Cinematic Universe Wiki*, n.d., http://marvelcinematicuniverse.wikia.com/wiki/Gamora.

133. Davis.

134. "Bill Clinton Plays Not My Job," Narrated by Peter Sagal, *Wait Wait...Don't Tell Me!*, NPR, June 25, 2011, http://www.npr.org/2011/06/25/137386121/bill-clinton-plays-not-my-job.

135. *Ibid.*

136. *Ibid.*

137. *Ibid.*

138. Alan Scherstuhl, "How Much of *The Hobbit* Can You Read During the Running Time of *The Hobbit*?," *Village Voice*, last modified December 7, 2012, http://www.villagevoice.com/news/how-much-of-the-hobbit-can-you-read-during-the-running-time-of-the-hobbit-668 5565.

139. "Wait Wait...Don't Tell Me!" NPR, n.d., http://www.npr.org/podcasts/344098539/wait-wait-don-t-tell-me.

140. "Bill Clinton Plays Not My Job," June 25, 2011.

141. *Ibid.*

142. James H, June 25, 2011 (12:42 p.m.), comment on "Bill Clinton Plays Not My Job," Narrated by Peter Sagal, *Wait Wait...Don't Tell Me!*, NPR, June 25, 2011, http://www.npr.org/2011/06/25/137386121/bill-clinton-plays-not-my-job.

143. Megan Gibson, "Guess Who's a Fan? Former President Bill Clinton Is a 'Brony,'" *Time*, last modified June 27, 2011, http://newsfeed.time.com/2011/06/27/guess-whos-a-fan-former-president-bill-clinton-is-a-brony/.

144. "Bill Clinton a Brony? Former President Knows My Little Pony Trivia," *Huffington Post*, last modified August 27, 2011, http://www.huffingtonpost.com/2011/06/27/bill-clinton-brony-my-little-pony-trivia_n_885509.html.

145. NPR, June 25, 2011.

146. *Ibid.*

147. *Ibid.*

148. William Harvey, "My Little Pony: Not Just for Little Girls," *Tampa Bay Times*, April 12, 2012.

149. T.L. Stanley, "Hey, It's Their 'Little Pony' Too," *Los Angeles Times*, April 22, 2012.

150. Margaret Hartmann, "The Unlikely Origins of the Brony, or Bros Who Like 'My Little Pony,'" *Jezebel*, last modified August 4, 2011, http://jezebel.com/5827591/the-unlikely-origins-of-the-brony-or-dudes-who-like-my-little-pony.

151. *Ibid.*

152. *Ibid.*

153. Margaret Hartmann, "Ryan Gosling Obviously Sings *My Little Pony* Theme Song," *Jezebel*, last modified January 4, 2011, http://jezebel.com/5724478/ryan-gosling-obviously-sings-my-little-pony-theme-song.

154. *Ibid.*

155. John Anderson, "As Tribeca Kicks Off, 'A Brony Tale' Leads Some Must-See Docs," *Indiewire*, last modified April 16, 2014, http://blogs.indiewire.com/thompsononhollywood/as-tribeca-turns-sweet-thirteen-a-roster-of-docs-looking-more-promising-than-ever.

156. *Ibid.*

157. Francois Marchand, "Filmmaker Riding High on My Little Pony," *Vancouver Sun*, April 23, 2014.

158. *Ibid.*

159. *Ibid.*

160. "Tigers and Furries," narrated by Steve Scher, *Weekday*, KUOW, March 30, 2011, http://www2.kuow.org/program.php?id=22994.

161. *Ibid.*

162. *Ibid.*

163. *Ibid.*

164. *Ibid.*

165. Shawn Conner, "Meet the Bronies at DOXA," *Vancouver Sun*, April 3, 2014.

166. Louis Emanuel, "Meet the Bronies: The Men (and Women) Who Love My Little Pony," *Bristol Post*, April 9, 2014.

167. *Ibid.*

168. Louis Emanuel, "Bristol Bronies: The Men Who Love My Little Pony," *Bristol Post*, last modified April 9, 2014, http://www.bristolpost.co.uk/Bristol-Bronies-men-love-Little-Pony/story-20931726-detail/story.html.

169. "Happening: Tribeca Film Festival," *Financial Times*, April 14, 2014.

170. Marianne Garvey, Brian Niemietz, and Lachlan Cartwright, "Photo Exhibition Clicks with Bono," *New York Daily News*, April 28, 2014.

171. LaMarche.

172. Caitlin Dewey, "Don't Laugh, But Bronies May Be Propping Up One of America's Favorite Companies," *Washington Post*, April 24, 2014.

173. *Ibid.*

174. Karen Kemmerle, "Brent Hodge on 'A Brony Tale' and What It Means to be a Man," *Tribeca Film Festival*, last modified April 30, 2014, https://tribecafilm.com/stories/brent-hodge-a-brony-tale-interview.

175. *Ibid.*

176. *Ibid.*

177. *Ibid.*

178. *Ibid.*

179. Carrie Goldman, "11-yr-old Boy Bullied for Being a Brony Fighting for Life After Suicide Attempt," *Chicago Now*, last modified February 2, 2014.

180. *Financial Times*, April 14, 2014.

181. Emily Le Coz, "11-Year-Old Boy's Suicide Attempt Part of Epidemic," *Clarion-Ledger*, April 14, 2014.

182. "School Bully Concerns," *WLOS-TV*, last modified March 12, 2014, https://web.archive.org/web/20140314044422/http://wlos.com/shared/news/features/top-stories/stories/wlos_-school-bully-concerns-15463.shtml.

183. Casey Blake, "School Will Allow Boy to Bring My Little Pony Backpack," *Citizen Times*, March 21, 2014.

184. Lee Moran, "North Carolina School Tells Boy, 9, to Ditch 'My Little Pony' Bag Because It's a Trigger for Bullying," *New York Daily News*, last modified March 19, 2014, http://www.nydailynews.com/news/national/boy-told-ditch-pony-bag-article-1.1726433.

185. Matt Labash, "The Dread Pony," *Weekly Standard*, last modified August 26, 2013, http://www.weeklystandard.com/article/dread-pony/748495.

186. *Ibid.*

187. *Weekly Standard*, "Media Kit," n.d., http://www.weeklystandard.com/advertising/pdf/TWS-media-kit-2013.pdf.

188. "Q3 2011 Hasbro Inc Earnings Conference Call," Hasbro Inc. press release, October 17, 2011.

189. Kidomo, "My Little Pony Tour 2011," n.d., http://www.kidomo.com/media/Special/Kidomo—Hasbro—MLP—2012.pdf.

190. Natasha Ann Zachariah, "Pony Posse," *Straits Times*, October 30, 2011.

191. *Ibid.*

192. Weinman.

193. LaMarche.

194. Watercutter.

195. Vauhini Vara, "Hey, Bro, That's My Little Pony! Guys' Interest Mounts in Girly TV Show; 'Bronies' Enthralled by Cartoon Equines; Characters 'Aren't One-Dimensional,'" *Wall Street Journal*, November 5, 2011.

196. Zachariah.

197. Natasha Ann Zachariah, "Bonding Over Magical Ponies," *Straits Times*, October 30, 2011.

198. *Ibid.*

199. Vara.

200. *Ibid.*

201. Reed Tucker, "Horsing Around! The My Little Pony Craze Is Back—But This Time Grown-Up Guys Are Leading the Charge," *New York Post*, January 11, 2012.

202. *Ibid.*

203. *Ibid.*

204. Weinman, "Ponies Do Sondheim," September 7, 2011.

205. Tucker..

206. Rob Wennemer, "Beer, Women and … My Little Pony? Men Profess Newest Love," *Pittsburgh Post-Gazette*, July 30, 2012.

207. *Ibid.*

208. *Ibid.*

209. *Ibid.*

210. Stephen Daultrey, "Bromancing the Ponies," *Bizarre* 215 (June 2014): 62.

211. *Ibid.*

212. *Ibid.*

213. *Ibid.*

214. "Hasbro, Inc. Investor Day," Hasbro Inc. press release, November 9, 2010.

215. "Hasbro Presents Array of Branded Lifestyle Goods for Entire Family at the International Licensing Expo," Hasbro Inc. press release, June 13, 2011.

216. "Hasbro Teams with Target to Create a Magical In-Store Experience for Girls," Hasbro Inc. press release, July 28, 2011.

217. "Hasbro Delivers Must-Have Products and Entertainment Experiences for the Holiday Season," Hasbro Inc. press release, October 24, 2011.

218. *Ibid.*

219. *Rarity's Carousel Boutique Playset (TV Commercial) | My Little Pony Toys for Kids*, YouTube Video, 0:20, posted by "My Little Pony Official," November 28, 2011, https://www.youtube.com/watch?v=sRSFsNbPp0o.

220. Hasbro Inc., October 24, 2011.

221. "Hasbro to Debut Innovative New Play Experiences from Its Expansive Portfolio of Iconic Brands at the American International Toy Fair," Hasbro Inc. press release, February 9, 2012.

222. "Hasbro Film, Television Programming and Licensed Merchandise Driving Global Retail Growth," Hasbro Inc. press release, June 11, 2012.

223. "Hasbro Returns to Comic-Con International to Showcase Its Iconic Pop-Culture Brands," Hasbro Inc. press release, July 9, 2012.

224. *Ibid.*

225. "MY LITTLE PONY Gallops into Comics," Hasbro Inc. press release, July 14, 2012.

226. "Guinness World Record® Achieved for Largest Coloring Book During Hub Tv Network's 'Playdate Premiere Party,'" Hasbro Inc. press release, November 12, 2012.

227. *PlaydatePremiereParty Preview File*, MPEG-4 Video, 3.30, November 10, 2012, http://premieretvmedia.com/Client/HUB/Playdate PremiereParty/.

228. "Hasbro Delivers Innovative and 'Must Have' Toys for the Holidays," Hasbro Inc. press release, November 14, 2012.

229. *Ibid.*

230. "Twilight Sparkle Becomes a Princess in Special Coronation Episode of 'My Little Pony Friendship Is Magic' on The Hub TV Network," Hasbro Inc. press release, January 30, 2013.

231. *Ibid.*

232. "MY LITTLE PONY Gallops into Build-a-Bear Workshop," Hasbro Inc. press release, March 26, 2013.

233. *Ibid.*

234. Hasbro Inc., March 7, 2005.

235. "CORRECTING and REPLACING Hasbro Builds on MY LITTLE PONY Brand Growth Catering to Fans Worldwide," Hasbro Inc. press release, June 19, 2013.

236. "Hasbro, Inc. 2013 Investor Day—Final," Hasbro Inc. press release, September 10, 2013.

237. *Ibid.*

238. *Ibid.*

239. "Hasbro and Shapeways Launch SuperFanArt, New Website That Empowers Fans to Be Creators Using Hasbro Brands," Hasbro Inc. press release, July 21, 2014.

Part 5

1. Katie Levine, "James Bonding #008: DIE ANOTHER DAY with Ben Blacker and Ben Acker," *Nerdist*, last modified October 24, 2013, http://nerdist.com/james-bonding-008-

die-another-day-with-ben-blacker-and-ben-acker/.

2. Edenthegamer, "Derpy Hooves," *Know Your Meme*, last modified in 2015, http://know yourmeme.com/memes/derpy-hooves.

3. Ashbot, "Derp," *Know Your Meme*, last modified in 2015, http://knowyourmeme.com/memes/derp.

4. Jayson Thiessen, "Hey Ponychan," *Ponychan*, last modified March 30, 2011, https://www.ponychan.net/arch/res/6286.html.

5. Edenthegamer.

6. Victorian R. Hellsly, "My Little Time Lord," *FanFiction*, last modified December 29, 2011, https://www.fanfiction.net/s/6700975/.

7. *Ibid.*

8. Soarin_the_Pegasus, "Where Did the Whole 'Mail Carrier Derpy' Thing Come From?" *Derpibooru*, last modified in 2013, https://derpibooru.org/pony/where-did-the-whole-mail-carrier-derpy-thing-come-from.

9. Thiessen.

10. fyre-flye, "MLP Art for Japan **UPDATE**," *DeviantArt*, last modified April 8, 2011, https://web.archive.org/web/20140216014638/http://fyre-flye.deviantart.com/journal/MLP-art-for-Japan-UPDATE-219997425.

11. "Derpy Hooves: Lauren Faust MLP:FIM Original Art," *eBay*, last modified April 15, 2011, http://www.ebay.com/itm/Derpy-Hooves-Lauren-Faust-MLP-FIM-Original-Art-/280662542214.

12. Michael O'Connell, "When 'The X-Files' Became A-List: An Oral History of Fox's Out-There Success Story," *Hollywood Reporter*, last modified January 7, 2016, http://www.hollywoodreporter.com/features/x-files-became-a-list-852398.

13. "I'm the Juggernaut, Bitch!" *Know Your Meme*, last modified in 2013, http://knowyourmeme.com/memes/im-the-juggernaut-bitch.

14. "Hachune Miku." *Vocaloid Wiki*, n.d., http://vocaloid.wikia.com/wiki/Hachune_Miku.

15. *Hatsune Miku Project Diva 2nd—Ievan Polkka*, YouTube video, 2:34, posted by "averageasian4292," July 29, 2010, https://www.youtube.com/watch?v=pQ4Z2VpuB-U.

16. KEI, *Mikucolor: KEI's Hatsune Miku Illustration Works* (Fujimi, Chiyoda, Tokyo: Kadokawa Shoten, 2012), 119.

17. "Amy Keating Rogers Responds," *Save Derpy*, n.d., http://savederpy.tumblr.com/AKR Response.

18. Lauren Faust (Fire_Flye), *Twitter* post, May 1, 2013, 8:53pm. https://twitter.com/Fyre_flye/status/329805944051625984.

19. Lauren Faust (Fire_Flye), *Twitter* post,

May 1, 2013, 8:54pm. https://twitter.com/Fyre_flye/status/329806111022653441.

20. *Save Derpy.*

21. *MLP FiM—Chat Reactions to Derpy in "The Last Roundup,"* YouTube video, 2:08, posted by swainize, January 21, 2012, https://www.youtube.com/watch?v=geTCP666Yf4.

22. Cereal Velocity, "DERPY DERPY DERPY DERPY DERPY DERPY," *Equestria Daily*, last modified January 21, 2012, http://www.equestriadaily.com/2012/01/oh.html.

23. Ponyceum, January 21, 2012 (6:41 p.m.), comment on Cereal Velocity.

24. Ponyceum, January 21, 2012 (9:01 p.m.), comment on Cereal Velocity.

25. Tora, January 21, 2012 (4:29 p.m.), comment on Cereal Velocity.

26. Susan Goodman, "What's in a Label?" *The Washington Post*, April 7, 1992.

27. sUiCiDaLn00b, January 21, 2012 (12:42 p.m.), comment on Cereal Velocity.

28. Vulcan539, January 21, 2012 (12:44 p.m.), comment on Cereal Velocity.

29. GumballCrash, January 21, 2012 (12:47 p.m.), comment on Cereal Velocity.

30. Senior Waffles, January 21, 2012 (3:55 p.m.), comment on Cereal Velocity.

31. Commander Hurricane, January 21, 2012 (4:18 p.m.), comment on Cereal Velocity.

32. hyreia, January 21, 2012 (6:03 p.m.), comment on Cereal Velocity.

33. ThinLine_3RX, January 21, 2012 (9:15 p.m.), comment on Cereal Velocity.

34. Jenna Pitman, "Make Amends for Hurtful Ableist Stereotype in My Little Pony," *Change.org*, last modified January 21, 2012, https://www.change.org/p/hasbro-hasbro-studios-the-hub-make-amends-for-hurtful-ableist-stereotype-in-my-little-pony.

35. *Ibid.*

36. *Ibid.*

37. *Ibid.*

38. *Save Derpy.*

39. *Ibid.*

40. *Ibid.*

41. Kelven486, "So I emailed Ms Germain (voice for Rarity, Luna, Derpy) and got a reply...," *Reddit*, last modified January 27, 2012. https://www.reddit.com/r/mylittlepony/comments/oynoa/so_i_emailed_ms_germain_voice_for_rarity_luna/.

42. *Save Derpy.*

43. Sethisto, "The Last Roundup's Mysterious iTunes Dissapearence," *Equestria Daily*, last modified January 30, 2012, http://www.equestriadaily.com/2012/01/last-roundups-mysterious-itunes.html.

44. Sethisto, "Derpy Has Been Modified," *Equestria Daily*, last modified, February 24, 2012, http://www.equestriadaily.com/2012/02/derpy-has-been-modified.html.

45. Prophet of Ponies, January 22, 2012 (3:28 p.m.), comment on Cereal Velocity.

46. Ragemoar, January 23, 2012 (10:24 a.m.), comment on Cereal Velocity.

47. Sethisto, "Small Update on Derpy Overall," *Equestria Daily*, last modified February 2, 2012, http://www.equestriadaily.com/2012/02/small-update-on-derpy-overall.html.

48. Jakep Chellen, "Keep Derpy Named Derpy!," *Change.org*, last modified February 2, 2012, https://www.change.org/p/hasbro-keep-derpy-named-derpy.

49. Andrew Holt, "Hasbro Studios/The Hub: Do Not Change Derpy's Name," *Change.org*, last modified February 2, 2012, https://web.archive.org/web/20120207085817/http.//www.change.org/petitions/hasbro-studiosthe-hub-do-not-change-derpys-name.

50. Andrew Holt, "Petition Update—Sent an Email to Hasbro, Waiting on Clarification about the Whole Issue," *Change.org*, last modified February 4, 2012, https://www.change.org/p/hasbro-studios-the-hub-return-derpy-s-scene-in-the-last-roundup-to-normal/u/814365.

51. Sethisto, "Important Message to the Community from Hasbro," *Equestria Daily*, last modified February 6, 2012, http://www.equestriadaily.com/2012/02/important-message-to-community-from.html.

52. Andrew Holt, "Regarding the Message from Hasbro," *Change.org*, last modified February 7, 2012, https://www.change.org/p/hasbro-studios-the-hub-return-derpy-s-scene-in-the-last-roundup-to-normal/u/828150.

53. Andrew Holt, "Reopening Petition," *Change.org*, last modified February 8, 2012, https://www.change.org/p/hasbro-studios-the-hub-return-derpy-s-scene-in-the-last-roundup-to-normal/u/833350.

54. "Q4 2011 Hasbro Inc Earnings Conference Call," Hasbro Inc. press release, February 6, 2012.

55. Sethisto, February 24, 2012.

56. *Save Derpy.*

57. Kreoss, "Derpy," *DeviantArt*, last modified February 24, 2012, http://kreoss.deviantart.com/journal/Derpy-287023334.

58. *Ibid.*

59. Yamino, "I Made a Response to the Ponychan Thread Regarding....," *tumblr*, last modified July 23, 2011, http://yamino.tumblr.com/post/7968862006/i-made-a-response-to-the-ponychan-thread-regarding.

60. Yamino, "Final Word on Brony Drama," *tumblr*, last modified March 1, 2012, http://yamino.tumblr.com/post/18558550747/final-word-on-brony-drama.

61. Derek July, "CG, EQLA, BronyCon, EFNW, Las Pegasus Unicon, Other Brony Conventions: Ban YAC from Performing, and from Appearing in Any Guest of Honor Role," *Change.org*, last modified February 2, 2012, https://www.change.org/p/cg-eqla-bronycon-efnw-las-pegasus-unicon-other-brony-conventions-ban-yac-from-performing-and-from-appearing-in-any-guest-of-honor-role.

62. Hawklaser, February 25, 2012 (7:28 p.m.), comment on Sethisto, February 24, 2012.

63. Dsludge, February 27, 2012 (8:53 p.m.), comment on Sethisto, February 24, 2012.

64. Mystic, February 25, 2012 (1:38 a.m.), comment on Sethisto, February 24, 2012.

65. keneticpest, February 25, 2012 (2:36 a.m.), comment on Sethisto, February 24, 2012.

66. Xeddrief, February 25, 2012 (2:27 a.m.), comment on Sethisto, February 24, 2012.

67. Alondro, February 25, 2012 (9:08 p.m.), comment on Sethisto, February 24, 2012.

68. Soapy5, February 25, 2012 (1:46 a.m.), comment on Sethisto, February 24, 2012.

69. Forb.Jok, February 25, 2012 (8:58 a.m.), comment on Sethisto, February 24, 2012.

70. Luna4life, February 25, 2012 (2:53 a.m.), comment on Sethisto, February 24, 2012.

71. Asterik, February 25, 2012 (4:08 a.m.), comment on Sethisto, February 24, 2012.

72. HappySquid, February 25, 2012 (8:53 a.m.), comment on Sethisto, February 24, 2012.

73. Turboblazer, February 25, 2012 (3:19 a.m.), comment on Sethisto, February 24, 2012.

74. ShadowofColosuss708, February 25, 2012 (2:29 a.m.), comment on Sethisto, February 24, 2012.

75. Kemmerle.

76. Shine, February 25, 2012 (4:23 a.m.), comment on Sethisto, February 24, 2012.

77. Thecrazyrabbidfangirl, February 25, 2012 (1:07 p.m.), comment on Sethisto, February 24, 2012.

78. "Age and Sex Composition in the United States: 2012," *United States Census Bureau*, n.d., http://www.census.gov/population/age/data/2012comp.html.

79. Andrew Holt, "Return Derpy's Scene in the Last Roundup to Normal," *Change.org*, last modified February 26, 2012. https://www.change.org/p/hasbro-studios-the-hub-return-derpy-s-scene-in-the-last-roundup-to-normal/u/932490.

80. brilliantspecter, February 25, 2012 (1:34 a.m.), comment on Sethisto, February 24, 2012.

81. Andrew Holt, "Derpy's Edit," *Change.org*, last modified February 25, 2012, https://www.change.org/p/hasbro-studios-the-hub-return-derpy-s-scene-in-the-last-roundup-to-normal/u/925345.

82. GuerreroPerdido, February 25, 2012 (1:35 a.m.), comment on Sethisto, February 24, 2012.

83. Kyli Rouge, February 25, 2012 (1:56 a.m.), comment on Sethisto, February 24, 2012.

84. Jenna Pitman, "Hasbro and Studio B Heard Our Cries!," *Change.org*, last modified February 25, 2012, https://www.change.org/p/hasbro-hasbro-studios-the-hub-make-amends-for-hurtful-ableist-stereotype-in-my-little-pony/u/924955.

85. *Ibid.*

86. Andrew Holt, "Return Derpy's Scene in the Last Roundup to Normal," *Change.org*, last modified February 26, 2012, https://www.change.org/p/hasbro-studios-the-hub-return-derpy-s-scene-in-the-last-roundup-to-normal.

87. Andrew Holt, "Slight Changes to the Petition Overall," *Change.org*, last modified February 26, 2012, https://www.change.org/p/hasbro-studios-the-hub-return-derpy-s-scene-in-the-last-roundup-to-normal/u/932490.

88. Alex Shen, "Save Derpy (and Hasbro's Creative Process)," *Change.org*, last modified February 26, 2012, https://www.change.org/p/save-derpy-and-hasbros-creative-process.

89. *Ibid.*

90. "Stellar Performance of My Little Pony Friendship Is Magic Fan-Favorite Marathon Powers the Hub to Strong Audience Gains," Discovery Communications press release, February 14, 2012.

91. *Ibid.*

92. Justin Jurek, "Change Derpy Back," *Change.org*, last modified February 25, 2012, https://www.change.org/p/hasbro-studios-the-hub-change-derpy-back.

93. Daniel Reinert, "Return Derpy Hooves! Name, Voice, and Eyes!," *Change.org*, last modified February 25, 2012, https://www.change.org/p/hasbro-return-derpy-hooves-name-voice-and-eyes.

94. Kylen Taskovic, "WE WANT DERPY HOOVES'S NAME BACK!," *Change.org*, last modified February 25, 2012, https://www.change.org/p/we-want-derpy-hoovess-name-back.

95. Sarah Patterson, "No Money for Hasbro Until Derpy Hooves's Name, Voice and Eyes Are Restored!," *Change.org*, last modified February 25, 2012, https://www.change.org/p/hasbro-no-money-for-hasbro-until-derpy-hooves-s-name-voice-and-eyes-are-restored. .

96. Charles "Shuttershade" Rhue, "Do Not Alter Derpy in 'The Last Roundup,'" *Change.org*, last modified February 2012, https://www.change.org/p/keep-derpy-no-ditzy-do-not-alter-derpy-in-the-last-roundup.

97. Sethisto, February 24, 2012.

98. Adrian Chen, "Bronies Furious After Minor My Little Pony Character Is Changed to Seem Less Mentally Disabled," *Gawker*, last modified February 28, 2012, http://gawker.com/5889084/bronies-furious-after-minor-my-little-pony-character-is-changed-to-seem-less-mentally-disabled.

99. HashUpAsshole, May 15, 2013, comment on Sethisto, "Reminder: My Little Pony Season 2 DVD Now Available," *Equestria Daily*, last modified May 15, 2013, http://www.equestriadaily.com/2013/05/reminder-my-little-pony-season-2-dvd.html.

100. Calpain, "An Appeal to the Fandom—Keep Calm and Trot On," *Equestria Daily*, last modified May 14, 2013, http://www.equestriadaily.com/2013/05/an-appeal-to-fandom-keep-calm-and-trot.html.

101. Dana Simpson, "Phoebe and Her Unicorn Comic Strip, March 17, 2013," *GoComics*, last modified March 17, 2013.

102. Dana Simpson, *Unicorn on a Roll: Another Phoebe and Her Unicorn Adventure* (Kansas City, MO: Andrews McMeel Publishing, 2015): vi-vii.

103. *Ibid.*

104. "Hasbro Delivers the Hottest Special Edition Toys at San Diego Comic-Con, Featuring Transformers, G.I. Joe, My Little Pony and More," Hasbro Inc. press release, June 27, 2012.

105. "Rare Ponies." *Strawberry Reef.*

106. *Ibid.*

107. "Comic Con 2012 (Ditzy Doo/Derpy Hooves)," *Strawberry Reef*, n.d., http://www.strawberryreef.com/Index/Name/derpyFIMstyle.html.

108. Sethisto, "Derpy Possibly This Year's Comic Con Exclusive!" *Equestria Daily*, last modified May 28, 2012, http://www.equestriadaily.com/2012/05/derpy-possibly-this-years-comic-con.html.

109. Cereal Velocity, "Derpy Toy Confirmed by USA Today," *Equestria Daily*, last modified May 30, 2012,. http://www.equestriadaily.com/2012/05/derpy-toy-confirmed-by-usa-today.html.

110. Travis Tucker, "Return Derpy Hooves in Season 4 of MLP: FiM," *Change.org*, last modified February 5, 2013, https://www.change.org/p/hasbro-return-derpy-hooves-in-season-4-of-mlp-fim.

111. *Ibid.*

112. *Gravity Falls*, "Between the Pines," produced by Emily Burton and Eric Beaudry, Disney XD, February 12, 2016.

113. Erik Adams, "There's One Secret the Rick and Morty Guys Will Never Reveal," *A.V. Club*, last modified July 23, 2015, http://www.avclub.com/article/theres-one-secret-rick-and-morty-guys-will-never-r-222269.

114. Sethisto, "Poll Results: Worst Pony Drama So Far This Year?" *Equestria Daily*, last modified June 27, 2013, http://www.equestriadaily.com/2013/06/poll-results-worst-pony-drama-so-far.html.

115. Chris Isaac, "Interview: Them's Fightin' Herds' Lauren Faust and the Mane6 Team on Their Fighting Game," *Mary Sue*, last modified October 19, 2015.
http://www.themarysue.com/lauren-faust-and-mane6-on-thems-fightin-herds/.

116. TheBiggestJim (Jim Miller), *Twitter* post, January 18, 2014, 8:42am. https://twitter.com/TheBiggestJim/status/424582482239832065.

117. "List of Strawberry Shortcake's Berry Bitty Adventures episodes," *Wikipedia*, last modified February 19, 2016, https://en.wikipedia.org/wiki/List_of_Strawberry_Shortcake's_Berry_Bitty_Adventures_episodes.

118. Eric Goldman, "Transformers Prime Ending with Season 3," *IGN*, last modified March 1, 2013.

119. *M.A. Larson's Deconstruction of Episode #100 Panel: MLP-MSP*, YouTube video, 38:47, posted by "ACRacebest," June 17, 2015, https://www.youtube.com/watch?v=MTJoTjeyqmA.

120. *Ibid.*

121. *Ibid.*

122. M_A_Larson (M.A. Larson), *Twitter* post, June 10, 2015, 11:40am. https://twitter.com/M_A_Larson/status/608705364377239552.

123. TheBiggestJim (Jim Miller), *Twitter* post, June 13, 2015, 9:21am. https://twitter.com/TheBiggestJim/status/609757573550612481.

124. CMC_Scootaloo, June 2015, comment on Sethisto, "M.A. Larson Reveals All Sorts of Fun Things Cut from Episode 100," *Equestria Daily*, last modified June 18, 2015.

125. *Ibid.*

126. Steven L. Kent, *The Ultimate History of Video Games* (Roseville, Calif: Prima, 2001), 142.

127. Murrison (Murrison), *Twitter* post, June 13, 2015, 9:19pm. https://twitter.com/Murrisson/status/609757108339363840.

128. TheBiggestJim (Jim Miller), *Twitter* post, June 13, 2015, 9:21am. https://twitter.com/TheBiggestJim/status/609757573550612481.

129. TheBiggestJim (Jim Miller), *Twitter* post, June 13, 2015, 11:04am. https://twitter.com/TheBiggestJim/status/609783439584157696.

130. Murrison (Murrison), *Twitter* post, June 13, 2015, 11:31am. https://twitter.com/Murrisson/status/609790193068064768.

131. TheBiggestJim (Jim Miller), *Twitter* post, June 13, 2015, 11:38am. https://twitter.com/TheBiggestJim/status/609791901198188546.

132. TheBiggestJim (Jim Miller), *Twitter* post, June 13, 2015, 11:38am. https://twitter.com/TheBiggestJim/status/609792045696159744.

133. "My Little Pony Soaring Pegasus Set," *Kmart*, last modified September 20, 2013, https://web.archive.org/web/20130926162906/http://www.kmart.com/hasbro-my-little-pony-soaring-pegasus-set/p-004W005184348013P?.

134. *Ibid.*

135. "My Little Pony Muffins Big Face Snapback Purple Trucker Hat," *Amazon*, last modified August 18, 2014, http://www.amazon.com/My-Little-Pony-Muffins-Snapback/dp/B00MU65O2G.

136. "THE GAME of LIFE: My Little Pony," *Amazon*, n.d., http://www.amazon.com/GAME-LIFE-My-Little-Pony/dp/B00K3EYVJO/.

137. "Boston America My Little Pony Derpy Muffin Flavored Lip Balm," *Amazon*, n.d., http://www.amazon.com/Boston-America-Little-Blueberry-Flavored/dp/B00VC1PAGU.

138. Sethisto, "Derpy Hooves Hits Build a Bear Site as Web Exclusive—Vinyl Scratch 'Coming Soon,'" *Equestria Daily*, last modified August 24, 2015, http://www.equestriadaily.com/2015/08/derpy-hooves-hits-build-bear-site-as.html.

139. *Ibid.*

140. CMC_Scootaloo, August 2015, comment on Sethisto, "Derpy Hooves Hits Build a Bear Site as Web Exclusive—Vinyl Scratch 'Coming Soon,'" *Equestria Daily*, last modified August 24, 2015, http://www.equestriadaily.com/2015/08/derpy-hooves-hits-build-bear-site-as.html.

141. *Cereal Velocity*, May 30, 2012.

142. "Rejoined (episode)," *Memory Alpha*, n.d., http://memory-alpha.wikia.com/wiki/Rejoined_%28episode%29.

143. "Our Charity," *Everfree Northwest*, n.d., https://everfreenw.com/archive/2013/charity.html.

144. "What Is Bronycon?" *BronyCon*, n.d., http://bronycon.org/about/what-is-bronycon/.

145. Chessie2003, "Friendship Is Magic," *Ponychan*, last modified July 8, 2011, https://web.archive.org/web/20110714015717/http://www.ponychan.net/chan/pony/res/35687258.html.

146. Razor Jack, "Redheart's Roundup,"

Bronies for Good, last modified August 23, 2011, http://broniesforgood.org/2011/08/redhearts-roundup/.

147. Razor Jack, "About BfG," *Bronies for Good*, last modified October 22, 2011, http://broniesforgood.org/about-us/.

148. *Ponychan*, July 8, 2011.

149. Gutis.

150. Hasbro Inc., "Trademark/Service Mark Application, Principal Register Serial Number: 85804403," December 17, 2012.

151. Hasbro Inc. "Trademark/Service Mark Application, Principal Register Serial Number: 85805634." December 18, 2012.

152. Gregory Schmidt, "Classic Toys Redesigned to Traverse Generations," *New York Times*, last modified March 1, 2013, http://www.nytimes.com/2013/03/02/business/hasbro-expands-transformers-brand-into-new-media.html.

153. Hasbro Inc. press release, October 7, 2010.

154. G. Ferro.

155. Schmidt.

156. "Hasbro to Showcase Its Iconic Pop Culture Brands at Comic-Con International," Hasbro Inc. press release, July 15, 2013.

157. "FashionApplejackBackcard.jpg."

158. *Advertising Age*, May 3, 2010.

159. Tekaramity.

160. Gregory Schmidt, "A New Direction for a Hasbro Stalwart," *New York Times*, last modified May 12, 2013, http://www.nytimes.com/2013/05/13/business/equestria-girls-a-my-little-pony-offshoot-in-its-movie-debut.html.

161. *Ibid.*

162. *Ibid.*

163. "My Little Pony: Equestria Girls," *Screenvision*, last modified June 7, 2013, https://web.archive.org/web/20130607121052/http://www.screenvision.com/cinema-events/my-little-pony-equestria-girls.

164. "My Little Pony: Equestria Girls." *Screenvision*. Last modified July 15, 2013, https://web.archive.org/web/20130721215156/http://www.screenvision.com/cinema-events/my-little-pony-equestria-girls.

165. *Ibid.*

166. Hasbro Inc. press release, September 10, 2013.

167. My Little Pony. *Facebook* post. May 12, 2013. https://www.facebook.com/mylittlepony/posts/645558932128214.

168. *Ibid.*

169. Hannah Alex Ford, May 12, 2013 (8:18 p.m.), comment on My Little Pony, May 12, 2013,

https://www.facebook.com/mylittlepony/posts/645558932128214.

170. Jade-Elise Newell, May 12, 2013 (7:03 p.m.), comment on My Little Pony, May 12, 2013.

171. Maria Inês Courinha, May 12, 2013 (7:05 p.m.), comment on My Little Pony, May 12, 2013.

172. Rachel Cantrell, May 12, 2013 (7:13 p.m.), comment on My Little Pony, May 12, 2013.

173. Kama Ogden, May 12, 2013 (6:56 p.m.), comment on My Little Pony, May 12, 2013.

174. Karen Mitchell, May 12, 2013 (9:34 p.m.), comment on My Little Pony, May 12, 2013.

175. Anthrocon, "What Is Furry?" n.d., http://www.anthrocon.org/files/anthrocon/2016-WhatIsFurry-brochure-web.pdf.

176. Kimberly Koppenhafer, May 13, 2013 (6:13 a.m.), My Little Pony, May 12, 2013.

177. Mary Canada, May 12, 2013 (7:52 p.m.), comment on My Little Pony, May 12, 2013.

178. Mario Barreiro, May 13, 2013 (7:58 a.m.), comment on My Little Pony, May 12, 2013.

179. Schmidt, May 12, 2013.

180. *Ibid.*

181. *Ibid.*

182. Benschachar, May 2013, comment on Cereal Velocity, "More 'Equestria Girls' Details Surface, Plus a Trailer," *Equestria Daily*, last modified May 12, 2013.

183. SweetieBot, May 2013, comment on Cereal Velocity, May 12, 2013.

184. Millstone, May 2013, comment on Cereal Velocity, May 12, 2013.

185. Chimakara, May 2013, comment on Cereal Velocity, May 12, 2013.

186. Dyxid, May 2013, comment on Cereal Velocity, May 12, 2013.

187. "Princess Twilight Sparkle and Rainbow Dash," *My Little Wiki*, last modified November 29, 2013, http://mylittlewiki.org/wiki/Princess_Twilight_Sparkle_and_Rainbow_Dash.

188. "File:Riding Along Twilight Sparkle MIB.jpg," *My Little Wiki*, last modified August 22, 2012, http://mylittlewiki.org/wiki/File:Riding_Along_Twilight_Sparkle_MIB.jpg.

189. "File:Twilightsparkletravel.JPG," *My Little Wiki*, last modified April 22, 2012, http://mylittlewiki.org/wiki/File:Twilightsparkletravel.JPG.

190. "My Little Pony Twilight Sparkle RC Car Vehicle," *Amazon*, n.d., http://www.amazon.com/My-Little-Pony-Twilight-Sparkle/dp/B00859GJXA.

191. Calpain.

192. Shen.

193. MoppyPuppy, May 14, 2013, comment on Calpain, "An Appeal to the Fandom—Keep Calm and Trot On," *Equestria Daily*, last modi-

fied May 14, 2013, http://www.equestriadaily.
com/2013/05/an-appeal-to-fandom-keep-calm-
and-trot.html.

194. z55177, May 14, 2013, comment on Calpain.

195. HMS_Celestia, May 14, 2013, comment
on Calpain.

196. "Muslim Convert Jesse Curtis Morton
Gets Nearly 12 Years for Posting Online Threats
Against 'South Park' Creators," *New York Daily
News*, June 22, 2012.

197. RDisBestPony, May 14, 2013, comment
on Calpain.

198. Squidward Tentacles, May 14, 2013,
comment on Calpain.

199. *Ibid.*

200. Ryan Gajewski, "'Jem and the Holograms' Director on Film Bombing, Getting
'Death Threats' from Show Fans," *Hollywood Reporter*, last modified October 24, http://www.
hollywoodreporter.com/news/jem-holograms-
director-film-bombing-834476.

201. Lauren Faust (Fire_Flye), *Twitter* post,
May 27, 2013, 4:35pm. https://twitter.com/Fyre_
flye/status/339163075146022912/photo/1.

202. Lauren Faust (Fire_Flye), *Twitter* post,
May 27, 2013, 5:26pm. https://twitter.com/Fyre_
flye/status/339175908558639104.

203. Lauren Faust (Fire_Flye), *Twitter* post,
May 27, 2013, 5:50pm. https://twitter.com/Fyre_
flye/status/339181827199729664/photo/1.

204. Maria Adcock, "Hasbro Plans Debut of
My Little Pony Equestria Girls Minis for the
New Year," *Examiner.com*, last modified December 17, 2015, http://www.examiner.com/article/
hasbro-plans-debut-of-my-little-pony-
equestria-girls-minis-for-the-new-year.

205. "'My Little Pony Equestria Girls' in Cinemas Nationwide Beginning June 16," Hasbro
Inc. press release, May 30, 2013.

206. Pesce.

207. *Ibid.*

208. *Ibid.*

209. *Ibid.*

210. Cooney.

211. Amanda Marcotte, "Triumph of the
Bronies: Hasbro Turning My Little Ponies into
Sexy Human Characters. Neigh," *Slate*, last
modified June 13, 2013. http://www.slate.com/
blogs/xx_factor/2013/06/13/triumph_of_the_
bronies_hasbro_turning_my_little_ponies_
into_sexy_human_characters.html.

212. *Ibid.*

213. *Ibid.*

214. "Rule 34," *Know Your Meme*, last modified March 25, 2015, http://knowyourmeme.
com/memes/rule-34.

215. Marcotte.

216. Kreoss, "MLP Human version ver. 1,"
DeviantArt, last modified December 24, 2010,
http://kreoss.deviantart.com/art/MLP-Human-
version-ver-1-190767778.

217. Danny Jones, May 12, 2013 (7:46 p.m.),
comment on My Little Pony, May 12, 2013.

218. Logan Houseman, May 12, 2013 (7:23
p.m.), comment on My Little Pony, May 12,
2013.

219. Melody Wilson, "Brony Love: Lauren
Faust, Creator of My Little Pony: Friendship Is
Magic, Live from Bronycon!" *Bitch Magazine*,
last modified July 3, 2012, http://bitchmagazine.
org/post/lauren-faust-creator-of-my-little-pony-
friendship-is-magic-live-from-bronycon-
feminist-magazine-bronies-gender-fandom.

220. *Ibid.*

221. Hasbro Inc. press release, June 19, 2013.

222. *Ibid.*

223. Anne Marie Chaker, "Toy Makers Look
to Extend the Run of Classic Girls' Characters,"
Wall Street Journal, December 17, 2013.

224. CouchCrusader, "Movie Followup:
'Equestria Girls,'" *Equestria Daily*, last modified
June 23, 2013, https://web.archive.org/web/
20130624065830/http://www.equestriadaily.
com/2013/06/movie-followup-equestria-girls.
html.

225. *Ibid.*

226. *Ibid.*

227. Sethisto, "Brony Shirts Now at the Actual Hot Topic Stores (UPDATED)," *Equestria
Daily*, last modified August 23, 2011, http://www.
equestriadaily.com/2011/08/stolen-design-
brony-shirts-now-at.html.

228. *Confound These Ponies—Rise of My Little Pony Fandom—Connecticon 2011.*

229. *Ibid.*

230. Sethisto, "Poll Results: What Is the Pony
DJ's Name?" *Equestria Daily*, last modified February 9, 2011, http://www.equestriadaily.com/
2011/02/poll-results-what-is-pony-djs-name.
html

231. *Ibid.*

232. MrOptimist666, June 23, 2013, comment
on CouchCrusader.

233. marshallhuffman, June 23, 2013, comment on CouchCrusader.

234. Marxon6, June 23, 2013, comment on
CouchCrusader.

235. Silver_Smoulder, June 23, 2013, comment on CouchCrusader..

236. CouchCrusader, "Movie Followup/Ed-
itorial/Opinion Piece: 'Equestria Girls,'" *Equestria Daily*, last modified February 18, 2014,
https://web.archive.org/web/20140218185303/

http://www.equestriadaily.com/2013/06/movie-followup-equestria-girls.html.

237. Sethisto, "Editorial: Hype. Equestria Girls, EQD, Episode Followups, and Twilight Sparkle," *Equestria Daily*, last modified June 24, 2013, http://www.equestriadaily.com/2013/06/editorial-hype-equestria-girls-eqd.html.

238. *Ibid.*

239. Dana Simpson, "Phoebe and Her Unicorn Comic Strip, August 11, 2013," *GoComics*, last modified August 11, 2013.

240. Marcy Vernier, e-mail message to author, June 12, 2013.

241. *Ibid.*

242. Hasbro Inc. press release, November 9, 2004.

243. "Celebrities Step out on the 'Pink Carpet' to Celebrate the Hollywood Premiere of MY LITTLE PONY LIVE!" Hasbro Inc. press release, March 13, 2007.

244. "The World's Biggest Tea Party Stock Photos," *Bigstock*, n.d., http://www.bigstockphoto.com/search/The-World's-Biggest-Tea-Party/.

245. Hasbro Inc. press release, June 19, 2007.

246. Hasbro Inc. press release, February 14, 2008.

247. "Los Angeles Film Festival—'My Little Pony: Equestria Girls' Premiere," *Getty Images*, n.d., http://www.gettyimages.com/detail/news-photo/anja-louise-ambrosio-mazur-and-alessandra-ambrosio-arrive-news-photo/170634483.

248. Meghan McCarthy, "Audio Commentary," My Little Pony: Equestria Girls—Rainbow Rocks, directed by Jayson Thiessen, Blu-ray (USA: Shout! Factory, 2014).

249. Hasbro Inc. press release, September 10, 2013.

250. "Hasbro Revolutionizing Branded Play and Lifestyle Experiences Through Rich Storytelling Across All Entertainment Platforms," Hasbro Inc. press release, June 17, 2014.

251. "Q2 2014 Hasbro Inc Earnings Call," Hasbro Inc. press release, July 21, 2014.

252. "My Little Pony: Equestria Girls," *Box Office Mojo*, n.d., http://www.boxofficemojo.com/movies/intl/?page=&id=_fMYLITTLEPONYEQUE01.

253. *Show Infantil My Little Pony Equestria Girls*, YouTube video, 1:52, posted by "Animanía Eventos," October 27, 2013, https://www.youtube.com/watch?v=-qve3F2SusE.

254. *Ibid.*

255. *Show Infantil Equestria Girls—Animania Show—Lima Peru*, YouTube video, 4:03, posted by "Animanía Eventos," February 17, 2015, https://www.youtube.com/watch?v=OrBB9T53cvE.

256. Kelsey Tarczanin, e-mail message to author, September 11, 2014.

257. Perdita Finn, *My Little Pony: Equestria Girls—Rainbow Rocks* (Boston: Little, Brown Books for Young Readers, 2014).

258. Tarcazanin.

259. Perdita Finn, *My Little Pony: Equestria Girls—The Mane Event* (Boston: Little, Brown Books for Young Readers, 2014), 118.

260. Maria Bustillos, "Friendship Is Complicated: Art, Commerce, and the Battle for the Soul of My Little Pony," *Longreads*, last modified January 28, 2015, http://blog.longreads.com/2015/01/28/friendship-is-complicated/.

261. *Ibid.*

262. *Ibid.*

263. Erickson, 1995, 350.

264. *Advertising Age*, May 3, 2010.

265. Bustillos.

266. *Ibid.*

267. "Meet the Characters," *Dork Diaries*, n.d., http://dorkdiaries.com/meet-the-characters/.

268. Bustillos.

269. *Ibid.*

270. *Ibid.*

271. *Ibid.*

272. *M.A. Larson's Deconstruction of Episode #100 Panel: MLP-MSP.*

273. Bustillos.

274. *Ibid.*

275. "My Little Pony Equestria Girls Minis Rainbow Dash Doll," *Amazon*, n.d., http://www.amazon.com/My-Little-Pony-Equestria-Girls/dp/B012CCAVKM.

276. Kat Brown, "Disney and Pixar's Female Characters All Have the Same Face," *Telegraph*, last modified June 29, 2015, http://www.telegraph.co.uk/film/inside-out/disney-pixar-characters-same-face/.

277. "Hasbro Reports Revenue and Earnings Growth for the First Quarter 2014," Hasbro Inc. press release, April 21, 2014.

278. *Ibid.*

279. "Hasbro Inc Annual Investor meeting at Toy Fair—Final," Hasbro Inc. press release, February 13, 2015.

280. *Ibid.*

281. *Ibid.*

282. *Ibid.*

283. *Ibid.*

284. "Screenvision Lands Event Cinema Pioneers Maxwell/Diamond—Former Ncm/Fathom Executives Head To Screenvision," Screenvision Media press release, December 17, 2015.

285. "My Little Pony: Equestria Girls—Friendship Games," Vue Big Screen Entertainment, n.d., http://www.myvue.com/latest-

movies/info/film/my-little-pony-equestria-girls-friendship-games.

286. Vue Cinemas, *Facebook* post, October 27, 2015, https://www.facebook.com/VueCinemas/photos/a.166763116690994.38166.147114011989238/1057748944259069.

287. *Ibid.*

288. Gemma Stephens, October 27, 2015 (12:04 p.m.), comment on Vue Cinemas, *Facebook* post, October 27, 2015, https://www.facebook.com/VueCinemas/photos/a.166763116690994.38166.147114011989238/1057748944259069.

289. "39th Annual Daytime Entertainment Emmy Award Nominations," *National Academy of Television Arts & Science*, last modified June 23, 2012, http://www.emmyonline.org/mediacenter/daytime_39th_nominations.html.

290. "Hasbro Brings Hotly-Anticipated Special Edition Toys to Comic-Con International, Featuring Transformers, My Little Pony, Jem and More," Hasbro Inc. press release, July 8, 2015.

291. *Ibid.*

292. "Stars Come out to Celebrate the Third Installment of MY LITTLE PONY EQUESTRIA GIRLS with the 'Friendship Games' Premiere from Hasbro Studios," Hasbro Inc. press release, September 18, 2015.

293. Rebecca Dart, "Audio Commentary," *My Little Pony: Equestria Girls—Friendship Games*, directed by Ishi Rudell, Blu-ray (USA: Shout! Factory, 2015).

294. Armando Reyes (Mandoreyes80), *Twitter* post, August 29, 2015, 7:50am. https://twitter.com/Mandoreyes80/status/637638499827499008.

295. Animania Show, *Facebook* post, September 19, 2015,. https://www.facebook.com/animaniashow/photos/a.958518407542740.1073741864.893809874013594/958518814209366.

296. "My Little Pony & Equestria Girls El Show En Vivo," *Cine Información y más*, last modified October 27, 2015, http://www.cineinformacionymas.com/eventos-especiales/my-little-pony-equestria-girls-el-show-en-vivo/.

297. *Ibid.*

298. "Show Equestria Girl," *Hasbro Activaciones*, last modified April 27, 2016, https://web.archive.org/web/20160427055445/http://hasbro-activaciones.com/showequestriagirl/.

299. *MLP Show en vivo Bienvenido al show*, YouTube video, 6:19, posted by "Fatima Blaze," February 21, 2016, https://www.youtube.com/watch?v=UzozHf9YV98.

300. *MLP:EG / La Música oficial del Show en Vivo*, YouTube video, 42:58, posted by "tan00k150," March 18, 2016, https://www.youtube.com/watch?v=XJSAo2PK1xY.

301. Sethisto, "Is Equestria Girls a Bad Thing for Pony?" *Equestria Daily*, last modified September 29, 2015, http://www.equestriadaily.com/2015/09/is-equestria-girls-bad-thing-for-pony.html.

302. *Ibid.*

303. Brown.

304. Weinman, September 7, 2011.

305. Sethisto, "Poll Results: Power Ponies Poll #1—Who Had the Best Costume?" *Equestria Daily*, last modified December 27, 2013, www.equestriadaily.com/2013/12/poll-results-power-ponies-poll-1-who.html.

306. "Hasbro Delivers the Hottest Special Edition Toys at Comic-Con International, Featuring Transformers, My Little Pony, Magic: The Gathering, Star Wars, Marvel and More," Hasbro Inc. press release, July 23, 2014.

307. Sethisto, "Full Power Ponies Brushable Set Revealed at Target," *Equestria Daily*, last modified July 5, 2015, http://www.equestriadaily.com/2015/07/full-power-ponies-brushable-set.html.

308. Sethisto, September 29, 2015.

309. *Ibid.*

310. *Ibid.*

311. Cereal Velocity, May 30, 2012.

312. Tekaramity.

313. Sethisto, "Lauren Faust Answers a Bunch of Questions (Update- More Added!)," *Equestria Daily*, last modified May 27, 2013, http://www.equestriadaily.com/2013/05/lauren-faust-answers-bunch-of-questions.html.

314. Sethisto, September 29, 2015.

315. Margaret Hartmann, January 4, 2011.

316. VanDerWerff.

317. Sethisto, September 29, 2015.

318. *Ibid.*

319. Cups, "My Little Pony Dog Tags Series 2 Announced!," *Equestria Daily*, last modified September 29, 2015.

320. Sethisto, "Kinder Reveals Full Lineup of Toys, Plus a 3D Animated Promo Showing Them Off—Now Available," *Equestria Daily*, last modified August 17, 2015, http://www.equestriadaily.com/2015/08/kinder-reveals-full-lineup-of-toys-plus.html.

321. Sethisto, "Kinder Egg MAXI Vs. Normal Size Figure Comparison,"*Equestria Daily*, last modified October 4, 2015, http://www.equestriadaily.com/2015/10/kinder-egg-maxi-vs-normal-size-figure.html.

322. Sethisto, September 29, 2015.

323. Rachel Abrams, "BB-8 Droid Offers Hint of Coming Crush of 'Star Wars' Toys," *New*

York Times, September 3, 2015, http://www.nytimes.com/2015/09/04/business/a-hint-of-star-wars-toys-in-the-form-of-a-little-droid.html.

324. Sethisto, September 29, 2015.

325. Dart.

326. Kevin Jagernauth, "Max Landis Wonders If the Flop of 'American Ultra' Means That Original Movies Are Dead," *Indiewire*, last modified August 24, 2015, 2015, http://www.indiewire.com/2015/08/max-landis-wonders-if-the-flop-of-american-ultra-means-that-original-movies-are-dead-260572/.

327. Schmidt.

328. Sethisto, September 29, 2015.

329. Josh Haber, "Audio Commentary," *My Little Pony: Equestria Girls—Friendship Games*, directed by Ishi Rudell, Blu-ray (USA: Shout! Factory, 2015).

330. *Ibid.*

331. Faust, December 24, 2010.

332. Tekaramity.

333. *My Little Pony: Friendship Is Magic—Canterlot Playset Target Exclusives Commercial*, YouTube video, 0:15, posted by "richfiles," August 18, 2011, https://www.youtube.com/watch?v=obo_9yyAIoA.

334. *Applejack's Sweet Apple Barn Playset—My Little Pony—Friendship Is Magic*, YouTube video, 0:20, posted by "MegaDyskont.pl—Toy Store—We Love Toys," March 14, 2014, https://www.youtube.com/watch?v=s5zMjpuUt88.

335. *MLP: Friendship Is Magic Toys—'Friendship Express Train' Official T.V. Spot*, YouTube video, 0:20, posted by "My Little Pony Official," February 13, 2012, https://www.youtube.com/watch?v=EPSY9QLNRY0.

336. *My Little Pony Pop Fluttershy Cottage Decorator Kit—Build Klip Design Ponies by FunToys*, YouTube video, 6:00, posted by "FunToyzCollector," October 13, 2014, https://www.youtube.com/watch?v=x1SRsjOOchw.

337. *My Little Pony North America Product Demo POP Playset Castle (Princess Twilight Sparkle's Kingdom)*, YouTube video, 0:58, posted by "My Little Pony Official," July 20 2015, https://www.youtube.com/watch?v=dZm4W1TREhg.

338. Sethisto, September 29, 2015.

339. *Rarity's Carousel Boutique Playset (TV Commercial) | My Little Pony Toys for Kids*.

340. *MLP: Friendship Is Magic Toys—My Little Pony Canterlot Wedding Toy & Playset!*, YouTube video, 1:07, posted by "My Little Pony Official," November 13, 2012, https://www.youtube.com/watch?v=R7612ozqgRM.

341. *girly girly product reviews pony ville school house*, YouTube video, 9:59, posted by "inuskypie," June 22, 2012, https://www.youtube.com/watch?v=BXZJ2fqrxTI.

342. Kate, "Royal Ball at Canterlot Castle Playset," *My Little Pony News*, last modified Tuesday, June 14, 2011, http://www.mylittleponynews.com/2011/06/royal-ball-at-canterlot-castle-playset.html.

343. *My Little Pony Applejack's Farm Truck from Hasbro*, YouTube video, 0:37, posted by "TTPM Toy Reviews," October 13, 2011, https://www.youtube.com/watch?v=r0h2wwnE2t4.

344. *MLP: Friendship Is Magic Toys—'Pinkie Pie RC Car' Official T.V. Spot*, YouTube video, 0:21, posted by "My Little Pony Official," November 28, 2011, https://www.youtube.com/watch?v=XTY3zJaA2Dc.

345. "My Little Pony Twilight Sparkle RC Car Vehicle," *Amazon*.

346. *Equestria Girls Canterlot High Pep Rally Set with Vice Principal LUNA! Review by Bin's Toy Bin*, YouTube video, 8:26, posted by "Bins Toy Bin," October 15, 2013, https://www.youtube.com/watch?v=9VtXZ3tVfpw.

347. *Equestria Girls Rainbow Rocks Mane Event Stage Playset! Review by Bin's Toy Bin*, YouTube video, 11:29, posted by "Bins Toy Bin," November 18, 2014, https://www.youtube.com/watch?v=it8vKMZiwK0.

348. *My Little Pony Equestria Girls Rainbow Rocks DJ Pon-3's Rockin' Convertible with Doll from Hasbro*, YouTube video, 1:12, posted by "TTPM Toy Reviews," August 31, 2014, https://www.youtube.com/watch?v=zDzGD9AfrYI.

349. *MLP: Equestria Girls Toys—Canterlot High Playset (Product Demo)*, YouTube video, 1:37, posted by "My Little Pony: Equestria Girls Official," July 27, 2015, https://www.youtube.com/watch?v=9vQsBoOSh-A.

350. Sethisto, February 9, 2011.

351. Ilona, "My Little Pony at the NY Toy Fair 2015 Wrap-up," All About MLP Merch, last modified February 18, 2015, http://www.mlpmerch.com/2015/02/my-little-pony-at-ny-toy-fair-2015-wrap.html.

352. Sethisto, "Friendship Is Magic Collection Apple Family Figures in the Packaging," *Equestria Daily*, last modified May 1, 2015, http://www.equestriadaily.com/2015/05/friendship-is-magic-collection-apple.html.

353. Sethisto, "Packaging and Stock Images of All the Friendship Is Magic Apple Family Set Ponies Arrives!" *Equestria Daily*, last modified May 2, 2015, http://www.equestriadaily.com/2015/05/packaging-and-stock-images-of-all.html.

354. Sethisto, "Friendship Is Magic Collec-

tion Mrs. Cake, Pinkie Pie, and Maud Pie Appear," *Equestria Daily*, last modified September 18, 2015, http://www.equestriadaily.com/2015/09/friendship-is-magic-collection-mrs-cake.html.

355. Sethisto, September 29, 2015.

356. Zer0C0re, September 2015, comment on Sethisto, "Is Equestria Girls a Bad Thing for Pony?" *Equestria Daily*, last modified September 29, 2015, http://www.equestriadaily.com/2015/09/is-equestria-girls-bad-thing-for-pony.html.

357. paladin3210, September 2015, comment on Sethisto, September 29, 2015.

358. CMC_Scootaloo, September 2015, comment on Sethisto, September 29, 2015.

359. *Ibid.*

360. "Powers of Persuasion: Use It Up, Wear It Out," *National Archives and Records Administration*, n.d., http://www.archives.gov/exhibits/powers_of_persuasion/use_it_up/use_it_up.html.

361. paladin3210, September 2015, comment on Sethisto, September 29, 2015.

362. Ael Davies, September 2015, comment on Sethisto, September 29, 2015.

363. CMC_Scootaloo, September 2015, comment on Sethisto, September 29, 2015.

364. Lauren Faust (Fire_Flye), *Twitter* post, October 17, 2015, 1:40pm. https://twitter.com/Fyre_flye/status/655483575660249088.

365. Zaelle (ZaelleLexil), *Twitter* post, October 17, 2015, 2:10pm. https://twitter.com/ZaelleLexil/status/655491110178062337.

366. Laura Moss, "Why Must We Hate the Things Teen Girls Love?" *Mother Nature Network*, last modified October 9, 2015. http://www.mnn.com/lifestyle/arts-culture/stories/why-do-we-hate-things-teen-girls-love.

367. *Ibid.*

368. Seiter, 9.

369. Sethisto, September 29, 2015.

370. Seiter, 7–8.

371. *'This Is MST3K' hosted by Penn Jillette 1/3*, YouTube video, 6:08, posted by "tnvince-sanity," May 30, 2009, https://www.youtube.com/watch?v=TH7dxROgpK4.

372. Hasbro Inc., *2014 Annual Report*, n.d., p. 6, http://investor.hasbro.com/common/download/download.cfm?companyid=HAS&fileid=819559&filekey=8A09F66A-4137–45A9–88BA-C16F08E1AF90&filename=Annual_Report_Website_FINAL.pdf..

373. *Ibid.*

374. *2015 Annual Report*. n.d., Hasbro Inc., p. 30, http://investor.hasbro.com/common/download/download.cfm?companyid=HAS&fileid=883653&filekey=E95A5C8D-DFAA-4ACB-BB2C-844E50306A01&filename=Annual_Report_for_Web.pdf.

375. "The Hub Network to Become Discovery Family Channel on October 13," Hasbro Inc. press release, September 25, 2014.

376. Marc Graser, "'My Little Pony' Movie in the Works at Hasbro Studios (EXCLUSIVE)," *Variety*, last modified October 20, 2014, http://variety.com/2014/film/news/my-little-pony-movie-in-the-works-at-hasbro-studios-exclusive-1201334144/.

377. Hilary Lewis, "Hasbro Working on 'My Little Pony' Movie," *Hollywood Reporter*, last modified October 20, 2014, http://www.hollywoodreporter.com/news/hasbro-working-my-little-pony-742126.

378. "Discovery Family Channel Leaps into 2015–16 Upfront Season," Discover Communications press release, March 31, 2015.

379. Hasbro Inc., *My Little Pony Equestria Girls 2016 Product Descriptions*, n.d. http://files.shareholder.com/downloads/HAS/1966905775x0x874895/7EC99304–1F36–4DB7-A2FE-3E650830DE11/My_Little_Pony_Equestria_Girls_2016_Product_Descriptions.pdf.

380. Anita Sarkeesian, "LEGO & Gender Part 1: Lego Friends," *Feminist Frequency*, last modified January 30, 2012, http://feministfrequency.com/2012/01/30/lego-gender-part-1-lego-friends/.

Bibliography

"About Me." *Chris Battle Art & Stuff*. n.d. http://chrisbattleart.tumblr.com/about_me.

Abrams, Rachel. "BB-8 Droid Offers Hint of Coming Crush of 'Star Wars' Toys." *New York Times*. September 3, 2015. http://www.nytimes.com/2015/09/04/business/a-hint-of-star-wars-toys-in-the-form-of-a-little-droid.html.

"Action for Children's Television." *Harvard Graduate School of Education*. https://www.gse.harvard.edu/library/collections/special/act.

Adams, Erik. "There's One Secret the Rick and Morty Guys Will Never Reveal." *A.V. Club*. Last modified July 23, 2015. http://www.avclub.com/article/theres-one-secret-rick-and-morty-guys-will-never-r-222269.

Adcock, Maria. "Hasbro Plans Debut of My Little Pony Equestria Girls Minis for the New Year." *Examiner.com*. Last modified December 17, 2015. http://www.examiner.com/article/hasbro-plans-debut-of-my-little-pony-equestria-girls-minis-for-the-new-year.

Advertisement. *Broadcasting* 114, no. 7 (February 15, 1988): 93.

_____. *The Los Angeles Times*, November 15, 1981: 8.

_____. *The Los Angeles Times*, December 18, 1982: 17.

_____. *The Los Angeles Times*, October 16, 1983: AC4.

"Age and Sex Composition in the United States: 2012." *United States Census Bureau*. n.d. http://www.census.gov/population/age/data/2012comp.html.

Amidi, Amid. *Amazon*. n.d. http://www.amazon.com/Amid-Amidi/e/B001JS6FGK/ref=sr_tc_2_0?qid=1436054748&sr=8-2-ent.

_____. "The End of the Creator-Driven Era in TV Animation." *Cartoon Brew*. Last modified October 18, 2010. http://www.cartoonbrew.com/ideas-commentary/the-end-of-the-creator-driven-era-29614.html.

_____. "Let's Talk About the Animation in 'The Lego Movie.'" *Cartoon Brew*. Last modified February 5, 2014. http://www.cartoonbrew.com/ideas-commentary/lets-talk-about-the-animation-in-the-lego-movie-95781.html.

_____. "My Little Bronies." *Cartoon Brew*. Last modified June 10, 2011. http://www.cartoonbrew.com/cartoon-culture/my-little-bronies-44016.html.

_____. "Ruby-Spears and Sid and Marty Krofft Team Up." *Cartoon Brew*. Last modified April 13, 2010. http://www.cartoonbrew.com/bad-ideas/ruby-spears-and-sid-and-marty-krofft-team-up-22390.html.

"Amy Keating Rogers Responds." *Save Derpy*. n.d. http://savederpy.tumblr.com/AKRResponse.

Anderson, John. "As Tribeca Kicks Off, 'A Brony Tale' Leads Some Must-See Docs." *Indiewire*. Last modified April 16, 2014. http://blogs.indiewire.com/thompsononhollywood/as-tribeca-turns-sweet-thirteen-a-roster-of-docs-looking-more-promising-than-ever.

Anderson, Monika. "Never Too Old for 'Thundercats?'" *Wall Street Journal*, August 12, 2011.

Andrews, Edmund L. "F.C.C. Adopts Limits on TV Ads Aimed at Children." *New York Times*, April 10, 1991.

Animania Show. *Facebook* post. September 19, 2015. https://www.facebook.com/animaniashow/photos/a.958518407542740.1073741864.893809874013594/958518814209366.

Annie N. Mouse. "Invisible Women: Why Marvel's Gamora & Black Widow Were Missing from Merchandise, and What We Can Do About It." *Mary Sue*. Last modified April 7, 2015. http://www.themarysue.com/invisible-women/.

Anthrocon. "What Is Furry?" n.d. http://www.anthrocon.org/files/anthrocon/2016-WhatIsFurry-brochure-web.pdf.

Arrant, Chris. "The Hub Announces 2011–2012 Program Line-Up, Including a Warren Buffet

Animated Series." *Cartoon Brew*. Last modified March 28, 2011. http://www.cartoonbrew.com/biz/the-hub-announces-2011–2012-program-line-up-including-a-warren-buffet-animated-series-39441.html.

Ashbot. "Derp." *Know Your Meme*. Last modified in 2015. http://knowyourmeme.com/memes/derp.

Beck, Jerry. *Animated Movie Guide*. Chicago: Chicago Review, 2005.

_____. "Day One: CTN-Expo Is a Hit!" *Cartoon Brew*. Last modified November 21, 2009. http://www.cartoonbrew.com/events/day-one-ctn-expo-is-a-hit-18381.html.

_____. "New from McCracken and Faust." *Cartoon Brew*. Last modified January 20, 2010. http://www.cartoonbrew.com/animators/new-from-mccracken-and-faust-19994.html.

Benitez Eves, Tina. "Buzz Report: Licensing Show 2007." *Gifts & Dec*. Last modified June 21, 2007. http://www.giftsanddec.com/article/429753-buzz-report-licensing-show-2007.

Bennett, Alanna. "Former President Bill Clinton Knows Everything About My Little Pony." *Mary Sue*. Last modified June 27, 2011. http://www.themarysue.com/bill-clinton-brony/.

Bennett, Catherine. "Inside Story: Private." *Guardian*, June 3, 1995.

"Bill Clinton Plays Not My Job." Narrated by Peter Sagal. *Wait Wait … Don't Tell Me!*. NPR. June 25, 2011. http://www.npr.org/2011/06/25/137386121/bill-clinton-plays-not-my-job.

Blake, Casey. "School Will Allow Boy to Bring My Little Pony Backpack." *Citizen Times*. March 21, 2014.

Bond, Paul. "DVD Players Pack Santa's Sleigh." *Hollywood Reporter* 381, no. 25 (December 1, 2003): 22.

"Boston America My Little Pony Derpy Blueberry Muffin Flavored Lip Balm." *Amazon*. n.d. http://www.amazon.com/Boston-America-Little-Blueberry-Flavored/dp/B00VC1PAGU.

Boucher, Geoff. "VHS Era Is Winding Down." *Los Angeles Times*, December 22, 2008.

Boyar, Jay. "Tell You What We Want, What We Really, Really Want: A Good Movie." *Orlando Sentinel*, January 23, 1998.

Brachmann, Kathleen. "*My Little Pony Under the Big Top!*" *School Library Journal* 32, no. 7 (1986): 153.

Brown, August. "Pop Music Review; Pure Confection from Katy Perry; the Singer Brings Sugary Pop Savvy to Her Three-Night Nokia Theatre Stand." *Los Angeles Times*, August 8, 2011.

Brown, Kat. "Disney and Pixar's Female Characters All Have the Same Face." *Telegraph*.

Last modified June 29, 2015. http://www.telegraph.co.uk/film/inside-out/disney-pixar-characters-same-face/.

Brown, Patricia Leigh. "When Child's Play Is Collecting, It's Serious Stuff." *New York Times*, December 14, 1989.

Buckleitner, Warren. "Teacher's Picks [Best New Tech]." *Scholastic Parent & Child* 12, no. 2 (October 2004): 20.

Burke, Timothy, and Kevin Burke. *Saturday Morning Fever: Growing Up with Cartoon Culture*. New York: St. Martin's Griffin, 1999.

Burn, Shawn Meghan, A. Kathleen O'Neil, and Shirley Nederend. "Childhood Tomboyism and Adult Androgyny." *Sex Roles* 34, no. 5–6 (1996): 419–428.

Bustillos, Maria. "Friendship Is Complicated: Art, Commerce, and the Battle for the Soul of My Little Pony." *Longreads*. Last modified January 28, 2015. http://blog.longreads.com/2015/01/28/friendship-is-complicated/.

Butnotblackwidow. "Reason for the Blog." *…But Not Black Widow*. Last modified September 12, 2012. http://butnotblackwidow.tumblr.com/post/31547288566/reason-for-the-blog/.

Cain, Scott. "Movie Review—'Transformers' a Bleak Commercial Mutant." *Atlanta Journal-Constitution*, August 12, 1986.

_____. "Movies—A G Rating the Kiss of Death? Most Kiddie Films Are Taking a Beating at the Box Office." *Atlanta Journal-Constitution*, June 6, 1987.

_____. "Video." *Atlanta Journal-Constitution*, November 8, 1986.

Calhoun, Pedro. "Bromance." *Urban Dictionary*. Last modified January 13, 2004. http://www.urbandictionary.com/define.php?term=Bromance&defid=444973.

Callison, Cleve. "Great American Songbook Memorial Day Special." *WHQR*. Last modified May 22, 2015. http://whqr.org/post/great-american-songbook-memorial-day-special.

Canemaker, John. "Fantasia in Eight Parts: 'The Pastoral Symphony.'" *Walt Disney Family Museum*. n.d. http://www.waltdisney.org/blog/fantasia-eight-parts-pastoral-symphony.

"Capsule Reviews." *Hartford Courant*, January 4, 2007.

Cardona, Mercedes M. "Toy Story: Nostalgia Sells Big." *Advertising Age* 74, no. 48 (December 1, 2003): 4.

Carter, Tim. "If You're into Physical Violence, This Is a Hard Target to Miss." *Ottawa Citizen*, August 26, 1993.

"Cathy Weseluck." *IMDB*. http://www.imdb.com/name/nm0921699/reference#musicX20department.

Cereal Velocity. "DERPY DERPY DERPY DERPY DERPY DERPY." *Equestria Daily.* Last modified January 21, 2012. http://www.equestriadaily.com/2012/01/oh.html.

_____. "Derpy Toy Confirmed by USA Today." *Equestria Daily.* Last modified May 30, 2012. http://www.equestriadaily.com/2012/05/derpy-toy-confirmed-by-usa-today.html.

_____. "More 'Equestria Girls' Details Surface, Plus a Trailer." *Equestria Daily.* Last modified May 12, 2013.

"Chain Store Age—General Merchandise Trends." *Western Theological Seminary.* http://cook.westernsem.edu/CJDB4/EXS/journal/39945.

Chaker, Anne Marie. "Toy Makers Look to Extend the Run of Classic Girls' Characters." *Wall Street Journal,* December 17, 2013.

Charren, Perry. "FCC Should Ban These Half-Hour Commercials." *USA Today,* October 8, 1987.

Chellen, Jakep. "Keep Derpy Named Derpy!" *Change.Org.* Last modified February 2, 2012. https://www.change.org/p/hasbro-keep-derpy-named-derpy.

Chen, Adrian. "Bronies Furious After Minor My Little Pony Character Is Changed to Seem Less Mentally Disabled." *Gawker.* Last modified February 28, 2012. http://gawker.com/5889084/bronies-furious-after-minor-my-little-pony-character-is-changed-to-seem-less-mentally-disabled.

Chessie2003. "Friendship Is Magic." *Ponychan.* Last modified July 8, 2011. https://web.archive.org/web/20110714015717/http://www.ponychan.net/chan/pony/res/35687258.html.

"Class D21: Games, Toys, and Sports Equipment." *United States Patent and Trademark Office.* n.d. http://www.uspto.gov/web/patents/classification/uspcd21/defsd21.htm.

Colby, Pamela. "From Hot Wheels to Teenage Mutant Ninja Turtles: The Evolution of the Definition of Program Length Commercials on Children's Television." Presentation at the Annual Meeting of the Broadcast Education Association, Las Vegas, NV, April 12–16, 1993.

Colvey, Scott. "My Little Pony: Best Friends Ball." *Computer Act!Ve,* November 23, 2006.

"Comic Con 2012 (Ditzy Doo/Derpy Hooves)." *Strawberry Reef.* n.d. http://www.strawberryreef.com/Index/Name/derpyFIMstyle.html.

Congress of the U.S., Washington, D.C. House Committee on Energy, and Commerce. *Bill Summary & Status, 101st Congress (1989–1990), H.R.1677, All Information,* 101st Congress.

_____. House Committee on Energy and Commerce. *Hearings on H.R. 3288, H.R. 3966, and H.R. 4125: Bills to Require the FCC to Reinstate Restrictions on Advertising During Children's Television, to Enforce the Obligation of Broadcasters to Meet the Educational Needs of the Child Audience, and for Other Purposes, Before the Subcommittee on Telecommunications and Finance of the Committee on Energy and Commerce, House of Representatives,* One Hundredth Congress, September 15, 1987 and March 17, 1988.

Conley, Lucas. "A Craving for Cool." *Fast Company.* Last modified July 1, 2006. http://www.fastcompany.com/57129/craving-cool.

Connelly, Sherilyn. "Interview: Daniel Ingram, Songwriter for *My Little Pony: Friendship Is Magic.*" *SF Weekly.* Last modified November 9, 2012. http://www.sfweekly.com/exhibitionist/2012/11/09/interview-daniel-ingram-songwriter-for-my-little-pony-friendship-is-magic.

_____. "*Jem and the Holograms* Isn't Even Close to Being the Worst Movie Ever Made." *SF Weekly.* Last modified October 27, 2015. http://www.sfweekly.com/exhibitionist/2015/10/27/jem-and-the-holograms-isnt-even-close-to-being-the-worst-movie-ever-made.

Conner, Shawn. "Meet the Bronies at DOXA." *Vancouver Sun,* April 3, 2014.

Cook, William. "Aladdin Working." *Guardian,* December 21, 1993.

Cooney, Joyceann. "My New Little Pony." *License!* 5, no. 12 (January 2003): 44.

CouchCrusader. "Movie Followup/Editorial/Opinion Piece: 'Equestria Girls.'" *Equestria Daily.* Last modified February 18, 2014. https://web.archive.org/web/20140218185303/http://www.equestriadaily.com/2013/06/movie-followup-equestria-girls.html.

_____. "Movie Followup: 'Equestria Girls.'" *Equestria Daily.* Last modified June 23, 2013. https://web.archive.org/web/20130624065830/http://www.equestriadaily.com/2013/06/movie-followup-equestria-girls.html.

Creager, Ellen. "Barbie Bares Her Belly to Compete with Bratz." *Detroit Free Press,* November 27, 2002.

Cups. "My Little Pony Dog Tags Series 2 Announced!" *Equestria Daily.* Last modified September 29, 2015.

D'Angelo, Joe. "*Billboard* Sours on Prince's *Musicology* Experiment." *MTV.* Last modified May 28, 2004. http://www.mtv.com/news/1488027/billboard-sours-on-princes-musicology-sales-experiment/.

Darnton, Nina. "*My Little Pony* Movie Review." *New York Times*, June 27, 1986.

Dart, Rebecca, Josh Haber, Daniel Ingram, Brian Leonard, Ishi Rudell, and Jayson Thiessen. "Audio Commentary." *My Little Pony: Equestria Girls—Friendship Games*. Directed by Ishi Rudell. USA: Shout! Factory, 2015. Blu-ray.

Daultrey, Stephen. "Bromancing the Ponies." *Bizarre* 215 (June 2014): 62–66.

DavidDavidsonic. "Brony." *Urban Dictionary*. Last modified December 23, 2010. http://www.urbandictionary.com/define.php?term=Brony&defid=5460072.

Davies, Margery. "Never Too Young to Buy." *Women's Review of Books*, 11 no. 6 (Mar. 1994): 6–7.

Davis, Bob. "Tough Game." *Wall Street Journal*, December 13, 1984.

Davis, John. "Acoustic Alchemy." *Austin American Statesman*, November 19, 1992.

Davis, Michael. *Street Gang: The Complete History of Sesame Street*. New York: Viking, 2008.

Davis, Patricia V. "Add Black Widow to the Avengers Action Figure Pack." *Change.Org*. Last modified May 2, 1015. https://www.change.org/p/hasbro-add-more-female-superhero-merc-add-black-widow-to-the-avengers-action-figure-pack.

"Davy Crockett Collectibles." *Disney Memorabilia*. Last modified March 5, 2007. http://disneymemorabilia.com/collectibles/davy-crockett-collectibles.

"Derpy Hooves: Lauren Faust MLP:FIM Original Art." *EBay*. Last modified April 15, 2011. http://www.ebay.com/itm/Derpy-Hooves-Lauren-Faust-MLP-FIM-Original-Art-/280662542214.

Dewey, Caitlin. "Don't Laugh, but Bronies May Be Propping Up One of America's Favorite Companies." *Washington Post*, April 24, 2014.

Diamond, John. "Advice to the Lovelorn: Don't Ask; Private Life." *Times*, July 16, 1992.

DiOrio, Carl. "Fat Rock Tooning Up Toy-Based Pix." *Daily Variety* 277, no. 54 (December 19, 2002): 5.

Discovery Communications. "Discovery Family Channel Leaps into 2015–16 Upfront Season." Discovery Communications press release, March 31, 2015.

_____. "Introducing the Hub—Discovery Communications and Hasbro Officially Unveil Children's Network Brand: New Joint Venture Children's Network to Launch in Fall 2010." Discovery Communications press release, January 14, 2010.

_____. "Stellar Performance of My Little Pony Friendship Is Magic Fan-Favorite Marathon Powers the Hub to Strong Audience Gains." Discovery Communications press release, February 14, 2012.

Disney Store. n.d. http://www.disneystore.com/.

Donahue, Christine. "A Limit on Children's Advertising?" *Adweek's Marketing Week* 30, no. 29 (July 17, 1989): 2.

Dougherty, Philip. "BBDO Direct Is Picked for Hasbro Toy Work." *New York Times*, November 25, 1983.

Douglas, John. "Impotence Killed the Cat, and Mouse." *Grand Rapids Press*, August 1, 1993.

Downing, Neil. "Guess Who? My Little Pony Trots into Soviet Toy Market." *Providence Journal*, December 23, 1989.

_____. "Hasbro Sees Record Sales and Profits." *Providence Journal*, May 21, 1987.

Dunphy, Caroline. "Magic Fable Eco-Dazzles." *Toronto Star*, April 16, 1992.

Dutka, Elaine. "The Brains Behind 'Beauty,'" *San Francisco Chronicle*, January 20, 1992.

Dyckman, Constance. "Audiovisual Review: My Little Pony." *School Library Journal* 33, no. 8 (1987): 66–67.

Dyess, Norma. "Musical Score, Vivid Animation Are Pony Highlights." *Advocate*, June 13, 1986.

_____. "Recapping the Summer's Best, Worst, and in Between." *Advocate*, September 12, 1986.

Dylan, Bob. *Chronicles: Volume One*. New York: Simon & Schuster, 2004.

Ebert, Roger. "Ebert's Guide to Practical Filmgoing: A Glossary of Terms for the Cinema of the '80s." *Roger Ebert's Journal*. n.d. http://www.rogerebert.com/rogers-journal/eberts-guide-to-practical-filmgoing-a-glossary-of-terms-for-the-cinema-of-the-80s.

"Editorial: A Reconsideration." *Baltimore Sun*. November 4, 2007. http://articles.baltimoresun.com/2007-11-04/news/0711040177_1_pony-cuteness-parents.

Ellery, Simon. "Analysis: Toy Revivals Must Look Beyond Adult Nostalgia." *PR Week (UK)*, August 15, 2003.

Ellin, Harlene. "Leafing Through the New Fall Shows for Kids." *Chicago Tribune*, September 6, 1998.

Emanuel, Louis. "Bristol Bronies: The Men Who Love My Little Pony." *Bristol Post*. Last modified April 9, 2014. http://www.bristolpost.co.uk/Bristol-Bronies-men-love-Little-Pony/story-20931726-detail/story.html.

_____. "Meet the Bronies: The Men (And Women) Who Love My Little Pony." *Bristol Post*, April 9, 2014.

Engelhardt, Tom. "The Shortcake Strategy." In *Watching Television*, edited by Tod Gitlin, 69–110. New York: Pantheon Books, 1986.

"Era: History." *Equal Rights Amendment*. http://www.equalrightsamendment.org/history.htm.

Erickson, Hal. *Television Cartoon Shows. An Illustrated Encyclopedia, 1949 Through 1993*. Jefferson, NC: McFarland, 1995.

_____. *Television Cartoon Shows: An Illustrated Encyclopedia, 1949 Through 2003*. Jefferson, NC: McFarland, 2005.

Everar. "Bronies." *Urban Dictionary*. Last modified April 15, 2008. http://www.urbandictionary.com/define.php?term=Brony&defid=3009740.

"'Evil Empire' Speech." *Miller Center*. http://millercenter.org/president/speeches/speech-3409.

Farrell, Ken. *Warman's Disney Collectibles Field Guide: Values and Identification*. Iola, WI: Krause Publications, 2006.

Faust, Lauren. "My Little Non-Homophobic, Non-Racist, Non-Smart-Shaming Pony: A Rebuttal." *Ms*. Last modified December 24, 2010. http://msmagazine.com/blog/2010/12/24/my-little-non-homophobic-non-racist-non-smart-shaming-pony-a-rebuttal/.

_____. (Fire_Flye). https://twitter.com/Fyre_flye/.

"Federal Judge Rules 'Happy Birthday' Is in the Public Domain." Narrated by Laura Sydell. *NPR News*. NPR. September 23, 2015. http://www.npr.org/2015/09/23/442907049/federal-judge-rules-happy-birthday-is-in-the-public-domain.

"Ferraro's Acceptance Speech, 1984." *CNN*. http://www.cnn.com/ALLPOLITICS/1996/conventions/chicago/facts/famous.speeches/ferraro.84.shtml.

Ferrigno, Robert. "These Cartoons Are Not Just for Kids." *Orange County Register*, September 21, 1987.

Finn, Perdita. *My Little Pony: Equestria Girls—Rainbow Rocks*. Boston: Little, Brown Books for Young Readers, 2014.

_____. *My Little Pony: Equestria Girls—The Mane Event*. Boston: Little, Brown Books for Young Readers, 2014.

Flint, Joe. "Sesame Street's Favorite New Letters: HBO." *Wall Street Journal*, August 13, 2015.

Flint, Joe, and Dawn Chmielewski. "Toys and TV: A Winning Pair?" *Los Angeles Times*, October 5, 2010.

"Fluttershy." *Strawberry Reef*. n.d. http://www.strawberryreef.com/Index/Name/fluttershy.html.

"For Drug Chains, Category Has Lots of Untapped Potential." *Chain Drug Review* 28, no. 20 (November 20, 2006): 36.

Franke, Katherine M. "Theorizing Yes: An Essay of Feminism, Law, and Desire." *Columbia Law Review* 101, no. 1 (2001): 181–208.

Frankel, Susannah. "Ready to Wear." *Independent*, August 7, 2006.

Freedman, Samuel G. "The Words and Music of Stephen Sondheim." *New York Times*, April 1, 1984.

"Friday." *Ocala Star-Banner*, February 18, 1995.

fyre-flye. "Comment on Fyre-Flye's Profile." *DeviantArt*. Last modified September 20, 2011. http://comments.deviantart.com/4/1603670/2203413634.

_____. "Comment on Fyre-Flye's Profile." *DeviantArt*. Last modified December 18, 2010. http://comments.deviantart.com/4/1603670/1787126283.

_____. "Galaxy Girls, My Little Pony and 2010." *DeviantArt*. Last modified March 31, 2010. https://web.archive.org/web/20130825231559/http://fyre-flye.deviantart.com/journal/Galaxy-Girls-My-Little-Pony-and-2010-228911071?offset=20#comments.

_____. "MLP Art for Japan **Update**." *DeviantArt*. Last modified April 8, 2011. https://web.archive.org/web/20140216014638/http://fyre-flye.deviantart.com/journal/MLP-art-for-Japan-UPDATE-219997425.

_____. "Ms. and MLP." *DeviantArt*. Last modified December 24, 2010. http://fyre-flye.deviantart.com/journal/Ms-and-MLP-222240234.

_____. "Thank You!!!" *DeviantArt*. Last modified May 8, 2011. http://fyre-flye.deviantart.com/journal/?catpath=%2F&offset=40.

G. Ferro. "Brony." *Urban Dictionary*. Last modified February 25, 2010. https://web.archive.org/web/20110603082349/http://www.urbandictionary.com/author.php?author=G.+Ferro.

Gajewski, Ryan. "'Jem and the Holograms' Director on Film Bombing, Getting 'Death Threats' from Show Fans." *Hollywood Reporter*. Last modified October 24. http://www.hollywoodreporter.com/news/jem-holograms-director-film-bombing-834476.

"The GAME of LIFE: My Little Pony." *Amazon*. n.d. http://www.amazon.com/GAME-LIFE-My-Little-Pony/dp/B00K3EYVJO/.

Garvey, Marianne, Brian Niemietz, and Lachlan Cartwright. "Photo Exhibition Clicks with Bono." *New York Daily News*, April 28, 2014.

Gehman, Geoff. "Dr. Who, That's Who." *Morning Call*, October 19, 1985.

Gerrie, David. "Turtle Hero Worship." *Marketing* (June 14, 1990): 28.

Gerrold, David. *The Trouble with Tribbles*. New York: Ballantine Books, 1973.

Gibson, Megan. "Guess Who's a Fan? Former

President Bill Clinton Is a 'Brony.'" Time.com. Last modified June 27, 2011. http://newsfeed. time.com/2011/06/27/guess-whos-a-fan-former-president-bill-clinton-is-a-brony/.

Gilligan, Eugene. "Retailers to Rely on Tried and True Licenses for '88." *Playthings* (December 1987): 62.

Gliatto, Tom. "My Little Obsession." *USA Today*, December 7, 1988.

Goldman, Carrie. "11-Yr-Old Boy Bullied for Being a Brony Fighting for Life After Suicide Attempt." *Chicago Now.* Last modified February 2, 2014. http://www.chicagonow.com/portrait-of-an-adoption/2014/02/11-yr-old-boy-bullied-for-being-a-brony-fighting-for-life-after-suicide-attempt-how-you-can-help/.

Goldman, Eric. "Transformers Prime Ending with Season 3." *IGN.* Last modified March 1, 2013.

Goodman, Susan. "What's in a Label?" *Washington Post*, April 7, 1992.

Gould, Jack. "Television in Review: 'Ding Dong School,' a Worthwhile Video Program Directed at Children, Stubs Toe on Commercialism." *New York Times,* April 1, 1953.

Graser, Marc. "'My Little Pony' Movie in the Works at Hasbro Studios (EXCLUSIVE)." *Variety.* Last modified October 20, 2014. http://variety.com/2014/film/news/my-little-pony-movie-in-the-works-at-hasbro-studios-exclusive-1201334144/.

Gravity Falls. "Between the Pines." Produced by Emily Burton and Eric Beaudry. Disney XD, February 12, 2016.

Gregg, Clark (ClarkGregg). https://twitter.com/clarkgregg/.

Grimes LLC. "Chapter 1: The History of Licensing." n.d. http://www.gandb.com/documents/Chapter-1-Licensing-101-The-History-of-Merchandising-and-Licensing.pdf.

Grimm, Matthew. "Toys Are No Fun in a Flat Year." *Adweek* 41, no. 39 (September 23, 1991): S117.

Gutis, Philip S. "Toy Makers Frolic in Fantasy Land." *New York Times*, Dec. 23, 1984.

Gweiswasser. "The Hub Arrives 10.10.10." *Discovery Blog*, October 8, 2010. https://corporate.discovery.com/blog/2010/10/08/the-hub-arrives-10-10-10/.

"Hachune Miku." *Vocaloid Wiki.* n.d. http://vocaloid.wikia.com/wiki/Hachune_Miku.

Hagen, Bill. "Critic's 'Aides' Like Slimy Stuff, Call 'Pony' Kids' Film." *San Diego Union-Tribune*, June 24, 1986.

Hall, Brian. "Lauren Burleson Wins Horsemanship Honors." *Orange County Register*, March 7, 1996.

"Halloween Treats." *People*, November 4, 2002.

Hanks, Robert. "This Was a Real Test of Manhood." *Independent*, July 25, 2008.

Hansen, Natalie Corinne. "Queering the Horse-Crazy Girl: Part II." Presentation, Annual Thinking Gender Conference, UCLA Center for the Study of Women, February 1, 2008.

"Happening: Tribeca Film Festival." *Financial Times*, April 14, 2014.

Harnick, Chris. "Rainbow Brite Rides Again! the Iconic '80s Character Gets New Cartoon." *E! Online*, October 14, 2014. http://www.eonline.com/news/588229/rainbow-brite-rides-again-the-iconic-80s-character-gets-new-cartoon.

HarperCollins Publishers. "My Little Pony Books Hit 3.5 Million Unit Mark for Harper-Collins Children's Books." HarperCollins Publishers press release, November 22, 2004.

Harrison, Bernice. "Spice Girls Set the Tone." *Irish Times*, November 23, 1996.

Hartl, John. "'My Little Pony' Is Ok Matinee Fare." *Seattle Times*, June 23, 1986.

Hartlaub, Peter. "Deadly Alliance Revives Kombat." *San Francisco Chronicle*, January 7, 2003.

Hartmann, Margaret. "Ryan Gosling Obviously Sings *My Little Pony* Theme Song." *Jezebel.* Last modified January 4, 2011. http://jezebel.com/5724478/ryan-gosling-obviously-sings-my-little-pony-theme-song.

_____. "The Unlikely Origins of the Brony, or Bros Who Like 'My Little Pony.'" *Jezebel.* Last modified August 4, 2011. http://jezebel.com/5827591/the-unlikely-origins-of-the-brony-or-dudes-who-like-my-little-pony.

Harvey, William. "My Little Pony: Not Just for Little Girls." *Tampa Bay Times*, April 12, 2012.

Hasbro, Inc. "Celebrities Step Out on the 'Pink Carpet' to Celebrate the Hollywood Premiere of My Little Pony Live!" Hasbro Inc. press release, March 3, 2007.

_____. "Correcting and Replacing Hasbro Builds on My Little Pony Brand Growth Catering to Fans Worldwide." Hasbro Inc. press release, June 19, 2013.

_____. "Correcting and Replacing It's Time to Celebrate! Hasbro's My Little Pony Brand Makes Its Long Anticipated Return; My Little Pony Now Available Nationwide." Hasbro Inc. press release, September 19, 2003.

_____. "Event Brief of Hasbro and Discovery Communications Announce Joint Venture." Hasbro Inc. press release, April 30, 2009.

_____. "Fall 2009 Investor Day." Hasbro Inc. press release, November 5, 2009.

_____. "Fans of My Little Pony Can Now Create

Their Own Play Experience—Hasbro and Disney Create a Build-Your-Own Program at Downtown Disney." Hasbro Inc. press release, March 7, 2005.

_____. "Guinness World Record® Achieved for Largest Coloring Book During Hub TV Network's 'Playdate Premiere Party.'" Hasbro Inc. press release, November 12, 2012.

_____. "Hasbro Accelerates the Leveraging of Company's Vast Global Brand Portfolio Through Entertainment and Licensing." Hasbro Inc. press release, June 2, 2009.

_____. "Hasbro and Shapeways Launch Superfanart, New Website That Empowers Fans to Be Creators Using Hasbro Brands." Hasbro Inc. press release, July 21, 2014.

_____. "Hasbro Brings Hotly-Anticipated Special Edition Toys to Comic-Con International, Featuring Transformers, My Little Pony, Jem and More." Hasbro Inc. press release, July 8, 2015.

_____. "Hasbro Continues to Build Global Lifestyle Brands Bringing Innovative Products to Market That Touch Every Aspect of Consumers' Lives." Hasbro Inc. press release, June 19, 2007.

_____. "Hasbro Continues to Expand Its Immersive Global Brand Experiences Through Entertainment and Lifestyle Licensing." Hasbro Inc. press release, June 7, 2010.

_____. "Hasbro Delivers Innovative and 'Must Have' Toys for the Holidays." Hasbro Inc. press release, November 14, 2012.

_____. "Hasbro Delivers Innovative Products and Brand Experiences This Holiday Season." Hasbro Inc. press release, September 28, 2010.

_____. "Hasbro Delivers Must-Have Products and Entertainment Experiences for the Holiday Season." Hasbro Inc. press release, October 24, 2011.

_____. "Hasbro Delivers the Hottest Special Edition Toys at Comic-Con International, Featuring Transformers, My Little Pony, Magic: The Gathering, Star Wars, Marvel and More." Hasbro Inc. press release, July 23, 2014.

_____. "Hasbro Delivers the Hottest Special Edition Toys at San Diego Comic-Con, Featuring Transformers, G.I. Joe, My Little Pony and More." Hasbro Inc. press release, June 27, 2012.

_____. "Hasbro Film, Television Programming and Licensed Merchandise Driving Global Retail Growth." Hasbro Inc. press release, June 11, 2012.

_____. "Hasbro Forms Business Sector Designed to Leverage Company's Intellectual Properties." Hasbro Inc. press release, September 30, 1999.

_____. "Hasbro Inc Annual Investor Meeting at Toy Fair—Final." Hasbro Inc. press release, February 13, 2015.

_____. "Hasbro Interactive Brings Kid's Favorite Toys and Games to Life in Three New CD-ROM Games, My Little Pony, Operation and Candy Land." Hasbro Inc. press release, October 6, 1998.

_____. "Hasbro Presents Array of Branded Lifestyle Goods for Entire Family at the International Licensing Expo." Hasbro Inc. press release, June 13, 2011.

_____. "The Hasbro Properties Group and VEE Corporation to Bring *My Little Pony Live: The World's Biggest Tea Party* to Venues Across the U.S. This Fall." Hasbro Inc. press release, June 16, 2006.

_____. "Hasbro Properties Group Creates 'Lifestyles' Based on the World's Most Entertaining Toy and Game." Hasbro Inc. press release, June 9, 2003.

_____. "Hasbro Properties Group Strikes Licensing Deals That Elevate Core Toy and Game Properties to New Levels of Global Brand Extension." Hasbro Inc. press release, June 20, 2006.

_____. "Hasbro Reports Revenue and Earnings Growth for the First Quarter 2014." Hasbro Inc. press release, April 21, 2014.

_____. "Hasbro Returns to Comic-Con International to Showcase Its Iconic Pop-Culture Brands." Hasbro Inc. press release, July 9, 2012.

_____. "Hasbro Revolutionizing Branded Play and Lifestyle Experiences Through Rich Storytelling Across All Entertainment Platforms." Hasbro Inc. press release, June 17, 2014.

_____. "Hasbro Showcases Top Entertainment Properties at San Diego Comic-Con." Hasbro Inc. press release, July 16, 2009.

_____. "Hasbro Teams with Target to Create a Magical In-Store Experience for Girls." Hasbro Inc. press release, July 28, 2011.

_____. "Hasbro to Debut Innovative New Play Experiences from Its Expansive Portfolio of Iconic Brands at the American International Toy Fair." Hasbro Inc. press release, February 9, 2012.

_____. "Hasbro to Showcase Its Iconic Pop Culture Brands at Comic-Con International." Hasbro Inc. press release, July 15, 2013.

_____. "Hasbro Unveils a World of Fun at American International Toy Fair." Hasbro Inc. press release, February 6, 1998.

_____. "Hasbro Unveils 'The My Little Pony Project: 25 Ponies for 25 Years' Collection." Hasbro Inc. press release, September 10, 2008.

_____. "Hasbro, Inc. 2013 Investor Day—Final." Hasbro Inc. press release, September 10, 2013.

_____. "Hasbro's Iconic Mr. Potato Head Character Celebrates 60th Birthday." Hasbro Inc. press release, February 14, 2012.

_____. "Hasbro's Iconic My Little Pony Brand Excites a New Generation of Girls with Its Message of Friendship and Adventure." Hasbro Inc. press release, October 7, 2010.

_____. "Hasbro's My Little Pony and the Starlight Starbright Children's Foundation Roll Out the "Pink" Carpet for Hundreds of Kids." Hasbro Inc. press release, November 9, 2004.

_____. "Hasbro's My Little Pony Brand Celebrates 25 Years of Magic and Imagination with a Year-Long Global Celebration." Hasbro Inc. press release, February 14, 2008.

_____. "The Hub Network to Become Discovery Family Channel on October 13." Hasbro Inc. press release, September 25, 2014.

_____. "Hub TV Network Scores Record High Audience with Outstanding Performance of Special Royal Wedding of the Year on 'My Little Pony Friendship Is Magic.'" Hasbro Inc. press release, April 24, 2012.

_____. "'My Little Pony Equestria Girls' in Cinemas Nationwide Beginning June 16." Hasbro Inc. press release, May 30, 2013.

_____. My Little Pony Equestria Girls 2016 Product Descriptions. n.d. http://files.shareholder. com/downloads/HAS/1966905775x0x874895/ 7EC99304–1F36–4DB7–A2FE-3E650830 DE11/My_Little_Pony_Equestria_Girls_2016_ Product_Descriptions.pdf.

_____. "My Little Pony Gallops into Build-A-Bear Workshop." Hasbro Inc. press release, March 26, 2013.

_____. "My Little Pony Gallops into Comics." Hasbro Inc. press release, July 14, 2012.

_____. "My Little Pony Holiday Film Climbs to Top of Billboard Charts." Hasbro Inc. press release, November 22, 2005.

_____. "My Little Pony Holiday Film to Premier at Special Family Matinees Nationwide." Hasbro Inc. press release, September 29, 2005.

_____. "My Little Pony Makes Its Highly Anticipated Return; Hasbro Celebrates Cherished Brand with Worldwide Launch in 2003." Hasbro Inc. press release, February 10, 2003.

_____. "My Little Pony Meets the Art World with the Unveiling of the Pony Project." Hasbro Inc. press release, October 21, 2005.

_____. "Q2 2014 Hasbro Inc. Earnings Call." Hasbro Inc. press release, July 21, 2014.

_____. "Q3 2003 Hasbro Inc. Earnings Conference Call." Hasbro Inc. press release, October 20, 2003.

_____. "Q3 2011 Hasbro Inc. Earnings Conference Call." Hasbro Inc. press release, October 17, 2011.

_____. "Q4 2011 Hasbro Inc. Earnings Conference Call." Hasbro Inc. press release, February 6, 2012.

_____. "Stars Come Out to Celebrate the Third Installment of My Little Pony Equestria Girls with the 'Friendship Games' Premiere from Hasbro Studios." Hasbro Inc. press release, September 18, 2015.

_____. "Trademark/Service Mark Application, Principal Register Serial Number: 85804403." December 17, 2012.

_____. "Trademark/Service Mark Application, Principal Register Serial Number: 85805634." December 18, 2012.

_____. "Twilight Sparkle Becomes a Princess in Special Coronation Episode of 'My Little Pony Friendship Is Magic' on the Hub TV Network." Hasbro Inc. press release, January 30, 2013.

_____. 2000 Annual Report. n.d. http://files. shareholder.com/downloads/HAS/1221912 837x0x456758/1BF7BB27-F652–4BD9–8263– 8D0890E2B8FE/2000AR.pdf.

_____. 2002 Annual Report. n.d. http://ccbn18. mobular.net/ccbn/7/182/190/.

_____. 2006 Annual Report. n.d. http://files. shareholder.com/downloads/HAS/1221912 837x0x472633/426B06DF-9610–45BB-ADEF-E42FE749E902/2006AR.pdf

_____. 2014 Annual Report. n.d. http://investor. hasbro.com/common/download/download. cfm?companyid=HAS&fileid=819559& filekey=8A09F66A-4137–45A9–88BA-C16F08 E1AF90&filename=Annual_Report_Website_ FINAL.pdf.

_____. 2015 Annual Report. n.d. http://investor. hasbro.com/common/download/download. cfm?companyid=HAS&fileid=883653& filekey=E95A5C8D-DFAA-4ACB-BB2C- 844E50306A01&filename=Annual_Report_ for_Web.pdf.

"Hasbro Campaign Will Push My Little Pony's Comeback." PR Week (UK), June 27, 2003.

"Hasbro, Inc." Capital District Business Review (November 12, 1990): 27.

"Hasbro Revamps My Little Pony to Draw Younger Girls." Marketing Week 28, no. 26 (July 10, 2003): 9.

"Hasbro Says Profit in Fiscal 1st Quarter Nearly Quadrupled." Wall Street Journal. April 20, 1984.

Hawkinson, Olivia. "In Sci-Fi's Mostly Male

Realm, `Star Wars' Blasts Gender Lines." *Orange County Register*, January 29, 1999.

Hayes, Summer. *The My Little Pony G2 Collector's Inventory*. Denville, N.J.: Priced Nostalgia Press, 2010.

_____. *The My Little Pony 2007–2008 Collector's Inventory*. Denville, N.J.: Priced Nostalgia Press, 2009.

"He-Man and the Masters of the Universe." *Epguides*. Last modified December 30, 2001. http://epguides.com/HeMan_1983/.

Hellsly, Victorian R. "My Little Time Lord." *FanFiction*. Last modified December 29, 2011. https://www.fanfiction.net/s/6700975/.

Hetherington, Janet. "Just Hit Play: Toy Brand Animated DVDS." Last modified March 30, 2007. http://www.awn.com/animationworld/just-hit-play-toy-brand-animated-dvds.

Hoggart, Simon. "Simon Hoggart's Week: Royals, Gazza, Spice Et Moi." *Guardian*, October 26, 1996.

Holden, Stephen. "Melodist and Minimalist in Harmony." *New York Times*, February 1, 2015.

Holledge, Richard. "An Independent Week." *Independent*, November 27, 1995.

Holt, Andrew. "Hasbro Studios/The Hub: Do Not Change Derpy's Name." *Change.org*. Last modified February 2, 2012. https://web.archive.org/web/20120207085817/http://www.change.org/petitions/hasbro-studiosthe-hub-do-not-change-derpys-name.

_____. "Return Derpy's Scene in the Last Roundup to Normal." *Change.org*. Last modified February 26, 2012. https://www.change.org/p/hasbro-studios-the-hub-return-derpy-s-scene-in-the-last-roundup-to-normal/u/932490.

Hopkinson, Nalo. "Maybe They're Phasing Us In." *Journal of the Fantastic in the Arts* 18, no. 1 (Winter 2007): 99–107.

Houston, David. "The Magical Techniques of Movie and TV Special Effects: Part IX, the Matte Artist: An Interview with P.S. Ellenshaw." *Starlog*, June 1978.

"The Hub." *Advertising Age*. May 3, 2010. http://brandedcontent.adage.com/cableguide10/network.php?id=16.

"Humbug! the London of 'A Christmas Carol' Has Gone Commercial. *Philadelphia Inquirer*, December 25, 1984.

Ilfiorelaluna. "Licensing Show News—Core Seven Ponies." *My Little Pony Arena*. Last modified June 2007. http://www.mlparena.com/archive/Forums//viewtopic/t=117990/.

_____. "Report from Licensing Show 'Core Seven' BAD NEWS FOR MLP." *My Little Pony Trading Post*. Last modified June 25, 2007.

http://www.mlptp.net/index.php?threads/report-from-licensing-show-core-seven-bad-news-for-mlp.31962/.

Ilona. "My Little Pony at the NY Toy Fair 2015 Wrap-Up." *All About MLP Merch*. Last modified February 18, 2015. http://www.mlpmerch.com/2015/02/my-little-pony-at-ny-toy-fair-2015-wrap.html.

"I'm the Juggernaut, Bitch!" *Know Your Meme*. Last modified in 2013. http://knowyourmeme.com/memes/im-the-juggernaut-bitch.

Imbrie, Katherine. "Holiday Gifts Rated: Love It or Loathe It." *Providence Journal*, January 25, 1989.

Isaac, Chris. "Interview: Them's Fightin' Herds' Lauren Faust and the Mane6 Team on Their Fighting Game." *Mary Sue*. Last modified October 19, 2015. http://www.themarysue.com/lauren-faust-and-mane6-on-thems-fightin-herds/.

Jackson, Alan. "This Little Pony." *Guardian*, November 21, 1993.

Jagernauth, Kevin. "Max Landis Wonders If the Flop of 'American Ultra' Means That Original Movies Are Dead." *Indiewire*. Last modified August 24, 2015. http://www.indiewire.com/2015/08/max-landis-wonders-if-the-flop-of-american-ultra-means-that-original-movies-are-dead-260572/.

"Jem and the Holograms." *Box Office Mojo*. n.d. http://www.boxofficemojo.com/movies/?id=jemandtheholograms.htm.

Johnston. Lisa. "*The Animated Movie Guide*." *Booklist* 102, no. 12 (February 15, 2006): 125.

Jubera, Drew. "Watching TV: Cartoon Network Exec Loves to Show His Daffy Side." *Atlanta Journal*, February 18, 2001.

July, Derek. "CG, EQLA, Bronycon, EFNW, Las Pegasus Unicon, Other Brony Conventions: Ban YAC from Performing, and from Appearing in Any Guest of Honor Role." *Change.org*. Last modified February 2, 2012. https://www.change.org/p/cg-eqla-bronycon-efnw-las-pegasus-unicon-other-brony-conventions-ban-yac-from-performing-and-from-appearing-in-any-guest-of-honor-role.

Jurek, Justin. "Change Derpy Back." *Change.Org*. Last modified February 25, 2012. https://www.change.org/p/hasbro-studios-the-hub-change-derpy-back.

Kate. "Royal Ball at Canterlot Castle Playset." *My Little Pony News*. Last modified Tuesday, June 14, 2011. http://www.mylittleponynews.com/2011/06/royal-ball-at-canterlot-castle-playset.html.

Kelven486. "So I Emailed Ms Germain (Voice for Rarity, Luna, Derpy) and Got a Reply…"

Reddit. Last modified January 27, 2012. https://www.reddit.com/r/mylittlepony/comments/oynoa/so_i_emailed_ms_germain_voice_for_rarity_luna/.

Kemmerle, Karen. "Brent Hodge on 'A Brony Tale' and What It Means to Be a Man." *Tribeca Film Festival.* Last modified April 30, 2014. https://tribecafilm.com/stories/brent-hodge-a-brony-tale-interview.

Kent, Steven L. *The Ultimate History of Video Games.* Roseville, Calif: Prima, 2001.

Kidomo. "My Little Pony Tour 2011." n.d. http://www.kidomo.com/media/Special/Kidomo—Hasbro—MLP-2012.pdf.

Kiley, David. "Mobilizing Mom and Dad for the War on Kids' TV." *Adweek's Marketing Week* 32, no. 36 (September 2, 1991): 4.

King, Marsha. "Channeling the Wish Lists—Parents Need Strategy to Fight TV's Influence Over What Their Kids Request for Christmas." *Seattle Times,* December 3, 1985.

Knoedelseder, William K., Jr. "De Laurentiis: Producer's Picture Darkens." *Los Angeles Times,* August 30, 1987.

Koski, Genevieve. "Friendship Is Magic Pony-Creator Offers Endless Permutations of Cuteness." *A.V. Club.* Last modified January 6, 2012. http://www.avclub.com/article/emfriendship-is-magicem-pony-creator-offers-endles-67298.

Kreoss. "Derpy." *DeviantArt.* Last modified February 24, 2012. http://kreoss.deviantart.com/journal/Derpy-287023334.

_____. "MLP Human Version Ver. 1." *DeviantArt.* Last modified December 24, 2010. http://kreoss.deviantart.com/art/MLP-Human-version-ver-1-190767778.

Krieger, Elliot. "Movie Review: 'My Little Pony' Trots Out Some Fun." *Providence Journal-Bulletin,* June 24, 1986.

Kunkel, Dale. "From a Raised Eyebrow to a Turned Back: The FCC and Children's Product-Related Programming." *Journal of Communication* 38, no. 4 (1998): 90–108.

Kurhi, Eric. "Cupertino Couple Rides to Raise Funds to Fight Rare Disease That Struck Daughter." *San Mateo County Times,* October 5, 2013.

Labash, Matt. "The Dread Pony." *Weekly Standard.* Last modified August 26, 2013. http://www.weeklystandard.com/article/dread-pony/748495.

LadyM. "Found an Interview with One of the MLP Creators!" *My Little Pony Trading Post.* Last modified February 9, 2008. http://www.mlptp.net/index.php?threads/found-an-interview-with-one-of-the-mlp-creators.42431/.

LaMarche, Una. "Pony Up Haters: How 4chan Gave Birth to the Bronies." *New York Observer,* August 3, 2011. http://observer.com/2011/08/pony-up-haters-how-4chan-gave-birth-to-the-bronies/.

Larson, M.A. (M_A_Larson). https://twitter.com/M_A_Larson/.

Lauren, Andrew. "The Oldest Case of Disco Fever." *New York Magazine,* January 14, 1991.

"Lauren Faust." *Internet Movie Database.* http://www.imdb.com/name/nm0269260/reference.

Lauter, D. "Children's TV Bill Will Become Law Without Bush's Signature." *Los Angeles Times,* October 8, 1990.

Le Coz, Emily. "11-Year-Old Boy's Suicide Attempt Part of Epidemic." *Clarion-Ledger,* April 14, 2014.

Leonard, Brian, Meghan McCarthy, Ishi Rudell, Jayson Thiessen, and Michael Vogel. "Audio Commentary." *My Little Pony: Equestria Girls—Rainbow Rocks.* Directed by Jayson Thiessen. USA: Shout! Factory, 2014. Blu-ray.

Levine, Katie. "James Bonding #008: DIE ANOTHER DAY with Ben Blacker and Ben Acker." *Nerdist.* Last modified October 24, 2013. http://nerdist.com/james-bonding-008-die-another-day-with-ben-blacker-and-ben-acker/.

Lewis, Hilary. "Hasbro Working on 'My Little Pony' Movie." *Hollywood Reporter.* Last modified October 20, 2014. http://www.hollywoodreporter.com/news/hasbro-working-my-little-pony-742126.

Lipton, James. "Stephen Sondheim, the Art of the Musical." *Paris Review,* Spring 1997. http://www.theparisreview.org/interviews/1283/the-art-of-the-musical-stephen-sondheim.

"List of *Strawberry Shortcake's Berry Bitty Adventures* Episodes." *Wikipedia.* Last modified February 19, 2016. https://en.wikipedia.org/wiki/List_of_Strawberry_Shortcake's_Berry_Bitty_Adventures_episodes.

Loftus, Johnny. "*My Little Pony: Friendship Songs.*" *Allmusic.* n.d. http://www.allmusic.com/album/my-little-pony-friendship-songs-mw0001375227.

Lohman, Sidney. "News of TV and Radio: New Pre-School Age Show—Other Studio Items." *New York Times,* November 16, 1952.

"Lorna Dounaeva." *Amazon.* n.d. http://www.amazon.com/Lorna-Dounaeva/e/B00BSQL9YG.

"Los Angeles Film Festival—'My Little Pony: Equestria Girls' Premiere." *Getty Images.* n.d. http://www.gettyimages.com/detail/news-photo/anja-louise-ambrosio-mazur-and-alessandra-ambrosio-arrive-news-photo/170634483.

Lovell, Glenn. "Super Star Summer Sequels, Sequels Kiddie Heroes and Space Cadets Are Back." *San Jose Mercury News*, May 18, 1986.

_____. "Taking a Careful Journey in Wonderland." *San Jose Mercury News*, August 7, 1987.

Low, Kathleen. "'Dumping' Adds to Spotty Traffic at Volume Show." *Footwear News* (June 11, 1984): 21.

Lowry, Brian. "How Peggy Charren Outflanked the Children's TV Establishment." *Variety*, January 22, 2015. http://variety.com/2015/tv/columns/how-peggy-charren-outflanked-the-childrens-tv-establishment-1201412528/.

Lynch, Stephen. "Re-Animated Television Cartoons, for So Long Moronic and Mundane, Are Cool Again Thanks to the Return of Creator-Driven Animation." *Orange County Register*, March 23, 2001.

Lyons, Teena. "Why Size Isn't Everything." *Sunday Mirror*, January 18, 1998.

MacDonald, Marianne. "Time of Freedom Tempered by an Adult 'Conspiracy' Over Finances." *Independent*, August 24, 1994.

Maltin, Leonard. *Leonard Maltin's TV Movies and Video Guide.* New York: New American Library, 1990.

Marchand, Francois. "Filmmaker Riding High on My Little Pony." *Vancouver Sun*. April 23, 2014.

Marquis, Simon. "The Young Ones." *Marketing* (March 10, 1994): 22.

Martin, Richard. "Movie Sure to Give Toy Sales a Boost." *Ottawa Citizen*, July 21, 1986.

"Marvel Productions." *Internet Movie Database.* http://www.imdb.com/company/co0106768/.

Maslin, Janet. "In Animation for Children, the Old Days Were Better." *New York Times*, January 18, 1987.

"Matthew Weiner's No Madman." *Adweek*. July 30, 2007. http://www.adweek.com/news/advertising/matthew-weiners-no-madman-89728.

McDonald, Marianna. "Interview: Demi Moore: Twice the Woman She Used to Be." *Observer*, October 12, 1997.

"Media Relations: Two Minutes—Jen Barker, Editor, My Little Pony." *PR Week (UK)*, June 23, 2006.

"Meet the Characters." *Dork Diaries.* n.d. http://dorkdiaries.com/meet-the-characters/.

Meyers, Richard. "The Selling of Star Wars." *Starlog*, August 1978.

Midnightthunder. "Core 7?" *My Little Pony Trading Post.* Last modified September 6, 2008. http://www.mlptp.net/index.php?threads/core-7.52123/.

"'Milagro Beanfield War' and a Fantasy with Aliens." *Philadelphia Inquirer*, September 15, 1988.

Miller, Jim (TheBiggestJim). https://twitter.com/TheBiggestJim/.

"Mini-Trend: Horses Run Wild." *Licensing Letter*, July 3, 2006.

"MLP Through the Years." *Hasbro.* n.d. https://web.archive.org/web/20120309232144/http://www.hasbro.com/mylittlepony/en_US/parents/through-the-years.cfm.

"MLPFAIR in VIVA LAS VEGAS, Just Around the Corner!!" *My Little Pony Arena.* Last modified May 28, 2004. http://www.mlparena.com/archive/Forums/viewtopic/p=63856.html.

Moloney, Kathleen. "Close Up." *Los Angeles Times*, March 15, 1992.

"Mon, April 9 Daytime Specials." *Daytona Beach Sunday News-Journal*, April 8, 1984.

"Monday." *Southeast Missourian*, March 24, 1985.

"Monday Television." *Sarasota Herald-Tribune*, October 6, 1986.

MoondancerMLP. "Princess Promenade in WA Theater!" *My Little Pony Trading Post.* Last modified January 21, 2006. http://www.mlptp.net/index.php?threads/princess-promenade-in-wa-theater.11981/.

Moore, Booth. "Saturday Cartoons: Taking the Good with the Bad." *Los Angeles Times*, January 6, 1999.

Moore, Suzanne. "Clash of Symbols." *Times*, April 11, 1993.

_____. "Dessie … Great Horse but Still Just a Horse." *Mail on Sunday*, November 19, 2006.

Moran, Lee. "North Carolina School Tells Boy, 9, to Ditch 'My Little Pony' Bag Because It's a Trigger for Bullying." *New York Daily News*. Last modified March 19, 2014. http://www.nydailynews.com/news/national/boy-told-ditch-pony-bag-article-1.1726433.

Moreton, Cole. "Scientist? Banker? My Little Pony Fanatic?" *Independent on Sunday*, October 12, 2008.

"Morning." *Los Angeles Times*. February 20, 1987.

"Morning." *New York Times*. September 16, 1986.

Morrall, Claire. "It's Pony Mane-ia; Fans Flock All the Way from Texas for Toy Show." *Sunday Mercury*, October 29, 2006.

Moss, Laura. "Why Must We Hate the Things Teen Girls Love?" *Mother Nature Network.* Last modified October 9, 2015. http://www.mnn.com/lifestyle/arts-culture/stories/why-do-we-hate-things-teen-girls-love.

Mouland, Bill. "My Little Comeback; Comeback Internet Petition Gives 1980s Toy New Lease of Life." *Daily Mail*, January 30, 1998.

"Movie Clock." *New York Times*, November 13, 2009.

Mowatt, Raoul V. "Improved 'He-Man' Series Heads to Cartoon Network." *Chicago Tribune*, August 16, 2002.

Murrison (Murrison). https://twitter.com/Murrison/.

"Muslim Convert Jesse Curtis Morton Gets Nearly 12 Years for Posting Online Threats Against 'South Park' Creators." *New York Daily News*, June 22, 2012.

"*My Little Pony: A Very Minty Christmas*." *Kidtoon Films*. Last modified November 11, 2007. https://web.archive.org/web/20071111170712/http://www.kidtoonfilms.com/.

"My Little Pony & Equestria Girls El Show En Vivo." *Cine Información Y Más*. Last modified October 27, 2015. http://www.cineinformacionymas.com/eventos-especiales/my-little-pony-equestria-girls-el-show-en-vivo/.

"My Little Pony Collectors' Convention." *Mylittleponyconvention.com*. Last modified October 20, 2004. https://web.archive.org, web/20041210121905/http://www.mylittleponyconvention.com/

"My Little Pony: Equestria Girls." *Box Office Mojo*. n.d. http://www.boxofficemojo.com/movies/intl/?page=&id=_fMYLITTLEPONYEQUE01.

"My Little Pony: Equestria Girls." *Screenvision*. Last modified June 7, 2013. https://web.archive.org/web/20130607121052/http://www.screenvision.com/cinema-events/my-little-pony-equestria-girls.

"My Little Pony: Equestria Girls." *Screenvision*. Last modified July 15, 2013. https://web.archive.org/web/20130721215156/http://www.screenvision.com/cinema-events/my-little-pony-equestria-girls.

"My Little Pony: Equestria Girls—Friendship Games." Vue Big Screen Entertainment. n.d. http://www.myvue.com/latest-movies/info/film/my-little-pony-equestria-girls-friendship-games.

"My Little Pony Equestria Girls Minis Rainbow Dash Doll." *Amazon*. n.d. http://www.amazon.com/My-Little-Pony-Equestria-Girls/dp/B012CCAVKM.

My Little Pony. *Facebook* post. May 12, 2013. https://www.facebook.com/mylittlepony/posts/645558932128214.

My Little Pony. *Friendship Songs*. Compact Disc. Genius Entertainment.

"MY LITTLE PONY Is Now on TV." *Hasbro*. Last modified September 27, 2010. https://web.archive.org/web/20101012212441/http://www.hasbro.com/mylittlepony/en_US/discover/MY-LITTLE-PONY-is-now-on-TV.cfm.

"MY LITTLE PONY—Meet the Ponies." *Hasbro*. https://web.archive.org/web/20101002222511/http://www.hasbro.com/mylittlepony/en_US/play/details.cfm?guid=1b03b79b-19b9-f369-10e8-d2d56966309c.

"My Little Pony Muffins Big Face Snapback Purple Trucker Hat." *Amazon*. Last modified August 18, 2014. http://www.amazon.com/My-Little-Pony-Muffins-Snapback/dp/B00MU65O2G.

My Little Pony. *Musical Treasures*. Compact Disc. Genius Entertainment.

"My Little Pony Newborn Cuties Family Convertible with DVD." *Amazon.Co.Uk*. n.d. http://www.amazon.co.uk/Little-Newborn-Cuties-Family-Convertible/dp/B0031U1SPW.

"My Little Pony: Pinkie Pie's Party Parade—Pc." *Amazon*. n.d. http://www.amazon.com/My-Little-Pony-Pinkie-Party-Parade/dp/B000VRH6TK/.

My Little Pony. *Pony Party Favorites*. Compact Disc. Genius Entertainment.

"My Little Pony: The Runaway Rainbow." *Amazon*. n.d., http://www.amazon.com/My-Little-Pony-Game-Boy-Advance/dp/B000FNY4SG/.

"My Little Pony: Short Features." *Hasbro*. https://web.archive.org/web/20080712015458/http://www.hasbro.com/mylittlepony/default.cfm?page=Entertainment/Videos/ShortFeatures.

"My Little Pony Soaring Pegasus Set." *Kmart*. Last modified September 20, 2013. https://web.archive.org/web/20130926162906/http://www.kmart.com/hasbro-my-little-pony-soaring-pegasus-set/p-004W005184348013P?.

My Little Pony. *Sweet Classics in Ponyland*. Compact Disc. Genius Entertainment.

My Little Pony Tales. "The Great Lemonade Stand Wars." Written by George A. Bloom. USA: Shout! Factory, 2015. DVD.

"My Little Pony Trots Back." *Evening Times*, February 9, 2002.

"My Little Pony Twilight Sparkle RC Car Vehicle." *Amazon*. n.d. http://www.amazon.com/My-Little-Pony-Twilight-Sparkle/dp/B00859GJXA.

"MY LITTLE PONY: Twinkle Wish Adventure in Theaters in November." *Hasbro*. Last modified November 14, 2009. https://web.archive.org/web/20091114121329/http://www.hasbro.com/mylittlepony/en_US/discover/MY-LITTLE-PONY-Twinkle-Wish-Adventure-in-Theaters-in-November.cfm

"Mylittlepony—Video_Rainbow." *Hasbro*. https://

web.archive.org/web/20060811181434/http://
www.hasbro.com/mylittlepony/default.
cfm?page=video_rainbow.

MyStuff. "The Great Mouse Detective." *Collector Stuff*. Last modified November 16, 2011. http://
bingksjunk.blogspot.com/2011/11/great-
mouse-detective.html.

"New for NATPE in a Nutshell." *Broadcasting* 123, no. 1 (January 4, 1993): 34.

"1983 Sayles Film Is Finally Released." *Philadelphia Inquirer*, September 14, 1989.

Nossiter, Bernard. "Licenses to Coin Money: The FCC's Big Giveaway Show." *Nation*, October 26, 1985.

Novak, Ralph V.R. Peterson, Campbell Geeslin, Joanne Kaufman, and Kristin McMurran. "Picks and Pans Review: Snow White and the Seven Dwarfs." *People*, October 12, 1987.

O'Connell, Michael. "When 'The X-Files' Became A-List: An Oral History of Fox's Out-There Success Story." *Hollywood Reporter*. Last modified January 7, 2016. http://www.
hollywoodreporter.com/features/x-files-
became-a-list-852398.

Ostroff, Joshua. "All-Ages Show; Mom and Dad Hipsters Are Just as All Right with the Indie-Infused Children's Programming of Today." *National Post*, August 4, 2011.

"Our Charity." *Everfree Northwest*. n.d. https://
everfreenw.com/archive/2013/charity.html.

"Outlook '88: Toy Manufacturers Search for New Masterpieces." *Playthings* (February 1988): 111.

"Parents Guide for the *Transformers: The Movie*." *Internet Movie Database*, http://www.
imdb.com/title/tt0092106/parentalguide.

Patinkin, Mark. "Let's Remember the Victim and Forget the Killer." *Providence Journal-Bulletin*, January 28, 1996.

Patterson, Sarah. "No Money for Hasbro Until Derpy Hooves's Name, Voice and Eyes Are Restored!" Change.org. Last modified February 25, 2012. https://www.change.org/p/hasbro-no-
money-for-hasbro-until-derpy-hooves-s-
name-voice-and-eyes-are-restored.

PegasisterDDZ. "Pegasister." *Urban Dictionary*. Last modified July 27, 2011. http://www.
urbandictionary.com/define.php?term=
Pegasister&defid=5979315.

Pereira, Joseph. "Toy Industry Faces a Lackluster Year—Absence of Runaway Hits Is a Major Factor." *Wall Street Journal*, July 27, 1987.

Perkins, Pamela. "Saddle Up Memphis: My Little Pony Fair Hitches Up Downtown." *Memphis Commercial Appeal*, July 29, 2007.

Perlmutter, David. *America Toons In: A History of Television Animation*. Jefferson, N.C.: McFarland, 2014.

Pesce, Nicole Lyn. "Gen X Moms Fear New 'My Little Pony' Feature Film Horses Are Too Hot to Trot." *New York Daily News*, June 13, 2013.

Phillips, Phil. *Turmoil in the Toybox*. Lancaster, PA: Starburst, 1986.

PixelKatties (M.A. Larson). https://twitter.com/
m_a_larson/.

"Plenty of Programming on NATPE Display." *Broadcasting* 108, no. 2 (January 14, 1985): 84–90.

Pollock, Dale. *Skywalking: The Life and Films of George Lucas*. New York: Harmony Books, 1983.

PoniesYeah. "Doing My Pony Duty. a Tiny Preview from the Toy Show!" *My Little Pony Arena*. n.d. http://www.mlparena.com/archive/
Forums//viewtopic/t=117990/.

"The Pony Project." *The Pony Project*. n.d. https://web.archive.org/web/20050804
003809/http://www.theponyproject.com/.

"Pony Project: White." *Strawberry Reef*. n.d. http://www.strawberryreef.com/Index/Name/
ponyprojectwhite.html.

"Powerpuff Girls." Narrated by Madeleine Brand. *Morning Edition*. NPR, November 15, 2000. http://www.npr.org/templates/story/
story.php?storyId=1114006.

"The Powerpuff Girls (1998–2005)." *Internet Movie Database*. http://www.imdb.com/title/
tt0175058/fullcredits.

"Powers of Persuasion: Use It Up, Wear It Out." *National Archives and Records Administration*. n.d. http://www.archives.gov/exhibits/
powers_of_persuasion/use_it_up/use_it_up.
html.

Rafferty, Terrence. "Elmore Leonard's Men of Few Words, in a Few Words." *New York Times*, September 2, 2007.

Rakstis, Ted J. "1984: Another Year of Product Scarcity?" *Playthings* (March 1984): 32.

Ramirez, Anthony. "Tonka Accepts Offer from Hasbro." *New York Times*, February 1, 1991.

"Rare Ponies." *Strawberry Reef*. n.d. http://www.
strawberryreef.com/Topics/rare.html.

Raugust, Karen. "Hasbro: A Toy Story." *Publishers Weekly* 253, no. 37 (September 18, 2006): 10.

_____. "Talking Trends." *Publishers Weekly* 247, no. 23 (June 5, 2000): 24.

_____. "What's Old Is New Again." *Publishers Weekly* 250, no. 33 (August 18, 2003): 30.

Ray, Michael. "Tea Party Movement." *Encyclopedia Britannica*. Last modified June 11, 2014. http://www.britannica.com/EBchecked/topic/
1673405/Tea-Party-movement.

Razor Jack. "About BFG." *Bronies for Good*. Last

modified October 22, 2011. http://bronies forgood.org/about-us/.

_____. "Redheart's Roundup." *Bronies for Good.* Last modified August 23, 2011. http://bronies forgood.org/2011/08/redhearts-roundup/.

"Rehash of Classic Properties Dominates Apparel Programs." *DSN Retailing Today* 42, no. 11 (June 9, 2003): 35.

Reinert, Daniel. "Return Derpy Hooves! Name, Voice, and Eyes!" *Change.Org.* Last modified February 25, 2012. https://www.change.org/p/hasbro-return-derpy-hooves-name-voice-and-eyes.

Reisman, Abraham. "Do You Have 'The Touch'? Learn the Bizarre History of the Greatest Transformers Song Ever." *Vulture*, June 26, 2014. http://www.vulture.com/2014/06/trans formers-song-history-the-touch-stan-bush-mark-wahlberg-boogie-nights.html.

"Rejoined (Episode)." *Memory Alpha.* n.d. http://memory-alpha.wikia.com/wiki/Rejoined_%28episode%29.

"Reviews." *FamilyPC* 6, no. 4 (April 1999): 104.

Reyes, Armando (Mandoreyes80). https://twitter.com/Mandoreyes80/.

Rhue, Charles "Shuttershade." "Do Not Alter Derpy in 'The Last Roundup.'" *Change.Org.* Last modified February 2012. https://www.change.org/p/keep-derpy-no-ditzy-do-not-alter-derpy-in-the-last-roundup.

Richmond, Ray. "Ren Breaks Cartoon Mold." *Austin American Statesman*, May 17, 1992.

Richter, Kathleen. "My Little Homophobic, Racist, Smart-Shaming Pony." *Ms.* Last modified December 9, 2010. http://msmagazine.com/blog/2010/12/09/my-little-homophobic-racist-smarts-shaming-pony/.

Rickey, Carrie. "Film: Autobots vs. Decepticons." *Philadelphia Inquirer*, August 8, 1986.

Riddell, Mary. "An Outsider Who Took the Hot Seat; Profile; Pat Roberts Cairns." *Times*, January 1, 1996.

Ringel, Eleanor. "Movie Review—Toy-into-Tot-Movie Trend Gallops in 'My Little Pony.'" *Atlanta Journal-Constitution*, June 11, 1986.

Rosemond, John. "Some Toy Makers Don't Turn Out Schlock, Some Do." *Wichita Eagle*, November 29, 1984.

Rosenblum, Constance. "Eerie Metamorphosis Is Turning Girls into Turtles." *New York Times*, October 31, 1991.

Ross, Val. "Striking a Chord." *Globe and Mail*, May 18, 1991.

Rourke, Bryan. "The Mane Event for Little Ones." *Providence Journal*, November 19, 2006.

_____. "A Pony Tale: 100 Million Sold and Climbing." *Providence Journal*, June 22, 2008.

Ruffalo, Mark (MarkRuffalo). https://twitter.com/MarkRuffalo/.

"Rule 34." *Know Your Meme.* Last modified March 25, 2015. http://knowyourmeme.com/memes/rule-34.

Rusoff, Jane Wollman. "Bart Is Just One of Many Roles for Voice-Over Actress." *Columbus Dispatch*, June 29, 2000.

Russell, Mark. "Uniting the Two Koreas, in Animated Films at Least." *New York Times*, August 31, 2005.

Rutherford, Jesse. "My Little Calliponian." *Bitch Magazine*, Spring 2007.

Rutherford, Kevin. "Behind the Music of Pop Culture Smash 'My Little Pony: Friendship Is Magic.'" *Rolling Stone.* Last modified April 20, 2012. http://www.rollingstone.com/music/news/behind-the-music-of-pop-culture-smash-my-little-pony-friendship-is-magic-20120420.

Ryan, Desmond. "Film: Disney Offering Has Artful Animation." *Philadelphia Inquirer*, July 2, 1986.

_____. "Film: Tale of Fantasy for Kiddies." *Philadelphia Inquirer*, June 28, 1986.

"Sandra Day O'Connor." *Supreme Court of the United States.* http://www.supremecourt.gov/visiting/SandraDayOConnor.aspx.

Sarkeesian, Anita. "Lego & Gender Part 1: Lego Friends." *Feminist Frequency.* Last modified January 30, 2012. http://feministfrequency.com/2012/01/30/lego-gender-part-1-lego-friends/.

"Saturday." *Hour*, April 7, 1984.

"Saturday—Sign on to 5 P.M." *Milwaukee Journal*, October 3, 1986.

"Saturday Television." *Sarasota Herald-Tribune*, October 25, 1986.

Schechner, Sam, and Joseph Pereira. "Hasbro and Discovery Form Children's TV Network--Toy Maker Says Deal Reflects Its Shift into Entertainment; Consumer Groups Fear Shows Will Be Long-Playing Ads." *Wall Street Journal*, May 1, 2009.

Scherstuhl, Alan. "How Much of the *Hobbit* Can You Read During the Running Time of the *Hobbit*?" *Village Voice.* Last modified December 7, 2012. http://www.villagevoice.com/news/how-much-of-the-hobbit-can-you-read-during-the-running-time-of-the-hobbit-6685565.

Schmidt, Gregory. "Classic Toys Redesigned to Traverse Generations." *New York Times.* Last modified March 1, 2013. http://www.nytimes.

com/2013/03/02/business/hasbro-expands-transformers-brand-into-new-media.html.
_____. "A New Direction for a Hasbro Stalwart." *New York Times.* Last modified May 12, 2013. http://www.nytimes.com/2013/05/13/business/equestria-girls-a-my-little-pony-offshoot-in-its-movie-debut.html.
"School Bully Concerns." *WLOS-TV.* Last modified March 12, 2014. https://web.archive.org/web/20140314044422/http://wlos.com/shared/news/features/top-stories/stories/wlos_-school-bully-concerns-15463.shtml.
Schwartz, Charles. *Cole Porter: A Biography.* New York: De Capo, 1992.
Screenvision Media. "Screenvision Lands Event Cinema Pioneers Maxwell/Diamond—Former NCM/Fathom Executives Head to Screenvision." Screenvision Media press release, December 17, 2015.
Seiter, Ellen. *Sold Separately: Children and Parents in Consumer Culture.* New Brunswick, N.J.: Rutgers University Press, 1993.
"Selected 1980s Relaunches: Here Are Some of the Licensed Properties That Are Being Reintroduced." *Publishers Weekly* 250, no. 33 (August 18, 2003): 32.
Sethisto. "Brony Shirts Now at the Actual Hot Topic Stores (Updated)." *Equestria Daily.* Last modified August 23, 2011. http://www.equestriadaily.com/2011/08/stolen-design-brony-shirts-now-at.html.
_____. "Derpy Has Been Modified." *Equestria Daily.* Last modified, February 24, 2012. http://www.equestriadaily.com/2012/02/derpy-has-been-modified.html.
_____. "Derpy Hooves Hits Build-a-Bear Site as Web Exclusive—Vinyl Scratch 'Coming Soon.'" *Equestria Daily.* Last modified August 24, 2015. http://www.equestriadaily.com/2015/08/derpy-hooves-hits-build-bear-site-as.html.
_____. "Derpy Possibly This Year's Comic Con Exclusive!" *Equestria Daily.* Last modified May 28, 2012. http://www.equestriadaily.com/2012/05/derpy-possibly-this-years-comic-con.html.
_____. "Editorial: Hype. Equestria Girls, EQD, Episode Followups, and Twilight Sparkle." *Equestria Daily.* Last modified June 24, 2013. http://www.equestriadaily.com/2013/06/editorial-hype-equestria-girls-eqd.html
_____. "Equestria Girls: Official Song by Pinkie Pie." *Equestria Daily.* Last modified May 24, 2011. http://www.equestriadaily.com/2011/05/equestria-girls-song-by-pinkie-pie.html.
_____. "Friendship Is Magic Collection Apple Family Figures in the Packaging." *Equestria*

Daily. Last modified May 1, 2015. http://www.equestriadaily.com/2015/05/friendship-is-magic-collection-apple.html.
_____. "Friendship Is Magic Collection Mrs. Cake, Pinkie Pie, and Maud Pie Appear." *Equestria Daily.* Last modified September 18, 2015. http://www.equestriadaily.com/2015/09/friendship-is-magic-collection-mrs-cake.html.
_____. "Full Power Ponies Brushable Set Revealed at Target." *Equestria Daily.* Last modified July 5, 2015. http://www.equestriadaily.com/2015/07/full-power-ponies-brushable-set.html.
_____. "Important Message to the Community from Hasbro." *Equestria Daily.* Last modified February 6, 2012. http://www.equestriadaily.com/2012/02/important-message-to-community-from.html.
_____. "Is Equestria Girls a Bad Thing for Pony?" *Equestria Daily.* Last modified September 29, 2015. http://www.equestriadaily.com/2015/09/is-equestria-girls-bad-thing-for-pony.html.
_____. "Kinder Egg Maxi Vs. Normal Size Figure Comparison." *Equestria Daily.* Last modified October 4, 2015. http://www.equestriadaily.com/2015/10/kinder-egg-maxi-vs-normal-size-figure.html.
_____. "Kinder Reveals Full Lineup of Toys, Plus a 3D Animated Promo Showing Them Off—Now Available." *Equestria Daily.* Last modified August 17, 2015. http://www.equestriadaily.com/2015/08/kinder-reveals-full-lineup-of-toys-plus.html.
_____. "The Last Roundup's Mysterious iTunes Disappearance." *Equestria Daily.* Last modified January 30, 2012. http://www.equestriadaily.com/2012/01/last-roundups-mysterious-itunes.html.
_____. "Lauren Faust Answers a Bunch of Questions (Update-More Added!)." *Equestria Daily.* Last modified May 27, 2013. http://www.equestriadaily.com/2013/05/!lauren-faust-answers-bunch-of-questions.html.
_____. "Lauren Faust Ponychan Q&A Compiled." *Equestria Daily.* Last modified June 8, 2013. http://www.equestriadaily.com/2013/06/lauren-faust-ponychan-q-compiled.html.
_____. "M.A. Larson Reveals All Sorts of Fun Things Cut from Episode 100." *Equestria Daily.* Last modified June 18, 2015.
_____. "Packaging and Stock Images of All the Friendship Is Magic Apple Family Set Ponies Arrives!" *Equestria Daily.* Last modified May 2, 2015. http://www.equestriadaily.com/2015/05/packaging-and-stock-images-of-all.html.
_____. "Poll Results: Power Ponies Poll #1—

Who Had the Best Costume?" *Equestria Daily*. Last modified December 27, 2013. http://www.equestriadaily.com/2013/12/poll-results-power-ponies-poll-1-who.html.

_____. "Poll Results: What Is the Pony DJ's Name?" *Equestria Daily*. Last modified February 9, 2011. http://www.equestriadaily.com/2011/02/poll-results-what-is-pony-djs-name.html.

_____. "Poll Results: Worst Pony Drama So Far This Year?" *Equestria Daily*. Last modified June 27, 2013. http://www.equestriadaily.com/2013/06/poll-results-worst-pony-drama-so-far.html.

_____. "Premiere: Extended Equestria Girls." *Equestria Daily*. Last modified May 27, 2011. http://www.equestriadaily.com/2011/05/extended-equestria-girls.html.

_____. "Reminder: My Little Pony Season 2 DVD Now Available." *Equestria Daily*. Last modified May 15, 2013. http://www.equestriadaily.com/2013/05/reminder-my-little-pony-season-2-dvd.html.

_____. "Small Update on Derpy Overall." *Equestria Daily*. Last modified February 2, 2012. http://www.equestriadaily.com/2012/02/small-update-on-derpy-overall.html.

Shapiro, Mitchell E. *Television Network Weekend Programming, 1959–1990*. Jefferson, N.C: McFarland, 1992.

Shea, Ellen. "Manufacturers Double as Licensors." *Playthings* (June 1984): 64+.

Shen, Alex. "Save Derpy (And Hasbro's Creative Process)." *Change.Org*. Last modified February 26, 2012. https://www.change.org/p/save-derpy-and-hasbros-creative-process.

Sherber, Anne. "Toy Fair Provides Video Inspirations." *Billboard* 111, no. 10 (March 6, 1999): 85.

Shone, Tom. "Katy Perry: 'You Have to Bust Your Ass at This.'" *Guardian*, August 7, 2010.

"Show Equestria Girl." *Hasbro Activaciones*. Last modified April 27, 2016. https://web.archive.org/web/20160427055445/http://hasbro-activaciones.com/showequestriagirl/.

Simpson, Dana. "Phoebe and Her Unicorn Comic Strip, August 11, 2013." *GoComics*. Last modified August 11, 2013.

_____. "Phoebe and Her Unicorn Comic Strip, March 17, 2013." *GoComics*. Last modified March 17, 2013.

_____. *Unicorn on a Roll: Another Phoebe and Her Unicorn Adventure*. Kansas City, MO: Andrews McMeel Publishing, 2015.

Soarin_the_Pegasus. "Where Did the Whole 'Mail Carrier Derpy' Thing Come From?" *Derpibooru*. Last modified in 2013. https://derpibooru.org/pony/where-did-the-whole-mail-carrier-derpy-thing-come-from.

Solomon, Charles. "Movie Review: 'Pony' Has a Bad Case of the Cutes." *Los Angeles Times*, June 20, 1986.

_____. "Syndication Threat: KidVid on the Way Out?" *Los Angeles Times*, November 15, 1986.

Soto, Monica. "One Reporter's Foray into the ABCs of Football." *Santa Fe New Mexican*, August 30, 1997.

"Specials." *Ellensburg Daily Record*, April 14, 1984.

"Sporting Goods, Toy Sales Gain." *Discount Store News* (April 30, 1984): 1.

Stanley, T.L. "Hey, It's Their 'Little Pony' Too." *Los Angeles Times*, April 22, 2012.

_____. "Irony Giants." *Brandweek* 44, no. 23 (June 9, 2003): 42.

_____. "Toying Around with Stardom on Video." *Video Business* 23, no. 25 (June 23, 2003): 10.

Stanley, T.L., and Karen Benezra. "Amid Takeover Buzz, Toy Schleppers Brace for Godzilla, Teletubbies and McD's Happy Meal Girl." *Brandweek* 39 no.7 (February 16, 1998): 9.

Station Manager Ken. "Seven Minutes in Deadwood." *WFMU's Beware of the Blog*. Last modified May 20, 2005. http://blog.wfmu.org/freeform/2005/05/seven_minutes_i.html.

Stern, Sydney, and Ted Schoenhaus. *Toyland: The High-Stakes Game of the Toy Industry*. Chicago: Contemporary Books, 1990.

Stice, Joel. "Jean-Claude Van Damme Is Now Kicking Ass with My Little Pony." *CollegeHumor*. Last Modified March 3, 2015. http://www.collegehumor.com/post/7013462/heres-the-jean-claude-van-dammemy-little-pony-mash-up-youve-been-waiting-for.

Strachan, Alan. "Teletoons Animate Ratings." *Vancouver Sun*, June 13, 1998.

"Strike Two for FCC Order on Children's TV." *Broadcasting* 113, no. 14 (1987): 36.

"Sunbow Productions [Us]." *Internet Movie Database*. http://www.imdb.com/company/co0023518/.

Sutter, Janet. "Kids Play Favorites as They Toy Around." *San Diego Union-Tribune*, December 3, 1984.

"Syndication Marketplace." *Broadcasting* 109, no. 20 (November 11, 1985): 60.

Takiff, Jonathan. "Plug into These Holiday Gifts." *Philadelphia Daily News*, December 19, 1984.

Taskovic, Kylen. "We Want Derpy Hooves's Name Back!" *Change.org*. Last modified February 25, 2012. https://www.change.org/p/we-want-derpy-hooves-name-back.

"TCFC Are at It Again." *Chain Store Age—General Merchandise Trends,* 57 (Nov. 1986).

Tekaramity. "Exclusive Season 1 Retrospective Interview with Lauren Faust." *Equestria Daily.* Last modified September 6. 2011. http://www.equestriadaily.com/2011/09/exclusive-season-1-retrospective.html.

"Television Programs Today." *Hour,* April 4, 1985.

Terrill, Ashley. "Ladies, Leading." *Elle,* n.d. http://www.elle.com/culture/movies-tv/g2297/ladies-leading-514518/?slide=4.

Tevlin, Jon. "My Little Pony Tales, the (Sweet, Happy) Collector's Edition." *Minneapolis Star Tribune,* August 4, 2005.

"Theater Screenings Promote DVD Release." *Entertainment Marketing Letter,* July 1, 2005.

Thielman, Sam. "The Rise and Fall and Rise of Hasbro's TV Strategy." *Adweek.* Last modified February 23, 2015. http://www.adweek.com/news/television/after-rocky-few-years-hasbro-s-tv-strategy-changing-again-163083.

Thiessen, Jayson. "Hey Ponychan." *Ponychan.* Last modified March 30, 2011. https://www.ponychan.net/arch/res/6286.html.

"39th Annual Daytime Entertainment Emmy Award Nominations." *National Academy of Television Arts & Science.* Last modified June 23, 2012. http://www.emmyonline.org/media center/daytime_39th_nominations.html.

Thompson, Jonathan. "My Little What?" *Independent on Sunday,* July 20, 2003.

Thorne, Tony. *Fads, Fashions & Cults.* London: Bloomsbury, 1993.

"Thursday—Sign on to 5 P.M." *Milwaukee Journal.* October 8, 1986.

"Tigers and Furries." Narrated by Steve Scher. *Weekday.* KUOW. March 30, 2011. http://www2.kuow.org/program.php?id=22994.

Todd, Jeffrey Adams. *the Cinema of the Coen Brothers: Hard-Boiled Entertainments.* New York: Columbia University Press, 2015.

"Top Kid DVD." *Billboard* 119, no. 9 (March 3, 2007): 64.

"Top 10 Money Makers." *San Francisco Chronicle,* June 25, 1986.

"Tour Dates." *My Little Pony Live.* Last modified January 12, 2008. https://web.archive.org/web/20080113225437/http://mylittleponylive.net/tourdates.asp.

Truffaut, Francois. *Hitchcock.* New York: Simon & Schuster, 1983.

"The Tube." *Baltimore Afro-American,* April 13, 1984.

Tucker, Reed. "Horsing Around! the My Little Pony Craze Is Back—But This Time Grown-Up Guys Are Leading the Charge." *New York Post,* January 11, 2012.

Tucker, Travis. "Return Derpy Hooves in Season 4 of MLP: FIM." *Change.Org.* Last modified February 5, 2013. https://www.change.org/p/hasbro-return-derpy-hooves-in-season-4-of-mlp-fim.

Turner, James. "Is TV Paying Too Much Attention to Fans?" *Christian Science Monitor,* March 20, 2012.

"TV Listings." *Newburgh-Beacon Evening News,* March 31, 1984.

Tyrrel, Rebecca. "Pony Tale." *Sunday Telegraph Magazine,* December 19, 2004.

Uscinski, Henry John. "Comments Deregulating Commercial Television: Will the Marketplace Watch Out for Children?" *American University Law Review* no. 34 (1984): 141–173.

VanDerWerff, Todd. "My Little Pony Friendship Is Magic." *A.V. Club.* Last modified April 29, 2011. http://www.avclub.com/tvclub/imy-little-pony-friendship-is-magici-55168.

Vara, Vauhini. "Hey, Bro, That's My Little Pony! Guys' Interest Mounts in Girly TV Show; 'Bronies' Enthralled by Cartoon Equines; Characters 'Aren't One-Dimensional.'" *Wall Street Journal,* November 5, 2011.

"Videos." Hasbro. Last modified March 4, 2010. https://web.archive.org/web/20100304160520/http://www.hasbro.com/mylittlepony/en_US/play/videos.cfm.

Vineberg, Gary. "Gremlins Debuts in Theaters, Stores." *Footwear News* (June 11, 1984): 6.

Viner, Katharine. "Women: Sidelines." *Guardian,* February 4, 1997.

"Vintage Barbie White Hanky." *Fashion Doll Guide.* n.d. http://www.fashion-doll-guide.com/Vintage-Barbie-White-Hanky.html.

"Vinyls: My Little Pony—Applejack." *Funko.* http://funko.com/products/vinyls-my-little-pony-applejack.

Volmers, Eric. "Split with Charlie Sheen Was 'Heartbreaking,' Producer Says; Chuck Lorre Receives Comedy Award at Banff Media Festival." *Vancouver Sun,* June 16, 2012.

Vonnegut, Kurt. *Novels & Stories 1963–1973.* New York: Library of America, 2011.

Vue Cinemas. *Facebook* post. October 27, 2015. https://www.facebook.com/VueCinemas/photos/a.166763116690994.38166.147114011 989238/1057748944259069.

Wade, Lisa. "More Sexy Toy Makeovers: My Little Pony, Rainbow Brite, and Candy Land." *Ms.* Last modified December 7, 2010. http://msmagazine.com/blog/2010/12/07/more-sexy-toy-makeovers-my-little-pony-rainbow-brite-and-candy-land/.

_____. "More Sexy Toy Makeovers: My Little Pony, Rainbow Brite, and Candy Land." *So-*

ciological Images. Last modified December 7, 2010. http://thesocietypages.org/socimages/2010/12/07/more-sexy-toy-makeovers-my-little-pony-rainbow-brite-and-candy-land/.

"Wait Wait … Don't Tell Me!" NPR n.d. http://www.npr.org/podcasts/344098539/wait-wait-don-t-tell-me.

"Wall to Wall Television at NATPE." *Broadcasting* 110, no. 4 (January 27, 1986): 36–44.

Watercutter, Angela. "My Little Pony Corrals Unlikely Fanboys Known as 'Bronies.'" *Wired.* Last modified June 9, 2011. http://www.wired.com/2011/06/bronies-my-little-ponys/.

_____. "Sincerely Ours: *Glee*'s Success Cements Age of Geeky 'New Sincerity.'" *Wired.* Last modified September 21, 1010. http://www.wired.com/2010/09/new-sincerity/.

"Weekly Specials." *Mohave Daily Miner,* April 6, 1984.

Weekly Standard. "Media Kit." n.d. http://www.weeklystandard.com/advertising/pdf/TWS-media-kit-2013.pdf.

Weinman, Jaime. "Men Who Love My Little Pony: Don't Mess with Guys Who Want to Talk About Pinkie Pie and Pretty Pony Tea Parties." *MacLean's.* Last modified September 7, 2011. http://www.macleans.ca/culture/television/men-who-love-my-little-pony/.

_____. "Ponies Do Sondheim." *MacLean's,* September 7, 2011. http://www.macleans.ca/authors/jaime-weinman/ponies-do-sondheim/.

"Welcome." *Dream Valley.* n.d. http://www.kimsites.net/dreamvalley/index.html.

Wennemer, Rob. "Beer, Women and … My Little Pony? Men Profess Newest Love." *Pittsburgh Post-Gazette,* July 30, 2012.

Werbner, Donna. "Campaign: Hasbro Resurrects My Little Pony Brand—Consumer PR." *PR Week (UK).* Last modified September 10, 2004. http://www.prweek.com/article/221751/campaign-hasbro-resurrects-little-pony-brand---consumer-pr.

_____. "Campaign: Second Opinion." *PR Week (UK),* September 10, 2004.

"What Is BronyCon?" *BronyCon.* n.d. http://bronycon.org/about/what-is-bronycon/.

"Where the Action Was: NATPE's Programing Panoply." *Broadcasting* 108, no. 3 (January 21, 1985): 42–54.

Whipp, Glenn. "If You Pick One Movie to Miss, Make It 'Spice World.'" *Los Angeles Daily News,* January 23, 1998.

White, Nancy. "Annie's as Good as It Gets for Kids." *Toronto Star,* March 25, 1990.

Whyte, Sasha. "Children's Express: Girl Talk Unplugged; Everything from Sex to Barbie to Toys." *New York Amsterdam News,* March 23, 1996.

Wile, John, Lois Therrien, and Amy Dunking. "Are the Programs Your Kids Watch Simply Commercials?" *Business Week,* March 1985.

Wilson, MacKenzie. "*My Little Pony: Musical Treasures.*" *Allmusic.* n.d. http://www.allmusic.com/album/my-little-pony-musical-treasures-mw0000450550.

Wilson, Melody. "Brony Love: Lauren Faust, Creator of My Little Pony: Friendship Is Magic, Live from BronyCon!" *Bitch Magazine.* Last modified July 3, 2012. http://bitchmagazine.org/post/lauren-faust-creator-of-my-little-pony-friendship-is-magic-live-from-bronycon-feminist-magazine-bronies-gender-fandom.

Wolfensberger, Beth. "Trouble in Toyland." *New England Business* 12, no 9 (September 1990): 28–36.

"The World's Biggest Tea Party Stock Photos." *Bigstock.* n.d. http://www.bigstockphoto.com/search/The-World's-Biggest-Tea-Party/.

Yamino. "Final Word on Brony Drama." *tumblr.* Last modified March 1, 2012. http://yamino.tumblr.com/post/18558550747/final-word-on-brony-drama.

_____. "I Made a Response to the Ponychan Thread Regarding…" *tumblr.* Last modified July 23, 2011. http://yamino.tumblr.com/post/7968862006/i-made-a-response-to-the-ponychan-thread-regarding.

"Yankee Doodle." *Library of Congress.* n.d. http://www.loc.gov/teachers/lyrical/songs/yankee_doodle.html.

"The Yankee Doodle Boy." *Library of Congress.* Last modified December 10, 2014. http://lcweb2.loc.gov/diglib/ihas/loc.natlib.ihas.200000020/default.html.

"Year 1 (1982–1983)." *Dream Valley.* n.d. http://www.kimsites.net/dreamvalley/1st_edition.html.

Zachariah, Natasha Ann. "Bonding Over Magical Ponies." *Straits Times,* October 30, 2011.

_____. "Pony Posse." *Straits Times,* October 30, 2011.

Zacherle, Bonnie D., Charles Muenchinger, and Steven D. D'Aguanno. "United States Patent: 269986-Toy Animal," August 2, 1983.

Zaelle (ZaelleLexil). https://twitter.com/ZaelleLexil/.

"Zayre: We're Sorry." *Evening News,* December 11, 1983.

Zimmerman, Ann, and Sam Schechner. "Toys Take a Star Turn." *Wall Street Journal,* October 6, 2010.

Index

245